The Global Cybercrime Industry

Nir Kshetri

The Global Cybercrime Industry

Economic, Institutional and Strategic Perspectives

Springer

Dr. Nir Kshetri
The University of North Carolina
  at Greensboro
Bryan School of Business and Economics
Greensboro, NC 27402-6165
USA
nbkshetr@email.uncg.edu

ISBN 978-3-642-11521-9   e-ISBN 978-3-642-11522-6
DOI 10.1007/978-3-642-11522-6
Springer Heidelberg Dordrecht London New York

Library of Congress Control Number: 2010924064

Cover design: WMXDesign GmbH, Heidelberg

Printed on acid-free paper

Springer is part of Springer Science+Business Media (www.springer.com)

Preface

The Internet's rapid diffusion and digitization of economic activities have led to the emergence of a new breed of criminals. Economic, political, and social impacts impacts of these cyber-criminals' activities have received considerable attention in recent years. Individuals, businesses, and governments rightfully worry about the security of their systems, networks, and IT infrastructures.

Looking at the patterns of cybercrimes, it is apparent that many underlying assumptions about crimes are flawed, unrealistic, and implausible to explain this new form of criminality. The empirical records regarding crime patterns and strategies to avoid and fight crimes run counter to the functioning of the cyberworld. The fields of hacking and cybercrime have also undergone political, social, and psychological metamorphosis.

The cybercrime industry is a comparatively young area of inquiry. While there has been an agreement that the global cybercrime industry is tremendously huge, little is known about its exact size and structure. Very few published studies have examined economic and institutional factors that influence strategies and behaviors of various actors associated with the cybercrime industry. Theorists are also debating as to the best way to comprehend the actions of cyber criminals and hackers and the symbiotic relationships they have with various players.

Our observations above highlight the emergent nature of the global cybercrime industry. Cybercrime is also a topic of considerable interest both theoretically and practically. This book aims to contribute to filling the research gaps discussed above and initiate further academic discussion on this topic. A major goal of the book is to examine economic processes associated with the cybercrime industry. The book would help us better understand cybercrime as a form of economic activity and could inform the development of strategies for crime prevention. A further goal of the book is to understand institutional processes in the cybercrime industry. More to the point, we analyze formal and informal institutions and associated feedback mechanisms influencing this industry. A third goal of the book is to provide insights into the entrepreneurial aspect of firms engaged in cyber-criminal activities. The book examines how criminal entrepreneurs in the cyberworld organize and manage essential ingredients needed for their businesses. We will also take a close look at cybercrime business models. A fourth goal of the book is to explain the global variation in the pattern of cybercrimes. As we have demonstrated, economic factors facing cyber-criminal and cybercrime victims are significantly different in developing and developed countries. They include nature and quality of hardware, software, and infrastructure; targetability of victims; stock of cybercrime skills; and associated opportunity costs and benefits. Finally, the proposed book seeks to understand threats and countermeasures taken by key actors in this industry.

In sum, by providing a comprehensive overview of the ingredients, institutions, cost–benefit aspects, and modus operandi of different actors involved in cybercrimes, it is hoped that this book will aid in better understanding and analyzing the rapidly transforming cybercrime landscape. The book also provides research, managerial, and policy implications associated with cybercrimes.

This book is inter-disciplinary in focus, orientation, and scope. It crosses disciplines such as economics, law, business and management, international affairs, sociology, anthropology, cultural studies, and criminology to develop theory and provide information that could move theory and practice forward in the study of cybercrimes. This book is also theory-based, but practical and accessible to the wider audience.

This book is primarily targeted to academic specialists, practitioners, professionals, and policy makers interested in and concerned about the evolution of cybercrime industry. Undergraduate and graduate students are also target audience. More broadly, this book is expected to be useful to all members of the cyberworld to understand the nature of vulnerabilities from cyberattacks and develop appropriate defense mechanisms.

As for the ideas, concepts, content, and theories presented in this book, I am indebted and grateful to several people for comments, suggestion, support, encouragement, and feedbacks. Various papers related to this book were presented at scholarly meetings such as: (a) Fourth Annual CPP International Conference on Public Policy and Management, August 9–12, 2009, Bangalore, India; (b) Seventh International Business Week Conference, University of Minho, Braga, Portugal, April 26–May 1, 2009; (c) the 5th Annual Mason Entrepreneurship Research Conference, March 27, 2009 at Fairfax, Virginia; (d) The Workshop on Secure Knowledge Management, Dallas, Texas, November 3–4, 2008; (e) Third Annual Forum on Financial Information Systems and Cyber Security, Robert H. Smith School of Business at the University of Maryland, May 24, 2006; and (f) Sixth Annual International Business Research Forum, Philadelphia, April 1–2, 2005. This book benefited greatly from the comments and suggestions of anonymous reviewers and participants of these meetings.

My major debt is to my doctoral dissertation advisor Nikhilesh Dholakia, who has provided me with constant intellectual stimulation, support, and encouragement. I have also benefitted greatly from interacting with my colleagues Ralf Bebenroth, Nicholas Williamson, and David Bourgoin. Katharina Wetzel-Vandai, Senior Editor, Economics/Management Science, Springer has been constructive, supportive, helpful, and encouraging in guiding and managing this project. I also received help and support from my graduate assistant Jun (Johnny) Situ. I wish to express my profound gratitude to my life's companion and best friend, Maya, for the patience and loving support during the endeavor to write this book. Finally, I'd like to dedicate this book to my mother Manamaya Kshetri, for her love, guidance, and support.

Greensboro, North Carolina   Nir Kshetri

Contents

About the Author

Nir Kshetri is Associate Professor at Bryan School of Business and Economics, The University of North Carolina-Greensboro. Nir holds a PhD in Business Administration from University of Rhode Island; an MBA from Banaras Hindu University (India); and an MSc (Mathematics) and an MA (Economics) from Tribhuvan University (Nepal). His undergraduate degrees are in Civil Engineering and Mathematics/Physics from Tribhuvan University. Nir is also a Visiting Professor at Bad Mergentheim Business School, Baden-Wuerttemberg, Germany. Nir's previously held positions include faculty member at Management School, Kathmandu University (Nepal), visiting lecturer at Management School, Lancaster University (UK), and visiting professor at European Business School in Paris. During 1997–1999, Nir was a consultant and a trainer for the Food and Agricultural Organization (FAO) of the United Nations, German Technical Cooperation (GTZ), and Agricultural Development Bank of Nepal.

Nir is the author of *The Rapidly Transforming Chinese High Technology Industry and Market: Institutions, Ingredients, Mechanisms and Modus Operandi* (Caas Business School, City of London and Chandos Publishing: Oxford) which was published in 2008. Nir's works have also been published in journals such as *Foreign Policy, European Journal of Marketing, Journal of International Marketing, Asia Pacific Journal of Marketing and Logistics, Journal of International Management, Communications of the ACM, IEEE Security and Privacy, IEEE Software, Electronic Markets, Small Business Economics, Journal of International Entrepreneurship, Electronic Commerce Research and Applications, IT Professional, Journal of Developmental Entrepreneurship, Journal of Technology Management in China, First Monday, Pacific Telecommunications Review, Journal of Interdisciplinary Mathematics, Journal of Computer Information Systems, Journal of Asia Pacific Business, and International Journal of Cases on Electronic Commerce*. He has also contributed chapters to several books including *Outsourcing and Offshoring* (Cambridge University Press, New York), *Handbook of Technology Management* (Wiley, 2009), *In the wave of M&A: Europe and Japan* (Kobe University, RIEB Center, Kobe, Japan, 2007), *M-commerce in North America, Europe and Asia-Pacific: Country Perspectives* (Idea Group Publishing, 2006), *Encyclopedia of Information Science and Technology* (Idea Group Publishing, 2005), *Indian Telecom Industry – Trends and Cases* (The ICFAI University

Press, 2005), *The Internet Encyclopedia* (John Wiley & Sons, 2004); *Wireless Communications and Mobile Commerce* (Idea Group Publishing, 2003); *The Digital Challenges: Information Technology in the Development Context* (Ashgate Publishing, 2003); *Architectural Issues of Web-enabled Electronic Business* (Idea Group Publishing, 2003), *Internet Marketing* (2nd edition, Stuttgart, Germany: Schaeffer-Poeschel, 2001). Nir has presented over 85 research papers at various national and international conferences in Canada, China, Czech Republic, Dominican Republic, Greece, India, Italy, Japan, Nepal, New Zealand, Portugal, South Africa, South Korea, Sweden, Thailand, the Philippines and the United States. He has also given invited talks at Harvard University, Cornell University, Duke University, Kobe University, University of Maryland (College Park), and Temple University. In 2008, the Kauffman Foundation awarded Nir a grant to study Entrepreneurial Firms in OECD Economies.

Nir was the winner of the 2008 Bryan School Teaching Excellence Award. He was also a finalist in the 2009 UNCG Alumni Teaching Excellence Award. His recent research related awards include Pacific Telecommunication Council's 2008 Meheroo Jussawalla Research Paper Prize for his work on the Chinese IPTV market and a finalist in *the Management and Organization Review* (MOR) Best Paper Award in the China Goes Global Conference organized by the Harvard University (October 10–11, 2008). Nir was also the runner up in the 2004 dissertation competition of the American Marketing Association's Technology and Innovations Special Interest Group and the winner of the 2001 Association of Consumer Research/Sheth Foundation dissertation award. He also won the first place in the Pacific Telecommunication Council's Essay competition in 2001 and second place in the same competition in 2000. In May, 2006, the Information Resources Management Association (IRMA) presented Nir with the Organization Service Award for the Best Track Chair in the IRMA 2006 International Conference. Nir ranks 13th among the most popular authors of the NetAcademy Universe.

Nir's works have been featured in *Foreign Policy's Global Newsstand* section (a publication of the Carnegie Endowment for International Peace) and in *Providence Journal*. He was pictured in the front page of *Global Perspective*, a publication of the Fox School's Temple CIBER and Institute of Global Management Studies (Fall 2004). Nir has been quoted in magazines and newspapers such as *Telecommunications*, *The Business Journal of the Greater Triad Area, Greensboro News and Record*, and *High Point Enterprise*.

List of Figures

List of Tables

Chapter 1
The Global Cybercrime Industry and Its Structure: Relevant Actors, Motivations, Threats, and Countermeasures

> *"Robbing banks is so 20th century. Stealing IDs is where the money is" (an editorial in the* The Miami Herald, *2009).*
> *"Cybercriminals stay in the shadows. They are people who don't know each other and who don't trust each other" Russian cybercrime expert Eugene Kaspersky (cf. Naidu, 2008).*

Abstract The meteoric rise in cybercrime has been an issue of pressing concern to our society. Cybercrime is global and organized. This chapter deals with definitional issues; analyses economic, social, and political impacts; and discusses methodological, conceptual, logical, and statistical problems in estimating the size of the cybercrime industry. The chapter also sheds light into different types of cybercrimes and relevant actors associated with the cybercrime industry.

1.1 The Rapidly Rising Global Cybercrime Industry

The meteoric rise in cybercrime has been an issue of pressing concern to our society. Mike Humphrey, Head of Information Assurance and Accreditation of the UK's Serious and Organised Crime Agency (SOCA), suggested that cybercrime is global and organized (Infosecurity-magazine.com, 2009). According to the US Federal Bureau of Investigation (FBI), organized cybercrimes are linked with other criminal activities such as drugs, gambling, prostitution, and terrorism (Antonopoulos, 2009). There are also reports that traditional organized crime groups have been involved in cybercrime. For instance, the Italian Mafia, Japanese Yakuza, Chinese gangs, Colombian cartels, and Russian and Malaysian organized crime groups have reportedly employed hackers, diverted their efforts from traditional activities to cybercrime, and expanded their businesses globally (Bell, 2002; Foreign Policy, 2005; Economist, 2009; Ismail, 2008; Katyal, 2001; Parker, 1998). Organized crime groups have also recruited young people in their cybercrime enterprises (BBC News, 2006b). The flourishing synergy between organized crimes and the Internet has thus increased the insecurity of the digital world (Kshetri, 2005; Williams, 2001).

N. Kshetri, *The Global Cybercrime Industry*, DOI 10.1007/978-3-642-11522-6_1,
© Springer-Verlag Berlin Heidelberg 2010

An estimate suggested that about 10 million computers worldwide are "hijacked" every day and connected to botnets[1] (Wolfe & Wade, 2008). Hackers have attacked computer networks of the Pentagon, the White House, NATO's military websites, and the Interpol. They have stolen secret source codes of Microsoft and credit card information from a number of US banks (Lunev, 2001; Walker, 2004). The US Secret Service called credit card fraud "the bank robbery of the future." In September 2009, a *Miami Herald* editorial commented how the Internet is making bank robbery obsolete: "Robbing banks is so 20th century. Stealing IDs is where the money is" (The Miami Herald, 2009). Cybercrime has also opened up new discourses in international relations. For instance, an FBI Assistant Director noted: "Cybercrime ... is the fastest-growing problem faced by China-US cooperation" (Schafer, 2006).

Below, we briefly discuss cybercrime situations in world's three major economies—the US, the UK, and Japan—which offer a glimpse of the seriousness of this issue:

The US: An FBI/McAfee study estimated that cybercrime costs the US economy over US $400 billion annually, which translates to 3.4% of the GDP (cf. Cardoso, 2007). A study conducted by *Gallup* in October 2009 indicated that 66% of US adults were worried "frequently" or "occasionally" about being an identity theft victim (Saad, 2009). The proportion was higher than the reported anxiety about 11 other crime types included in the *Gallup* survey. Internet-related frauds accounted for 53% of all consumer-fraud complaints made to the Federal Trade Commission in 2004 and 46% in 2005. Total losses of Internet-fraud victims reporting to FTC increased from US $205 million in 2003 to US $336 million in 2005. Likewise, victims, who reported to a hotline operated by the FBI and the National White Collar Crime Center, lost US $239 million in 2007, which increased to US $265 million in 2008. Cybercrime and cyber-terrorism have been the FBI's No. 3 priority[2]—behind counterterrorism and counterintelligence (Verton, 2002).

The UK: The size of the UK cybercrime industry is estimated to be the world's second highest (M2 PressWIRE, 2008). The number of cybercrimes in the country rose by 50% during 2004–2006 (Jones, 2006). A study found that the United Kingdom experienced an estimated 1.9 million incidents of cybercrime in 2006, or one every 10 s (ITU, 2007). The UK cybercrime industry was estimated at around GB £6 billion a year in 2008 (M2 PressWIRE, 2008). Surveys conducted among UK consumers indicated that 18% would not shop online because of cybercrime concerns, more people in the country fear a cybercrime than burglary, and a fifth of them fear a cybercrime more than any other crimes (BBC News, 2006a).

Japan: The number of cybercrime-related cases reported in 2004 was 2,081 (Xinhua, 2009); 4,425 instances of cybercrimes were reported in the country in 2006, which was 40% higher than in 2005 (The Daily Yomiuri February 23, 2007). According to a survey released by the National Police Agency (NPA), Japan's cybercrime cases rose by 15.5% to reach 6,321 in 2008.

Given the size of its economy, Japan accounts for a relatively small proportion of the global cybercrime industry (Businessweek.com, 2009). That being said, it is also the case that organized crime groups in the country are rapidly expanding into the cyberworld. There are reports that Japanese Yakuza have diverted their efforts from traditional activities to cybercrime and have sponsored cyber-criminals in other countries such as Malaysia and Russia (Economist, 2009; Ismail, 2008).

1.1.1 Cybercrime: Definitional Issues

At the outset, it is important to bear in mind that there is no universally accepted definition of the term—cybercrime. The conceptual definitions of cybercrime vary considerably across surveys and studies with regard to their clarity, comprehensiveness, and currency. In some cases, definitions of cybercrimes and related terms are not stated in surveys.

The analysis in this book is intended to be sufficiently general to cover not just felonies, but all types of violations on the cyberspace. A practical definition of a cybercrime is offered in Kshetri (2009): a cybercrime is defined as a criminal activity in which computers or computer networks are the *principal* means of committing an offense or violating laws, rules, or regulations. This definition of cybercrime is similar to that of Becker's (1968) approach of defining a crime. Examples of cybercrimes include denial-of-service attacks, cyber-theft, cyber-trespass, cyber-obscenity, critical infrastructure attacks, online fraud, online money laundering, criminal uses of Internet communications, ID fraud, use of computers to further traditional crimes, and cyber-extortions (Kshetri, 2006). Some authors have restricted the definition of cybercrime to only "an unlawful activity committed by a private individual in cyberspace" (Rho, 2007).

Government's some measures to deal with various forms of cyberattacks such as those committed by private individuals as well as cyber-terrorism and government-promoted cyberwarfare are lumped together in indistinguishable fashion. Some of our discussions in this book thus have been around a cyberattack, which can be considered as a conceptual superset of a cybercrime.

Cybercrimes are offences conducted in the "cyberspace" and the term "cyberspace" is ambiguous in the first place (Rho, 2007). A diverse range of acts such as the spread of computer viruses, visiting an obscene website, and cyberstalking may qualify as a cybercrime (Katyal, 2001; Jones, 2007).

Potentially even more problematic are inter-jurisdictional comparisons of cybercrimes. Regulators and policy makers in some countries, for instance, would prefer not to condemn some activities such as piracy, which are considered as cybercrimes in other countries (Rho, 2007). For instance, web contents that are considered to be obscene in Arab countries are socially acceptable in Western countries. At the same time, an "obscene" website in the United Kingdom may be acceptable in Scandinavian countries (Wall, 1998). When conceptual definitions vary, surveys conducted and their results across countries would not be amenable to equitable comparisons.

Similarly, differencing definitions of cyberwarfare exist and experts debate over whether cyberattacks on Georgia in 2008 and those on Estonia in 2007 qualify as cyberwarfare. Bruce Schneier of British Telecoms, for instance, considers many cyberattacks as vandalism or hooliganism. The actors involved and their motivations determine whether a cyberattack on a power station could be an act of war or of terrorism (The Economist, 2008). Some observers argue that a cyberattack qualifies as a "cyberwar" only if it is combined with conventional military operations. According to this view, the attacks on Georgia might qualify as cyberwarfare but those on Estonia would not (The Economist, 2008). Others argue that the effects of the 2007 cyberattacks in Estonia "were potentially just as disastrous as a conventional attack on this country" (Shackelford, 2009, p. 193). According to the strongest definition, a cyberattack is considered to be a cyberwar only if it causes "widespread harm, rather than mere inconvenience" (The Economist, 2008). Viewing from this perspective, even the 2008 cyberattacks against Georgia may not qualify as cyberwar as unlike the military operations, they did not cause a physical harm.

If certain forms of cyberattacks such as "cybervandalism" and "cyberhooliganism" are treated as cybercrimes, such attacks may fall within the scope of international treaties and conventions, such as the Council of Europe Convention on Cybercrime (The Economist, 2008). National and international law-enforcement agencies thus have frameworks to follow. On the other hand, if such attacks are as a form of warfare, there are no formal international frameworks to address them.

1.2 Economic, Social, and Political Impacts of Cybercrimes

Estimating economic, social, and political impacts of cybercrimes and web attacks to a reasonable level of accuracy has been a challenge. One view is that since many web attacks go unreported, such impacts tend to be underestimated. The opposite argument is that there may be vested interests among security companies to exaggerate the level of cybercrimes. Triangulation of data from various sources indicates substantial economic losses associated with cyberattacks.

Economic impacts: Before we proceed, it is important to note that "crime" can be considered as an "economically important activity" or an "industry" (Becker, 1968, p. 170). Recent estimates regarding the size of the global cybercrime industry vary from about US $100 billion (Voigt, 2009) to US $1 trillion (Acohido, 2009; Harris, 2009). A popular view is that cybercrimes have more severe economic impacts than most conventional crimes. According to the 2007 PricewaterhouseCoopers' biennial Global Economic Crime Survey, over 43% of the companies interviewed reported suffering one or more significant economic crimes. The average loss from fraud per company increased nearly 40% in 2 years from roughly US $1.7 million in 2005 to approximately US $2.4 million in 2007 (Africa News, 2007).

Below we consider economic impacts of some representative forms of cyber-crimes:

Identity theft: The FTC estimated that 10 million Americans became identity theft victims in 2008. Identity theft is unique among serious cybercrimes (Cheney, 2005; Pike, 2006). According to the FBI, 30 million credit card numbers were stolen through computer-security breaches during 1999–2003, resulting in US $15 billion in losses. In August 2009, in what is probably the highest-profile case in this category, a federal grand jury indicted a Florida man and two of his co-conspirators for allegedly stealing 130 million credit and debit card information (Claburn, 2009a).

A study conducted by the Federal Trade Commission (FTC) indicated that losses associated with identity theft including the time and out-of-pocket costs to US consumers amounted US $61 billion in 2006 (Schreft, 2007). Cyber-criminals are increasingly involved in the *"synthetic identity fraud,"* which involves combining information from different sources to open an account in the name of a "fictitious" identity (Cheney, 2005; Roberds & Schreft, 2009).

Spam: An estimate of MailFrontier, an e-mail security company, suggested that fraudulent e-mail messages (spam) totaled 80 million in September 2003. The number of spam messages around the world was estimated at 200 billion a day globally by the mid-2009 (Qatar-tribune.com, 2009). According to a May 2009 report from Symantec, spam accounted for 90% of all e-mails. Another estimate suggested that e-mail spam accounted for 87% of all e-mails in August 2009 (Shiels, 2009). As to the economic impact of spam, the European Union estimated that in 2001, spam cost Internet users €10 billion annually worldwide (Europa.eu, 2001). Another estimate suggested that in 2003, US consumers and businesses lost over US $10 billion to spam (Swartz, 2004).

Phishing: Phishing involves the uses of fraudulent e-mails and websites, which are designed to trick consumers to reveal personal information such as passwords, credit card information, and other personal data. Phishing schemes are considered among the biggest threats. In 2003, US consumers and businesses lost about US $2 billion to phishing (Swartz, 2004). Phishing scams have become far more prominent in the past few years. According to Gartner Research, in 2008, over 5 million Americans became phishing victims and lost money, which was a 40% increase from 2007 (Greenberg, 2009). According to the Anti-Phishing Working Group, in June 2009, there were about 50,000 active phishing websites (McMillan, 2009). Likewise, about a quarter of businesses in Australia had been attacked through phishing (Andrews, 2009).

1.2.1 Social Impacts

Cybercrime's adverse social impact is felt across all social and age spectrums. One estimate suggested that 20–25% of young people have been victims of cyberbullying (nasuwt.org, 2009). According to WiredSafety.org, more than half of 9–13-year-olds "have either cyberbullied or been cyberbullied, or had a close friend who was" (Saroyan, 2005). Likewise, Japan's Education, Science and Technology Ministry reported that of the 38,000 Internet bulletin boards operated by children in the country, about 20% harass other children (Salud, 2009).

There is also a heightened sense of fear and anxiety about cybercrimes among individuals and businesses. A survey conducted by IBM found that US businesses worry more about cybercrimes than about physical crimes (Christian Science Monitor, 2006). An IBM survey released in 2006 also found that there were three times more Americans who thought they would be victims of a computer crime "in the next year" than of a physical crime (Keizer, 2006). Likewise, according to a survey conducted by University of Calgary's Rozsa Centre, the average citizen is more likely to be a cybercrime victim than that of a physical crime (Zickefoose, 2008). Another survey conducted by TNS Sofres indicated that about 60% of Americans were fearful that their passwords would be stolen when they bank online, and 38% do not trust making payments online (Swartz, April 11, 2008).

1.2.2 Political and National Security Impacts

According to the US Homeland Security Department, compared to 2006, there was a 152% increase in cyberattacks against US federal agencies in 2007 (United Press International, 2009). The Pentagon detected over 79,000 attempted intrusions in its network in 2005 (Reid, 2007) and more than 80,000 in 2007 (Hamilton, 2009).

In a discussion of the national security impacts, attacks against the Department of Defense (DoD) networks merit mention. Note that the DoD information network represents about 20% of the entire Internet (GAO Reports June 22, 2007). In 1999, Department of Defense (DoD) networks detected 22,144 attacks on its networks compared to 5,844 in 1998 (Wolf, 2000). In 2008, the DoD estimated that its networks experienced more than 3 million attacks annually (Hess, 2008). The DoD networks were reported to receive about 6 million probes/scans a day (GAO Reports June 22, 2007).

Entire infrastructure including those of emergency services call centers, electricity, nuclear power plants, communications, dams, air traffic control and transportation, commercial databases and information systems for financial institutions and health care providers, and military applications are vulnerable to attacks by cyberterrorists or hostile state actors (Ronfeldt & Arquilla, 2003, p. 314; Shackelford, 2009; The Economist, 2008). For many years, technology and policy analysts have been talking about the possibility of a "digital Pearl Harbour"—an unexpected cyberattack on a nation's infrastructure. Some reports have indicated US electricity grid infrastructures and F-35 fighter jet programs had been the target of cyberattacks (Beatty, 2009). The US President Obama noted: "We know that cyber-intruders have probed our electrical grid and that in other countries, cyberattackers have plunged entire cities into darkness" (cf. Harris, 2009). The FBI has ranked cybercrime as the third-biggest threat to US national security—after nuclear war and weapons of mass destruction (Sloane, 2009).

In a 2007 testimony to the US Congress, an analyst working on cyber defense systems for the Pentagon told that a mass cyberattack could leave up to 70% of the

United States without electrical power for 6 months (Reid, 2007). Another estimate suggested that a loss of 4% of the North American power grid will disconnect almost two-thirds of the entire grid in the region (Cetron & Davies, 2009). Likewise, a study of US Cyber Consequences Unit indicated that the costs of a single wave of cyberattacks on US infrastructures could exceed US $700 billion, which is about the same as the costs associated with 50 major hurricanes (Sloane, 2009).

In a discussion of the Internet's national security impacts, cyberattacks against Estonia in April–May 2007 and those against Georgia in 2008 deserve special attention. The cyberattacks against Georgia by civilians were coordinated with physical attacks by a military force (Claburn, 2009b). Likewise, in a high-profile Distributed Denial of Service (DDOS)[3] attacks in 2007, a botnet of up to 1 million computers attacked Estonian computer networks, which shut down the country's government ministries, parliament, and major banks (Grant, 2008). The attacks against Estonia were launched after the Estonian government moved the Soviet memorial to the "Great Patriotic War" (1941–1945) (as well as the soldiers buried there) from downtown Tallinn to a suburb location. Obviously, Russia was unhappy with this decision. Some cyberattack experts noted that they saw the involvement of the Russian government in the attacks (Economist.com, 2007). Some analysts observed that the effects of the 2007 cyberattacks in Estonia "were potentially just as disastrous as a conventional attack" (Shackelford, 2009, p. 193).

1.3 Methodological, Conceptual, Logical, and Statistical Problems in Estimating Cybercrime

As is the case of any underground economy (Naylor, 2005), estimating the size of the global cybercrime industry has been a challenge. No reliable statistics exist. Empirical findings regarding various indicators related to cybercrime are remarkably inconsistent. For instance, an estimate suggested that cybercrime costs companies and consumers about US $100 billion worldwide in 2009 (Voigt, 2009). However, a study conducted by PricewaterhouseCoopers indicated that as early as in 2000, businesses' costs to fight hackers and viruses, which are a part of the total cybercrime costs, were US $300 billion.

As another example, consider estimates related to average costs to deal with virus-infected computers. An FBI report released in January 2006 indicated that the average attack cost around US $24,000, which included expenses related to repairing infected machines and networks and lost work time (Regan, 2006). Another study, however, suggested that costs to repair virus-inflicted computers averaged US $81,000 per incident per company in 2002 (Roush, 2003).

Estimations vary widely even for indicators related to concepts having fairly straightforward definitions. For instance, estimates of the proportion of computers used in botnets vary from 7 to 25%. At the World Economic Forum in 2007, Vinton Cerf (best known as the Father of the Internet), the co-designer of the Internet's basic architecture, noted that up to a quarter of computers connected to the Internet might be linked to botnets by cyber-criminals (Rodier, 2007). Other estimates are much smaller. In 2006, participants in meetings of high-tech's Messaging Anti-Abuse Working Group estimated that 7% of the PCs connected to the Internet were controlled by botnets (Acohido & Swartz, 2006). Experts at the Georgia Tech Information Security Center, however, estimated that 10% of the world's computers were used in botnets by the end of 2007, which was estimated to increase to 15% by the end of 2008 (Wolfe & Wade, 2008). Another estimate suggested that 11% of computers connected to the Internet contain botnet programs (Pappas, 2008).

Next consider, auction frauds. eBay claims that users face only a 1 in 10,000 risk of fraud in online auctions (Consumer Reports, 2007, p. 12). According to FBI, however, the auction fraud rate on eBay website is in the range of 1 in 100 (Bauerly, 2009). Indeed, in 2006, online auction fraud was the most reported cybercrime category, which comprised of 45% of complaints made to the Internet Crime Complaint Center (IC3, 2007).

The above inconsistencies regarding the estimates of the global cybercrime industry may be attributable to the fact that there are many methodological, logical, conceptual, and statistical problems in estimating the level and pattern of cybercrimes. While many associations, groups, and company publish their estimates on a regular basis, it is impossible to compare them meaningfully and evaluate their consequences (Rush, Chris, Erika, & Puay, 2009). Different combinations of direct, indirect, and opportunity costs such as actual money and intellectual property stolen, costs of fixing or replacing infected networks and equipment, lost work time, and intangible losses associated with the lack of customer confidence in doing business with the affected company are included under cybercrimes' projected losses (GAO Reports June 22, 2007).

There are many logical issues with measuring the cybercrime-related indicators in an economy and comparing them across jurisdictions. For instance, the country of origination of a cyberattack is extremely fuzzy. Many cybercrimes originate in one country but are initiated by criminals in different jurisdictions and territories. For instance, in 1999, two members of a US-based "Phonemasters" were convicted for attacking the networks of US telecom companies. One of them downloaded thousands of Sprint calling card numbers that were sold to intermediaries in Canada and Switzerland, and finally ended up with an organized crime group in Italy (Williams, 2001). Likewise, consider the July 2009 cyberattacks on major websites in the United States and South Korea. It was suggested that about 167,000 compromised computers in 74 countries were used in the attacks. A command-and-control server was on an UK-based IP address. The master server, which distributed instructions to eight other command-and-control servers, however, was located in Miami, USA (Kirk, 2009).

Definitions and estimates of cybercrime also differ due to heterogeneity in institutional differences, preferences, and constraints across jurisdictions. For instance, while British, French, and German laws prohibit contents on the Internet related to race hatred or Holocaust denial, the US Constitution protects free speech (Werth, 2009). Likewise, estimates of reported cybercrimes also vary across jurisdictions because governments across the world differ significantly in terms of statutes and administrative regulations related to reporting of cybercrimes. For instance, since the mid-2004, South Korea's National Cyber Security Center has mandated that all Internet-related hacking incidents must be reported (Ho, 2004). Likewise, as of 2006, more than 30 US states had laws that require businesses to report cyber-crimes (Greenemeier, 2006). Inter-jurisdictional comparison of various forms of cybercrimes is thus difficult and uniquely controversial.

Different cybercrimes also differ in terms of the probability of being reported. For instance, unlike most other types of identity thefts, the "synthetic identity fraud" victimizes only businesses (Cheney, 2005; Roberds & Schreft, 2009), which is less likely to be reported to authorities.

Finally, different estimates related to cybercrime have been widely criticized on the ground that there may be vested interests of the organization which may lead to over- or under-estimation of the true level of cybercrime (Rush et al., 2009). For instance, many security and consulting companies may have vested interests in exaggerating risks involved with cyberattacks. The law-enforcement agencies may use "purported evidence" of the rapid cybercrime growth "to justify larger budgets and more arbitrary powers" (Naylor, 2005, p. 131). For e-commerce companies such as eBay, on the other hand, there may be an incentive in underreporting cybercrimes related to their businesses.

1.4 Trends in Cybercrimes

Cyber-criminals' business models are maturing. They are using increasingly novel and creative methods to victimize businesses and consumers (Bridis, 2006; BBC News, 2004). An estimate suggested that more than 2 million new malicious pro-grams such as viruses, worms, and Trojans were created in 2007, which increased to more than 20 million in 2008 (Wattanajantra, 2008). Estimates also suggest that, in the early 2007, there were up to 45,000 different botnets involved in cybercrimes (Sullivan, 2007).

What is more, botnets are becoming more sophisticated. Initially they were run via Internet Relay Chat with a clear command-and-control structure that was easy to close down. But recent botnets employ peer-to-peer techniques that lack a central point of control (Vallance, 2008).

They have also widened the latitude in terms of the technologies they can perpetrate. In November 2007, malware[4] written for financially motivated pur-poses such as phishing and identity theft targeted consumers using Apple's Mac computers (Sophos.com, 2008). Note that while there were malware for Macs before, the earlier versions were not financially motivated (Sophos.com, 2008). Estimates suggested that 30% of malicious software was distributed through Internet ads in 2008 (Wolfe, 2008). Experts also predict possible increase in cyberattacks tar-geting new mobile technologies and Wi-Fi-enabled devices such as iPhone and iPod Touch (Sophos.com, 2008).

As evidenced by the recent attacks on Twitter, Facebook, and MySpace, cyber-criminals are exploiting the viral nature of Web 2.0. Cybercrime is spreading rapidly through social networking sites. In June 2009, laptops of several business school students at Yale University were infected, which was suspected to spread through Facebook (Finkle, 2009). Cyber-criminals have also targeted Twitter users by using links with malware that tag current topics (Voigt, 2009).

1.4.1 Social Engineering Skills

The basic idea behind social engineering is as follows: in many cases, it would be easier and more effective to trick potential victims to provide information than to steal it from them. Cyber-criminals persuade potential victims with emotional appeals such as excitement or fear or establishing interpersonal relationships or create a feeling of trust and commitment.

Deception is a psychological rather than a technological exercise (Vidalis & Kazmi, 2007). Zhou et al. (2004) note: "deception in human communication occurs when information senders attempt to create a false impression in receivers." To create such an impression, one requires an understanding of how the world functions.

Cyber-criminals possess skills in areas such as psychology and linguistics (PR Newswire, February 21, 2008). They are combining their technological and social engineering skills. Such skills have helped them achieve their ends by creating false impressions in victims by managing their perceptions and disrupting their decision making processes (Waltz, 1998). Kevin Mitnick, arguably the world's most famous hacker, employed social engineerin tactics in order to illegally access organizations' computer networks (Mitnick & Simon, 2002). Notable events such as the 2004 Indian Ocean tsunami,[5] Samoan tsunami of September 2009, the 2006 FIFA World Cup, Air France crash, the NBA finals, and launch of the new iPhone led to e-mail scams and phishing sites (PR Newswire, February 21, 2008; Voigt, 2009).

Cross-cultural and linguistic skills have helped cyber-criminals operate across borders efficiently. In the European Union countries, for instance, one of the most important barriers for cyber-criminals centered on languages. Note that the EU economies have 23 official languages and about 60 regional and minority languages (Orban, 2009). What seems to have happened was that consumers in non-English speaking countries tended to delete English-language spam and phishing e-mails. They have created malware specific to each country. Cyber-criminals have geared up to respond by making adaption to the malicious websites and scam message according to the language of the Internet domain site of the target victim.

1.5 Types and Classification of Cybercrimes

Glaser (1971) identified and classified various types of crimes such as predatory crimes against property, predatory crimes against person, illegal service crimes, and public disorder crimes. Most of these can be extended in the context of the cyberspace. Cyberattacks can be classified by various criteria. One way to classify cyberattacks is to consider whether they are directed against an intended target (e.g., targeted and opportunistic attacks). Cyberattacks can also be classified into two categories based on whether they are predatory or market-based. A further way to classify cybercrimes is related to the relative roles of human and technology elements. Gordon and Ford (2006) have divided cybercrime into distinct categories. In their categorization, Type I cybercrime mostly contains technological elements while Type II cybercrimes have mainly human elements (Gordon & Ford, 2006). We discuss some of the types in this section.

1.5.1 Targeted vs. Opportunistic Attacks

Targeted attacks: In targeted attacks, specific tools are used against specific cyber targets. Targeted attacks are carried out by skilled hackers with expertise to do serious damages. Some of them are motivated by financial gains (see Box 1.1). Targeted attacks are also initiated by terrorists, rival companies, ideological hackers, or government agencies. For instance, in August 2004, six hackers were convicted by a Californian court for their involvement in DoS attacks against business rivals (Leyden, 2004).

Box 1.1 Hacking the Odds[6]

In the early 2004, VIP Management Services, an online sports betting and gambling company based on the tiny Caribbean island of Curaçao, received an unnerving e-mail (Onlinecasinonews.com, 2004). Criminals had hacked into its computer system and offered an ultimatum: Pay US $30,000 in ransom or have its computer systems grind to a halt. The website of VIP Management Services was first targeted in September 2003 and was regularly attacked since then (Walker, 2004).

As the company's computer servers are its sole platform for doing business, VIP paid up. And it is not alone. Based primarily in Russia and Eastern Europe, organized criminal groups are increasingly targeting corporations for large-scale extortion schemes. In recent years, such plots have also been uncovered in Australia, Britain, Canada, Thailand, and the United States.

Businesses with a high dependence on digital technologies—such as online casinos, banks, and e-commerce hubs—are the most likely to fall victim to this form of online hijacking. The attacks are carefully planned. After cracking into victims' computer systems, extortionists normally send e-mails demanding that ransoms as high as US $100,000 be sent via money transfer agencies, such as Western Union. It is difficult to estimate how much money is extorted globally each year, because experts say only 10% of extortion cases are reported to law-enforcement agencies. But monetary losses are substantial. Reports suggest that gambling sites alone pay out millions of dollars in extortion money each year.

Some companies prefer to take their chances with a cyberattack. In 2004 fall, credit card payment processor Authorize.net refused to pay an extortion demand of a "substantial amount of money" and faced repeated denial-of-service attacks that disrupted business for more than 100,000 clients. That is why many companies choose to negotiate or simply pay up, rather than lose customers' trust, attract media attention face legal action for failing to adequately protect their patrons' private information.

Britain's SOCA and the US National White Collar Crime Center are teaming up with similar agencies in Russia and Eastern Europe to help prosecute online extortionists. But success is making some criminal outfits more brash. And many nations lack the resources to investigate, let alone prosecute, this new form of cyber-terrorism. Which means for small Caribbean operations such as VIP, its paradise lost.

Hackers that were involved in mass attacks before are moving toward more focused attacks that target mainly e-commerce sites. Targeted web attacks are not limited to networks of large organizations. Such attacks accounted for 10% of total attacks in small businesses in the first half of 2004 compared to 3% in the second half of 2003 (Symantec, 2004, p. 17).

Opportunistic attacks: Opportunistic attacks, on the other hand, entail releasing worms and viruses that spread indiscriminately across the Internet. Opportunistic attacks are less dangerous than targeted attacks and have smaller financial ramifications. The proportion of opportunistic cyberattacks is decreasing (see Box 1.2).

Box 1.2 Mpack

Cyber-criminals are employing increasingly sophisticated tools. The virus creation tool Mpack provides a remarkable example of the sophisticated nature of cybercrime. Mpack was sold on the websites of Russian Business Network (RBN),[7] probably the most notorious cybercrime outfit. Mpack is a computer program, which is designed to extract data from Internet users' PCs. Mpack, packaged with personal tech support from the software developers, cost US $500–US $1,000. Mpack can exploit known software security holes in several different kinds of Internet browsers (Krebs, 2007).

Here is how Mpack works. Cyber-criminals hack a website and install malicious programs created with Mpack. It then scans the user's computer for vulnerabilities related with web browser, operating system as well as other programs (Kendall, 2009). When an Internet user visit such sites with a web browser unequipped with the latest software security updates, the site silently installs a password-stealing program on the visitor's computer.

The victim's stolen data were then forwarded to a "drop site," which were located in a set of servers of RBN. Mpack monitors the success of a cybercrime operation through various metrics on its online, password protected control, and management console (Symantec, 2007).

1.5.2 Predatory Cybercrimes vs. Market-Based Cybercrimes

Cybercrimes can also be grouped into two types: predatory cybercrimes for profit and market-based cybercrimes (see Naylor, 2005). Predatory cybercrimes can be defined as illegal acts in the cyberspace in which "someone definitely and intentionally takes or damages the person or property of another" (Glaser, 1971, p. 4). Examples include stealing money from someone's bank account and intellectual property infringement. From the national GNP point of view, these acts do not produce new goods or services. They simply redistribute the existing wealth. Market-based cybercrimes, on the other hand, generate new incomes rather than redistributing the existing wealth (Naylor, 2005). Such crimes occur, for example, in the sales of stolen credit card information and illegal drugs online.

1.6 Relevant Actors Associated with Cybercrimes

1.6.1 Cyber-Criminals, Cyber-Terrorists, and State Actors Involved in Cyberattacks

Who are the cyberattackers? In light of the stereotypically different expectations that surround cyber-criminals, it is important to note that this new breed of criminals does not consist of isolated individuals working on home computers. Indeed, cyber-criminals resemble criminals in the conventional world.

A survey conducted among the members of the Confederation of British Industry indicated that the attackers in the most serious cybercrimes in 2000 were hackers (44.8%), former employees (13.4%), organized criminal groups (12.8%), current employees (11.5%), customers (7.9%), competitors (5.8%), political and protest groups (2.6%), and terrorists (1.4%) (BBC News, 2001). We now further examine some of these groups:

Employees: According to a report released by the FBI in January 2006, over 40% of attacks came from inside an organization (Regan, 2006). In a high-profile case in this category, in 2001, two accountants at Cisco Systems pled guilty for breaking and accessing into unauthorized parts of the company's network and issuing themselves nearly US $8 million in company stock. Each was sentenced to 34 months in prison (Tedeschi, 2003). An analyst of the technology consulting firm Gartner estimated employees accounted for about 70% of computer system intrusions that resulted in a loss (Tedeschi, 2003). Likewise, a survey conducted among Irish businesses in 2007 indicated that about 40% of respondents said that internal cybercrime investigations led to firing or resignation of their employees (Madden, 2007).

Organized crime groups: It is reported that organized crime groups are increasingly involved in cybercrimes (Coviello & Holleyman, 2008). Some Japanese gangs, for instance, hire Russian hackers to attack law-enforcement agencies' databases (The Economist, 1999). Likewise, Australian scammers have established links with Russian and Malaysian organized crime networks to transfer stolen money from overseas banks they have cracked into (Foreign Policy, 2005).

Cyber-terrorists: Experts say that cyber-terrorism, which can be considered as "the marriage of terrorism and cyberspace" has been relatively absent in the world (Gabrys, 2002). A survey indicated that there were at least 4,300 websites serving terrorists and their supporters (Michael, 2009). Cyber-terrorism related worries are, however, cropping up in the policy circle. According to the US Central Intelligence Agency (CIA), there are at least two terrorist organizations that possess the capability and the competence and are likely to use cyberattacks against the US infrastructures (GAO Reports June 22, 2007). It is argued that a cyberattack coordinated with physical attacks could compound the fallout by "disrupting communications, distracting the government response, and exacerbating the psychological damage from terrorism"[8] (Harvard Law Review, 2006).

Almost two decades ago, National Research Council (1991) noted, "Tomorrow's terrorist may be able to do more with a keyboard than with a bomb." An *Economist*

(December 6, 2008) article put the issue this way: "Why bomb your enemy's power-stations or stockmarkets if you can disable them with software?"

State actors as cyberattackers: Reports suggest that between 100 (Swartz, March 12, 2007) and 120 countries are planning and developing cyberattack strategies and infowar capabilities (Robertson, 2007; Cetron & Davies, 2009). These governments believe that such capabilities would help them maintain control over the domestic and international agenda. ITU secretary-general, Hamdoun Toure noted, "... the next world war could happen in the cyber space and that would be a catastrophe" (cf. Schlein, 2009).

Some authoritarian regimes are exploiting the new technologies to gain political control (Ronfeldt & Arquilla, 2003, p. 314). They use cyberattack against their critics. For instance, there are reports that the Chinese government sends viruses to attack websites that are banned in the country (Guillén & Suárez, 2005). Likewise, it is reported that the governments of Myanmar and Mauritania have hired botnet operators to attack their critics' websites with denial-of-service attacks (Cetron & Davies, 2009). Similarly, the Government of Myanmar has reportedly built up an advanced cyberwarfare department within the police force, which tracks its online critics and sends virus attached e-mails to exiled activists (Havely, 2000). In 2008, just before the anniversary of the Saffron Revolution,[9] at least three websites associated with Burmese exiles experienced the distributed denial-of-service attacks (Lunau, 2008).

1.6.2 Cybercrime Victims and Targets

1.6.2.1 Businesses

The US Federal Bureau of Investigation (FBI) reported that cyber-criminals have attacked almost all of the Fortune 500 companies (Pollock & May, 2002). According to the market research firm International Data Corporation (IDC), 39% of Fortune 500 companies suffered a security breach in 2003 and 40% of global IT managers have rated security as their number one priority. Likewise, according to the FBI, 9 out of 10 US companies experienced computer-security incidents in 2005 which led to a loss of US $67.2 billion (United States Government Accountability Office, 2007).

An estimate of the European Network Information Security Agency (ENISA) indicated that cybercrimes cost businesses in the European Union €65 billion annually (Darkreading.com, 2008). A survey conducted among Irish businesses in 2007 indicated that 98% of respondents indicated that they were cybercrime victims (Madden, 2007). The survey also found that their most serious cybercrimes cost over €100,000 for more than one in five companies.

1.6.2.2 Consumers

The fact that many consumers have weak technological and behavioral defenses against cybercrimes makes them vulnerable to such crimes. A 2005 survey by

America Online and the National Cyber Security Alliance found that 80% of computers in the test group were infected by spyware and almost all of them were completely unaware of it (US Fed News Service, Including US State News, 2005).

According to a report released by the FBI in January 2006, the respondents believed many of the incidents did not rise to the level of criminal activity or that reporting them would not lead to a positive outcome. A study of VeriSign indicated that most of the Australian web users lacked skills and knowhow in protecting their personal information (Businessweek.com, 2009).

Strategies to Avoid Being Victimized

Businesses and consumers are taking some measures in protecting themselves from becoming victims and targets by cyber-criminals. They are getting help and supports from government agencies and online security companies. In a July 2007 interview with *USA Today*, McAfee CEO reported that his company received 3,000–5,000 threat submissions per day from customers and 10% of them were new. The Federal Trade Commission (FTC) received about 15,000–20,000 contacts per week from victims and those who want to avoid becoming victims (GAO Reports June 17, 2009). A survey of US consumers found that 67% of respondents in the 18–24 age group, who became ID fraud victims in 2007, responded by putting fraud alerts on their credit reports and 47% purchased ID fraud insurance (Euromonitor.com, 2008).

1.6.3 Regulators and Governments

1.6.3.1 Government Agencies

In order to prevent and combat cybercrimes, governments across the world have created various agencies. These agencies have devoted resources to strengthen regulative institutions. Governments across the world have also promised to make further efforts to improve the regulative institutions by enacting new laws and to enforce existing laws. Government agencies have also taken measures to create public awareness about cybercrimes. In addition, government agencies' roles in stigmatizing cybercrimes by acting as legal arbiters are discussed in Chapter 5.

1.6.3.2 The US FTC

The FTC distributes security information through its website. It has also formed partnerships with other government agencies and the private sector. Dewie the e-Turtle, is the FTC's mascot, which helps to "promote a culture of security."[10] Likewise, the Department of Homeland Security promotes educational programs from the grade school through university levels. It also has a National Cyber Alert System to distribute information to computer users. The Department of Homeland Security also has awareness programs, which include encouraging citizens to "review and improve their cyber readiness" during Daylight Savings Time.[11]

1.6.3.3 The US Secret Service

The agency had about 1,000 trained agents in 2008 (Swartz, 2008). During 2004–2005, the Secret Service investigated and shut down an online organization, which had 4,000 members in a number of countries including Bulgaria, Canada, Poland, Sweden, and the United States (Grow & Bush, 2005). It was reported that the organization functioned as an international clearinghouse for 1.7 million stolen credit cards and identity documents, which led to a loss of over US $4 million for businesses and consumers (GAO Reports June 22, 2007). In 2007, the Secret Service official stated that the agency's Electronic Crimes Special Agent Program would have 770 trained and active agents by the end of the fiscal year (GAO Reports June 22, 2007).

1.6.3.4 The US FBI

In 2005, FBI spent US $150 million on cybercrimes out of its US $5 billion budget for that year (Grow & Bush, 2005). In 2007, FBI funded 1,151 employees for cybercrime and 659 among them were agents (Blitstein, 2007). Scott O'Neal computer intrusion head of the FBI's cyber division noted that as of 2008 every field office had "at least one dedicated cyber squad" (Heath, 2008).

1.6.3.5 The White House Cybersecurity Office

Perhaps the most notable regulative development in the United States concerns the creation of the White House office in May 2009, by President Obama, which will be led by a Cybersecurity Coordinator (cyber-czar). This office will be devoted to the security of the nation's digital infrastructure. The President outlined the responsibilities that the new office would fulfill: "orchestrating and integrating all cybersecurity policies for the government; working closely with the Office of Management and Budget to ensure agency budgets reflect those priorities; and, in the event of major cyber incident or attack, coordinating our response" (The White House, 2009). The new cyber-czar will report to the national security adviser and the director of the National Economic Council and would have "regular access" to the President (Harris, 2009). The Cybersecurity Office will work to strengthen the cooperation between the public and private sectors. The President emphasized that his Administration "will not dictate security standards for private companies. On the contrary, we will collaborate with industry to find technology solutions that ensure our security and promote prosperity" (cf. Asner & Kleyna, 2009).

1.6.3.6 The UK's National Hi-Tech Crime Unit (NHTCU) and Serious Organized Crime Agency (SOCA)

In the UK, the National Hi-Tech Crime Unit (NHTCU) was formed in 2001. NHTCU had built up an extensive network of international contacts and had impressive links with Russia and Eastern European countries (Computer Weekly, 2009). The Serious Organized Crime Agency (SOCA) was formed in 2006. In the same year, the NHTCU was merged with SOCA (Blakely & O'Neill, 2007). SOCA's annual budget was GB £400 million in 2008 (Giannangeli, 2008). SOCA's priority areas, however, are drugs, fraud, and human-trafficking. Critics argue that cybercrime and web-based industrial espionage are relatively low-priority areas. In 2007, SOCA had to cut about 400 staff because of budget cut (Blakely & O'Neill, 2007). The agency had more than 4,000 staff in 2008 (Giannangeli, 2008). The Metropolitan Police also announced a plan to establish a new cybercrime unit (Blakely &d O'Neill, 2007).

1.6.3.7 The Dutch Plainclothes High-Tech Unit

As of the early 2008, the Dutch plainclothes high-tech unit employed about 25 people (Carvajal, 2008). The chief inspector of the unit reported that the police were in the process of developing training programs for everyone in the unit (Birmingham Post, 2007).

1.6.4 Supranational Organizations

Given the global nature of cybercrimes, international institutions are likely to carry enormous power that can be harnessed to fight such crimes. International legal and regulatory frameworks to deal with cybercrimes and cyberattacks in general, however, are arguably severely underdeveloped (Shackelford, 2009). However, it is worth noting that there have been several noteworthy initiatives at the international level to combat cybercrimes. Some highly visible examples of supranational organizations working on cybercrimes include the United Nations, the Council of Europe and the G8 High Tech Crime Working Group.

1.6.4.1 The United Nations

In the early 1990s, the UN Resolution 45/121 endorsed the recommendations of the Eighth United Nations Congress on the Prevention of Crime and the Treatment of Offenders. It called upon Member States to intensify efforts to combat computer crimes. In 2001, UN General Assembly Resolutions 55/63 and 56/121 on "Combating the criminal misuse of information technologies" were passed. The resolutions advocated a global framework to counter cybercrimes. Resolutions 57/239 in 2002 and 58/199 in 2004 encouraged Member States to create a global culture of cybersecurity and to take action to protect critical infrastructure. The ITU, which is a *UN* Chartered organization, has developed the Toolkit for Cybercrime Legislation. The Toolkit intends to help develop "cybercrime legislation that is globally applicable and interoperable with existing national and regional legislative measures" (ITU, 2009; p. 8). As of October 2009, the ITU had 191 countries and 700 organizations as its members. In 2007, the ITU announced a 2 years plan to combat cybercrime. The ITU collaborated with the Malaysian company IMPACT to develop a system to help prevent, defend, and respond to cyber threats. In 2009, the ITU and IMPACT announced that they developed the Global Response Center. The Center provides an early warning system by bringing the global threat intelligence on a near real-time basis and helps identify threats associated with a country (Schlein, 2009).

1.6.4.2 Council of Europe (CoE)

In 1997, the 41-nation Council of Europe (CoE) started working on international cooperation on cybercrime. The ambition of the group was to build on its binding International Treaty on Cybercrime. In November 2000, the Council released the 22nd draft of its treaty (BBC News Online, 2000). In April 2008, the Council settled on voluntary guidelines to strengthen cooperation between the police and Internet service companies (Carvajal, 2008). Its Cybercrime Convention asks signatory countries to enact legislation criminalizing the Convention-specified cybercrime categories (Council of Europe, 2001).

As of August 2009, 46 nations including four non-member states of the CoE (Canada, Japan, South Africa, and the United State) had signed the Treaty and 26 of them including the United State ratified it (COE, 2009). The US Senate had approved the Treaty in August 2006 (Chertoff, 2009).

One of the goals of the CoE is to harmonize laws against cybercrime. It also aims to ensure that police forces and investigators in individual countries follow standard evidence-gathering techniques and promote the use of latest technology for tracking and catching cyber-criminals.

In its 4th annual Octopus Conference against Cybercrime held in Strasbourg, France, in March 2009, the CoE launched the second phase (March 2009–June 2011) of its project. The CoE intends to help countries worldwide to implement its Convention. For instance, as of the early 2009, Laos and Cambodia had no computer crime laws. However, the Council translated the Convention into the *Lao language*, which provided a groundwork for cybercrime laws in the country (Kirk, 2009). In May 2007, the European Commission pledged to support the implementation of the Convention on Cybercrime worldwide. Over 100 countries in the world are using the Convention as a framework to develop their cybercrime-related regulative institutions (COE, 2009). Countries outside the CoE have been invited to join the Treaty. That is, a non-CoE member conforms to the Treaty like a CoE member. Many non-CoE countries such as Argentina, Brazil, Colombia, Egypt, India, Indonesia, Nigeria, Sri Lanka, and the Philippines are soon expected to join the Convention (Britt, 2008; Cybercrime Law, 2009).

1.6.4.3 G8 High Tech Crime Working Group

The G8's Subgroup on High Tech Crime is one of the five subgroups of the "Lyon Group" created to implement the Forty Recommendations adopted by G8 in 1996.[12] The Subgroup was created in January 1997, which adopted the "Ten Principles" to combat computer crimes. This Subgroup's mission is to enhance the abilities to combat high-technology crimes. It was subsequently expanded to include non-G8 countries. In May 2001, the G8 Government/Private Sector High Level Meeting on High Tech Crime held in Tokyo covered five major themes: data retention, data preservation, threat assessment and prevention, protection of electronic commerce, and user authentication and training (Miyake, 2001).

1.6.5 Voluntary, Nonprofit, and Non-government Organizations

Voluntary, nonprofit, and non-government organizations define the parameters of acceptable behaviors of various actors in reference to fight against cybercrimes. Some organizations such as WiredSafety (Box 1.3) are providing help and safety online.

Box 1.3 WiredSafety

WiredSafety (WiredSafety.org) is a Seattle, Washington-based nonprofit Internet safety advocacy group. WiredSafety was formerly known as CyberAngels (Frechette, 2005). WiredSafety is arguably the world's largest organization to provide help and safety online. In 2002, it had 1,000 volunteers worldwide, which increased to over 9,000 in 2007 (Joseph, 2007). WiredSafety's various Internet safety groups include WiredPatrol, WiredKids.org, WiredTeens, Teenangels, CyberMoms and CyberDads, WiredCops.org. These groups regularly "patrol" the Internet for child pornography, child molesters, and cyber stalkers (Frechette, 2005). Many of the WiredSafety volunteers are also trained by the FBI.

WiredSafety focuses on four areas: helping cybercrime victims, assisting law-enforcement agencies, education, and providing information about privacy and security online (Joseph, 2007). Child pornography is a major focus of WiredSafety. In 2002, average number of illegal sites in this category reported by WiredSafety to authorities was over 600 a month. In 2004, it provided services to over 1,000 victims in areas such as information and education (Aftab, 2004). WiredSafety also trains police officers on investigative techniques (Hauser, 2007). As part of the education component, WiredSafety volunteers review family friendly websites, filter software products and Internet services, and make their findings available online (Frechette, 2005). The site offers resources to keep children safe online and maintains an updated list of "not-for-children" websites (Frechette, 2005; Joseph, 2007). Teenangels.org is comprised of teen and preteen volunteers trained by law enforcement.

1.6.5.1 Civil-Liberties Organizations

The effectiveness of anti-cybercrime activities undertaken by an institutional actor is a function of how it fits with the "higher" level institutions and exogenous parameters (Snidal, 1994, 1996). In this regard, civil-liberty groups have opposed some national laws and international treaties arguing that they give too much power to the government and law-enforcement agencies. For instance, in the US, in 2001, technology-industry lobbyists and consumer and civil-liberties activists including the American Civil Library Association, Electronic Privacy Information Centre, and Consumer Federation of America circulated a letter to members of Congress and the president, which criticized the government's measures to deal with cybercrimes and called for a stronger set of privacy rules (Benson & Simpson, 2001).

Likewise, civil-liberty groups and some industry associations have vigorously opposed the Council of Europe's cybercrime treaty since the early 2000, when it became public. They argued that the CoE's proposed cybercrime fighting measures are not within the parameters of established constitutional requirements. A draft CoE treaty on cybercrime was condemned as "appalling" by civil-liberty groups, which was arguably contrary to well-established norms for the protection of the individual Global Internet Liberty Campaign (BBC News Online, 2000). According to a provision in the draft treaty, people could be charged with computer crimes although the country where they lived did not consider their acts as crimes.

In 2000, 23 organizations signed a letter, which warned that the treaty would do serious damage to civil liberties under the guise of helping law-enforcement agencies catch cyber-criminals (BBC News Online, 2000). They argued that it would endanger privacy rights and grant too much power to government investigators (McCullagh, 2003). Thirty-five organizations coordinated by the umbrella organization the Global Internet Liberty Campaign urged the Council to change the treaty saying, "The draft treaty is contrary to well-established norms for the protection of the individual" (BBC News Online, 2000). Industry groups such as Americans for Computer Privacy and the Internet Alliance have also raised concerns that the treaty could limit anonymity or impose vague record-keeping requirements on US Internet providers (McCullagh, 2003).

1.7 Motivations Associated with Cybercrimes

A deeper understanding of web attacks requires an examination of motivation that energizes a hacking unit's behaviors (Coates, 2002). The nature of web attacks allows us to draw an analogy with conventional wars. As is the case of the physical world, wars on the web are fought for material ends as well as for intangible goals such as honor, dominance, and prestige (Hirshleifer, 1998).

As early as in the mid-1990s, Rasch (1996, pp. 141–142) noted the involvement of a wide range of individuals in cybercrimes with varied motivations: "[C]omputer criminals are not of a discrete type. They range from the computer world equivalent of a juvenile delinquent, the hacker or cyberpunk, to the sophisticated white-collar embezzler attacking financial institution computers, and include cyberterrorists, extortionists, spies, petty thieves and joyriders."

Literatures in psychology and economics suggest two types of motivations.

1.7.1 Intrinsic Motivation

The theory of intrinsic motivation is based on the premise that human need for competence and self-determination are linked with interest and enjoyment (Deci & Ryan, 1985, p. 35). According to Ryan and Deci (2000), intrinsically motivated individuals do activities for "inherent satisfactions rather than for some separable consequence." They argue that "when intrinsically motivated, a person is moved to act for the fun or challenge entailed rather than because of external prods, pressures or rewards." Intrinsic motivation can be separated into two separate constituents: (1) enjoyment-based intrinsic motivation and (2) obligation/community-based intrinsic motivation (Lindenberg, 2001).

1.7.1.1 Enjoyment-Based Intrinsic Motivation

Central to the concept of intrinsic motivation is having fun or enjoying oneself when taking part in an activity (Deci & Ryan, 1985). Csikszentmihalyi (1975), one of the first psychologists to study the enjoyment dimension, emphasized that some activities were pursued for the sake of enjoyment derived from doing them. Csikszentmihalyi refers it to a satisfying flow of activity. Shapira (1976) argues that this category of motivation is related with fulfilling a challenging task without an external reward. Maverick hackers, for instance, attack websites because of the perceived challenges and without any desire for financial incentives.

1.7.1.2 Obligation/Community-Based Intrinsic Motivation

Lindenberg (2001) argues that acting on the basis of principle is also a form of intrinsic motivation. He argues that individuals may be socialized into acting appropriately and in a manner consistent with the norms of a group. The goal to act consistently within the norms of a group can trigger a normative frame of action (Lakhani & Wolf, 2005).

Hackers may associate themselves with various groups such as a nation, a territory, a terrorist organization, an association of hackers, or other ideological groups. The Zapatista movement in Chiappas state in southern Mexico was arguably the first high-profile group to employ cyberattacks against the web servers of Mexican officials to pursue its political goals (Lee, 2000).

Likewise, the Electrohippies Collective (http://www.fraw.org.uk/ehippies/index. shtml) encouraged individuals to attack the World Trade Organization (WTO) web servers. The obligation/community goal is strongest when gain seeking (gaining personal advantage at the expense of other group members) by individuals within the reference community is minimized (Lakhani & Wolf, 2005).

1.7.2 Extrinsic Motivation

Economists have contributed to our understanding of how extrinsic motivations drive human behavior. Economic theory suggests that human behavior is a result of "incentives applied from outside the person" (Frey, 1997, p. 13). The benefits accruing to the individual may be immediate or delayed. The amount of financial incentives and the amount of motivation driving a hacker's behavior co-vary positively.

Many security researchers suggest that there has been a rise of professional cybercrime (Antonopoulos, 2009). Peter Tippett, of Verizon Business, noted, "Today's online data thieves don't just run automatic scanners and jump on any network hole they find. They're more likely to first choose a target that has data they can turn into cash, and then figure out how to break in" (Larkin, 2009, p. 33).

Extrinsically motivated hackers are thus likely to attack networks of companies with higher digitization of values (higher potential financial incentives). For instance, online casinos, banks, and e-commerce hubs are an industry sweet spot for cyber extortionists (also see Box 1.1).

1.7.3 Combination of Motivations

In many cases, human behavior is driven by multiple motivations—different forms of intrinsic and extrinsic (Lindenberg, 2001). Thus, a person who wants to make money and also have fun is likely to choose opportunities that give economic reward (ransom from hacking an e-commerce website) with a sense of having fun (Lakhani & Wolf, 2005). To take one example, the hackers protesting India's nuclear weapons tests in 1998 fought for ideology (community-based intrinsic motivation), but also admitted they attacked the website for thrills (enjoyment-based intrinsic motivation) (Denning, 2000).

1.7.4 Trend Toward Extrinsically Motivated Crimes

It was apparent from our review of the cybercrime industry that the combination of motivations has changed drastically over time. Derek Manky, security researcher at Fortinet, noted, "Hacking has escalated from a destructive nature to financial gain through phishing, targeting people for bank account details, and siphoning accounts from there" (cf. Fong, 2008). In a 1991 survey conducted by the Communications Managers Association, 55% of the respondents reported problems with computer viruses and 48% reported a computer-security breach by a hacker (Harler & Fox,

1992). Note that most of these crimes were not financially motivated. Likewise, by 1992, about 1,300 computer viruses existed and most of them were harmless (Hansen, 2002).

Surveys that are more recent have found consumers' experiences of dramatically increased pervasiveness of extrinsically motivated cybercrimes. For example, in an UCLA-sponsored study completed in 2001, 90% respondents stated that they were concerned about putting their credit card numbers online (cf. Smith, 2004). Likewise, in a 2002 survey conducted by San Francisco-based Computer Security Institute among computer-security experts working for the US private sector and federal government, 90% of the respondents said that they experienced a computer-security breach within the past year and 80% of those resulted in financial losses (Davis, 2006). Blau (2004) quoted a Russian hacker: "There is more of a financial incentive [extrinsic motivation] now for hackers and crackers as well as for virus writers to write for money and not just for glory or some political motive [intrinsic motivation]."

1.8 Businesses' Countermeasures to Combat Cybercrimes

In addition to regulative measures discussed above, there have also been corporate-level initiatives to fight cybercrimes. Some organizations have invested in alternative networks, which are insulated from the conventional Internet. The Internet2 consortium, for instance, has created a high-performance backbone network, known as the Abilene network. Only Internet2 members may connect to the Abilene network.

Companies such as Microsoft, Google, and eBay have their own teams of investigators to deal with cybercrimes. For instance, eBay claimed that the company had "2,000 staff members policing its site around the clock" (*Consumer Reports*, 2007). More importantly, businesses have initiated collaborations with law-enforcement agencies in fighting against cyber threats. For instance, in order to gather information to help law enforcement, some financial institutions' employees pose as buyers and sellers in underground e-marketplaces (Sutherland, 2008). Microsoft finances cybercrime conferences and training programs to judges and law-enforcement agencies (Birmingham Post, 2007). For instance, in 2009, Microsoft spent GB £325,000 in the United Kingdom to organize a 3-day training in IT forensics, in which 190 police and law-enforcement officers participated (Grant, 2009). Likewise, eBay has been educating Romanian prosecutors about cybercrimes including explaining to a judge using layman's language (Wylie, 2007).

Another way in which businesses are helping develop anti-cybercrime institutions is by aggressively pursuing cyber-criminals under the existing laws. For instance, in 2008, MySpace filed at least five lawsuits against spammers. One of the lawsuits resulted in a US $230 million judgment for violation of the federal anti-spam law (Swartz, 2008). Likewise, in June 2009, Microsoft filed a lawsuit over click fraud against three Canadians (Business Week, 2009). These measures have undoubtedly helped strengthen the regulative institutions.

There have also been industry level efforts to fight cybercrimes. For instance, the Corporate IT Forum, which represents 150 companies in the UK, reported that it was considering for the establishment of a confidential channel through which cybercrimes incidents could be reported (Carvajal, 2008).

1.9   Concluding Comments

Hacking and cybercrime are going through a rapid transition phase. In recent years, cybercrimes have increased dramatically in terms of quantity, diversity, and sophistication. Some analysts have rightfully argued that while the Western countries have declared war on terrorism, they have failed to pay enough attention to this even more serious threat (Glenny, 2008; Wiltenburg, 2008).

One observation is that proportion of extrinsically motivated cyberattacks has increased. Extrinsically motivated cyber-criminals ruthlessly and efficiently exploit the weaknesses of their victims and targets. What is more, a number of purely symbolic cyberattacks (e.g., those directed toward challenging some forms of ideologies) also entail significant economic losses.[13]

All businesses and consumers are not equally aware of the threats associated with cybercrimes. They also vary considerably in terms of the level of preparedness and the barriers and facilitators to improving preparedness to fight cybercrimes. Some victims and targets are thus particularly prone to cybercrime. Businessees and consumers that are unprepared, unaware, or inadequately aware are more likely to be victimzed by cyber-criminals.

Anti-cybercrime measures are being taken at various levels. As observed above, there appears to be a far greater achievement in fighting cybercrimes than might at first appear. On the bright side, anti-cybercrime formal and informal institutions have thickened in recent years. Governments have devoted substantial resources in creating and developing formal institutions to fight and prevent cybercrimes. Yet, notwithstanding these accomplishments government measures are far from sufficient to deal with cybercrimes.

Some argue that law enforcement is losing the battle against cyber-criminals (Zeller, 2005). Many governments have underestimated the potential impacts of cybercrimes and neglected to pay enough attention to combating this new form of criminality. Cybercrime fighting efforts are under-funded. Cybercrime has been a relatively low-priority area among the world's top crime-fighting agencies such as SOCA and FBI. They have devoted more resources to other conventional crimes such as counterterrorism, drugs, fraud, and human-trafficking. For instance, The UK's National Hi-Tech Crime Unit, which was formed in 2001 to fight against computer crime, could not convince cybercrimes' seriousness to the government. The unit could secure only half the funds needed (Goodwin, 2004). SOCA allocated only 5% of its 2008–2009 budget on cybercrime (Giannangeli, 2008). In the same manner, SOCA has been criticized for its low cybercrime prosecution rates. There is also a lack of coordination among various government agencies established to deal with cybercrimes. A complete overhaul of the structures, organization, functions, and activities of various cybercrime-related government agencies may be needed to fight with cybercrimes.

As discussed above, some international level efforts are being directed against cybercrimes. However, institutions vary widely across countries with respect to cybercrimes. The above discussion indicates that there has been a lack of international agreement on definitions of various terms related to cybercrimes, which has hindered efforts to deal with such crimes at the global levels. On the bright side, there have been some international level initiatives such as CoE's Treaty on Cybercrimes. Note too that many of the signatories of the Treaty are developing countries. Their participation in the Treaty would help developing countries to cooperate efficiently with CoE members and non-members in fighting against cybercrimes.

Notes

1. A botnet (robot network) is a network of computers infected with worms and Trojans, which is controlled by a cyber-criminal. A botnet is used to deliver spam and malware applications to victims.
2. In 2007, 5,987 employees were assigned to counterterrorism and 4,479 to counterintelligence. Cybercrime and cyber-terrorism are thus "a distant third."
3. There are two categories of DoS attacks: operating system (OS) attacks and network attacks. OS attacks entail discovering holes in the security of the OS and bringing down the system. Network attacks disconnect a network from the Internet services provider (ISP). The attackers use mis-configured networks to perform such attacks.
4. Malware (malicious + software) is software program used by cyber criminals to infiltrate or damage a computer system without the owner's informed consent.
5. In an e-mail, which claimed to be from a Philippino dying of cancer, the sender said he needed help to distribute $26 million to "people of the tsunami disaster." He offered a 20% commission to anyone who could help him (Iwata and Kasindorf, 2005).
6. This is an updated version of the author's article published in *Foreign Policy* magazine in May/June 2005.
7. The RBN stopped operations in November 2007.
8. US Gen. Accounting Office, Information Security: Computer Attacks at Department of Defense Pose Increasing Risks 15 Fig. 1.2 (1996), available at http://www.pbs.org/wgbh/pages/frontline/shows/hackers/risks/1996dod.pdf
9. The massive monk-led protests against the Buremese military junta in 2007 is also referred as the Saffron Revolution.
10. Protecting Our Nation's Cyber Space: Educational Awareness for the Cyber Citizen: Hearing Before the House Subcommittee on Technology, Information Policy, Intergovernmental Relations and the Census, 108th Cong. 12–13 (2004) (statement of FTC Comm'r Orson Swindle).
11. Protecting Our Nation's Cyber Space: Educational Awareness for the Cyber Citizen: Hearing Before the House Subcommittee on Technology, Information Policy, Intergovernmental Relations, and the Census, 108th Cong. 12–13 (2004) (statement of Amit Yoran, Director, National Cyber Security Division, US Department of Homeland Security).
12. The G8 (Group of Eight) consists of Canada, France, Germany, Italy, Japan, Russia, the UK, and the US.

13. For instance, hackers that attacked India's Bhabha Atomic Research Center (BARC) network in 1998 also downloaded thousands of pages of e-mail and research documents and erased huge amount of data (Denning, 2000).

References

Acohido, B. (2009, February 17). Experts eager to hear Hathaway's advice for Obama on cyber-security. *USA Today.* http://blogs.usatoday.com/technologylive/2009/02/experts-eager-t.html. Accessed 1 October 2009.

Acohido, B., & Swartz, J. (2006, October 11). Cybercrime flourishes in online hacker forums. *USA Today.* http://www.usatoday.com/tech/news/computersecurity/infotheft/2006-10-11-cybercrime-hacker-forums_x.htm. Accessed 1 October 2007.

Africa News. (2007, October 24). South Africa; Internet banking fraud on the increase.

Aftab, P. (2004, August 23). Understanding the Cyberharassment Problem. *InformationWeek.* http://www.informationweek.com/news/security/privacy/showArticle.jhtml?articleID=29116 706#at. Accessed 1 October 2009.

Andrews, L. (2009). Online scams go unreported and unpunished. *Cybercriminals beating the law Canberra Times (Australia) Section A* (p. 5).

Antonopoulos, A. (2009). ATM hack: Organized crime or market forces? *Network World. Southborough, 26*(8), 20.

Asner, M. A., & Kleyna, M. (2009). The new white house cyber czar. *Computer & Internet Lawyer, 26*(7), 1–4.

Bauerly, R. J. (2009). Online auction fraud and ebay. *Marketing Management Journal, 19*(1), 133–143.

BBC News. (2001, August 29). Business leaders are calling on the government to set up a national database to combat internet fraud. http://news.bbc.co.uk/hi/english/business/newsid_1514000/1514215.stm. Accessed 9 October 2001.

BBC News. (2004, December 22). Santy Worm Makes Unwelcome Visit. http://news.bbc.co.uk/1/hi/technology/4117711.stm. Accessed 1 October 2005.

BBC News. (2006a, October 8). Net crime 'big fear' for Britons. http://news.bbc.co.uk/2/hi/technology/5414696.stm. Accessed 1 October 2007.

BBC News. (2006b, December 8). Criminals 'target tech students'. http://news.bbc.co.uk/2/hi/technology/6220416.stm. Accessed 20 June 2008.

BBC News Online. (2000, December 18). Cybercrime treaty condemned. http://news.bbc.co.uk/1/hi/sci/tech/1072580.stm. Accessed 1 October 2001.

Beatty, A. (2009, June 17). Agence France Presse – English. US cybersecurity chief warns of 'market' in malware.

Becker, G. (1968). Crime and punishment: An economic approach. *Journal of Political Economy, 76*(2), 169–217.

Bell, R.E. (2002). The prosecution of computer crime. *Journal of Financial Crime, 9*(4), 308–325.

Benson, M., & Simpson, G. R. (2001, January 18). Privacy measure for US is backed by trade group. *Wall Street Journal,* B.6.

Birmingham Post. (2007, September 16). Politics: Cybercrime victim every 10 seconds, 4.

Blakely, R., & O'Neill, S. (2007, December 4). Cybercrime agency faces cuts as computer raid threats grow. *The Times* (London), 41.

Blau, J. (2004, May 26). Russia – a happy haven for hackers. http://www.computerweekly.com/Article130839.htm. Accessed 1 October 2005.

Blitstein, R. (2007, November 14). Cybercops: US targets terrorists as online thieves run amok. *San Jose Mercury News.*

Bridis, T. (2006). Computer Researchers Warn of Net Attacks, Yahoo! Fin. Accessed 1 October 2009. http://biz.yahoo.com/ap/060316/internet attack.html. Accessed 1 October 2007.

Britt, P. (2008). International Cybercrime Convention Gains Adherents around the World, Info Tech & Telecom News, The Heartland Institute.

Business Week. (2009). Microsoft Sues, *137*, 9.

Businessweek.com. (2009). Countries with the most cybercrime. http://images.businessweek.com/ss/09/07/0707_ceo_guide_security/17.htm. Accessed 1 October 2009.

Cardoso, L. S. (2007). Cyber crime and critical information infrastructure impact. *ITU*. http://www.itu.int/ITU-D/cyb/events/2007/praia/docs/cardoso-cybercrime-impact-praia-nov-07.pdf. Accessed 1 October 2009.

Carvajal, D. (2008, April 7). Cybercrime evolves as it grows. *The International Herald Tribune*, 10.

Cetron, M. J., & Davies, O. (2009). Ten critical trends for cybersecurity. *Futurist, 43*(5), 40–49.

Cheney, J. S. (2005). Identity theft: Do definitions still matter? Federal Reserve Bank of Philadelphia, Payment Cards Center, Discussion paper, No. 05–10 August.

Chertoff, M. (2009). The responsibility to contain: Protecting sovereignty under international law. *Foreign Affairs, 88*(1), 130–148.

Christian Science Monitor. (2006, March 17). *When the Law Chases the Internet, 98*(77), 6.

Claburn, T. (2009a). Hacker indicted for stealing 130 million credit cards. *InformationWeek*. http://www.informationweek.com/news/security/attacks/showArticle.jhtml?articleID=219400277.

Claburn, T. (2009b). Cyber attack against Georgia Blurred civilian and military. *InformationWeek*. http://www.informationweek.com/news/government/security/showArticle.jhtml?articleID=219400248&subSection=All+Stories. Accessed 11 October 2009.

Coates, J. F. (2002). What's next? Foreseeable terrorist acts. *The Futurist, 36*(5), 23–26.

COE. (2009). Convention on Cybercrime: CETS No.:185. http://conventions.coe.int/Treaty/Commun/ChercheSig.asp?NT=185&CM=&DF=&CL=ENG. Accessed 11 October 2009.

Computer Weekly. (2009, April 16). Does government have the will to win against e-crime? http://www.computerweekly.com/blogs/editors-blog/2009/04/does-government-have-the-will.html#at. Accessed 30 October 2009.

Consumer Reports. (2007). Winning at eBay: How to bid smart & play safe. *72*(8), 12–14.

Council of Europe. (2001). Convention on cybercrime, arts 2–13, ETS No 185, available at http://conventions.coe.int/Treaty/en/Treaties/Html/185.htm. Accessed 1 October 2009.

Coviello, A., & Holleyman, R. (2008). Tougher cybercrime legislation needs OK from congress, President, 2008. http://www.mercurynews.com/opinion/ci_7984798. Accessed 1 October 2009.

Csikszentmihalyi, M. (1975). *Beyond boredom and anxiety: The experience of play in work and games*. San Francisco: Jossey-Bass, Inc.

Cybercrime Law. (2009). News. http://www.cybercrimelaw.net.

Darkreading.com. (2008, June 11). Cybercrime outranks other crimes on Europeans' worry list: Almost half of German PC users believe they will eventually fall victim. http://www.darkreading.com/document.asp?doc_id=156206. Accessed 1 October 2009.

Davis, J. B. (2006). Cybercrime fighters. *ABA Journal, 89*, 36.

Deci, E. L., & Ryan, R. M. (1985). *Intrinsic motivation and self-determination in human behavior*. New York: Plenum Press.

Denning, D.E. (2000). Hacktivism: An emerging threat to diplomacy. American Foreign Service Association. www.afsa.org/fsj/sept00/Denning.cfm. Accessed 1 October 2009.

Economist.com. (2007). The mouse that roared; Cyberwarfare: Is cyberwarfare a serious threat?

Euromonitor.com. (2008). Cybercrime: The global impact on consumer behavior. http://www.portal.euromonitor.com/passport/ResultsList.aspx. Accessed 1 October 2009.

Europa.eu. (2001). Data protection: "Junk" e-mail costs internet users 10 billion a year worldwide – Commission study. http://europa.eu/rapid/pressReleasesAction.do?reference=IP/01/154&format=HTML&aged=0&language=EN&guiLanguage=en. Accessed 1 October 2009.

Finkle, J. (2009, July 1). The Globe and Mail (Canada) Friend or cyber criminal? Cybercrime growing on Facebook, Reuters P. L3.

Fong, C. (2008, May 8). Fighting the agents of organized cybercrime. *CNN.com*.

Foreign Policy. (2005, March/April). Caught in the net: Australian teens, 92.

Frechette, J. (2005). Cyber-democracy or cyber-hegemony? Exploring the political and economic structures of the internet as an alternative source of information. *Library Trends, 53*(4), 555–575.

Frey, B. (1997). *Not just for the money: An economic theory of Brookfield*. VT: Edward Elgar Publishing Company.

Gabrys, E. (2002). The international dimensions of cyber-crime, Part 1. *Information Systems Security, 11*(4), 21–32.

GAO Reports. (2007). *Public and private entities face challenges in addressing cyber threats*. RPT-NUMBER: GAO-07-705.

GAO Reports. (2009, June 17). *Identity theft: Governments have acted to protect personally identifiable information, but vulnerabilities remain (preceding)* (pp. 1–20).

Giannangeli, M. (2008). Are we ready for Russian Mafia's crime revolution? Sunday Express, June 8, 2008, Scottish Edition, p. 3.

Glaser, D. (1971). *Social deviance*. Chicago, IL: Markham.

Glenny, M. M. (2008). *A journey through the global criminal underworld, Knopf*.

Goodwin, B. (2004, February 10). Victims must speak up to beat cybercrime. *Computer Weekly*, 18.

Gordon, S., & Ford, R. (2006). On the definition and classification of cybercrime. *Journal in Computer Virology, 2*,13–20.

Grant, I. (2008). The UK's dependence on the internet is putting more than half of its economy at risk, says the government, ComputerWeekly.com, 19 March, 2008. http://www.computerweekly.com/Articles/2008/03/19/229932/uk-government-warns-of-economys-reliance-on-internet.htm. Accessed 1 October 2009.

Grant, I. (2009). *Microsoft gives police training in IT forensics Computer Weekly*, 6 pp.

Greenberg, A. (2009). Cybercops without borders. *Forbes*, June 4.

Greenemeier, L. (2006, October 30). New from Cybercrooks: Fake chrome, pump-and-dump. *InformationWeek, 1112*, 26.

Grow, B., & Bush, J. (2005, May 30). Hacker hunters. *Business Week*.

Guillén, M. F., & Suárez, S. L. (2005). Explaining the global digital divide: Economic, political and sociological drivers of cross-national internet use. *Social Forces, 84*(2), 681–708.

Hamilton, L. (2009). Cyber-attack just a click away, IndyStar.com. http://www.indystar.com/article/20090824/OPINION12/908240315/1002/OPINION/Cyber-attack+just+a+click+away. Accessed 1 October 2009.

Hansen, B. (2002). Early hackers wanted to advance technology, not diminish it. *CQ Weekly, 60*(26).

Harler, C., & Fox, B. (1992). Network security communications news. *Nokomis, 29* (1), 20–24.

Harris, S. (2009, June 15). Digital security in an Analog Bureaucracy. *National Journal*, 9. http://www.nationaljournal.com/njmagazine/nj_20090613_8035.php. Accessed 1 October 2009.

Harvard Law Review. (2006, June). Note: Immunizing the internet, Or: How I learned to stop worrying and love the worm, *119*, 2442.

Hauser, C. (2007, December 7). A video posted online poses a riddle for police. http://www.nytimes.com/2007/12/07/nyregion/07video.html?pagewanted=print. Accessed 1 October 2009.

Havely, J. (2000, February 16). Online's when states go to cyber-war. *BBC News*.

Heath, N. (2008, April 15). FBI cyber crime chief on botnets, web terror and the social network threat: Q&A: Scott O'Neal, computer intrusion head, FBI cyber division. http://management.silicon.com/government/0,39024677,39188638,00.htm. Accessed 1 October 2009.

Hess, P. (2008). Pentagon puts hold on USAF cyber effort. *Associated Press*. http://www.boston.com/news/nation/washington/articles/2008/08/13/pentagon_puts_hold_on_usaf_cybcr effort/. Accessed 1 October 2009.

Hirshleifer, J. (1998). The bioeconomic causes of war. *Managerial and Decision Economics, 19*(7/8), 457–466.

Ho, S. (2004, November/December). Haven for hackers. *Foreign Policy*.

IC3. (2007). Internet fraud crime report, January 1, 2006–December 31, 2006. National White Collar Crime Center and the Federal Bureau of Investigation. www.ic3.gov/media/annualreport/2006_IC3Report.pdf. Accessed 1 October 2009.

Infosecurity-magazine.com. (2009, September 29). SOCA: Cybercrime is global and organised. http://www.infosecurity-magazine.com/view/4246/soca-cybercrime-is-global-and-organised. Accessed 1 October 2009.

Ismail, I. (2008, February 18). Understanding cybercriminals. *New Straits Times* (Malaysia), 12.

ITU. (2007). New study estimates an online crime is committed every 10 seconds in the UK. http://www.itu.int/osg/csd/newslog/default,date,2007-11-21.aspx. Accessed 1 October 2009.

ITU. (2009). ITU Toolkit For Cybercrime Legislation, April 2009, International Telecommunication Union. http://www.itu.int/ITU-D/cyb/cybersecurity/docs/itu-toolkit-cybercrime-legislation.pdf. Accessed 1 October 2009.

Iwata, E., & Martin, K. (2005). Crooks faking Web sites to bilk unwitting donors. *USA Today*.

Jones, B. R. (2007). Comment: Virtual neighborhood watch: Open source software and community policing against cybercrime. *Journal of Criminal Law & Criminology, 97*(2), 601–629.

Jones, M. (2006, September 15). Cybercrime becoming more organized. *Baseline.com*.

Joseph, L. C. (2007). Keeping Safe in Cyberspace. *MultiMedia & Internet@Schools, 14*(1), 17–20.

Katyal, N. K. (2001). Criminal law in cyberspace. *University of Pennsylvania Law Review, 149*(4), 1003–1114.

Keizer, G. (2006, January 25). Cybercrime feared 3 times more than physical crime. *InformationWeek*.

Kendall, N. (2009). What the cybercrime fraudsters get up to, Times Online. http://www.timesonline.co.uk/tol/news/uk/crime/article6735761.ece. Accessed 1 October 2009.

Kirk, J. (2009, March 11). Countries move forward on cybercrime treaty. *PC World*. http://www.pcworld.com/article/161067/countries_move_forward_on_cybercrime_treaty.html. Accessed 1 October 2009.

Kirk, J. (2009). Cyberattack Probe Goes Global. http://www.csoonline.com/article/497242/Cyberattack_Probe_Goes_Global. Accessed 1 October 2009.

Krebs, B. (2007, October 13). Taking on the Russian Business Network. http://blog.washingtonpost.com/securityfix/2007/10/taking_on_the_russian_business.html. Accessed 27 October 2009.

Kshetri, N. (2005). Pattern of global cyber war and crime: A conceptual framework. *Journal of International Management, 11*(4), 541–562.

Kshetri, N. (2006). The simple economics of cybercrimes. *IEEE Security and Privacy, 4*(1), 33–39.

Kshetri, N. (2009). Positive externality, increasing returns and the rise in cybercrimes. *Communications of the ACM, 52*(12).

Lakhani, K. R., & Wolf, R. G. (2005). Why hackers do what they do: Understanding motivation and effort in free/open source software projects. In Feller, J., Fitzgerald, B., Hissam, S., & Lakhani, K. R. (Eds.), Perspectives on Free and Open Source Software. Cambridge, MA: MIT Press.

Larkin, E. (2009). Organized crime moves into data theft. *PC World, 27*(7), 33–34.

Lee, J. K. (2000). *The e-citizen, social education*. Arlington, *64*(6), 378–380.

Leyden, J. (2004, September 23). US credit card firm fights DDoS attack. http://www.theregister.co.uk/2004/09/23/authorize_ddos_attack. Accessed 1 October 2009.

Lindenberg, S. (2001). Intrinsic motivation in a new light. *Kyklos, 54*(2/3), 317–342.

Lunau, K. (2008). *Burma sets its sights on online critics Maclean's, 121*(39), 51.

Lunev, S. (2001, October 1). 'Red Mafia' operating in the US – Helping Terrorists. http://www.newsmax.com/archives/articles/2001/9/28/90942.shtml. Accessed 1 October 2002.

Madden, C. (2007). Firms trying to crack down on cyber-crime. *The Irish Times*, 14.

M2 PressWIRE. (2008). BCS: BCS Launches Special Cybercrime 'Think Tank' ahead of London 2012.

McCullagh, D. (2003). Bush backs international cybercrime plan. *CNET News.com*. http://news.zdnet.co.uk/itmanagement/0,1000000308,39117978,00.htm. Accessed 1 October 2004.

McMillan, R. (2009, October 7). Citing cybercrime, FBI director doesn't bank online. *computerworld.com*. http://www.computerworld.com/s/article/9139106/Citing_cybercrime_FBI_director_doesn_t_bank_online. Accessed 11 October 2009. Accessed 11 October 2009.

Michael, G. (2009). Adam Gadahn and Al-Qaeda's internet strategy. *Middle East Policy, 16*(3), 135–152.

Mitnick, K. D., & Simon, L. W. (2002). *The art of deception: Controlling the human element of security*. John Wiley & Sons, Inc.

Miyake, K. (2001). G8 concludes Tokyo high-tech crime meeting, May 31. http://archives.cnn.com/2001/TECH/internet/05/31/g8.cyber.crime.idg/index.html. Accessed 1 October 2009.

Naidu, E. (2008, May 11). Cybercrime expert comes to SA. http://www.iol.co.za/index.php?set_id=1&click_id=139&art_id=vn20080511082218330C406913 Accessed 1 October 2008.

Nasuwt.org. (2009). Prejudice-related bullying. http://www.nasuwt.org.uk/consum/groups/public/@equalityandtraining/documents/nas_download/nasuwt_002942.pdf. Accessed 1 October 2009.

Naylor, R. T. (2005). The rise and fall of the underground economy. *Brown Journal of World Affairs, Winter/Spring, 11*(2), 131–143.

Onlinecasinonews.com. (2004, February 3). Mob's extortion attempt on Internet bookies. http://www.onlinecasinonews.com/ocnv2_1/article/article.asp?id=4748 Accessed 1 October 2005.

Orban, L. (2009). Multilingualism: A policy for uniting Europeans, London School of Economics. http://ec.europa.eu/commission_barroso/orban/news/docs/speeches/090519_London_School_Economics/London_School_Economics_May_2009_en.pdf. Accessed 1 October 2009.

Pappas, K. (2008). Back to basics to fight botnets. *Communications News, 45*(5), 12.

Parker, D. B. (1998). *Fighting computer crime: A new framework for protecting information*. New York: John Wiley & Sons, Inc.

Pike, G. H. (2006). Lost data: The legal challenges. *Information Today, 23*(10), 1–3.

Pollock, J., & May, J. (2002). Authentication Technology Identify Theft and Account Takeover. *The FBI Law Enforcement Bulletins*, 71(6), United States Department of Justice Federal Bureau of Investigation. http://www.fbi.gov/publications/leb/2002/june2002/june02leb.htm. Accessed 1 October 2003.

PR Newswire. (2008, February 21). New McAfee research shows regionalized malware rising; More attacks tailored to different cultures and technologies.

Qatar-tribune.com. (2009). Over 42% netizens in Qatar prone to cybercrime, qatar-tribune.com. www.qatar-tribune.com/data/20090520/pdf/nation.pdf. Accessed 1 October 2009.

Rasch, M. D. (1996). Criminal law and the internet, in the internet and business: A lawyer's guide to the emerging legal issues. In J. F. Ruh, Jr. (ed.), Computer Law Ass'n 1996 (http://www.cla.org/RuhBook). Accessed 1 October 2007.

Regan, K. (2006). FBI: Cybercrime Causes Financial Pain for Many Businesses, technewsworld. http://www.technewsworld.com/story/48417.html. Accessed 1 October 2007.

Reid, T. (2007). China's cyber army is preparing to march on America, says Pentagon. http://technology.timesonline.co.uk/tol/news/tech_and_web/the_web/article2409865.ece. Accessed 1 October 2008.

Rho, J. J. (2007). Blackbeards of the twenty-first century: Holding cybercriminals liable under the Alien tort statute. *Chicago Journal of International Law, 7*(2), 695–719.

Roberds, W., & Schreft, S. L. (2009). Data security, privacy, and identity theft: The economics behind the policy debates. *Economic Perspectives, 33*(1), 22–30.

Robertson, J. (2007). *China disputes report calling it a key cyber warfare instigator*. Worldstream: Associated Press.

Rodier, M. (2007). Thwarting Hackers; As hacking increases, experts say firms must use a blend of multifactor authentication, risk analysis and people to protect themselves. Wall Street & Technology, October 1, P. 17.

Ronfeldt, D., & Arquilla, J. (2003). Chapter ten: What next for networks and netwars? In J. Arquilla & D. Ronfeldt (Eds.), *Networks and netwars: The future of terror, crime, and militancy, rand corporation.* Monograph/Report MR-1382. http://www.rand.org/pubs/monograph_reports/ MR1382/index.htm. Accessed 1 October 2009.

Roush, W. (2003). The internet reborn: The internet has transformed the way we find information, shop, and do business. But it is a dumb network built for a bygone age. A university-industry coalition is designing a vastly smarter and more secure Internet: PlanetLab, Technology Review, 1 October 2003.

Rush, H., Chris, S., Erika, K. M., & Puay, T. (2009). Crime online: Cybercrime and illegal innovation, Research report: July 2009, CENTRIM, University of Brighton. http://eprints.brighton.ac.uk/5800/01/Crime_Online.pdf. Accessed 1 October 2009.

Ryan, R. M., & Deci, E. L. (2000). Intrinsic and extrinsic motivations: Classic definitions and new directions. *Contemporary Educational Psychology, 25*(1), 54–67.

Saad, L. (2009, October 16). Two in three Americans worry about identity theft. *Gallup.* http://www.gallup.com/poll/123713/Two-in-Three-Americans-Worry-About-Identity-Theft.aspx. Accessed 16 16 October 2009.

Salud, J. P. (2009, September 12). Grabbing the bully by the horns: Violence in schools. *ABS-CBN News.* http://www.abs-cbnnews.com/features/09/11/09/grabbing-bully-horns-violence-schools. Accessed 1 October 2009.

Saroyan, S. (2005). Mean girls online The Internet has made almost everything easier, faster, and more intense-including bullying. *Teen Vogue*, 158–159.

Schafer, S. (2006). A piracy culture; Beijing continues to defy US and European efforts to stop IP theft. *Newsweek* (International ed.).

Schlein, L. (2009, October 7). ITU tackles global cyber attacks. *VOANews.com.* http://www.voanews.com/english/2009-10-07-voa51.cfm. Accessed 11 October 2009.

Schreft, S. L. (2007). Risks of identity theft: Can the market protect the payment system? *Economic Review*, Federal Reserve Bank of Kansas City, Fourth Quarter, 5–40.

Shackelford, S. J. (2009). From nuclear war to net war: Analogizing cyber attacks in international law. *Berkeley Journal of International Law, 27*(1), 192–251.

Shapira, Z. (1976). Expectancy determinants of intrinsically motivated behavior. *Journal of Personality and Social Psychology, 34*, 1235–1244.

Shiels, M. (2009, October 1). US urges 'cyber hygiene' effort, BBC News. http://news.bbc.co.uk/2/hi/technology/8279867.stm. Accessed 1 October 2009.

Sloane, S. (2009). The US needs a Cybersecurity Czar now. *businessweek.com.* http://www.businessweek.com/technology/content/aug2009/tc20090813_393090.htm. Accessed 1 October 2009.

Smith, A. D. (2004). Cybercriminal impacts on online business and consumer confidence. *Online Information Review, 28*(3), 224–234.

Snidal, D. (1994). The politics of scope: Endogenous actors, heterogeneity and institutions. *Journal of Theoretical Politics, 6*(4), 449–472.

Snidal, D. (1996). Political economy and international institutions. *International Review of Law and Economics, 16*(1), 121–137.

Sophos.com. (2008). Sophos security threat report reveals cybercriminals moving beyond Microsoft. http://www.sophos.com/pressoffice/news/articles/2008/01/security-report.html. Accessed 1 October 2009.

Sullivan, B. (2007, April 10). Who's behind criminal bot networks? http://redtape.msnbc.com/2007/04/whos_behind_cri.html. Accessed 1 October 2009.

Sutherland, B. (2008). The rise of black market data; Criminals who steal personal data often don't exploit it. Instead, they put it up for sale on one of the many vibrant online markets. *Newsweek* (International ed.)*, 152*(24).

Swartz, J. (2004, October 21). Crooks slither into Net's shady nooks and crannies crime explodes as legions of strong-arm thugs, sneaky thieves log on. *USA Today.* www.usatoday.com/printedition/money/20041021/cybercrimecover.art.htm. Accessed 1 October 2005.

Swartz, J. (2007). Chinese hackers seek US access; Attacks highlight weaknesses in Internet security, USA Today, March 12, P. 3B.

Swartz, J. (2008). Cybercriminals can't get away with it like they used to USA Today.

Symantec. (2004). *Symantec internet security threat report* (Vol. VI). http://www.4law.co.il/L138.pdf. Accessed 1 October 2005.

Symantec. (2007, September 17). Symantec reports cyber criminals are becoming. http://www.prwire.com.au/pdf/symantec-reports-cyber-criminals-are-becoming-increasingly-professional. Accessed 1 October 2009.

Tedeschi, B. (2003, January 27). Crime is soaring in cyberspace, but many companies keep it quiet. *New York Times*, C.4.

The Daily Yomiuri. (2007, February 23). (Tokyo) NPA: Cybercrime jumped 40% in 2006. Net fraud tops list, 1.

The Economist. (1999). Crime without punishment: Special article. *Russian Organized Crime, 352*(134), 17–19.

The Economist. (2008, December 8). Marching off to cyberwar. *389*(8609), 20.

The Economist. (2009). International: It may make life easier and cheaper. East Africa gets broadband. *391*(8636), 46.

The Miami Herald. (2009). Businesses must beware of cybercrime: OUR OPINION: Cybercrime sends wake-up message to business world, 09.01.0. http://www.miamiherald.com/opinion/editorials/story/1211476.html. Accessed 1 October 2009.

The White House. (2009, May 29). Office of the press secretary, remarks by the president on securing our nation's cyber infrastructure. http://www.whitehouse.gov/the_press_office/Remarks-by-the-President-on-Securing-Our-Nations-Cyber-Infrastructure/. Accessed 11 July 2009.

United Press International. (2009, August 4). High-tech Northrop Grumman center to fight cybercrime. http://www.upi.com/Security_Industry/2009/08/04/High-tech-Northrop-Grumman-center-to-fight-cybercrime/UPI-48401249417676. Accessed 1 October 2009.

United States Government Accountability Office. (2007, June). GAO report to congressional requesters, cyber crime, public and private entities face challenges in addressing cyber threats.

US Fed News Service, Including US State News. (2005, May 20). *Cracking down on cyber crime.* Washington, DC.

Vallance, C. (2008, February 21). The battle against the botnet hordes. http://news.bbc.co.uk/1/hi/technology/7256501.stm. Accessed 1 October 2009.

Verton, D. (2002, October 31). FBI chief: Lack of incident reporting slows cybercrime fight. *Computerworld.* http://computerworld.com/securitytopics/security/cybercrime/story/0,10801,75532,00.html. Accessed 1 November 2002.

Vidalis, S., & Kazmi, Z. (2007). Security through deception. *Information Systems Security, 16*(1), 34–41.

Voigt, K. (2009, June 21). Dangerous Internet search terms grow with cybercrime. *CNN.com.*

Walker, C. (2004, June). Russian Mafia extorts gambling websites. http://www.americanmafia.com/cgi/clickcount.pl?url=www.americanmafia.com/Feature_Articles_270.html. Accessed 1 October 2005.

Wall, D. S. (1998). Catching cybercriminals: Policing the internet, international review of law. *Computers & Technology, 12*(2), 201–218.

Waltz, E. (1998). *Information warfare.* Norwood, MA: Artech House.

Wattanajantra, A. (2008, April 11). Ten-fold increase in malware predicted for 2008. http://www.itpro.co.uk/news/186723/tenfold-increase-in-malware-predicted-for-2008.html. Accessed 1 October 2009.

Werth, C. (2009). Software crackdown. *Newsweek* (International ed.), *154*(5).

Williams, P. (2001, August 13). *Organized crime and cybercrime: Synergies, trends, and responses*, Office of International Information Programs, US Department of State, http://usinfo.state.gov. Accessed 1 October 2002.

Wiltenburg, M. (2008, April 22). McMAFIA: Coming soon to a location near you. *Christian Science Monitor.*

Wolf, J. (2000, August 9). Hacking of pentagon persists. *Washington Post*, A23.

Wolfe, D. (2008, January 2). Cybercrime. *American Banker*, *173*(1), 5.

Wolfe, D., & Wade, W. (2008). Security Watch. *American Banker, 173*(237), 5.

Wylie, I. (2007, December 26). Internet; Romania home base for EBay scammers; The auction website has dispatched its own cyber-sleuth to help police crack fraud rings. *Los Angeles Times*, C.1.

Xinhua. (2009). Japan's cybercrime cases hit record high in 2008: Survey 2009-02-26. http://tianjin.chinadaily.com.cn/world/2009-02/26/content_7515827.htm. Accessed 1 October 2009.

Zeller, T., Jr. (2005, June 21). Black market in credit cards thrives on web. *New York Times*, A.1.

Zhou, L., Burgoon, J. K., Twitchell, D. P., Qin, T., & Nunamaker, J. F., Jr. (2004). A comparison of classification methods for predicting deception in computer-mediated communication. *Journal of Management Information Systems*, 20(4): 139–165.

Zickefoose, S. (2008, May 22). Cybercrime 'escalating': Police: Most Canadians think they've been targeted: Survey, Calgary Herald. http://www.canada.com/calgaryherald/story.html?id=5a8ff98a-719a-441e-b7ea-e9234a3c6a51. Accessed 1 October 2009.

Chapter 2
Simple Economics of Cybercrime and the Vicious Circle

"Today's online data thieves don't just run automatic scanners and jump on any network hole they find. They're more likely to first choose a target that has data they can turn into cash, and then figure out how to break in" (Peter Tippett of Verizon Business, cf. Larkin, 2009, p. 33).

"Law enforcement is presently 5 to 10 years behind the global crime curve in relation to technological capabilities" (Alexander, 2002).

Abstract Cybercrimes are becoming increasingly pervasive and sophisticated and have more severe economic impacts than most conventional crimes. Technology and skill-intensiveness; a higher degree of globalization than conventional crimes; and the newness make cybercrimes structurally different. In this chapter, we examine how characteristics of cyber-criminals, cybercrime-victims, and law-enforcement agencies have reinforced each other and formed the vicious circle. Next, we build on key elements of the vicious circle and some additional characteristics of cybercrimes to assess the cost–benefit calculus of a hacker.

2.1 Introduction

The underlying causal mechanisms may differ across types of crime (Clarke, 1983). A clearer understanding of such mechanisms, that is, the structures of costs, benefits, and attractiveness of cybercrimes, is crucial to combat against this new form of criminality. Three factors contribute to structural uniqueness of cybercrimes: technology and skill-intensiveness; a higher degree of globalization than conventional crimes; and the newness. First, unlike conventional crimes against persons or property such as arson, burglary, and murder, most cybercrimes are very skill-intensive. At this point, it must be emphasized that even script kiddies that use someone else's tools to commit victimless and/or marginal cybercrimes possess more skills than most of their conventional world counterparts do. Second, given the global nature of the Internet, cybercrimes entail important procedural and jurisdictional issues. Third, mostly due to newness of cybercrimes, law-enforcement authorities across the world are relatively inexperienced to deal with these crimes. Fourth, another implication of newness is that the legal system is not well-developed to deal with cybercrimes. Brenner (2004, p. 22) notes: "... the traditional model of law enforcement is a compilation of past practices that have been deemed effective in dealing with the phenomena it confronts. The model's general strategy, the reactive approach, is one that has been in use since antiquity." Some scholars argue that "first principles of law" need rethinking in the cyberspace (Katyal, 2001). Moreover, some countries have not yet enacted laws related to cybercrimes. Fifth, still another dimension of newness is a lack of previously developed mechanisms and established codes, policies, and procedures. These factors are likely to result in much less guilt in cybercrimes compared to conventional crimes.

This chapter examines the structure of cybercrimes and assesses the cost–benefit structure of cyber-criminals. From a potential victim's perspective, it is widely recognized that economic analysis can help explain the optimum investment as well as types of measures needed to prevent hackers' cracking into an organization's computer network (Anderson & Schneier, 2005). We offer a simple economic analysis from the perspectives of a cyber-criminal. Such an analysis provides insight into factors encouraging and energizing a cyber-criminal's behavior.

2.2 Economic Factors Affecting Crimes

Prior researchers have suggested that "offences are most imminent if their technological viability coincides with a high level of economic temptation to break the rules" (Hirschauer & Musshoff, 2007, p. 248). People can perceive the criminal law system as legitimate and fair, accept the legitimacy of anti-cybercrime norms and internalize them, but may violate them when they have a powerful temptation (Morgan, 2005). An important question then is: what factors make the commission of a crime tempting?

2.2.1 Target Attractiveness

Target attractiveness depends on offenders' perceptions of victims. Prior research indicates that crime opportunity is a function of target attractiveness, which is measured in monetary or symbolic value and portability (Clarke, 1995). The general affluence of an area as well as the value of a particular target influences attractiveness. Empirical research has demonstrated that in a given area, more affluent residents' cars are more likely to be targeted (Clarke, 1995). Likewise, some goods are "hot products" in terms of being targeted (Clarke, 1999). Target attractiveness is also related to accessibility—visibility, ease of physical access, and lack of surveillance (Bottoms & Wiles, 2002; Clarke, 1995).

Weakness of Defense Mechanisms: Weakness of defense mechanism co-varies positively with the likelihood of becoming a crime victim (Glaeser & Sacerdote, 1999). A low informal surveillance (e.g., not watching out for suspicious-looking activities in a neighborhood) is related to a high crime rate (Taylor, Koons, Kurtz, Greene, & Perkins, 1995). Because of a low surveillance, sparsely populated neighborhoods tend to have a high rate of violent crimes (Browning, Feinberg, & Dietz, 2004; Wilson, 1987). Individuals and organizations, however, can reduce the probability of becoming victims and losses by buying insurance policies or by using safety measures such as anti-burglar systems and safety deposit boxes, or by living in safe neighborhoods (Ehrlich & Becker, 1972). Likewise, middle classes tend to avoid "high crime areas" by moving away from crime hot spots (Lianos & Douglas, 2000).

2.2.2 Economic Conditions Facing an Offender

In general, crime rates are tightly linked to the lack of economic opportunities. Becker (1995, p. 10) comments on the increased number of crimes committed by teenagers: "[L]ow earnings are a factor behind crime, and teenagers have lower earnings and fewer opportunities."

Scholars have examined how certain "land use" types act as crime generators by bringing potential offenders and potential victims together (McCord, Ratcliffe, Garcia, & Taylor, 2007; Swope, 2001). Schuerman and Kobrin (1986) observed a three-stage process in the emergence of a high offender area. The first stage involved an increase in the number of renting and apartment units. Stage II was characterized by changes in population-related feature such an increase in the proportion of unrelated individuals or a higher residential mobility. The final stage concerned a change in socio-economic status such as more unskilled people and a higher proportion of unemployed population (Schuerman & Kobrin, 1986).

Recent studies provide a growing body of evidence to support and extend Schuerman and Kobrin's findings. McCord et al. (2007) found that some businesses, institutions, and facilities act as "crime generators" by bringing potential offenders and victims. Concentrated poverty has been linked to a high crime rate (Kupersmidt, Griesler, DeRosier, Patterson, & Davis, 1995; Oberwittler, 2007; Hawkins et al., 1998; Valdez, Kaplan, & Curtis, 2007). Likewise, Deas and Thomas (2002) reported that poverty and living in an urban environment predicted substance abuse among adolescents.

2.3 Economic Processes Motivating a Cyber-Criminal's Behavior

Unlike conventional crimes against persons or property such as arson, burglary, and murder, cybercrimes are skill-intensive. In industrialized countries, people with IT skills can more easily find legitimate jobs. A large number of cyberattacks originate from Eastern Europe and Russia because students there are good at mathematics, physics, and computer and have difficulties finding jobs (Blau, 2004). Economies of the former Soviet Union are too small to absorb the existing computer talent (Serio & Gorkin, 2003). Beyond all that, a 1998 financial crash in Russia left many programers unemployed (Serio & Gorkin, 2003). In some countries, organized crime groups reportedly pay up to 10 times as much as legitimate IT jobs to top graduates (Warren, 2007). A self-described hacker from Moscow noted: "Hacking is one of the few good jobs left here" (Walker, 2004). Likewise, regarding computer attacks originating from Romania, the US-based Internet Fraud Complaint Center noted: "Frustrated with the employment possibilities offered in Romania, some of the world's most talented computer students are exploiting their talents online."

Notwithstanding India's huge IT talents, the country accounts for proportionately fewer cybercrimes compared to most developing countries. The primary reason behind India's low cybercrime profile is the development of legitimate IT industry in the country. Speaking of a low rate of cybercrimes in the country, Nandkumar Saravade, director of cybersecurity for India's National Association of Software and Service Companies (NASSCOM) noted: "Today ... any person in India with marketable computer skills has a few job offers in hand" (Greenberg, 2007).

2.3.1 Selection of Targets

Businesses with a high dependence on digital technologies such as online casinos, banks, and e-commerce hubs are the most likely to fall victim to cybercrimes (Kshetri, 2005). These seem to be attractive targets, which provide a powerful temptation to cyber-criminals (Clarke, 1995; Morgan, 2005). A study by IDC indicated that over 60% of cybercrimes targeted financial institutions in 2003 (Swartz, 2004).

It is also apparent that cybercrimes targeting developing economies exhibit a concentration in e-commerce ready industries such as the online gaming industry in China (Greenberg, 2007; Fong, 2008), banking industry in Brazil (Miller, 2008), and the offshoring sector in India (Fest, 2005).

2.4 Structure of Cybercrimes: The Vicious Circle

Characteristics of cyber-criminals, cybercrime-victims, and law-enforcement agencies have reinforced each other and formed the vicious circle of cybercrime. Key elements of the vicious circle are presented in Fig. 2.1.

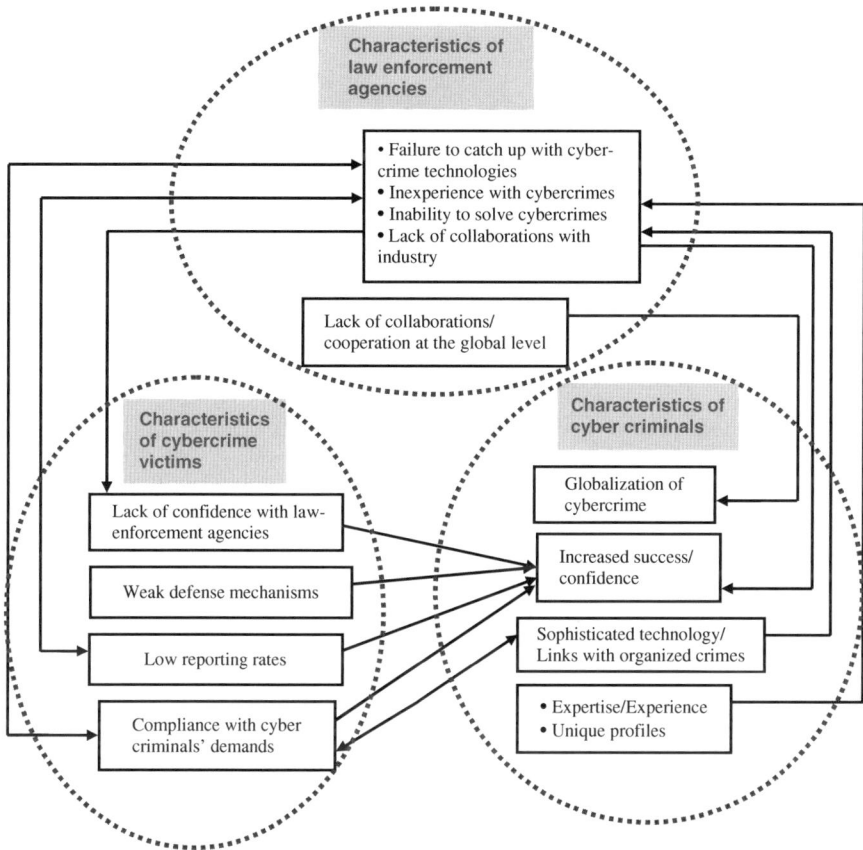

Fig. 2.1 The vicious circle of cybercrimes: a proposed framework

2.4.1 The Cybercrime Market

We begin by considering the "market" for cybercrime. Following, Ehrlich (1996), cybercrime "market" can be considered as a Walrasian market in which "the aggregate behavior of suppliers and demanders is coordinated and made mutually consistent through adjustments in relevant prices." Note that Walrasian market is among the most common models used to describe the operation of the virtual market (Toshiya, Susumu, & Noriyasu, 2003). In Becker's (1968) model of the crime market, criminals and law enforcers are the only actors involved. Interactions between these two sets of actors determine equilibrium. It is important to note that actors other than criminals and law enforcers are also involved in the game. For conventional crimes, they include consumers of illicit and illegally sold goods and services in specific crimes and victims (Ehrlich, 1996).

2.4.2 Law-Enforcement Agencies

First, laws as well as enforcement mechanisms lag in their response to cybercrimes' challenges (Brenner, 2004; Jones, 2007). Law-enforcement agencies such as Police forces and the FBI are inexperienced with these new forms of crimes. Police forces in most countries are highly localized and are not well equipped to deal with the global nature of cybercrimes (Walden, 2005). Alexander (2002) noted: "Law enforcement is presently 5 to 10 years behind the global crime curve in relation to technological capabilities."

The failure to change structures and practices fast enough to deal with the rapidly growing cybercrimes can be attributed to the organizational inertia. Organizational inertia can be defined as formal organizations' tendency to resist internal changes to respond to external changes (Larsen & Lomi, 2002). Prior research indicates that established and matured organizations tend to stick with the traditional business model (Matsumoto, Ouchi, Watanabe, & Griffy-Brown, 2002; Watanabe & Tokumasu, 2003). Wall (2007) comments on police forces' failure to change organizational structures to deal with cybercrimes: "But, it is one thing to possess the technological capabilities and another to be able to utilize them, and there are a number of institutional obstacles to this task. The public police, like the other criminal justice agencies are deeply conservative institutions that have been moulded by time-honored traditions, and therefore do not respond readily to rapid change."

They are also facing a short supply of manpower to handle cybercrimes. A senior official of the Internet Crime Complaint Center (I3C) reported in November 2004 that the FBI has been unable to recruit and retain the best available IT talent. Based on his interviews with current and former agents Blitstein (2007) noted that "there are too few federal cyber-investigators, and that too little is done to retain detectives with advanced technical training."

According to the American Prosecutors Research Institute, the FBI's San Diego lab in 2005 had a 6-month backlog for forensic examinations (Blitstein, 2007). Moreover, cybercrimes are increasingly sophisticated and new forms and methods of such crimes are developing at an increasing rate. Law-enforcement agencies lack resources and have failed to catch up with technologies enabling such crimes. Grow and Bush (2005) note: "[C]ops don't have all the weapons they need to fight back [cyber-criminals]. They clearly lack the financial resources to match their adversaries' technical skills and global reach."

As is the case of any transnational crime, dealing with cybercrimes, especially those with international dimensions, is a resource intensive task (Walden, 2005). As noted above, cybercrime investigations are highly complex, as well as resource and expertise intensive. Many small countries thus do not investigate all reported cybercrimes. In Indonesia, for instance, only 15% of reported incidents are investigated. Law-enforcement agencies' lack of ability to solve cybercrimes reinforces cyber-criminal's confidence as well as victims' unwillingness to report such crimes (Fig. 2.1).

There is a lack of collaboration and coordination among various government agencies and between government and the private sector. Rivalries among various law-enforcement agencies have hindered information dissemination (Joshi, 2009). The US president put the issue this way: "Indeed, when it comes to cybersecurity, federal agencies have overlapping missions and don't coordinate and communicate nearly as well as they should—with each other or with the private sector" (The New York Times, 2009). Given that up to 90% of all critical infrastructures in the United States are owned by private sectors, many cybercrimes cannot be solved without their help. An estimate suggests that 80% of global email traffic including the majority of the spam scams comes via the Webmail services of global providers such as AOL, MSN, and Yahoo. Law-enforcement agencies have expressed concern over service providers' unwillingness to cooperate in cybercrime investigations.

2.4.3 Cyber-Criminals

Cyber-criminals' unique profiles are significantly different from those of conventional criminals. Non-existence of cyber-criminals' database with law-enforcement agencies has also hampered the latter's ability to solve cybercrimes. In Russia, for instance, most hackers are young, highly educated, and work independently and thus do not fit the conventional Police profiles of criminals.

Cyber-criminals are also inventing various forms of markets. Some, for instance, have created a hybrid market consisting of online and offline market activities, with each having different roles. For instance, it was estimated that there were over 300 cashiers in Paris, who regularly steal payment-card details from their customers. Most of the stolen data were sold face-to-face between fraudsters who met online (Sutherland, 2008). Likewise, in first- and second-tier cities in India, data brokers and data merchants reportedly buy data from people working in offshoring companies (Aggarwal, 2009).

Evidence indicates that criminals' skill, intelligence, and experience co-vary positively with the odds of getting away with crimes. Some serious cyber-criminals are highly skillful and thus face very low odds of getting caught. For instance, in recent years, the Russian mafia has developed expertise in cybercrime (Giannangeli, 2008). Russian mafia hack rings are reportedly operated by former KGB agents (Bell, 2002). There is evidence that some less skillful criminals get help from experienced hackers and transnational organized crime groups thereby minimizing the probability of getting caught.

Increased success is making cyber-criminals more brash. Barnes (2004) notes: "There is, then, a justifiable perception among worm authors that only exceptionally careless authors get caught, and this causes authors to deeply discount the occasional law enforcement success." There is some evidence of cyber-criminals becoming disrespectful of law-enforcement agencies. A number of international hackers, for instance, do not even conceal their real identities and the origin of their mailings. What is more, many organized criminals have invested illegally earned incomes in new technologies and to globalize their operations making it further difficult to solve cybercrimes. Experts suggest that international collaboration among cyber-criminals will further grow in the future (Rush, Smith, Mbula, & Tang, 2009).

2.4.4 Cybercrime Victims

Cybercrimes are also among the most under-reported forms of criminality. Cybercrime victims' unwillingness to report such crimes to law-enforcement agencies further encourages cyber-criminals' behavior (Fig. 2.1). Some experts say that less than 10% of cybercrimes are reported (Bednarz, 2004). An FBI report released in January 2006 indicated that only 9% businesses reported cybercrimes to authorities (Regan, 2006). Likewise, another study conducted in the United Kingdom indicated that no formal complaint was made in 90% of online harassment cases (Birmingham Post, 2007). Similarly, a survey conducted among Australian businesses indicated that only 8% of respondents reported computer security breaches to police and most preferred to deal with them internally (Andrews, 2009).

Many victims are unwilling to report cybercrimes because they think going to law-enforcement does not stop an attack. Most Internet fraud victims are embarrassed to report that they have been victimized (Salu, 2004). Other factors contributing to low reporting rates could be the fear of losing customer trust; the damage in corporate credibility; and potential stock prices fall. Especially banks, financial institutions, and others businesses that deal with sensitive data are reluctant to turn over the investigation to the authorities. According to the *Seventh Annual Computer Crime and Security Survey* 70% of those not reporting cybercrimes cited negative publicity as a reason. Difficulties related to documentation and proofs further discourage businesses reporting cybercrimes. Finally, enterprises do not always know when their networks have been attacked, which results in under-reporting of cybercrimes (Regan, 2006). In some cases, it may also take cybercrime victims some time to realize that they have been victims (Wall, 1998; Richtel, 1999). Studies have found that terminologies such as "breaches" or "security incidents" were used to refer to cyberattacks, which meant that businesses were less likely to treat the attacks as cybercrimes (Andrews, 2009).

For many online transactions, the costs of enforcing a contract tend to be higher than the transaction's value (McDonald & Slawson, 2002). For instance, many online auctions are of low value, averaging under US \$25 per item (Bauerly, 2009). For many defrauded buyers, the costs of pursuing a claim may outweigh the potential gains of a desired outcome.

Weakness of defense mechanisms co-varies positively with the likelihood of attack. While some weaknesses are technological, others are behavioral or perceptual in nature. The public's lack of education to recognize cybercrime has been a major challenge. Cyber-criminals take advantage of Internet users' ignorance (GAO Reports, 2007). Consider, for instance, phishing—acquisition of personal information fraudulently by tricking an Internet user. Experts say that the key to combat phishing lies in consumer's ability to distinguish between real and fraudulent e-mails. A study conducted by MailFrontier in the early 2003 indicated that 40% of people who read a fraudulent Citibank e-mail considered it as a real one (Salkever, 2003). Another study suggested that 60% of people clicked on phishing e-mails within the first hour of receiving them (Shiels, 2009).

An understanding of manipulative techniques used by various creatures to fool their enemies is of particular relevance for cybercrimes. In particular, a phenomenon proposed by Dawkins (1982) called the *rare enemy syndrome*, provides a helpful theoretical perspective for understanding how victims often fall to new unfamiliar baits or lure. The basic idea behind rare enemy syndrome is simple. The enemy's manipulation is so rare that evolutionary development has not yet progressed to the point that the victim has an effective counter poison (de Jong, 2001). Similar processes happen in the cyberworld. Many targets and victims lack a strong protection against cyber-criminals' novel manipulation tactics. Several examples provided by Schneier (2009), which have been used by fraudsters to frame their enemies, are rare manipulations. For instance, Google's anti-fraud systems detect and shut down advertisers if they attempt to inflate their commission by repeatedly clicking on their own AdSense ads. In response, some fraudsters built bots, which repeatedly clicked on their competitors' AdSense ads. To take another example, Google penalizes a website's search engine rankings if the site is linked with bad sites such as adult or gambling sites, blog spam, and link farms.[1] Some fraudsters spotted an opportunity to build link farms, where they posted blog comment spam to their competitors' sites (Schneier, 2009).

Beyond all that some criminal organizations are highly skillful in carrying out cybercrime activities. For instance, the Russian group, Rock Phish, which is estimated to be responsible for over half of all phishing sites worldwide, arguably has a " proven technical prowess" and sends "baited hooks written in perfect English—as well as French, German and Dutch" (Fong, 2008). Rock Phish uses "impeccable" counterfeit design of brand logos and styles of financial companies, retailers, and government agencies (Bulkeley, 2008; Fong, 2008). The Riga, Latvia-based company, Real Host, which was found to have 3.6 million PCs involved in a botnet called Zeus, was reported to have links to Rock Phish (The Baltic Times, 2009).

Similarly, a survey by the US National Cyber Security Alliance (NCSA) found that 61% of computers were infected with adware and spyware but only 8% of users knew that they were infected (Edelman, 2007). In another study conducted by McAfee and the NCSA, about half the respondents erroneously believed their computers were protected by anti-virus software and 71% never heard the word "botnet" (Claburn, 2008).

Moreover, some companies choose to negotiate with cyber-criminals by paying ransom. Estimates suggest that online gambling sites alone have paid millions of dollars to cyber-extortionists. To take one example, in September 2003, Antigua-based World Wide Tele-Sports (BetWWTS.com) paid ransoms as high as US $30,000 to cyber-extortionists after attacks to the company's networks resulted in customers not being able to place wagers estimated at US $5 million. Similarly, UK's National Hi-Tech Crime Unit (NHTCU) estimated extortion of "hundreds of thousands of pounds" paid by UK-based online bookmakers during October 2003–January 2004. For some companies, it is cheaper to pay up to online extortionists than to face an attack. For instance, estimates suggest that a few hours downtime on a peak time (e.g., Super Bowl weekend) costs online casinos up to US $1 million.

2.4.5 Inter-jurisdictional Issues

In the conventional world, most crimes are committed close to home. Criminals travel far only if there are sufficient incentives to leave known territory (van Koppen & Jansen, 1998). Some crimes such as kidnapping, attacking a bank are "attractive" enough to do so. These crimes require much more planning. Crimes in the digital world differ significantly on this dimension. Most cybercrimes, on the other hand, are conducted away from a criminal's home. For instance, in California, which accounted for most reported cyber-fraud cases in the United States in 2007, only in 18.3% of the cases, both the victim and perpetrator lived in the state (IC3, Internet Crime Complaint Center, 2007). A high proportion of cybercrime investigations thus have significant jurisdictional issues. In many cases, cybercrimes crossing borders slow down responses to such crimes.

National boundaries have thus created serious obstacles to law-enforcement agencies. Collaborations and cooperation among law-enforcement agencies in different jurisdictions are far from sufficient to solve cybercrimes. To take one example, although Russia has signed an agreement with the United States to help in investigating a number of crimes, cybercrimes are not among them (Lemos, 2001). In 2000, the FBI arrested two Russian hackers by luring them to the United States with job offers. FBI Agents handling the case later downloaded data from the two hackers' computers located in Chelyabinsk, Russia. In 2002, Russia filed hacking charges against the FBI arguing that it was illegal to download data from computers physically located in Russia. Similarly, in 2001, the US Department of Justice requested the help of Russian authorities but received no response. More recently, US law-enforcement officials have reported improving cooperation from Russian authorities. In 2005, it was reported that US law-enforcement officials received help from their Russian counterparts on about one out of six cybercrime-related requests (Bryan-Low, 2005).

The police's association with corruption and crime association with corruption in some countries further complicate the problems. Law-enforcement agencies from other countries tend to be reluctant to share information with them (Joshi, 2009).

There is also a high degree of international heterogeneity in cybercrime laws. The Council of Europe's Convention on cybercrime is, for example, the first international treaty on cybercrimes. As noted in Chap. 1, although 46 nations signed the treaty as of August 2009, only 26 members had ratified it by that time (COE, 2009). Likewise, industrialized countries are discussing about international cooperation to combat cybercrimes, many poor countries are not yet involved in the discussions. What is more, many countries have not yet enacted cybercrime laws. One estimate suggested that in 2000, more than 60% of Interpol members lacked the appropriate legislation to deal with cybercrimes (cnn.com, 2000). Likewise, as of May 2008, out of the 35 Organization of American States (OAS) member states, only 15 had "substantive cybercrime legislation in place" and only 12 had enacted procedural cybercrime legislation (Caribbean Press Releases, 2008). In April 2008, Bryan Tan, director of Keystone Law Corporation, noted that in many countries in Asia, laws to deal with cybercrime are "either are very basic or have not been passed" (Ye, 2008).

A lack of cross-border collaboration in cybercrime investigations, international heterogeneity in cybercrime laws, and weakness and even non-existence of such laws in some countries have facilitated the globalization of cybercrimes. A report released by the UK government at its first national security strategy noted how the Internet is being used by spies, terrorists, and transnational organized criminal groups: "Organized crime groups are becoming more organized and professional and increasingly operate a portfolio approach, switching focus to wherever risk is lowest and profit highest" (Grant, 2008). It is, for instance, reported that some Japanese gangs hire Russian hackers to attack law-enforcement agencies' databases. Likewise, some Australian swindlers have established links with Russian and Malaysian organized crime networks to transfer stolen money from overseas banks they have cracked into (Foreign Policy, 2005).

2.5 A Cyber-Criminal's Cost–Benefit Calculus

In this section, we integrate key elements of the simplified framework representing the vicious circle discussed above and some additional characteristics of cybercrimes to examine a hacker's perceived cost–benefit structure. Following the economic approach, a cyber-criminal weighs benefits and costs to make decision about engaging in a crime (Becker, 1968; also see Probasco, Clark, & Davis, 1995). A cybercrime is committed if

$$M_b + P_b > O_{cp} + O_{cm}P_aP_c \qquad (2.1)$$

where

   M_b = The monetary benefits of committing the crime;
   P_b = The psychic benefit of committing the crime;
   O_{cm} = Monetary opportunity costs of conviction;
   O_{cp} = Psychic costs of committing a cybercrime;
   P_a = The probability of arrest;
   P_c = The probability of conviction.

The product term in the right side: O_{cm} P_a P_c in (2.1) is also referred as the expected penalty effect. Equation (2.1) captures costs and benefits associated with macro- and micro-level factors such as arrest, stigma, and illegal earnings, which are found to influence an individuals' engagement in a crime (Aguilar-Millan, Foltz, Jackson, & Oberg, 2008; McCarthy, 2002).

2.5.1 The Benefit Side

2.5.1.1 Monetary Benefits

The cybercrime landscape is rapidly changing in terms of hackers' monetary motives. A Russian hacker employed as a security expert noted: "There is more of a financial incentive now for hackers and crackers as well as for virus writers to write for money and not just for glory or some political motive" (Blau, 2004). For instance, IT graduates with legitimate job in Romania earn about US $400 per month compared with several thousand per month in the cybercrime economy. A "security exploiter" can earn 10 times as much a security researcher (Claburn, 2008). Terri Forslof of TippingPoint Technologies put the issue this way: "Over a ten year period hack for fun and hack for fame has become hack for profit" (Webwire, 2008).

2.5.1.2 Psychic Benefit (P_b)

The potential psychological benefits provide strong incentives for some individuals to engage in cybercrimes. Psychological benefits can be better explained in terms of intrinsic motivations. For instance, maverick hackers testing their skills and looking for fun act for purely psychological rather than monetary benefits. As noted in Chap. 1, acting on the basis of principle is also a form of intrinsic motivation. First, the respect of one's peer hackers acts as a source of psychological benefit for some hackers.

Second, a feeling of vindication against symbolic enemy also provides psychological benefits to hackers. Many ideological hackings fall in this category. An organization becomes a hacking unit's symbolic foe for many reasons. In addition to nationalism and religion, hackers' interests are also framed by fight against global capitalism. Such hackers are likely to attack networks of big multinationals.

Government backed cyber-wars in some countries also fall in this category. A number of such wars are fought for intangible goals such as dominance and prestige rather than material goals.

2.5.2 The Cost Side

2.5.2.1 Psychic (Psychological) Costs of Committing a Cybercrime (O_{cp})

Psychological costs are intangible, but can, however, be considered as costs. These costs are associated with the psychological and mental energy needed in committing cybercrimes. They result from the fear or apprehension of punishment, guilt, etc. A potential criminal's taste or distaste for crime, and moral values also influence O_{cp} (Ehrlich, 1996). Some scholars argue that moral values, which are associated with social costs, are more important than monetary opportunity costs of conviction (O_{cm}) related to imprisonment and loss of wages (Nagin, 1998).

An important question is: Do cyber-criminals have a feeling of guilt or remorse after cracking into a victim's computer? Experts argue that most of those who make unethical uses of computer networks arguably do not really perceive the ethical implications of their actions (Kallman & Grillo, 1996). Put differently, the novelty of the technology; a lack of previously developed mechanisms and established codes, policies, and procedures; and non-existence of an easily identifiable victims in many cases (Phukan, 2002) are likely to lead to much less in cybercrimes guilt compared to conventional crimes. An official of India's Cyber Crime Investigation Cell (CCIC) noted that many young people in the country have committed cybercrimes for fun "without actually realising the gravity of their actions" (cf. Sawant, 2009).

Some argue that widely shared norms, values, and beliefs of Napster users contradicted the existing copyright laws and legitimized file-swapping services provided by the company (Webb, Tihanyi, Ireland, & Sirmon, 2009). Napster users did not feel guilty about their file sharing activities.

In the medical world, for instance, there arguably is a lack of clear guidelines as to what constitutes an unethical or unprofessional online conduct for physicians (Lagu, Kaufman, & Asch, 2008; Thompson et al., 2008). In a survey conducted among US medical schools to assess professionalism in medical students' online posts, 60% of the respondents reported incidents of their students posting online content that were unprofessional and 13% violated patient confidentiality (Chretien, Ryan, Chretien, & Kind, 2009). The study also found that only few schools had policies to deal with such violations. Illegal or questionable activities such as violation of patient confidentiality are taking place in the cyberspace without the violators' intent.

Likewise, it is argued that online child pornography "reduces the social stigma" as individuals do not have to go to stores, which eliminates the chance of meeting other criminals engaged in child pornography (Shelley, 1998). Others note that "consumer indifference to the stigma of intellectual property theft" has contributed to such crimes (McIllwain, 2005, p. 35). This is contrary to most conventional crimes such as drug dealings, which are characterized by social stigma (Whitlock, 1979; Harler & Fox, 1992).

Research on crimes in the conventional world has indicated that socio-cultural practices and political and economic systems are tightly linked to crimes. We thus hypothesize that the feeling of guilt is not equally pervasive across hackers in different socio-cultural backgrounds. Put differently, the psychological cost of a cybercrime is a function of a cyber-criminal's socio-cultural background.

2.5.2.2 Monetary Opportunity Costs of Conviction (O_{cm})

It is the foregone monetary income incurred by serving out a criminal sentence. For instance, if a hacker is sentenced to a 3-year prison term, and if he/she could legally earn US $20,000 per year, the sentence would cost US $60,000. In recent years, many countries have enacted stricter laws against cybercrimes, which have increased the opportunity costs of conviction. Nonetheless, many countries have no laws enacted to fight cybercrimes, which means a very low or no opportunity cost of conviction. To take one example, when a Philippino hacker launched the "Love Letter" virus in 2000, estimated loss of damage in the United States was in the range of US $4–15 billion. But the US government could not do anything to prosecute the hacker or to recover the damages because at that time the Philippines had no laws prohibiting such crimes (Adams, 2001). In sum, costs to criminals of their deviant behaviors on the Internet have been remarkably low (Shelley, 1998).

As noted above, crime rates are related to the lack of economic opportunities. Additionally, unlike conventional crimes, most cybercrimes are skill-intensive. The most relevant issues thus concern expectations from education. Note that if societal expectations related to educational attainment are unmet, people are likely to engage in crimes (McCleary, 2008).

Cybercrimes are thus likely to originate if the legitimate IT industry is too small to absorb available talents. Consistent with history and theory, serious cyber-criminals tend to be from countries that emphasize on physics, mathematics, and computer science educations, but lack high-paying legitimate IT jobs (Sullivan, 2007).

Speaking of emphasis on mathematics in Romania, a scientist in Bucharest put the issue this way: "The respect for math is inside every family, even simple families, who are very proud to say their children are good at mathematics" (Wylie, 2007). In the former Soviet Union economies, computer specialists gained experience in "disassembling, examining and hacking American systems to see how they worked in order to make them functional on Soviet systems" (Serio & Gorkin, 2003).

2.5.2.3   The Probability of Arrests (P_a) and the Probability of Conviction (P_c)

As discussed above, only a small proportion of cybercrimes are reported. For small transactions in Internet auctions, for instance, buyers often avoid criticizing sellers for their opportunistic behavior because they are afraid of possible reprisal from the seller (Clemons, 2007). Because of concerns related to retaliation by the seller, buyer satisfaction statistics published by websites tend to be higher than the actual satisfaction level (Dellarocas & Wood, 2008).

Among reported crimes, arrest rates are vanishingly small. Arrest entails identi-fying the pool of potential suspects and narrowing the pool by eliminating innocents. The structure of cybercrimes discussed in the previous section makes it difficult to identify the pool of potential suspects. The FBI estimates that the probability of cyber-criminal's being caught is less than 1 in 20,000 (Gabrys, 2002). Another estimate suggests that the proportion of identity thefts (most of which employ the Internet) that are even investigated is estimated to be fewer than 1 in 700 (Boal, 2005).

The low probability of arrests can also be attributed to the huge global e-marketplace with a large number of vendors (Webb et al., 2009). This means that most informal and underground economy entrepreneurs that operate online are invisible to law-enforcement agencies (Zimmerman, 2006).

In order to minimize the probability that they are caught, some cyber-criminals avoid victimizing people in the country where they live. Benjamin Edelman of Harvard Business School noted: "By declining to hurt people in their own country, they discourage law enforcement from pursuing them" (cf. Messmer, 2009).

The conviction phase of a cybercrime is equally complex. Difficulties related to documentation and proof compound the problems at this phase (Casey, 2004). The newness of cybercrimes has also presented a challenge to the court system. For small cases, it is difficult to find an attorney in who takes cyber-fraud cases. Experts also say that explaining Internet-related crimes to judges is difficult. Estimates suggest that if a cyber-criminal is caught, the probability that the criminal would be convicted is 1 in 22,000 (Gabrys, 2002).

The situation is worse in developing countries. Mohammad Khairuddin Abdullah, Malaysia's HeiTech Padu Berhad's director noted: "As long as they [cyber-criminals] are within the country, the criminals can be brought to court, but you'll be lucky if you can find the judge, who can write the warrant and understands the issue. Even though cyberlaws are in place, you need to have people who are able to apply the laws, as most cybercrime cases will get cold in just 24 hours" (cf. Ismail, 2008).

2.6 Concluding Comments

The above discussion indicates that there is a temptation to engage in opportunistic behavior in the cyberspace. Compared to the physical world, the detection of opportunism is difficult in the cyberworld. Some also commit a cybercrime due to ignorance.

The concept of manifest and latent functions (Merton, 1968) can be very helpful in understanding the behaviors of some cyber-criminals. Manifest functions are explicitly stated and understood by the participants in the relevant action and the consequences can be observed or expected. Latent functions, on the other hand, are those that are not explicitly stated by the people involved (Merton, 1968). In the Napster example above, for instance, the manifest posture may be the users' argument that free file sharing services provided by Napster are consistent with their norms, values, and beliefs. Below the surface deeply ingrained, however, may be a powerful economic temptation of free music (latent function).

In the absence of appropriate measures, the elements of the vicious circle reinforce each other and lead to public distrust of law-enforcement agencies and increased confidence of cyber-criminals, which results in more and serious cybercrimes. A Global Security Survey conducted by *Deloitte Touche Tohmatsu* in 2003, for instance, found that respondent companies spent 6% of their IT budgets on security. Nevertheless, cyberattacks are increasing rapidly.

Where should we start to break the vicious circle of cybercrime and to alter the cost/benefit calculus associated with committing cybercrimes? There is no pure technological solution for security-related problems involving technologies. Micro- and macro-level measures combining technological and non-technological fixes are thus needed to combat cybercrimes.

In the conventional world, individuals and organizations can reduce the probability of becoming victims and their losses by buying insurance policies or by using safety measures such as anti-burglar systems and safety deposit boxes, or by living in safe neighborhoods (Ehrlich & Becker, 1972). Not all of these have their equivalents in the cyberworld. As noted above, certain "land use" types act as crime generators (McCord et al., 2007; Swope, 2001). While formal control mechanisms such as "hot spots policing" can be used to deal with land uses associated with high crime rates (Weisburd, Bushway, Lum, & Yang, 2004), there are no equivalents of such mechanisms in the cyberspace.

At the macro-level, development of national technological and manpower capabilities; enactment of new laws; a higher level of industry-government collaborations; and international coordination are critical for combating this new form of crime. Investment in the skills of law-enforcement authorities is likely to enhance national capabilities to fight cybercrimes and thus increasing the probability of arrest and conviction. Like most other criminals (Becker, 1995), we can assume that cyber criminals are risk takers, not risk avoiders. Measures taken so far have mainly emphasized on increasing penalty rather than on increasing the probabilities of arrest and conviction. This is arguably because law-enforcement agencies have been unable to catch up technologically with cyber-criminals (Downes, 2007). It is suggested that private citizens may be especially effective at combating cybercrimes as the costs are much less for individuals and private firms to protect their electronic records than those for the government to identify and prosecute criminals (Katyal, 2001; Mikos, 2006).

Note

1. A link farm is "any group of web sites that all hyperlink to every other site in the group" (Wikipedia definition of Link farm, http://en.wikipedia.org/wiki/Link_farm, accessed 19 October 2009).

References

Adams, J. (2001, May/June). Virtual defense. *Foreign Affairs, 98*–112.
Aggarwal, V. (2009). Lead: Cyber crime's rampant, Express Computer, 03 August 2009. http://www.expresscomputeronline.com/20090803/market01.shtml. Accessed 1 October 2009.
Aguilar-Millan, S., Foltz, J. E., Jackson, J., & Oberg, A. (2008). The globalization of crime. *Futurist, 42*(6), 41–50.
Alexander, D. (2002, June). Policing and the global paradox. *FBI Law Enforcement Bulletin, 71*(6), 6–13, 00145688.
Anderson, R., & Schneier, B. (2005). Counterpane internet security guest editors introduction: Economics of information security. *IEEE Security & Privacy, 3*(1), 12–13.
Andrews, L. (2009, June 9) Online scams go unreported and unpunished. *Cybercriminals beating the law Canberra Times (Australia) SECTION: A*, p. 5.
Barnes, D. A. (2004). Note, Deworming the Internet, 83 TEX. L. REV. 279, 322–329.
Bauerly, R. J. (2009). Online auction fraud and ebay. *Marketing Management Journal, 19*(1), 133–143.
Becker, G. (1968). Crime and punishment: An economic approach. *Journal of Political Economy, 76*(2), 169–217.

Becker, G. S. (1995, Fall). The economics of crime. *Cross Sections*, 8–15. http://www.rich.frb.org/pubs/cross/crime/crime.pdf. Accessed 1 October 2006.

Bednarz, A. (2004). Profiling cybercriminals: A promising but immature science, Network World, November 29. http://www.nwfusion.com/supp/2004/cybercrime/112904profile.html?page=2. Accessed 1 October 2005.

Bell, R. E. (2002). The prosecution of computer crime. *Journal of Financial Crime, 9*(4), 308–325.

Birmingham Post. (2007). Politics: Cybercrime victim every 10 seconds, 4.

Blau, J. (2004). Russia - a happy haven for hackers, 26 May 2004. http://www.computerweekly.com/Article130839.htm. Accessed 1 October 2005.

Blitstein, R. (2007, November 14). Cybercops: US targets terrorists as online thieves run amok. *San Jose Mercury News.*

Boal, M. (2005). Being Bill Gates Steven Spielberg, Martha Stewart, George Soros Charles Schwab: How the Most Brazen Identity Thief In US Almost Get Away With It. *Readers Digest,* 161–173.

Bottoms, A. E., & Wiles, P. (2002). Environmental criminology. *Oxford Handbook of Criminology,* 620–656.

Brenner, S. W. (2004). Toward a criminal law for cyberspace: A new model of law enforcement? *30 Rutgers Computer and Technology Law Journal, 30,* 1–9.

Browning, C. R, Feinberg, S. L., & Dietz, R. D. (2004). The paradox of social organization: Networks, collective efficacy, and violent crime in urban neighborhoods. *Social Forces, 83*(2), 503–534.

Bryan-Low, C. (2005, July 13). Fraud Inc.: As identity theft moves online, crime rings mimic big business; Russian-led Carderplanet steals account numbers; Mr. Havard hits ATMs; 'Common Punk' to 'Capo'. *Wall Street Journal*, A.1.

Bulkeley, W. M. (2008). Quiz; Tech IQ: How well do you know...the digital world. *Wall Street Journal*, R.14.

Caribbean Press Releases. (2008). Trinidad and Tobago to Host OAS Cyber-Crime Workshop, 13 May 2008. http://www.caribbeanpressreleases.com/articles/3236/1/Trinidad-and-Tobago-To-Host-OAS-Cyber-Crime-Workshop/Page1.html. Accessed 1 October 2009.

Casey, E. (2004). *Digital evidence and computer crime.* Cambridge: Academic Press.

Chretien, K. C., Ryan, G. S., Chretien, J. P., & Kind, T. (2009). Online posting of unprofessional content by medical students. *JAMA, 302*(12), 1309–1315.

Claburn, T. (2008). The Cybercrime Economy, April 9, 2008. http://www.informationweek.com/blog/main/archives/2008/04/the_cyber_crime.html. Accessed 1 October 2009.

Clarke, R. V. (1983). Situational crime prevention: Its theoretical basis and practical scope. In M. Tonry & N. Morris (Eds.), *Crime and justice: An annual review of research* (p. 14). Chicago: University of Chicago Press.

Clarke, R. V. (1995). Situational crime prevention. In M. Tonry & D. P. Farrington (Eds.), *Building a safer society. Strategic approaches to crime* (pp. 91–150). University of Chicago Press.

Clarke, R. V. (1999). Hot products: Understanding, anticipating, and reducing demand for stolen goods. *Police Research Paper 112.* London: Home Office.

Clemons, E. K. (2007). An empirical investigation of third-party seller rating systems in e-commerce: The case of buySAFE. *Journal of Management Information Systems, 24*(2), 43–71.

CNN.com. (2000, July 26). Many countries said to lack computer crime laws. CNN.com. http://www.cnn.com/2000/TECH/computing/07/26/crime.internet.reut.

COE. (2009). Convention on Cybercrime: CETS No.:185. http://conventions.coe.int/Treaty/Commun/ChercheSig.asp?NT=185&CM=&DF=&CL=ENG. Accessed 1 October 2009.

Dawkins, R. (1982). *The extended phenotype.* Oxford University Press.

de Jong, W. M. (2001). Manipulative tactics in budgetary games: The art and craft of getting the money you don't deserve. *Knowledge, Technology & Policy, Spring, 14*(1), 50–66.

Deas, D., & Thomas, S. (2002). Comorbid psychiatric factors contributing to adolescent alcohol and other drug use. *Alcohol Research and Health, 26,* 116–121.

Dellarocas, C., & Wood, C. A. (2008). The sound of silence in online feedback: Estimating trading risks in the presence of reporting bias. *Management Science, 54*(3), 460–476.

Downes, L. (2007, March 6). Cybercrime treaty: What it means to you. *Baseline.com.*

Edelman, B. (2007, January 25). Why I can never agree with adware and spyware. *The Guardian.*

Ehrlich, I. (1996). Crime, punishment, and the market for offenses. *Journal of Economic Perspectives, 10*(1), 43–67.

Ehrlich, I., & Becker, G. (1972). Market insurance, serf-insurance and serf-protection. *Journal of Political Economy, 80*(4), 623–648.

Fest, G. (2005, September 1). Offshoring: Feds take fresh look at India BPOs; Major theft has raised more than a few eyebrows. *Bank Technology News, 18*(9), 1.

Fong, C. (2008, May 8). Fighting the agents of organized cybercrime. *CNN.com.*

Foreign Policy. (2005, March/April). Caught in the net: Australian teens, 92.

Gabrys, E. (2002). The international dimensions of cyber-crime, Part 1. *Information Systems Security, 11*(4), 21–32.

GAO Reports. (2007). Public and private entities face challenges in addressing cyber threats, RPT-NUMBER: GAO-07-705.

Giannangeli, M. (2008, June 8). Are we ready for Russian Mafia's crime revolution? *Sunday Express,* Scottish Edition, 3.

Glaeser, E. L., & Sacerdote, B. (1999). Why is there more crime in cities? *The Journal of Political Economy, 107*(6), Part 2, 225–258.

Grant, I. (2008, March 19). The UK's dependence on the internet is putting more than half of its economy at risk, says the government. *ComputerWeekly.com.* http://www.computer weekly.com/Articles/2008/03/19/229932/uk-government-warns-of-economys-reliance-on-inte rnet.htm. Accessed 1 October 2009.

Greenberg, A. (2007). The top countries for cybercrime, Forbes.com. http://www.forbes.com/ 2007/07/13/cybercrime-world-regions-tech-cx_ag_0716cybercrime.html. Accessed 1 October 2008.

Grow, B., & Bush, J. (2005, May 30). Hacker hunters. *Business Week,* 74.

Harler, C., & Fox, B. (1992). Network security communications news. *Nokomis, 29*(1), 20–24.

Hawkins, J. D., Herrenkohl, T., Farrington, D. P., Brewer, D., Catalano, R., & Harachi, T. W. (1998). A review of predictors of youth violence. In R. Loeber & D. P. Harrington (Eds.), *Serious & violent juvenile offenders: Risk factors and successful interventions* (pp. 106–146). Thousand Oaks, CA: Sage.

Hirschauer, N., & Musshoff, O. (2007). A game-theoretic approach to behavioral food risks: The case of grain producers. *Food Policy, 32*(2), 246–265.

Internet Crime Complaint Center. (2007). Internet Crime Report, 2007. http://www.ic3.gov/media/ annualreport/2007_IC3Report.pdf. Accessed 1 October 2008.

Ismail, I. (2008, February 18). Understanding cybercriminals. *New Straits Times* (Malaysia), 12.

Jones, B. R. (2007). Comment: Virtual neighborhood watch: Open source software and community policing against cybercrime. *Journal of Criminal Law & Criminology, 97*(2), 601–629.

Joshi, V. (2009, October 12). Officials: Criminals cooperate better than police. *The Boston Globe.* http://www.boston.com/news/world/asia/articles/2009/10/12/officials_criminals_coop-erate_better_than_police/ Accessed 27 October 2009.

Kallman, E. A., & Grillo, J. P. (1996). *Ethical decision making and information technology,* 2e. New York: McGraw Hill.

Katyal, N. K. (2001). Criminal law in cyberspace. *University of Pennsylvania Law Review, 149*(4), 1003–1114.

Kshetri, N. (2005). Pattern of global cyber war and crime: A conceptual framework. *Journal of International Management, 11*(4), 541–562.

Kupersmidt, J. B., Griesler, P. C., DeRosier, M. E., Patterson, C. J., & Davis, P. W. (1995). Childhood aggression and peer relations in the context of family and neighborhood factors. *Child Development, 66,* 360–375.

Lagu, T., Kaufman, E. J., & Asch, D. A. (2008). Armstrong, K. Content of weblogs written by health professionals. *Journal of General Internal Medicine, 23*(10), 1642–1646.

Larkin, E. (2009). Organized crime moves into data theft. *PC World, 27*(7), 33–34.

Larsen, E., & Lomi, A. (2002). Representing change: A system model of organizational inertia and capabilities as dynamic accumulation processes. *Simulation Model Practice and Theory, 10*(5), 271–296.

Lemos, R. (2001, May 1). FBI "hack" raises global security concerns. *CNet News*. http://news.com.com/2100-1001-950719.html

Lianos, M., & Douglas, M. (2000). Dangerization and the end of deviance. *The British Journal of Criminology, 40*(2), 261–278.

Matsumoto, K., Ouchi, N., Watanabe, C., & Griffy-Brown, C. (2002). Optimal timing of the development of innovative goods with generation. *Technovation, 22*(3), 175–185.

McCarthy, B. (2002). New economics of sociological criminology. *Annual Review of Sociology, 28*, 417–442.

McCleary, R. M. (2008). Religion and economic development. *Policy Review, 148*, 45–57.

McCord, E. S., Ratcliffe, J. H., Garcia, R. M., & Taylor, R. B. (2007). Nonresidential crime attractors and generators elevate perceived neighborhood crime and incivilities. *Journal of Research in Crime and Delinquency, 44*(3), 295–320.

McDonald, C. G., Slawson, C. V., Jr. (2002, October). Reputation in an internet auction market. *Economic Inquiry, 40*(4), 633–650.

McIllwain, J. S. (2005). Intellectual property theft and organized crime: The case of film piracy. *Trends in Organized Crime, 8*(4), 15–39.

Merton, R. (1968). *Social theory and social structure*. New York: Free Press.

Messmer, E. (2009, October 6). Malware flea market pays hackers to hijack PCs. *The Industry Standard*. http://www.thestandard.com/news/2009/10/06/malware-flea-market-pays-hackers-hijack-pcs. Accessed 14 October 2009.

Mikos, R. A. (2006). "Eggshell" victims, private precautions, and the societal benefits of shifting crime. *Michigan Law Review, 105*(2), 307–351.

Miller, N. (2008). Casting a wide net for cyber crimes. *The Age*. Melbourne, Australia.

Morgan, P. M. (2005). Taking the long view of deterrence. *Journal of Strategic Studies, 28*(5), 751–763.

Nagin, D. S. (1998). Criminal deterrence–research at the outset of the twenty-first century. In M. Tondry (Ed.), *Crime and justice: A review of research, 23*, 1–42.

Oberwittler, D. (2007). The effects of neighborhood poverty on adolescent problem behaviors: A multi-level analysis differentiated by gender and ethnicity. *Housing Studies, 22*, 781–803.

Phukan, S. (2002, June). IT ethics in the Internet age: New dimensions. *InSITE*. http://proceedings.informingscience.org/IS2002Proceedings/papers/phuka037iteth.pdf

Probasco, J., Clark, R., & Davis, W. L. (1995). A human capital perspective on criminal careers. *Journal of Applied Business Research, 11*(3), 58–64.

Regan, K. (2006). FBI: Cybercrime causes financial pain for many businesses. *TechNewsWorld*. http://www.technewsworld.com/story/48417.html. Accessed 1 October 2009.

Richtel, M. (1999, June 2). Federal cybercrime unit hunts for hackers. *New York Times*, A16.

Rush, H., Smith, C., Mbula, E. K., & Tang, P. (2009). Crime online: Cybercrime and illegal innovation, Research report: July 2009, CENTRIM, University of Brighton. http://eprints.brighton.ac.uk/5800/01/Crime_Online.pdf. Accessed 1 October 2009.

Salkever, A. (2003, October 21). "Phishing" is foul on the Net. *Business Week Online*. http://www.businessweek.com/technology/content/oct2003/tc20031021_8711_tc047.htm. Accessed 1 October 2004.

Salu, A. O. (2004). Online crimes and advance fee fraud in nigeria – Are available legal remedies adequate? *Journal of Money Laundering Control, 8*(2), 159–167.

Sawant, N. (2009, October 5). Virtually speaking, crime in the city on an upward spiral. *The Times of India*. http://timesofindia.indiatimes.com/news/city/mumbai/Virtually-speaking-crime-in-the-city-on-an-upward-spiral/articleshow/5087668.cms.

Schneier, B. (2009, October 15). Why framing your enemies is now virtually child's play. *The Guardian*. http://www.guardian.co.uk/technology/2009/oct/15/bruce-schneier-internet-security.

Schuerman, L., & Kobrin, S. (1986). Community careers in crime. In A. J. Reiss, Jr. & M. Tonry (Eds.), *Communities and crime* (pp. 67–100). Chicago: University of Chicago Press.

Serio, J. D., & Gorkin, A. (2003). Changing lenses: Striving for sharper focus on the nature of the 'Russian Mafia' and its impact on the computer realm. *International Review of Law, Computers and Technology, 17*(2), 191–202.

Shelley, L. I. (1998). Crime and corruption in the digital age. *Journal of International Affairs, 51*(2), 605–620.

Shiels, M. (2009, October 1). US urges 'cyber hygiene' effort, BBC News. http://news.bbc.co.uk/2/hi/technology/8279867.stm. Accessed 1 October 2009.

Sullivan, B. (2007). Who's Behind Criminal Bot Networks?, April 10. http://redtape.msnbc.com/2007/04/whos_behind_cri.html. Accessed 1 October 2008.

Sutherland, B. (2008). The Rise of Black Market Data; Criminals who steal personal data often don't exploit it. Instead, they put it up for sale on one of the many vibrant online markets. *Newsweek (International ed.), 152*(24).

Swartz, J. (2004, October 21). Crooks slither into Net's shady nooks and crannies crime explodes as legions of strong-arm thugs, sneaky thieves log on. *USA Today*. www.usatoday.com/printedition/money/20041021/cybercrimecover.art.htm. Accessed 1 October 2005.

Swope, R. E. (2001). Criminal theory on the street: Analyzing why offenses take place. *Law and Order, 49*(6), 121–128.

Taylor, R. B., Koons, B., Kurtz, E., Greene, J., & Perkins, D. (1995). Streetblocks with more nonresidential landuse have more physical deterioration: Evidence from baltimore and philadelphia. *Urban Affairs Review, 30*, 120–136.

The Baltic Times. (2009, August 4). Cyber criminals found in Latvia. http://www.baltictimes.com/news/articles/23283. Accessed 1 October 2009.

The New York Times. (2009). Text: Obama's Remarks on Cyber-Security. http://www.nytimes.com/2009/05/29/us/politics/29obama.text.html?pagewanted=2. Accessed 1 October 2009.

Thompson, L. A., Dawson, K., & Ferdig, R., Black, E., Boyer, J., & Coutts, J. (2008). The intersection of online social networking with medical professionalism. *Journal of General Internal Medicine, 23*(7), 954–957.

Toshiya, K., Susumu, F., & Noriyasu, Y. (2003). A validation on Pareto optimality of Walrasian virtual market. *IEIC Technical Report (Institute of Electronics, Information and Communication Engineers), 102*(613), 13–18.

Valdez, A., Kaplan, C. D., & Curtis, R. L. (2007). Aggressive crime, alcohol and drug use, and concentrated poverty in 24 US urban areas. *American Journal of Drug and Alcohol Abuse, 33*, 595–603.

Van Koppen, P. J., & Jansen, R. W. J. (1998). The road to the robbery: Travel patterns in commercial robberies. *The British Journal of Criminology, 38*(2), 230–246.

Walden, I. (2005). Crime and security in cyberspace. *Cambridge Review of International Affairs, 18*(1), 51–68.

Walker, C. (2004, June). *Russian Mafia extorts gambling websites.* http://www.americanmafia.com/cgi/clickcount.pl?url=www.americanmafia.com/Feature_Articles_270.html. Accessed 1 October 2005.

Wall, D. S. (1998). Catching cybercriminals: Policing the internet. *International Review of Law, 12*(2), 201–218.

Wall, D. S. (2007). Policing cybercrimes: Situating the public police in networks of security within cyberspace. *Police Practice & Research, 8*(2), 183–205.

Warren, P. (2007, November 15). Hunt for Russia's web criminals. The Russian Business Network – Which some blame for 60% of all internet crime – Appears to have gone to ground. *The Guardian*. http://www.guardian.co.uk/technology/2007/nov/15/news.crime. Accessed 1 October 2009.

Watanabe, C., & Tokumasu, S. (2003). Optimal timing of R&D for effective utilization of potential resources in innovation. *Journal of Advances in Management Research, 1*(1), 11–27.

Webb, J. W., Tihanyi, L., Ireland, R. D., & Sirmon, D. G. (2009). You say illegal, I say legitimate: Entrepreneurship in the informal economy. *Academy of Management Review, 34*(3), 492–510.

Webwire. (2008, June 25). First told of Chinese PC hijack explosion. http://www.webwire.com/ViewPressRel.asp?aId=68776. Accessed 1 October 2009.

Weisburd, D., Bushway, S., Lum, C., & Yang, S. M. (2004). Trajectories of crime at places: A longitudinal study of street segments in the city of Seattle. *Criminology, 42*(2), 283–320.

Whitlock, R. A. (1979). Witch crazes and drug crazes: A contribution to the social pathology of credulity and scapegoating. *Australian Journal of Social, 14*(1), 43–54.

Wilson, W. J. (1987). *The truly disadvantaged*. Chicago: University of Chicago Press.

Wylie, I. (2007, December 26). Internet; Romania home base for EBay scammers; The auction website has dispatched its own cyber-sleuth to help police crack fraud rings. *Los Angeles Times*, C.1.

Ye, V. (2008, April 15). Asia hindered by lack of cybercrime laws. *businessweek.com*. http://www.businessweek.com/globalbiz/content/apr2008/gb20080415_220378.htm?campaign_id=rss_daily. Accessed 12 October 2009.

Zimmerman, A. (2006, October 25). Creative crooks: As shoplifters use high-tech scams, retail losses rise; Theft rings alter bar codes, work gift-card swindles; Fencing the loot online; Target snares a Lego bandit. *Wall Street Journal*, A1.

Chapter 3
An Institutional Perspective on Cybercrimes

"The draft treaty is contrary to well-established norms for the protection of the individual" (The Global Internet Liberty Campaign's comment on Council of Europe's Treaty on Cybercrime, BBC News online December 18, 2000).
   "Why are Brazil's hackers so strong and resourceful? Because they have little to fear legally" (Smith, 2003, quoting a Brazilian Internet security expert).

Abstract There are persuasive arguments for thinking that institutional processes have enormous power to explain cyberattacks. This chapter examines how macro- and micro-level institutions provide regulative, normative, and cognitive legitimacy to hackers', organizations', and governments' actions that facilitate or hinder cyberattacks. More specifically, we analyze institutions at supra-national, national, professional, industry, organizational, informal network, and intra-organizational levels in terms of their impacts on cyberinfrastructure, network, and computer attacks.

3.1 Introduction

The nature of activities of cyber-criminals fits squarely with what Baumol (1990) calls destructive entrepreneurship. Baumol (1990) hypothesized that the distribution of productive, unproductive, and destructive entrepreneurs in a society is a function of the "relative payoffs" offered to these activities by the society's "rules of the game." Note that these rules are referred as institutions (North, 1990). An entrepreneur's acts in an economy depend on the rules of the game and the reward structure in the economy (Baumol, 1990, p. 894).

Prior researchers have recognized that economic activities and actors are embedded in formal and informal institutions (Granovetter, 1985; Parto, 2005). There are persuasive arguments for thinking that institutional processes have enormous power to explain the degree and patterns of cyberattacks. An institutional perspective helps us link cyberattacks with rules and laws as well as values, norms, and cognitive assessment of actors related to cyberattacks.

N. Kshetri, *The Global Cybercrime Industry*, DOI 10.1007/978-3-642-11522-6_3,   57
© Springer-Verlag Berlin Heidelberg 2010

Social and policy-related factors and institutional logics powerfully moderate the effects of economic forces (Schneiberg, King, & Smith, 2008). It is apparent that cybercrimes differ from other crimes in terms of permissiveness of regulatory regimes (Mittelman & Johnston, 1999), regulatory arbitrage (Levi, 2002), and culture and ethical attitudes that influence external and internal stigma (Aguilar-Millan, Foltz, Jackson, & Oberg, 2008; Donaldson, 1996; Kwong, Yau, Lee, Sin, & Tse, 2003).

In this chapter, we draw upon literatures on institutional theory to develop a framework on the institution-cybercrime nexus. More to the point, we provide a framework for key institutional factors at different levels of analysis that influence cyberattacks.

3.2 Institutional Theory

We begin by considering a broad approach to institutions, which defines the concept in terms of an equilibrium of a game. Three factors that determine an equilibrium include "(i) technologically determined external constraints; (ii) humanly devised external constraints, and; (iii) constraints developed within the game through patterns of behavior and the creation of expectations" (Snidal, 1996, p. 128). This section mainly deals with the second factor, which corresponds to the "rules of the game" and includes "formal constraints (rules, laws, constitutions), informal constraints (norms of behavior, conventions, and self-imposed codes of conduct), and their enforcement characteristics" (North, 1996, p. 344).

Scott (1995) proposed three institutional pillars—regulative, normative, and cognitive—which relate to "legally sanctioned," "morally governed," and "recognizable, taken-for-granted" behaviors, respectively (Scott, Ruef, Mendel, & Caronna, 2000, p. 238). Formal constraints can be mapped with Scott's (2001) regulative pillar while informal constraints can be mapped with normative and cognitive pillars. To put things in context, formal and informal institutions influence the perceived threats of shame and embarrassment and that of legal sanctions for a criminal (Blackwell, 2000; Grasmick & Robert, 1990).

3.2.1 Regulative Institutions

Regulative institutions consist of "explicit regulative processes: rule setting, monitoring, and sanctioning activities" (Scott, 1995, p. 35). These institutions focus on the pragmatic legitimacy concerns in managing the demands of regulators and governments (Kelman, 1987). In the context of this chapter, regulative institutions consist of regulatory bodies (such as the US Department of Justice and the US Department of Homeland Security) and existing laws and rules (e.g., *the Patriot Act* and *the Gramm Leach Bliley (GLB) Act* in the United States) that influence individuals and organizations to behave in certain ways (Scott, 1995). Individuals and organizations adhere to the rules so that they would not suffer the penalty for noncompliance (Hoffman, 1999).

3.2.2 Normative Institutions

Normative components introduce "a prescriptive, evaluative, and obligatory dimension into social life"[1] (Scott, 1995, p. 37). This component focuses on the values and norms held by individuals, organizations, and government agencies that influence the ICT-national security nexus. Practices that are consistent with and take into account the different assumptions and value systems of the national cultures are likely to be successful (Schneider, 1999). The basis of compliance in the case of normative institutions derives from social obligations, and non-adherence can result in societal and professional sanctions. Normative institutions also include trade associations, professional associations (e.g., the Honker Union of China, also known as the Red Hackers), or non-profit organizations (e.g., ACLU in the US) that can use social obligation requirements (e.g., ethical codes of conduct) to induce certain behavior.

3.2.3 Cognitive Institutions

Cognitive institutions are associated with culture (Jepperson, 1991). These components represent culturally supported habits that influence governments', firms', and hackers' behaviors. In most cases, they are based on subconsciously accepted rules and customs as well as some taken-for-granted cultural account of computer use (Berger & Luckmann, 1967). Scott (1995, p. 40) suggests that "cognitive elements constitute the nature of reality and the frames through which meaning is made."

Although carried by individuals, cognitive programs are social in nature (Berger & Luckmann, 1967). Compliance in the case of cognitive legitimacy concerns is due to habits. Political elites, organizational decision makers, and hackers may not even be aware that they are complying.

3.2.4 Interrelationships Among Institutional Pillars

It is quite possible that formal and informal institutions with respect to some issues may be incongruent for some groups (Webb, Tihanyi, Ireland, & Sirmon, 2009). That is, what some groups in a society may consider some activities legitimate, as specified by their norms, values, and beliefs, which are in fact illegal, that, they violate existing laws and regulations (Dowling & Pfeffer, 1975; Webb et al., 2009).

It is, however, worth keeping in mind that an institutional pillar both reflects and determines the nature of the other pillars (Hayek, 1979). In the "real world," thus it is difficult to isolate them. North (1994) argues that informal rules such as values and norms provide legitimacy to formal rules. Likewise, political scientist Robert Axelrod (1997, p. 61) comments on the relationship between regulative and normative institutions:

> Social norms and laws are often mutually supporting. This is true because social norms can become formalized into laws and because laws provide external validation of norms.

3.2.5 Exogenous and Endogenous Institutions

Another approach to analyze institutions is to focus on the exogenous and endogenous natures (Davis & North, 1971). According to this approach, the exogenous institutional environment consists of formal and informal macro-level rules such as the judicial system, cultural norms, and kinship patterns (Davis & North, 1971). The exogenous institutional environment is slow to change and defines the world in which firms and people interact. Some refer these as *fundamental institutions*, which "are taken for granted and are difficult to change through purposive design" (Bresser & Millonig, 2003).The endogenous institutional arrangement, on the other hand, consists of the formal and informal micro-level rules of exchange devised by specific parties to a specific exchange (Davis & North, 1971; Carson, Timothy, Grahame, & George, 1999) or to regulate specific societal problems (Bresser & Millonig, 2003). These are also known as *secondary institutions*. They include laws, contracts, organizations, and organizational rules and procedures and are more amenable to conscious design (Bresser & Millonig, 2003).

3.2.6 Neoinstitutionalism

Neoinstitutionalism is characterized by both macro- and micro-level approaches, which complement each other (Scott, 1987). One way to differentiate these two approaches is whether the sources of institutionalization are external or internal to the organization. Macro-institutionalism considers the sources of institutionalization in the external environment of organizations and argues that organizations exhibit isomorphism with respect to external institutional pressures by adopting institutionally desirable structures and processes. Micro-institutionalism, on the other hand, assumes that these sources are internal to organizations (Bresser & Millonig, 2003). Scott (1995, p. 40) observes the existence of external and internal dimensions in institutions by stating that values and norms "... are both internalized and imposed by others." Inter-firm differences in behavior can be explained in terms of an "institutional filter," which determines the extent to which specific environmental demands are compatible with an organization's system of norms and values and should therefore be adopted (Bresser & Millonig, 2003). Theorists have provided evidence, which indicates that organizations may engage in non-isomorphic responses if they perceive that such responses are likely to minimize a potential loss of resources (George, Chattopadhyay, Sitkin, & Barden, 2006).

Many micro-level rules that govern cyber-criminals' and victims' decisions and have extremely large macro-level consequences are embedded in the social and cultural institutions. Macro-level heterogeneity can thus arguably be attributed to "homophilic microlevel rules" (Macy & Willer, 2002, p. 13). Deinhart (2000) illustrates how macro- and micro-level institutions are related:

> ... [M]arkets ... are embedded in social institutions that guide behavior, involve organizations, that have internal structures (institutions) that guide behavior, and involve individuals making decisions in the context of market and organizational institutions and relationships.

3.2.7 Institutions Operating at Various Levels

Institutions influencing cyberattacks operate at different levels—global, national, local, social network, professional, industry, inter-organizational, and intra-organizational (Atkinson, 1991; Giddens, 1984; Kalipeni & Feder, 1999; Oppong & Kalipeni, 2005; Strang & Sine, 2002).

On institutions at the international/global level, Louis Henkin (1979) noted that "almost all nations observe almost all principles of international law and almost all of their obligations almost all of the time." Thanks to globalization, governments are turning to supra-national institutions to resolve transnational problems (Smith & Wiest, 2005) such as cyberattacks. It should, however, be noted that although some commentators have argued that supra-national institutions are playing a crucial role in solving transnational problems (Dingwerth, 2005) and are reducing the power and autonomy of the state (Smith & Wiest, 2005), others have suggested that these institutions lack legitimacy as they lack a democratic mandate and have failed to represent broad interests (Castles, 2005).

Of greatest relevance here are national-level institutions—also known as the "country-level effects" or the "societal effects" (Zaheer & Zaheer, 1997)—which include political, legal, cultural, and other environmental factors specific to a country that influence cyberattacks. The state is arguably the most important external institutional actor and powerful drivers of institutional isomorphism since a violation of laws and regulations can have harsh economic and social sanctions (Bresser & Millonig, 2003).

At the industry/professional/inter-organizational level, external institutional actors exert pressure by threatening punishment in cases of noncompliance (Bresser & Millonig, 2003). Ethical codes of conduct set by different institutions and governing bodies such as professional associations and other private sector organizations are examples of institutions residing at inter-organizational level. The codes of conduct generally require members to maintain higher standards of conduct than required by law (Backoff & Martin, 1991).

At the societal network level, participants are encouraged to comply with the norms and values of the networks (Chung, 2004). A network can be defined as a group of "autonomous" actors "purposively involved in the group's activities" (Bieje & Groenewegen, 1992, p. 90). Some institutionalists refer traditional institutions consisting of custom and limited social networks (intragroup networks) of the pre-industrial era as the true forms of institutions (Sjostrand, 1992). Indeed, Gehlen (1957/1980) argued that modem society is being increasingly deinstitutionalized. In some societies, informal networks are still more effective than formal laws and regulations in dealing with local problems (Mol & Van Den Burg, 2004). An individual's social network is related to the obligation to be trustworthy and follow the norms of equity (Granovetter, 1985).

Different theoretical contributions and various empirical studies have led to the accepted view that that institutions within organizations or intra-organizational institutions have important consequences for organizations and their members including implementation of organizational knowledge and technology (Elsbach,

2002). These are associated with internal structures of organization (Deinhart, 2000). To take one example, in 2001, eBay announced a global ban on the sale of hate-related items on the company's websites (Wolverton, 2001).

3.3 Viewing Cybercrimes Through the Prism of the Literature on Institutions

The contexts of the economic activities were considered to influence the meaning and significance of institutions (Holm, 1995). In this chapter we consider formal and informal institutions from the standpoint of criminal activities.

3.3.1 Formal Constraints and Crimes

In prior literature, researchers have found organized crime groups thrive in a country with a weak state (Levi, 2002). Note that organized crime groups are increasing using the Internet to facilitate criminal activities (Finckenauer, 2005). The Italian Mafia, Japanese Yakuza, Chinese gangs, Colombian cartels, and Russian and Malaysian organized crime groups have reportedly employed hackers (Foreign Policy, 2005; Ismail, 2008; Katyal, 2001; Parker, 1998). The Business Software Alliance (BSA) urged US Congress to enact legislation to treat "cyber crime as organized crime" (Natividad, 2008).

A related concept is regulatory arbitrage, which exists when regulative institutions differ across countries in their permissiveness and conduciveness to crimes. Prior researchers have noted that transnational criminal groups' knowledge of regulatory variation in European countries allows them to use clever strategies to avoid prosecution (Levi, 2002). Likewise, financial frauds occur more in locations with less reporting obligations (Stewart, 2006).

3.3.2 Informal Constraints and Crimes

Studies of informal sanctions constitute a notable stream in the criminology literature. Prior researchers have noted the roles of informal psychological and social sanctions (e.g., shame, guilt, embarrassment, and rejection) in deterring socially undesirable and illegal behaviors (Aguilar-Millan et al., 2008; Blackwell, 2000; Clark & Davis, 1995; Paetzold, Dipboye, & Elsbach, 2008; Rasmussen, 1996; Smith, Simpson, & Chun-Yao, 2007). Proponents of "gay rights" legislation, for instance, argue that the real battle centers on gaining cultural acceptability and social legitimacy of such rights (Hu, 2001; Shilts, 1991) and stigmatizing "orthodox religious believers" (Duncan, 1994). Likewise, it is argued that culture and ethical attitudes may be a more crucial factor in driving software piracy than the level of economic development (Donaldson, 1996; Kwong et al., 2003).

Galtung (1958, p. 127) distinguishes two types of informal constraints facing a person (P): Institutionalized norms are "norms from other members from the social system to P" and internalized norms are "norms from P to himself." These are captured by Scott's (1995) normative and cognitive pillars. Institutionalized and internalized norms are related to external and internal stigma, respectively (Aguilar-Millan et al., 2008), which increase the psychic cost of feeling embarrassment and shame (Blackwell, 2000; Clark & Davis, 1995).

Institutionalized norms: Institutionalized norms are related to embarrassment, which is a socially imposed sanction that occurs when individuals violate norms endorsed by the society, especially by significant others (Blackwell, 2000; Paetzold et al., 2008). An external or social stigma is related to resentment against a criminal activity, which can lead to a deterrence of crimes (Rasmussen, 1996).

Prior researchers have also noted that from the society's point of view, whether crimes and victimization "elicit a stigma or a sympathy effect may depend on the evaluator's characteristics" (Lyons, 2006). The social identity theory points to the possibility of ethnocentric bias (Hamner, 1992; Tajfel & Turner, 1986). This means that ingroup victims and offenders are likely to be perceived sympathetically, while out-group ones may be stigmatized (Howard & Pike, 1986; Lyons, 2006). In a related vein, prior research also seems to indicate that racial prejudice leads to crimes (Hawkins et al., 1998).

Internalized norms: Internalized norms are related to internal stigma or a feeling of guilt and shame (Aguilar-Millan et al., 2008) and a negative evaluation of the self or a specific behavior (Harris, 2006; Lewis, 1971, 1992). Note that shame is a self-imposed sanction, which occurs as a reaction to individuals' violation of their internalize standards (Benedict, 1946; Freud, 1949/1930; Mead, 1937). Scholars also suggest that condemnation of a criminal act leads to internalization of norms against the act among the "condemners" and as well as the "condemned" (Kahan, 1996).

3.4 Institutions at Different Levels Influencing Cyberattacks

Table 3.1 illustrates how formal and informal institutions at different levels influence cyberattacks.

3.4.1 International-Level Institutions and Cyberattacks

Cyberattacks are global problems and for this reason, global-level institutions are likely to be effective to deal with such problems. As discussed in Chap. 1, supranational institutions such as International Telecommunications Union (ITU) and Interpol are working to strengthen regulative institutions related to cybercrime laws across the world.

Table 3.1 Institutions at different levels impacting cybercrimes

Level	Formal institutions	Informal institutions
Global/International	o International laws and treaties	
National	o National rules and laws	o Political-normative views
		o Political-cognitive factors
		o Nationalism/patriotism-related hackings
		o National subculture and cybercrime patterns
Industry/profession/Inter-organizational		o Pressure to deploy defense mechanisms (e.g., NASSCOM)
		o Engaging in cyberattacks to gain respect from peer hackers (e.g., red hackers)
Informal networks		o Norms related to information sharing among hackers
		o Ideology: cyberattacks related to religion, fight against capitalism and nuclear proliferation, etc.
		o Cognitive legitimacy from parents and teachers
Intra-organizational		o Norms related to reporting
		o Norms related to defense measures
		o Cognitive assessment of reporting cyberattacks

Given the global nature of cybercrime, fighting them more effectively would require global institutions with more effective compliance mechanisms. As are the cases of most global-level institutions and processes, international institutions designed to deal with cybercrime are, however, relatively underdeveloped. International treaties on cybercrime are weak and unenforceable.

3.4.2 National-Level Institutions and Cyberattacks

Compared to international institutions, the state arguably is more dominant in most areas of policy (Tarrow, 2001). National-level institutions provide a number of mechanisms to influence the cybercrime landscape.

Rules and laws: Cyberattack have benefited from jurisdictional arbitrage. Thanks to the newness, jurisdictional arbitrage is higher for cybercrimes compared to other conventional crimes. In a 2003 *Newsweek* article, Piore (2003, p. 48) argued that only the United States and the United Kingdom had "laws that come even close to adequate in defining cybercrimes and leveling penalties." The lack of a strong rule of law is associated with the origination of more cyberattacks. A country with a strong rule of law is characterized by a strong court system and effective punishment and legal sanctions against criminals (Oxley & Yeung, 2001), which increase the expected probability of apprehension and conviction for criminals (see Eq. (2.1) in Chap. 2) (Ehrlich, 1996). A weak rule of law, on the other hand, is characterized by a lack of trust between the government and the citizens (Levi, 2002). Countries with weak rule of law and permissiveness of regulatory regimes thus provide a fertile ground for criminal activities (Mittelman & Johnston, 1999; Vassilev, 2003). Citizens' willingness to accept the established institutions and to obey the laws is equally important (The FBI Law Enforcement Bulletin, 2007).

Not surprisingly, organized cybercrimes are initiated from countries that have few or no laws directed against cybercrimes and little capacity to enforce existing laws (Grow & Bush, 2005; Williams, 2001). Eastern Europe and Russia's weak cybercrime laws have provided a fertile ground for computer crimes. Although many countries in Eastern Europe[2] have enacted cybercrime laws, they lack enforcement mechanisms.

A nation's laws also determine what is considered a cybercrime. For instance, in 2002, Germany announced that anyone promoting Holocaust denial, anywhere in the world, is liable under German law (Gabrys, 2002). Similarly, the Malaysian government announced that online insults to Islam would be punished (Perera, 2000).

National laws also facilitate or restrict law-enforcement agencies' ability to act on cybercrimes. In the United States, for instance, the FBI considers militant Islamist websites lawful as the First Amendment permits even the most hateful Internet speech, as long as they do not directly incite violence or raise money (Stephens, 2006). On the contrary, consider Singapore. In the cyber conflict with the Think Centre (Asia), an NGO, the state authorities reportedly employed surveillance and intimidation (Gomez, 2002, p. 76). There are reports that the government of Singapore actively scans and monitors e-mails and there are instances of breaking into a number of computers used by various groups and individuals (Gomez, 2002, pp. 43–44).

Law-enforcement agencies' responses also differ across types of cybercrimes. Experts argue that law-enforcement officials in some countries such as China and Russia do not take major actions against hackers attacking international websites and are more interested in protecting national security (Blau, 2004; Vardi, 2005).

Political cognitive factors: Mental maps of political elites or "persons who by virtue of their institutional positions have a high potential to influence national policy making" (Moore, 1979, p. 674) determine a nation's approach to cyberattacks. Political elites include legislators, governmental officials, political party officials, leaders of various interest groups, military leaders, etc.

An article published in *China Economic Times* on June 12, 2000 discussed three mechanisms that Xu Guanhua, then Chinese vice minister of the science and technology, thought high technology affects national security—military security, economic security, and cultural security. Regarding military security, Guanhua forcefully argued that developed countries have put many hi-tech arms into actual battles and discussed the likelihood of ICT exporting countries installing software for "coercing, attacking or sabotage." Ironically, the truth or falsity of such claims is less relevant than the fear itself, which can significantly alter the equation of global security.

Some US observers, on the other hand, think that countries like China, Russia, and North Korea are systematically probing the computer networks in the United States to find weaknesses that can be exploited later (Bickers, 2001). A group of US defense analysts also argued that the growing use of Linux (open source software) in US defense systems presents an urgent national security threat. They have maintained that Linux companies have deployed development centers with programers from China and Russia, on one hand, and open nature of Linux enables hackers or cyber-terrorists to exploit the system, on the other hand. According to the US National Security Agency, some foreign governments have developed computer attack capabilities. Some US officials believe Iran, North Korea, Russia, and China have trained hackers in Internet warfare (Lenzner & Vardi, 2004). From the standpoint of national security, the truth or falsify of such fear is less relevant than the fear itself, which influences a nation's approach to deal with possible attacks on cyberinfrastructure and networks.

Political-normative effects: Political elites also differ on political-normative paths, which lead to variation to approaches to cybercrimes across nations. While there are government-backed cyber-terrorisms in some countries (Comité Européen Des Assurances, 2004), others have followed different approaches. A comparison of the United States and Burma illustrates this point. For instance, the United States has reportedly developed cyber-weapons capable of destroying an enemy's computer network, but there are disagreements about the appropriateness of employing such weapons (Adams, 2001). The Government of Burma, on the other hand, uses its advanced cyberwarfare department within the police force to track its online critics and sends virus-attached e-mails to exiled activists (Havely, 2000). A 2002 survey of Australian firms indicated that foreign governments were perceived as sources of attacks for 24% respondents (Deloitte Touche Tohmatsu, 2002).

National subculture and cybercrime patterns: Skorodumova (2004) provides a useful set of distinctions for characterizing hacking cultures associated with different nationalities. The American hackers, for instance, are characterized by personal motives such as self-advertising compared to Russians or Europeans. European hackers refrain from attacking well-known sites and advertising themselves. The US specialists believe that European hackers more often attack websites in protest or in defense of human rights. Likewise, Russian hackers see the authority and laws as hostile.

3.4.3 Institutions at the Industry/Professional/Inter-organizational Level and Cyberattacks

Some professional and trade associations can use social obligation requirements to induce certain behavior within organizations and the hacking community. There are instances of professional and trade associations exerting isomorphic pressure to deploy appropriate defense measures. In India, the National Association of Software and Services Companies (NASSCOM) has played a critical role in the development of cybercrime-related institutions.

Motivation to earn respect from peer hackers also drives their actions. For instance, the members of the Honker Union of China (also known as the Red Hackers) are required to behave according to the guidelines set by the organization. The basis of compliance in such case thus derives from social obligations, and non-adherence can result in professional sanctions.

3.4.4 Institutions at the Network Level and Cyberattacks

Informal networks organized along a number of different lines also have values and norms that influence cyberattacks. First, consider families and broader social networks. There is some evidence that parents, and even teachers, advocate certain computer crimes, particularly software piracy among students (Bowker, 2000).

Other informal networks engaged in cyberinfrastructure, network, and computer attack spread across a wide geographical area. Some informal networks are organized along some type of ideology such as religion, fight against nuclear proliferation, and capitalism.

The networks of Islamic activists deserve special attention. Except for occasional India–Pakistan and Israel–Palestine cyber-wars, hacking by Islamist activists was insignificant before September 11, 2001. *mi2g Intelligence Unit* reported increasing Islamist hacking, the targets being networks of the United States, Britain, Australia, and other coalition partners, as well as domestic networks of Russia, Turkey, Indonesia, Pakistan, Saudi Arabia, Morocco, and Kuwait.[3] Even more intriguing is the Society for Internet Research's finding which indicated that 70% of militant Islamist websites are hosted on computers based in the United States (Stephens, 2006).

Some act against the nation-state where they live. For instance, in the mid-2001, Cyberjihad, a group of hackers in Indonesia attacked the website of the Indonesian police to force them to free a militant Muslim leader (Antariksa, 2001, p. 15).

To take another example of ideological hacking, in June 1998, six hackers from the United States, the United Kingdom, the Netherlands, and New Zealand (identifying themselves as *Milworm*) hacked India's Bhabha Atomic Research Center's website (Denning, 2000). Similarly, in South Korea, 58 Internet servers were attacked by a Japanese student in November 2003 to protest the US-led war on Iraq (Duk-kun, 2003). In addition to nationalism and religion, hackers' interests are also framed by fight against global capitalism (de Kloet, 2002). Such hackers are likely to attack networks of big multinationals.

Informal networks related to criminal organizations generally restrict membership according to various criteria such as ethnicity, kinship, race, and criminal background (Finckenauer, 2005) and in some cases corrupt public officials (Maltz, 1994, p. 27). The hawala system widely used in Middle East and Asia to move money internationally, which also uses the Internet, relies on brokers linked by clan-based networks of trust (Homer-Dixon, 2002).

The hacking community is also characterized by a high degree of information sharing. Members in the community are willing to help fellow hackers to solve problems such as accessing a router and getting through a firewall (Bednarz, 2004). Typically, swapping and sharing of hacking tools and secrets take place in closed chat rooms (Acohido & Swartz, 2005).

3.4.5 Institutions at the Intra-organizational Level and Cyberattacks

Organizational idiosyncrasy may lead to varying responses to influences from the external environment (Zucker, 1991). The intra-organizational level is dominated by the normative component of institutions. An organization may voluntarily adhere to such norms, which may be subsequently internalized to be reflected in the organization's structures, strategies, and routines (Scott, 1995).

An important dimension of organizational norm related to cyberattacks is the organization's defense approach. We illustrate this point with Indian outsourcing firms' approach to prevent attacks on computers by current and former employees. In an attempt to address their clients' fear that customer data will be stolen and even sold to criminals (Lucas, 2004), Indian firms engaged in outsourcing have taken measures to prevent attacks on computers by current and former employees. For instance, call center employees have to undergo security checks which are considered to be "undignified" (The Economist, 2005). Firms have established biometric authentication controls for workers and banned cell phones, pens, paper, and Internet/e-mail access for employees (Fest, 2005). Computer terminals at Mphasis, an Indian outsourcing firm, lack hard drives, e-mail, CD-ROM drives, or other ways to store, copy, or forward data[4] (Engardio, Puliyenthuruthel, & Kripalani, 2004). Indian outsourcing firms also extensively monitor and analyze employee logs (Fest, 2005). Outsourcing firms in developing countries consider relationships with clients as important resources that can provide long-term returns on investment. To win and maintain legitimacy from their clients, structures and practices of Indian outsourcing firms have become non-isomorphic with respect to the local culture. Recall that organizations may engage in non-isomorphic responses if they perceive that such responses are likely to minimize a potential loss of resources (George et al., 2006).

To take another example, consider *The New York Times'* response after the company was duped into running a fake malware-loaded advertisement in September 2009. Following the security breach, the company suspended its practice of serving online ads directly from an advertiser's website (Kravets, 2009).

Organizations' cognitive assessment and norms related to reporting cyberattacks to authorities also influence law-enforcement agencies' ability to solve such crimes. As noted earlier, proportionally, much less cybercrimes than conventional crimes are reported to law-enforcement agencies.

3.5 Concluding Comments

The foregoing discussion provides a framework for understanding how institutions at various levels influence cyberattacks. An institutional perspective used in this chapter provides insights into factors and mechanisms that energize hackers' behaviors, nations' development, and deployment of cyber-weapons, law-enforcement agencies' responses to cyberattacks, organizations' defense mechanisms, and propensity to report cyberattacks on their networks, etc. From a theoretical perspective, our framework helps further explain patterns of cyberattacks.

As noted above, formal and informal institutions influence each other. Social and moral condemnation of cybercrime is thus likely to strengthen regulative institutions related to cybercrime. Likewise, legal system and legal discourse in relation to cybercrime are likely to influence social perception of cybercrimes.

Anti-cybercrime norms have not been fully institutionalized and internalized in the cyber-space. Institutions building efforts need to be carried out within the parameters of established culture, practices, discourses, power structures, and other institutions.

Notes

1. Deinhart (2000, p. xv) notes that "...business ethics is prescriptive while business and society is descriptive."
2. For instance, a law enacted in Romania in 2003 punishes convicts with up to 15 years in prison (Romania Gateway, 2003).
3. See "The rise of extremist hacking, criminal syndicates," http://star-techcentral.com/tech/story.asp?file=/2004/10/26/technology/9225925&sec=technology. Accessed 1 October 2009.
4. Since data theft is often committed by disgruntled former employees, Mphasis can lock an employee out and cut access to PCs and phones 3 minutes after a resignation. In 2003, the process took 3 days (Engardio et al., 2004).

References

Acohido, B., & Swartz, J. (2005, December 15). Meth addicts' other habit: Online theft. *USA Today*.

Adams, J. (2001). Virtual defense. *Foreign Affairs, 80*(3), 98–112.

Aguilar-Millan, S., Foltz, J. E., Jackson, J., & Oberg, A. (2008). The globalization of crime. *Futurist, 42*(6), 41–50.

Antariksa. (2001, July). I am a thief, not a hacker: Indonesia's electronic underground. *Latitudes Magazine*, 12–17.

Atkinson, A. (1991). *Principles of political ecology*. London: Belhaven Press.

Axelrod, R. (1997). *The complexity of cooperation*. New Jersey: Princeton University Press.

Backoff, J. F., & Martin, C. L., Jr. (1991). Historical perspectives: Development of the codes of ethics in the legal, medical and accounting professions. *Journal of Business Ethics, 10*, 99–110.

Baumol, W. J. (1990). Entrepreneurship: Productive, unproductive, and destructive. *Journal of Political Economy, 98*(5), 893–921.

Bednarz, A. (2004, November 29). Profiling cybercriminals: A promising but immature science. *Network World.* http://www.nwfusion.com/supp/2004/cybercrime/112904profile.html?page=2. Accessed 5 October 2006.

Benedict, R. (1946). *The chrysanthemum and the sword; Patterns of Japanese culture.* Boston: Houghton Mifflin.

Berger, P. L., & Luckmann, T. (1967). *The social construction of reality: A treatise in the sociology of knowledge.* New York: Doubleday.

Bickers, C. (2001). Combat on the web. *Far Eastern Economic Review, August 16,* 30–33.

Bieje, P.R., & Groenewegen, J. (1992). A network analysis of markets. *Journal of Economic Issues, 26*(1), 87–114.

Blackwell, B. S. (2000). Perceived sanction threats, gender, and crime: A test and elaboration of power-control theory, criminology. *Beverly Hills, 38*(2), 439–489.

Blau, J. (2004, May 26). Russia – A happy haven for hackers. http://www.computerweekly.com/Article130839.htm. Accessed 5 October 2006.

Bowker, A. L. (2000). The advent of the computer delinquent. *FBI Law Enforcement, 69*(12), 7–11.

Bresser, R. K. F., & Millonig, K. (2003). Institutional capital: Competitive advantage in light of the new institutionalism in organization theory. *Schmalenbach Business Review, 55*(3), 220–241.

Carson, S. J., Timothy, M. D., Grahame, R. D., & George, J. (1999). Understanding institutional designs within marketing value systems. *Journal of Marketing, 63,* 115–130.

Castles, S. (2005). Nation and empire: Hierarchies of citizenship in the new global order. *International Politics, 42*(2), 203.

Chung, K. H. (2004). Business groups in Japan and Korea: Theoretical boundaries and future direction. *International Journal of Political Economy, 34*(3), 67–98.

Clark, R., & Davis, W. L. (1995). A human capital perspective on criminal careers. *Journal of Applied Business Research, 11*(3), 58–64.

Comité Européen Des Assurances. (2004, February). Terrorist acts against computer installations and the role of the Internet in the context of international terrorism property insurance committee. *IT Risks Insurance Sub-committee.* http://www.cea.assur.org/cea/v1.1/actu/pdf/uk/annexe180.pdf. Accessed 5 October 2006.

Davis, L., & North, D. C. (1971). *Institutional change and American economic growth.* Cambridge: Cambridge University Press.

de Kloet, J. (2002). Digitisation and its Asian discontents: The internet, politics and hacking in China and Indonesia. *First Monday, 7*(9). http://firstmonday.org/issues/issue7_9/kloet/index.html. Accessed 5 October 2006.

Deinhart, J. W. (2000). *Business, institutions, and ethics.* New York: Oxford University Press.

Deloitte Touche Tohmatsu. (2002). *Australian computer crime and security survey.* http://www.4law.co.il/346.pdf. Accessed 5 October 2006.

Denning, D. E. (2000). *Acktivism: An emerging threat to diplomacy.* American Foreign Service Association. www.afsa.org/fsj/sept00/Denning.cfm. Accessed 5 October 2006.

Dingwerth, K. (2005). The democratic legitimacy of public-private rule making: What can we learn from the world commission on dams? *Global Governance, 11*(1), 65–83.

Donaldson, T. (1996). Values in tension: Ethics away from home. *Harvard Business Review, 74*(5), 48–57.

Dowling, J., & Pfeffer, J. (1975). Organizational legitimacy: Social values and organizational behavior. *Pacific Sociological Review, 18,* 122–136.

Duk-kun, B. (2003, November 19). Largest Internet hacking ring uncovered. *The Korea Times.*

Duncan, R. (1994). Who wants to stop the church: Homosexual rights, legislation, public policy, and religious freedom. *Notre Dame Law Review, 69,* 393.

Ehrlich, I. (1996). Crime, punishment, and the market for offenses. *Journal of Economic Perspectives, 10*(1), 43–67.

Elsbach, K. D. (2002). Intraorganizational Institutions. *Blackwell Companion to Organizations,* 37–57.

Engardio, P., Puliyenthuruthel, J., & Kripalani, M. (2004, August 16). Fortress India? *Business Week, 3896,* 42–43.

Fest, G. (2005, September 1). Offshoring: Feds take fresh look at India BPOs; Major theft has raised more than a few eyebrows. *Bank Technology News, 18*(9), 1.

Finckenauer, J. O. (2005). Problems of definition: What is organized crime? *Trends in Organized Crime, 8*(3), 63–83.

Foreign Policy. (2005, March/April). Caught in the net: Australian teens, 92.

Freud, S. (1949/1930). *Civilization and its discontents.* London: Hogarth Press and Institute of Psycho-Analysis.

Gabrys, E. D. (2002). The international dimensions of cyber-crime, Part 2. *Information Systems Security, 11*(5), 24–32.

Galtung, J. (1958). The social functions of a prison. *Social Problems, 6,* 127–140.

Gehlen, A. (1957/1980). *Man in the age of technology* (Reprint). New York: Columbia University Press.

George, E., Chattopadhyay, P., Sitkin, S. B., & Barden, J. (2006). Cognitive underpinnings of institutional persistence and change: A framing perspective. *Academy of Management Review, 31*(2), 347–385.

Giddens, A. (1984). *The constitution of society: Outline of the theory of structuration.* Berkely, CA: University of California Press.

Gomez, J. (2002). *Internet politics: Surveillance and intimidation in Singapore.* Bangkok and Singapore: Think Centre (Asia).

Granovetter, M. (1985). Economic action and social structure: The problem of embeddedness. *American Journal of Sociology, 91*(3), 481–510.

Grasmick, H. G., & Robert, J. B. (1990). Conscience, significant others, and rational choice: Extending the deterrence model. *Law and Society Review, 24,* 837–862.

Grow, B., & Bush, J. (2005, May 30). Hacker hunters. *Business Week.*

Hamner, K. M. (1992). Gay-bashing: A social identity analysis of violence against lesbians and gay men. In G. M. Herek & K. Berrill (Eds.), *Hate crimes: Confronting violence against lesbians and gay men* (pp. 179–190). Newbury Park, CA: Sage.

Harris, N. (2006). Reintegrative shaming, shame, and criminal justice. *Journal of Social Issues, 62*(2), 327–346.

Havely, J. (2000, February 16). Online's when states go to cyber-war. *BBC News.*

Hawkins, J. D., Herrenkohl, T., Farrington, D. P., Brewer, D., Catalano, R., & Harachi, T. W. (1998). A review of predictors of youth violence. In R. Loeber & D. P, Harrington (Eds.), *Serious & violent juvenile offenders: Risk factors and successful interventions* (pp. 106–146). Thousand Oaks, CA: Sage.

Hayek, F. A. (1979). *Law, legislation and liberty* (3 vols.). Chicago: University of Chicago Press.

Henkin, L. (1979). *How nations behave.* New York: Council on Foreign Relations.

Hoffman, A. J. (1999). Institutional evolution and change: Environmentalism and the US chemical industry. *Academy of Management Journal, 42*(4), 351–371.

Holm, P. (1995). The dynamics of institutionalization: Transformation processes in Norwegian fisheries. *Administrative Science Quarterly, 40*(3), 398–422.

Homer-Dixon, T. (2002, January/February). The rise of complex terrorism. *Foreign Policy, 128,* 52–62.

Howard, J. A., & Pike, K. C. (1986). Ideological investment in cognitive processing: The influence of social statuses on attribution. *Social Psychology, 49,* 154–167.

Hu, V. T. (2001). Nondiscrimination or secular orthodoxy? Religious freedom and breach of contract at Tufts University. *Texas Review of Law & Politics, 6*(1), 289–333.

Ismail, I. (2008, February 18). Understanding cybercriminals. *New Straits Times* (Malaysia), 12.

Jepperson, R. (1991). Institutions, institutional effects, and institutionalism. In W. W. Powell & P. J. DiMaggio (Eds.), *The new institutionalism in organizational analysis* (pp. 143–163). Chicago: University of Chicago Press.

Kahan, D. M. (1996). What do alternative sanctions mean? 63 U. *Chicago Law Review, 591,* 603–604.

Kalipeni, E., & Deborah, F. (1999). Environmental change in the Blantyre Fuelwood project area in Malawi: A political ecology perspective. *Politics and Life Sciences, 18*(1), 37–54.

Katyal, N. K. (2001). Criminal law in cyberspace. *University of Pennsylvania Law Review, 149*(4), 1003–1114.

Kelman, S. (1987). *Making public policy: A hopeful view of American government.* New York: Basic Books.

Kravets, D. (2009, September 14). New York Times reforms online ad sales after malware scam. *wired.com.* http://www.wired.com/threatlevel/2009/09/nyt-revamps-online-ad-sales-after-malware-scam/. Accessed 27 October 2009.

Kwong, K. K., Yau, O. H. M., Lee, J. S. Y., Sin, L. Y. M., & Tse, A. C. B. (2003). The effects of attitudinal and demographic factors on intention to buy pirated CDs: The case of Chinese consumers. *Journal of Business Ethics, 47*(3), 223–235.

Lenzner, R., & Vardi, N. (2004, September 20). The next threat. *Forbes, 174*(5), 15–21.

Levi, M. (2002). The organization of serious crimes. *Oxford handbook of criminology* (pp. 878–913). Oxford: Oxford University Press.

Lewis, H. B. (1971). *Shame and guilt in neurosis.* New York: International Universities Press.

Lewis, M. (1992). *Shame: The exposed self.* New York: Free Press.

Lucas, P. (2004). Outsourcing: The good, the bad & the ugly. *Collections & Credit Risk, 9*(12), 22–24.

Lyons, C. J. (2006). Stigma or sympathy? Attributions of fault to hate crime victims and offenders. *Social Psychology Quarterly, 69*(1), 39–60.

Macy, M. W., & Willer, R. (2002). From factors to actors: Computational sociology and agent-based modeling. *Annual Review of Sociology, 28*, 143–166.

Maltz, M. (1994). Defining organized crime. In R. J. Kelly, K.-L. Chin, & R. Schatzberg (Eds.), *Handbook of organized crime in the United States.* Westport, CT and London: Greenwood Press.

Mead, M. (1937). *Cooperation and competition among primitive peoples.* New York: McGraw-Hill.

Mittelman, J. H., & Johnston, R. (1999). The globalization of organized crime, the courtesan state, and the corruption of civil society. *Global Governance, 5*(1), 103–126.

Mol, A. P. J., & Van Den Burg, S. (2004). Local governance of environmental flows in global modernity. *Local Environment, 9*(4), 317–324.

Moore, S. (1979). The structure of a national elite network. *American Sociological Review, 44*, 673–691.

Natividad, K. F. (2008). Stepping it up and taking it to the streets: Changing civil and criminal copyright enforcement tactics. *Berkeley Technology Law Journal, 2008 Annual Review, 23*(1), 469–501.

North, D. C. (1990). *Institutions, institutional change and economic performance.* Cambridge, UK: Cambridge University Press.

North, D. C. (1994). Economic performance through time. *American Economic Review, 84*(3), 359–368.

North, D. C. (1996). Epilogue: Economic performance through time. In L. J. Alston, T. Eggertsson & D. C. North (Eds.), *Empirical studies in institutional change* (pp. 342–355). Cambridge, PA: Cambridge University Press.

Oppong, J. R., & Kalipeni, E. (2005). The geography of landmines and implications for health and disease in Africa: A political ecology approach. *Africa Today, 52*(1), 2–26.

Oxley, J. E., & Yeung, B. (2001). E-commerce readiness: Institutional environment and international competitiveness. *Journal of International Business Studies, 32*(4), 705–723.

Paetzold, R. L., Dipboye, R.L., & Elsbach, K. D. (2008). A new look at stigmatization in and of organizations. *Academy of Management Review, 33*(1), 186–193.

Parker, D. B. (1998). *Fighting computer crime: A new framework for protecting information.* New York: John Wiley & Sons, Inc.

Parto, S. (2005). Economic activity and institutions: Taking stock. *Journal of Economic Issues, 39*(1), 21–52.

Perera, R. (2000, November 26). Executives call for delay in cybercrime pact. *CNN.com.* http://www.cnn.com/2000/TECH/. Accessed 5 October 2006.

Piore, A. (2003, December 22). Computer Geeks: Hacking for dollars. *Newsweek International.* http://www.msnbc.msn.com/id/3706599/site/newsweek/print/1/displaymode/1098. Accessed 5 October 2006.

Rasmussen, E. (1996). Stigma and self-fulfilling expectations of criminality. *Journal of Law and Economics, 39*, 519–543.

Romania Gateway. (2003). Romania emerges as nexus of cybercrime. http://ro-gateway.ro/node/185929/comnews/item?item_id=223937. Accessed 5 October 2006.

Schneiberg, M., King, M., & Smith, T. (2008). Social movements and organizational form: Cooperative alternatives to corporations in the American insurance, dairy, and grain industries. *American Sociological Review, 73*(4), 635–667.

Schneider, A. (1999). US neo-conservatism: Cohort and cross-cultural perspective. *The International Journal of Sociology and Social Policy, 19*(12), 56–86.

Scott, R. (1987). The adolescence of institutional theory. *Administrative Science Quarterly, 32*, 493–511.

Scott, R. (1995). *Institutions and organizations.* Thousand Oaks, CA: Sage.

Scott, R. (2001). *Institutions and organizations.* Thousand Oaks, CA: Sage.

Scott, W. R., Ruef, M., Mendel, P. J., & Caronna, C. A. (2000). *Institutional change and health-care organizations: From professional dominance to managed care.* Chicago, IL: University of Chicago Press.

Shilts, R. (1991, January 1). The queering of America. *The Advocate*, 32–38

Sjostrand, S. E. (1992). On the rationale behind "irrational" institutions. *Journal of Economic Issues, 26*(4), 1007–1040.

Skorodumova, O. (2004). Hackers as information space phenomenon. *Social Sciences, 35*(4), 105–113.

Smith, T. (2003, October 27). Technology; Brazil Becomes a Cybercrime Lab. http://query.nytimes.com/gst/fullpage.html?res=9F02E3DA1131F934A15753C1A9659C8B63&sec=&spon=&pagewanted=2. Accessed 5 October 2006.

Smith, J., & Wiest, D. (2005). The uneven geography of global civil society: National and global influences on transnational association. *Social Forces, 84*(2), 621–651.

Smith, N. C., Simpson, S. S., & Chun-Yao, H. (2007). Why managers fail to do the right thing: An empirical study of unethical and illegal conduct. *Business Ethics Quarterly, 17*(4), 633–667.

Snidal, D. (1996). Political economy and international institutions. *International Review of Law and Economics, 16*(1), 121–137.

Stephens, H. (2006). Hosting Terror. *Foreign Policy, 155*, 92.

Stewart, J. (2006). White collar crime: Fraud, bribery and corruption—all alive and well? *Credit Control, 27*(4/5), 50–60.

Strang, D., & Sine, W. D. (2002). Interorganizational institutions. In J. Baum (Ed.), *Companion to organizations* (pp. 497–519). Oxford: Blackwell.

Tajfel, H., & Turner, J. C. (1986). The social identity theory of intergroup behavior. In S. Worchel & W. G. Austin (Eds.), *Psychology of intergroup relations* (pp. 7–24). Chicago, IL: Nelson-Hall.

Tarrow, S. (2001). Transnational politics: Contention and institutions in international politics. *Annual Review of Political Science, 4*, 1–20.

The Economist. (2005, September 10). Business: Busy signals; Indian call centres. *The Economist, 376*(8443), 66.

The FBI Law Enforcement Bulletin. (2007). Legitimizing criminal justice policies and practices, speech of Mark H. Moore as part of the Perspectives on Crime and Justice Series of the National Institute of Justice – Transcript.

Vardi, N. (2005, July 25). Chinese take out. *Forbes*, 54.

Vassilev, R. (2003). De-development problems in Bulgaria. *East European Quarterly, 37*(3), 345.

Webb, J. W., Tihanyi, L., Ireland, R. D., & Sirmon, D. G. (2009). You say illegal, I say legitimate: Entrepreneurship in the informal economy. *Academy of Management Review, 34*(3), 492–510.

Williams, P. (2001, August 13). *Organized crime and cybercrime: Synergies, trends, and responses.* Office of International Information Programs, US Department of State, http://usinfo.state.gov. Accessed 5 October 2006.

Wolverton, T. (2001, November 8). Court shields Yahoo from French laws. *CNET News.* http://news.cnet.com/2100-1017-275564.html. Accessed 5 October 2006.

Zaheer, S., & Zaheer, A. (1997). Country effects on information seeking in global electronic networks. *Journal of International Business Studies, 28*(1), 77–100.

Zucker, L. (1991). The role of institutionalization in cultural persistence. In W. W. Powell & P. J. DiMaggio (Eds.), *The new institutionalism in organizational analysis* (pp. 83–107). Chicago: University of Chicago Press.

Chapter 4
Increasing Returns and Externality in Cybercrimes

> *"Hacking is one of the few good jobs left here"*
> *(A self-described hacker from Moscow, cf. Walker, 2004).*
> *   "Whoever it is definitely worked in online ad sales at some*
> *point," a Gawker salesperson commenting on the fraudster who*
> *duped Gawker Media into running a fake Suzuki ad in October*
> *2009 (cf. Poulsen, 2009).*

Abstract This chapter employs increasing returns and externality approaches to explain cybercrimes' escalation. We focus on three positive or self-reinforcing feedback systems to examine increasing returns in cybercrime-related activities. They are related to economic, sociopolitical, and cognitive systems. We also examine three mechanisms that may give positive feedback to cyber-criminals: inefficiency and congestion in the law-enforcement system, acceleration of the diffusion of cybercrime know-how and technology, and increase in potential criminals' predisposition toward cybercrimes.

4.1 Introduction

This chapter analyzes various feedback systems and externality mechanisms associated with cybercrime-related activities. In Chap. 2, we observed that the most notable features of the cybercrime environment include newness, technology and skill-intensiveness, and a high degree of globalization. Factors such as a wide online availability of hacking tools, information sharing in the cyber-criminal community, availability of experienced hackers' help to less skillful criminals, and congestion in law-enforcement systems produce externality effects within the cyber-criminal community as well as across society and businesses. In this chapter, we focus on three positive or self-reinforcing feedback systems to examine increasing returns in cybercrime-related activities.

N. Kshetri, *The Global Cybercrime Industry*, DOI 10.1007/978-3-642-11522-6_4,
© Springer-Verlag Berlin Heidelberg 2010

4.2 Increasing Returns and Feedback Loops in Cybercrimes

Increasing returns approach help explain how firms, innovations, industries, and the environment influence each other. The law of increasing returns argues that economies of scale, decreasing costs, and feedback mechanisms lead to a further success of already successful entities. Arthur (1996) notes: "Increasing returns are ... mechanisms of positive feedback that operate—within markets, businesses, and industries—to reinforce that which gains success or aggravate that which suffers loss." This chapter explores evidence of increasing returns in cybercrime activities.

There are three types of self-reinforcing feedback systems: economic, sociopolitical, and cognitive (Arthur, 1996; Noda & Collis, 2001).

4.2.1 Economic Feedback

Cybercrimes' significant financial benefits provide a positive economic feedback to cyber-criminals. A low probability of cyber-criminals being caught and prosecuted (Kshetri, 2006) and less severity of punishment give them a high positive economic feedback (Becker, 1995). Some of the sources of economic feedback include the following.

4.2.1.1 Inefficiencies Associated with Electronic Channels

Indicators such as brand names, guarantees, certification, and licensure, which provide quality assurance in most physical transactions (Akerlof, 1970), tend to be absent in a significant proportion of online transactions. The issue probably is more a matter of inefficiencies of online channels than of reputation of players involved in the channel. Indeed, economists disagree about whether reputation has value (McDonald, Slawson, & Carlos, 2002; p. 634).

Various inefficiencies associated with electronic channels such as anonymity and a lack of product and process transparency[1] create a positive economic feedback for cyber-criminals (Chatterjee & Datta, 2008; Strader & Shaw, 1999; Kalakota & Whinston, 1996; Hsu & Soo, 2002). That is, electronic markets tend to be inefficient because it is difficult to judge seller performance due to a lack of true identity of transacting entities and the buyers' inability to monitor the process (Williamson, 1975). Some sellers and buyers use these inefficiencies to engage in opportunistic behaviors (Chatterjee & Datta, 2008).

The temptation to depreciate quality, commonly known as the "lemons problem," is more powerful in electronic channels which increases the possibility of adverse selection, moral hazard, and fraud (Akerlof, 1970; Barkhi, Belanger, & Hicks, 2008; Darby & Kami, 1973).[2] There tends to be a lack of information about the true nature of the product, so a fraudster can misstate the quality of the products or breach the contract, for instance, by not delivering the product (Gregg & Scott, 2008).

In order to avoid market failure, there have been attempts to make universal availability of market information through mechanisms such as online auction reputation systems, which consist of feedbacks related to prior transactions. The reputation systems, however, have their own limitations and inherent flaws, which cannot resolve the information asymmetry problems (Bolton, Katok, & Ockenfels, 2004; Ghose, 2009). For instance, it is reported that some eBay users artificially boost their reputations by selling products at low prices in exchange for positive feedbacks (Brown & Morgan, 2006). There are also reports that eBay accounts with pre-existing positive feedback can be bought in the electronic underground (Kendall, 2009). Opportunistic behaviors through manipulation of information as well as failure to fulfill obligations are more likely to occur in electronic channels than in conventional channels (John, 1984).

4.2.1.2 Low Entry Barriers

In e-commerce, barriers to entry are low, which allow the participation of buyers and sellers of all sizes and reputation (Chatterjee & Datta, 2008; Grazioli & Jarvenpaa, 2003). It is argued that this situation is even more so with some online activities such as Internet auctions, which are especially more susceptible to fraud and moral hazard (Gregg & Scott, 2008).

4.2.2 Sociopolitical Feedbacks

Sociopolitical feedbacks are related to formal and informal institutions (North, 1990; Scott, 2001). Specifically, sociopolitical feedbacks are related to Scott's (1995, 2001) regulatory and normative institutions (Aldrich & Fiol, 1994). Social feedbacks are linked to normative institutions. For instance, informal sanctions applied by a social group such as exclusion of a cyber-criminal from one's circle of friends send negative social feedback to the criminal (Property Rights & Competition, 2000). Cybercrimes are more justifiable in some societies compared to others. Quoting a Russian hacker-turned-teacher, Blau (2004) describes how he and his friends hacked programs and distributed them for free during their childhood: "It was like our donation to society, it was a form of honor; [we were] like Robin Hood bringing programs to people."

Political feedbacks, on the other hand, are applied by regulative institutions. One way of viewing legal and political institutions would be to consider them as the government's efforts to minimize the social loss from illegal activities (Becker, 1968; Becker, Murphy, & Grossman, 2004). In this regard, of all the characteristics of cybercrimes reviewed here, perhaps the most important one is their cross-border focus. In this regard, it is worth noting that most cyber-frauds, at least superficially, can simply be viewed as the "loss to victims as being compensated by equal gains to criminals" (Becker, 1968, p. 171). Most obviously, from a government's standpoint, there is no social loss if the victim is from another country. For instance, observers have noted that some countries such as China and Russia ignore cybercrimes unless such crimes are against their national interests (Voigt, 2009). The probability of a successful prosecution of a Russia-based hacker attacking a US-based computer is very low (Serio & Gorkin, 2003). Benjamin Edelman of Harvard Business School noted: "Why would Russian law enforcement want to pursue [cyber]attacks that never hurt Russians?" (cf. Messmer, 2009). Cyber-criminals in such countries thus receive positive political feedback.

4.2.3 Cognitive Feedback

The cognitive feedback loops are associated with cognitive programs that are built on the mental maps of individual hackers and thus function primarily at the individual level (Huff, 1990). Many effects can serve as cognitive feedback depending on the nature and motivation of the actor. In the case of hackers, for instance, they include enjoyment from cybercrimes and less guilt in such crimes. Put differently, cognitive systems influence the lens through which existing and potential criminals view cybercrimes (Scott, 2001). For instance, it is reported that many Indonesian hackers feel that cyber-fraud is "wrong" but acceptable, especially if the credit card owner is rich and not an Indonesian. A carder reportedly said: "Yes, it's wrong but it really only hurts other rich countries that were dumb enough to let us. Why should an Indonesian get arrested for damaging American business?" (Shubert, 2003). Another carder said: "I only choose those people who are truly rich. I'm not comfortable using the money of poor people. I also don't want to use credit cards belonging to Indonesians. Those are a carder's ethics" (Antariksa, 2001, p. 16). Likewise, the Chinese hackers involved in the China–US cyber-wars in 2001 argued that they were patriotic and thus did not do anything wrong (Kshetri, 2005).

4.3 Mechanisms Associated with Externality in Cybercrimes

It is well established in the literature that externalities can be positive as well as negative (Calabresi & Melamed, 1972). According to Demsetz, "[e]very cost and benefit associated with social interdependencies is a potential externality" (1967, p. 348). Put differently, economic actors with interdependent relations jointly produce an externality and whether it is positive or negative is a function of how and who produces it (Frischmann & Lemley, 2007).

4.3.1 Path Dependence and Externality

One of the central tenets of the path-dependence approach is that "history matters." This approach focuses on choices or conditions that influence options and steer history in a particular direction (David & Arthur, 1985; Arthur, 1989; North, 1990). Path dependence is related to externalities. In this book's context, externalities are external benefits or costs generated by a criminal activity to third parties, that is, individuals or businesses other than the criminal and the victim.

Criminal behaviors may have self-reinforcing effects. Criminals may generate externalities by making crime-related specialized inputs and services available, forming a specialized "labor market"; and facilitating the exchanges and spillovers of information and technology (Marshall, 1920). These externalities, which originate from other firms in the same industry, are also called MAR externalities (Marshall, 1890; Arrow, 1962; Romer, 1986). MAR externalities represent the positive role of specialization on growth through knowledge spillovers (Bun & Makhloufi, 2007).

Return to crime is positively related to the concentration of criminals (Deutsch et al., 1984). Highest rates of victimization are thus often found in poorest neighborhood with low levels of target attractiveness (Bottoms & Wiles, 2002; Clarke, 1995). Criminals tend to focus efforts in crime hot spots and overwhelm law-enforcement agencies (Freeman, Grogger, & Sonstelie, 1996; Weisburd, Bushway, Lum, & Yang, 2004). Inefficiency and congestion in the law-enforcement system generates positive externalities for criminals and negative externalities for the society (Gaviria, 2000; Sah, 1991).

Organized criminal groups across cultures and nations vary greatly in the nature of their ventures (New Zealand Ministry of Justice, 2008). The externality these criminal groups generate may differ. The idea of the "intergenerational externality" may be helpful to explain specialization in specific crimes. Prior research indicates that because of "intergenerational externality," past criminal activities influence current criminal activities (Freeman et al., 1996). It can be argued that, due to path dependence of crimes, other things being equal, the more a particular type of crime a society previously had, the higher the odds of observing crimes of the type in the society. Preliminary evidence consistent with this proposition emerged from De La Calle Robles' (2007) study of street violence. The study found that past pattern of street violence-related crimes influenced detentions related to such crimes, providing evidence of a "subculture of violence," which led to the perpetuation of violence (De La Calle Robles, 2007).

4.3.1.1 Externalities Generated by Conventional Crimes and Cybercrimes

Note that a cybercrime may require crime skills, technical skills, social engineering skills, and access to network of other criminals. Some serious cyber-criminals are highly skillful and thus face very low odds of getting caught. As noted in Chap. 2, Russian mafia hack rings are reportedly operated by former KGB agents (Bell, 2002). Likewise, after the fall of the communism, Bulgaria's secret service agents engaged in organized crimes (Bulgaria Political Risk Yearbook, 2007). Because of their law-enforcement experiences, these organized crime groups have special skills on their hands which have been a key asset for success in cybercrimes. There have thus been "inter industry knowledge spillovers" (between law-enforcement agencies and organized crime groups). Such spillovers are referred as Jacobs (1969) externalities as opposed to MAR externalities. As noted above, MAR externalities are related to firms in the same industry.

As is the case of crime subculture observed in the conventional world (De La Calle Robles, 2007), what seems to be happening is region-specific specialization in cybercrime activities. Evidence indicates that cybercrimes originated in Asia exploit vulnerabilities in common software applications to steal personal information. Eastern European criminals are linked with organized crimes and identity theft (Fitzgerald, 2008). Romanian criminals, for instance, have distinctive advantage in online auction frauds. In auctions for big-ticket items, Romanians arguably "own the game" (Wylie, 2007). They have developed an ecosystem specific to auction fraud bringing together various players and technologies. Likewise, Ukrainian criminal world is considered to be a "leader" in online credit card crime (Wylie, 2007). Hackers from the Middle East, on the other hand, deface websites (Fitzgerald, 2008). Likewise, Skorodumova (2004) linked national subculture with different characteristics of intrinsically motivated hacking.

Criminals' skill, organization, and intelligence co-vary positively with the odds of getting away with crimes (National Center for Policy Analysis, 2002). As noted above, organized crime groups in Russia and Eastern Europe have special skills on their hands, which have been valuable to expand in the cyberworld (Bell, 2002). Organized crimes have thus fueled the growth of cybercrimes.

Different types of cybercrimes such as online auctions frauds, Nigerian check scams, child pornography, and denial of services (DoS) attacks require different combinations of crime skills, technical skills, social engineering skills, and access to networks of other criminals (e.g., money mules). Cyber-criminals in a country may "invent" new tools and skills needed for certain types of cybercrimes (e.g., auction fraud-related ecosystem developed by Romanian cyber-criminals). Specialized inputs and services and exchanges and spillovers of information and technology (Marshall, 1920) may lead to a country's specialization in certain cybercrimes.

Given the cybercrime environment and feedback loops, increasing returns could manifest themselves in many ways. For instance, cyber-criminals may "invent" sophisticated and new tools that law-enforcement agencies face increased difficulty in tracing. Cyber-criminals could also operate from countries with weak cybercrime laws. The externality could also arise because at a given level of law-enforcement resources, an increase in the number of cyber-criminals reduces the probability that a cyber-criminal will be caught (Freeman et al., 1996).

We examine three mechanisms that may give positive feedback to cyber-criminals: inefficiency and congestion in the law-enforcement system, acceleration of the diffusion of cybercrime know-how and technology, and increase in potential criminals' predisposition toward cybercrimes (Gaviria, 2000; Sah, 1991). From victims' perspective, there is arguably a vicious circle of cybercrimes linking characteristics of cyber-criminals, cybercrime victims, and law-enforcement agencies (Kshetri, 2006) and a corresponding virtuous circle for cyber-criminals. These externality mechanisms strengthen the elements of the vicious circle for victims and of the virtuous circle for criminals.

Table 4.1 presents how the externality mechanisms and the feedback systems described above are intertwined.

Table 4.1 Externality mechanisms and feedback systems producing increasing return in cybercrime-related activities

Externality mechanisms ⇒ ———————— Feedback system ⇓	Inefficiency and congestion in the law-enforcement system (Assessment of risks related to cybercrimes)	Diffusion of cybercrime know-how and technology (Ability to commit cybercrimes)	Increased predisposition toward cybercrime (Willingness to commit cybercrimes)
Economic	• Law-enforcement agencies' lack of resources • Sophistication in cybercrimes • No cyber-criminal database • Difficult to explain in courts	• Easily available hacking tools • Schools teaching hacking skills in some countries	• Over-educated and under-employed workforce in some countries • Increasing financial incentives for hackers
Sociopolitical	• Weak cybercrime laws in some countries • Jurisdictional arbitrage • Lack of industry-government collaboration • Lack of international cooperation	• Less skillful criminals get help from experienced hackers/crime groups • Information sharing among hackers	• Ideological hackers: obligation-based intrinsic motivations • Social obligations • Cybercrimes are acceptable in some societies
Cognitive	• Victims' lack of confidence with law-enforcement: unwillingness to report cybercrimes	• Ease of use of hacking tools	• Enjoyment-based intrinsic motivations • Compliance with cyber-criminals' demands: more confidence • Less guilt

4.4 Inefficiency and Congestion in the Law-Enforcement System

Congestion and inefficiency in law-enforcement systems arise from factors such as the scale (Jones, 2007), newness of cybercrimes, a low-governmental priority, a lack of cross-border and industry–government cooperation, and victims' unwillingness to report (Kshetri, 2006). Cyber-criminals can "commit crimes on a scale far surpassing what is possible in the real-world, where one-to-one victimization and serial crimes are the norm. As a result, the absolute scale of cybercrime, in terms of incidence of discrete crimes, exponentially exceeds that of real-world crime" (Brenner, 2004, p. 15).

In the United States, attempts to regulate cyber-space to protect children faced oppositions from groups, which argue that such measures undermine free speech. Some countries are also slow to enact cybercrime laws.

Law-enforcement agencies such as police forces and the FBI are inexperienced with cybercrimes. Cyber-criminals and victims tend to be scattered across the country and the world, posing logistical challenges. At the same time, while large law-enforcement agencies such as FBI have developed some capacity to deal with cybercrimes, localized police forces are not equipped to deal with national and global nature of cybercrimes. They are also facing manpower shortages. An estimate suggested that only 2% of US Police personnel were trained in cyberforensics in 2000 (Swardson, 2000). Likewise, among Canada's 62,000 police officers, only 250 (or about 0.4%) work on cybercrimes, who mainly focus on child pornography (The Canadian Press, 2008).

Alack of sufficient resources has thus led to congestion in law-enforcement. Experts also argue that too little attention has been focused on tracking down the Internet's illegal contents at the source (Honig, 2005).

As discussed earlier, law-enforcement agencies lack sufficient resources to fight cybercrimes (Chap. 2). The failure to allocate enough resources to fight cybercrimes can be partly attributed to organizational inertia. Organizational inertia can be defined as formal organizations' tendency to resist internal changes to respond to external changes (Larsen & Lomi, 2002). Notwithstanding a meteoric growth in cybercrimes, budgets allocated to agencies established to fight cybercrimes have not grown at the same rate. For instance, the UK's National HiTech Crime Unit is planning to spend only 5% of its 2008–2009 budgets to combat cybercrime (Giannangeli, 2008).

Beyond all that, conventional crimes have overburdened law-enforcement agencies. For instance, at a US Senate Judiciary Subcommittee on Crime and Drugs meeting in May 2007, leaders of national law-enforcement organizations noted that budgetary cuts to programs such as the Community Oriented Policing Service (COPS) have led to escalation in violent crimes and "adversely affected local crime prevention and local law enforcement initiatives" (US Fed News Service, Including US State News, 2007). Similarly, street gangs, organized crime, and terrorism top Canadian Police force's list of priorities and cybercrimes are at the bottom (The Canadian Press, 2008). Likewise, in Brazil violent crimes in cities such as São Paulo, Rio de Janeiro, and Brasília have diverted law-enforcement agencies' attention away from cybercrimes (Smith, 2003).

In developing nations, fighting cybercrime gets a lower priority. In Indonesia, the police say they lack expertise and resources to fight against cybercrimes. The country's Information Technology Sub-Directorate of the Directorate of Special Crimes of the National Police Headquarters had only one dial-up connection in 2002. Moreover, Indonesian police use a "red book," a manual to conduct credit card investigations, to handle Internet credit card frauds. Estimates suggest that only 15% of reported incidents are investigated in Indonesia.

As noted earlier, cybercrimes are increasingly sophisticated and new forms and methods are developing rapidly. Speaking to the Commonwealth Club of California in October 2009, FBI Director Robert Mueller noted that he was almost fooled by a phishing scam. Mueller said that he received an e-mail, which looked like coming from his bank and asked him to confirm his account's status. He answered few questions and stopped before he entered his account's password (Egelko, 2009). It explains the level of sophistication of cyber-criminals' combination of technology and social engineering skills.

Law-enforcement agencies have failed to catch up with the constant progressive nature of such crimes. A further congestion in the law-enforcement system is caused by unavailability of cyber-criminals' database. Most of the new breed of criminals' profiles differ from those of conventional criminals. In Russia, for instance, most hackers are young, educated, and work independently and thus do not fit conventional criminal profiles.

Digital criminals are also more difficult to catch and prosecute than conventional ones. In fact, collection and retention of evidence has been a critical challenge facing law-enforcement agencies. Estimates suggested that in the late 1990s, the US Department of Justice declined to prosecute up to 78% of cases mainly because of a lack of evidence (Banisar, 1999).

Cybercrimes' newness has also presented challenges to the court system. For small cybercrime cases, it is difficult to find an attorney (Katz, 2005). Experts also say that explaining cybercrimes to judges is difficult.

Another point to bear in mind is increasingly transnational and international nature of cybercrimes, which benefit from jurisdictional arbitrage. Organized cybercrimes are initiated from countries with few or no laws and little enforcement capacity. For instance, the United States could not prosecute the Philippino hacker, who launched the "Love Letter" virus in 2000 because the Philippines had no laws prohibiting cybercrimes that time. Due to newness, jurisdictional arbitrage is higher for cybercrimes compared to conventional crimes.

Additional externality effects concern national boundaries. Collaborations and cooperation among law-enforcement agencies in different jurisdictions have been insufficient and "notoriously slow and bureaucratic" (Walden, 2005). For example, Russia and the United States have signed agreements in many crimes, but not in cybercrimes. Experts also argue that countries such as China and Russia ignore cybercrimes unless such crimes jeopardize their national interests (Vardi, 2005).

A lack of industry–government collaboration has also hampered law-enforcement agencies' ability to solve cybercrimes. For instance, estimates suggest that 80% of global e-mail traffic including most spam e-mails come via Webmail services of global providers such as AOL, MSN, and Yahoo. Law-enforcement agencies have expressed concern over these providers' unwillingness to cooperate.

Proportionally less cybercrimes than conventional crimes are reported. Some estimates suggest that less than 10% of cybercrimes are reported to authorities. Most businesses do not report cybercrimes because they are embarrassed; think doing so would undermine their credibility, likely lead to bad public relations and damage reputation; and fear their stock prices would drop. Especially financial institutions and businesses dealing with sensitive data such as e-commerce companies are reluctant to turn over the investigation to authorities. Complications related to documentation and proofs further discourage reporting cybercrimes.

4.5 Diffusion of Cybercrime Know-How and Technology

How do cybercrime know-how and technology diffuse? What factors lead to increased width and depth of cybercrime adoption among criminals? Diffusion of cybercrimes can be explained in terms of *relative advantage, compatibility, complexity, observability, and trialability* (Rogers, 1995). Table 4.2 briefly explains these dimensions and illustrates how cybercrime performs on each dimension.

Table 4.2 Cybercrime characteristics influencing its diffusion rate

Dimension	Explanation	Cybercrimes' characteristics
Relative advantage	• Perceived benefits of a technology over previous technologies	• Less likely to be caught and prosecuted • Can be committed without leaving home
Compatibility	• The degree to which a technology and the tasks it performs are perceived as being consistent with the existing values, beliefs, past experiences, and needs of potential adopters	• Digitizability of virtually all crimes.
Complexity	• Level of difficulty in using a technology	• Most hacking tools require little or no expertise • Less skillful criminals get help from experienced hackers and/or transnational organized crime groups • Information sharing in the hacking community • Availability of hackers for hire
Observability	• The degree to which the features and benefits of a technology are visible, noticeable and understandable to self/others and the results can be described to non-users	• Cybercrimes are easy to commit and rewards are high: significant financial benefits
Trialability	• The ability to experiment or try (on a limited basis) before formally adopting	• Free availability of hacking tools: risk free trial • Most college students may gain illegal access to a computer system

Cybercrimes' principal source of *relative advantage* stems from the Internet's "generativity" (Zittrain, 2006), which allows cyberattackers to "leverage limited resources into massive attacks with ease" (*Harvard Law Review*, 2006). The Internet arguably is "exceptionally generative" because its architecture is "amenable to a large number of applications," is "easy to master," has no "central gatekeeper," and uses publicly available protocols (Zittrain, 2006). For instance, when a hacker sends out hundreds of millions of spam e-mails, a small proportion of users are naive enough to answer them.

An additional source of *relative advantage* concerns the nature of business model in electronic transactions. For instance, consumers are required to give the business personal details for payment or delivery. Electronic transactions thus expose the consumer to identity theft or fraud (Morton, 2006).

Moreover, it is argued that in the digital world, it is "far more difficult to catch the criminal and almost impossible to successfully prosecute them if they are caught" (Lack, 2002, p. 4). An estimate of PricewaterhouseCoopers indicated that only about 5% of cyber-criminals are caught. Moreover, cybercrimes can be committed without leaving home. This is contrary to most conventional crimes, for which criminals leave a known territory only for sufficient incentives.

Next, consider *compatibility*. The Internet has facilitated carrying out of most traditional crimes. The Internet has thus become most criminals' tool. Orlans (2002) comments: "Internet is an excellent vehicle for drug trafficking,[3] gambling, money laundering, and tax evasion; for fraudulent charitable solicitations, credit card purchases, sales, investments, pyramid schemes, and lotteries; for pirating publications, films, and music; for spreading extremist messages, false alarms, and information about making bombs and setting fires; and for promoting prostitution, pornography, and perversions."

The natures of the technology and of hacking communities and organized crime groups have greatly reduced the *complexity* of cybercrime know-how and technology. Most hacking tools are widely available online and require little or no expertise. Less skillful criminals also get help from experienced hackers.

Information sharing in the cyber-criminal community also reduces the *complexity*. Members in the community help fellow hackers accessing a router and getting through a firewall (Bednarz, 2004). Typically, swapping and sharing of hacking tools and secrets take place in closed chat rooms (Acohido & Swartz, 2005). Information sharing among members in the cyber-criminal community is more pervasive in some societies. A security expert at Banco Itaú, one of Brazil's largest private banks, noted that hackers in the country are sociable and share more information than hackers in developed countries. He said: "It's a cultural thing. I don't see American hackers as willing to share information among themselves" (Smith, 2003).

Moreover, in some countries, specialized schools teach hacking skills. There are also reports that US-based low-end criminals get cybercrime-related helps from Russian and Eastern European professional criminals. An estimate suggested that, in 2004, there were over 50 gangs of professional criminals operating in Russia and Eastern European countries (Goldman, 2004).

Cybercrimes also induce a perception of a high degree of *observability* for criminals as they are easy to commit and rewards are high. It was reported that one spam organization alone generated US $40 million in a year (Fong, 2008). Some criminals in the conventional world are cashing in on the trend of increased sophistication in cybercrime technologies.

Online availability of hacking tools offers risk-free *trial* to would be hackers. Recently, quantity and availability of hacking tools have increased, and the quality has improved (Ashley, 2004). Some sources of externalities thus exist in the technology. Evidence also indicates that many college students pirate software and gain illegal access to a computer system to browse and/or exchange information (Fream & Skinner, 1997). Such experiences provide "trialability" and help them get their foot in the door of the cybercrime world (Lack, 2002).

4.6 Increased Predisposition Toward Cybercrime

What factors contribute to an individual's willingness to commit cybercrimes? First, crime rates are linked to economic opportunities. According to a March 2007 *McAfee Virtual Criminology Report* produced with the United States and European high-tech crime units, 88% of computer science students at a US university admitted committing an illegal act online. A McAfee analyst noted that crime gangs are recruiting and training teenagers as young as 14 for cybercrimes.

In some economies, the lack of employment opportunities has led to increase in cybercrimes. In Russia and Eastern Europe, students good in mathematics, physics, and computer science are having difficulty to find jobs (Bryan-Low, 2005).

An article published in *The Chronicle of Higher Education* (2007, p. B.29) forcefully put the issue this way:

> Parents and teachers are increasingly relying on new technology to enhance education both in and out of the classroom. Employers are badly in need of competent and ethically responsible computer users. Meanwhile, our schools have failed to systematically incorporate Internet safety, information security, and cyberethics instruction into curricula.

Even worse, there is some evidence that parents, and even teachers, advocate certain computer crimes, particularly software piracy among students (Bowker, 2000). These actions provide social legitimacy to cybercrimes. Note that condemnation of an act such as a cybercrime leads to internalization of norms against the act among the "condemners" and as well as the "condemned" (Kahan, 1996).

Cybercrimes are even more justifiable in some societies. An *IDG News Service* article describes how a Russian hacker-turned-teacher and his friends hacked programs and distributed for free: "It was like our donation to society, it was a form of honor; [we were] like Robin Hood bringing programs to people."

Behaviors of ideological hackers interested in political goals can be explained by obligation/community-based intrinsic motivations. Chinese hackers, for instance, have expressed patriotic and nationalistic longings in cyber-wars. They have fought cyber-wars with Taiwanese, Indonesians, Japanese, and US hackers. Chinese hackers involved in cyber-wars argued that they were patriotic and did not do anything wrong. Patriotism and nationalism thus provided cognitive legitimacy of these hackers' activities. Other factors energizing ideological hackers include motivation to fight against global capitalism and religion.

Technological, behavioral, and perceptual weaknesses in defense are tightly linked with cybercrimes. Cyber-criminals are taking advantage of computer users' ignorance. A 2003 MailFrontier study indicated that 40% of people reading a fraudulent Citibank e-mail believed it to be a real. Similarly, a 2005 survey by America Online and the National Cyber Security Alliance found that 80% of the respondents' computers were infected by spyware and almost all were unaware of it (US Fed News Service, Including US State News, 2005). Another survey found that 56% of US home computers have either no or outdated anti-virus software. It is important to note that, according to Symantec, home users account for 95% of all attacks related to botnet (Vallance, 2008).

Some companies negotiate with cyber-criminals by paying ransom. Estimates suggest that online gambling companies have paid millions of dollars to cyber-extortionists. Increased success is sending positive cognitive messages and making cyber-criminals disrespectful of law-enforcement agencies. Many international hackers, for instance, do not conceal their real identities or mailings' origin.

As discussed in Chap. 2, compared to other criminals, cyber-criminals are less likely to feel guilt for their actions. It is also argued that standards of rules and conducts guiding actions are based on the notion of face-to-face relations. More generally, human being and other creatures develop ethical norms and stick to them if this increases their fitness in some way (Ruse, 1998; Ruse & Maienschein, 1999). People normally try to fit in their society. It can thus be argued that lying and cheating behaviors tend to be more common in the cyberworld than in the conventional world. McCabe (2000) quotes a philosophy professor: "The standards of conduct that guide our lives are premised on the notion that we are going to have face-to-face relations with people. But in the virtual world, that reinforcement practically disappears."

The cyber-space is similar to urban areas in one important aspect—a high proportion of unrelated individuals (Deas & Thomas, 2002; McCord, Ratcliffe, Garcia, & Taylor, 2007; Schuerman & Kobrin, 1986). Note that in prior literature researchers have found that opportunistic behaviors lead to high crime rates in large cities. In such cities, individuals are less likely to be long-term residents and the anonymity protects criminals from the social stigma (Glaeser & Sacerdote, 1999). A reduction in face-to-face interactions between neighbors leads to an increased crime rates in the neighborhood (Putnam, 2000). In this regard, the cyber-space provides a conducive environment for crimes. The cyber-space has brought potential offenders and potential victims together.

Compared to conventional crimes, people involved in cybercrimes are thus less likely to see their actions' negative impacts. A final concern regards the trend of declining morality. For instance, in the United States, two-thirds of respondents in a 2004 *USA Today*/CNN/Gallup Poll said that "the state of moral values is getting worse" (Drinkard, 2004). Only 27% of the respondents said that it was getting better. A government-sponsored survey in China, which was conducted with 4,500 people and was reported in the early 2007 found a similar trend in the country (Cody, 2007). Likewise, Special Agent Palmer Mallari of the Anti-Fraud and Computer Crimes Division at the Philippines National Bureau of Investigation (NBI) noted that the rise in cybercrimes in the Philippines can be attributed to the decline in people's ethical standards (Sulaiman, 2007). In sum, the rapid rise in cybercrimes is associated with and facilitated by declining morality and values.

4.7 Concluding Comments

In this chapter, we examined synergies between increasing return activities in cybercrimes. Our analysis of economic, sociopolitical, and cognitive legitimacy to cyber-criminals, which influence the degree of increasing to returns to these criminals, helps understand why instances of buyers' engagement in opportunism are also very common in e-marketplaces.

Cybercrimes can be carried anonymously, which increases the chance of the occurrence of opportunism. Opportunism provides the possibility of the deliberate creation of information advantage through guile, deception, trickery, disguise, lies, and manipulation (Williamson, 1975, 1985). Attempts to make universal availability of market information through mechanisms such as online auction reputation systems have done little to reduce the problem of informational disadvantage of the consumers.

Technological and non-technological measures can reduce the externality effects and can provide negative cognitive feedback to cyber-criminals. These are discussed in detail in Chap. 11.

On the bright side, some recent technological developments have also prompted a shift in the structure of the computing industry, which is likely to lead to a decline in some forms of computer crimes. For instance, cybercrimes involving counterfeit software are reported to decline with the diffusion of cloud computing (Rubenking, 2009).

Notes

1. Even when there is a one-to-one correspondence between the workflows in a physical and an electronic channel, the latter tends to be less transparent. Chatterjee and Datta (2008) provide a useful example to compare process transparencies in electronic and physical channels. For example, a credit card swipe at a gas station uses similar workflows as an online purchase with a credit card. The gas station, however, uses a dedicated channel instead of an open Internet-based connection. Second, in an electronic channel, a buyer is required to make a payment before the product is shipped (McDonald et al., 2002). While pre-payment is required in some physical transactions such as a gas station, the time lag between the card swipe and order fulfillment in the gas station is shorter compared to the time taken from order placement and delivery in an online channel. Finally, any problems can be traced more easily in the gas station. For instance, the customer can talk with the store clerk. The clerk's body language, physical interaction,

and other cues can be used to assess seller quality (Gefen, Karahanna, & Straub, 2003). Most electronic channels are characterized by an absence of such cues, which increased the chance for an opportunistic behavior.

2. Adverse selection (anti-selection, or negative selection) arises from information asymmetry between buyers and sellers. In such a case, one party is unable to determine if the other party is lying. Likewise, moral hazard is the problem of not being able to determine if the other party is cheating or acting dishonestly.

3. By the early 2000, over 1,000 websites worldwide were selling illicit drugs (Foreign Policy, 2002).

References

Acohido, B., & Swartz, J. (2005, December 15). Meth addicts' other habit: Online theft. *USA Today*.

Akerlof, G. A. (1970). The Market for 'Lemons': Qualitative uncertainty and the market mechanism. *Quarterly Journal of Economics, 84*, 488–500.

Aldrich, H. E., & Fiol, C. M. (1994). Fools rush in? The institutional context of new industry creation. *Academy of Management Review, 19*, 645–670.

Antariksa. (2001, July). I am a thief, not a hacker: Indonesia's electronic underground. *Latitudes Magazine*, 12–17.

Arrow, K. J. (1962). The economic implications of learning by doing. *Review of Economic Studies, 29*, 155–173.

Arthur, W. B. (1989). Competing technologies, increasing returns, and lock-in by historical events. *Economic Journal, 99*, 116–131.

Arthur, W. B. (1996, July/August). Increasing returns and the New World of Business. *Harvard Business Review*, 101–109.

Ashley, B. K. (2004, March). The United States is vulnerable to cyberterrorism. *SIGNAL Magazine*. http://www.afcea.org/signal/articles/anmviewer.asp?a=32. Accessed 21 September 2006.

Banisar, D. (1999, August 3). Computer Hacker's sentence spotlights high-tech crime prosecutions. *Criminal Justice Weekly*.

Barkhi, R., Belanger, F., & Hicks, J. (2008). A model of the determinants of purchasing from virtual stores. *Journal of Organizational Computing & Electronic Commerce, 18*(3), 177–196.

Becker, G. (1968). Crime and punishment: An economic approach. *Journal of Political Economy, 76*(2), 169–217.

Becker, G. S. (1995, Fall). The economics of crime. *Cross Sections*, 8–15, http://www.rich.frb.org/pubs/cross/crime/crime.pdf. Accessed 21 September 2006.

Becker, G. S., Murphy, K. M., & Grossman, M. (2004, December). *The economic theory of illegal goods: The case of drugs*. NBER Working Paper No. 10976. http://home.uchicago.edu/~gbecker/illegalgoods_Becker_Grossman_Murphy.pdf. Accessed 21 September 2006.

Bednarz, A. (2004, November 29). Profiling cybercriminals: A promising but immature science, *Network World*. http://www.nwfusion.com/supp/2004/cybercrime/112904profile.html?page=2. Accessed 21 September 2006.

Bell, R. E. (2002). The prosecution of computer crime. *Journal of Financial Crime, 9*(4), 308–325.

Blau, J. (2004, May 26). Russia – A happy haven for hackers. http://www.computerweekly.com/Article130839.htm. Accessed 21 September 2006.

Bolton, G. E., Katok, E., & Ockenfels, A. (2004). How effective are electronic reputation mechanisms? An experimental investigation. *Management Science, 50*(11), 1587–1602.

Bottoms, A. E., & Wiles, P. (2002). Environmental criminology. *Oxford Handbook of Criminology*, 620–656.

Bowker, A. L. (2000). The advent of the computer delinquent. *FBI Law Enforcement, 69*(12), 7–11.

Brenner, S. W. (2004). Toward a criminal law for cyberspace: A new model of law enforcement? *30 Rutgers Computer and Technology Law Journal, 30*, 1–9.

Brown, J., & Morgan, J. (2006). Reputation in online markets: The market for trust. *California Management Review, 49*(1), 61–81.

Bryan-Low, C. (2005, September 1). Digital trails: In Eastern Europe, a Gumshoe chases Internet villains; Microsoft deploys Mr. Fifka to hunt cyber felons amid rise in online crime; tailing 'Benny' in a Czech city. *Wall Street Journal*, A.1.

Bulgaria Country Report. (2007). The PRS Group, Inc., Bulgaria, ISSN: 1054–5298.

Bun, M. J. G., & Makhloufi, A. E. (2007). Dynamic externalities, local industrial structure and economic development: Panel data evidence for morocco. *Regional Studies, 41*(6), 823–837.

Calabresi, G., & Melamed, A. D. (1972). Property rules, liability rules, and inalienability: One view of the cathedral. *Harvard Law Review, 85*, 1089, 1102–1105.

Chatterjee, S., & Datta, P. (2008). Examining inefficiencies and consumer uncertainty in e-commerce. *Communications of AIS, 22*, 525–546.

Clarke, R. V. (1995). Situational crime prevention. In M. Tonry & D. P. Farrington (Eds.), *Building a safer society strategic approaches to crime* (pp. 91–150). Chicago: University of Chicago Press.

Cody, E. (2007, February 8). Poll finds surge of religion among Chinese. *The Washington Post*, A.15.

Darby, M. R., & Kami, E. (1973). Free competition and optimal amount of fraud. *Journal of Law and Economics, 16*(April), 67–86.

darkreading.com. (2008, June 11). Cybercrime outranks other crimes on Europeans' worry list: Almost half of German PC users believe they will eventually fall victim. http://www.darkreading.com/document.asp?doc_id=156206. Accessed 21 September 2008.

David, P., & Arthur, B. (1985). Clio and the economics of QWERTY. *American Economic Review, 75*, 332–337.

De La Calle Robles, L. (2007). Fighting for local control: Street violence in the basque country. *International Studies Quarterly, 51*(2), 431–455.

Deas, D., & Thomas, S. (2002). Comorbid psychiatric factors contributing to adolescent alcohol and other drug use. *Alcohol Research and Health, 26*, 116–121.

Deutsch, J., Hakim, S., & Weinblatt, J. (1984). Interjurisdictional criminal mobility: A theoretical perspective. *Urban Studies, 21*, 451–458.

Demsetz, H. (1967). Toward a theory of property rights. *The American Economic Review, 57*(2), 347–359.

Drinkard, J. (2004, November 23). Nation's moral values declining, most say; Poll: Majority see USA as deeply split. *USA Today*, A.11.

Egelko, B. (2009, October 8). FBI chief urges vigilance against cybercrime. *San Francisco Chronicle*. http://www.sfgate.com/cgi-bin/article.cgi?f=/c/a/2009/10/07/BA061A2HG7.DTL. Accessed 21 October 2009.

Fitzgerald, P. (2008, September/October). Crash of civilizations. *Foreign Policy*, 122.

Fong, C. (2008, May 8). Fighting the agents of organized cybercrime. *CNN.com*.

Foreign Policy. (2002). *Web Trafficking, 129*, 96.

Fream, A. M., & Skinner, W. F. (1997). Social learning theory analysis of computer crime among college students. *Journal of Research in Crime and Delinquency, 24*(4), 495–518.

Freeman, S., Grogger, J., & Sonstelie, J. (1996). The spatial concentration of crime. *Journal of Urban Economics, 40*(2), 216–231.

Frischmann, B. M., & Lemley, M. A. (2007). Spillovers. *Columbia Law Review, 107*(1), 257–301.

Gaviria, A. (2000). Increasing returns and the evolution of violent crime: The case of Colombia. *Journal of Development Economics, 61*(1), 1.

Gefen, D., Karahanna, E., & Straub, D. (2003). Trust and TAM in online shopping: An integrated model. *MIS Quarterly, 27*(1), 51–90.

Ghose, A. (2009). Internet exchanges for used goods: An empirical analysis of trade patterns and adverse selection. *MIS Quarterly, 33*(2), 263–291.

Giannangeli, M. (2008, June 8). Are we ready for Russian Mafia's crime revolution? *Sunday Express*, Scottish Edition, 4.

Glaeser, E. L., & Sacerdote, B. (1999). Why is there more crime in cities? *The Journal of Political Economy, 107*(6), Part 2, 225–258.

Goldman, L. (2004, October 4). Cybercon. *Forbes, 174*(6).

Grazioli, S., & Jarvenpaa, S. L. (2003). Deceived: Under target online, Association for computing machinery. *Communications of the ACM, 46*, 196.

Gregg, D. G., & Scott, J. E. (2008, April). A typology of complaints about ebay sellers. *Communications of the ACM, 51*(4), 69–74.

Harvard Law Review. (2006, June). Note: Immunizing the Internet, or: How I learned to stop worrying and love the worm. *119*, 2442.

Honig, D. (2005). Can illegal content be regulated or prosecuted? *Intermedia, 33*(1), 30–33.

Hsu, M., & Soo, M. (2002). A secure multi-agent vickrey auction scheme. In *International conference on Autonomous Agents and Multi-Agent Systems*.

Huff, A. S. (1990). Mapping strategic thought. In A. S. Huff (Ed.), *Mapping strategic thought* (pp. 11–49). Chichester, England: Wiley.

Jacobs, J. (1969). *The economy of cities*. New York: Vintage.

John, G. (1984). An empirical investigation of some antecedents of opportunism in a marketing channel. *Journal of Marketing Research, 21*(3), 278–289.

Jones, B. R. (2007). Comment: Virtual neighborhood watch: Open source software and community policing against cybercrime. *Journal of Criminal Law & Criminology, 97*(2), 601–629.

Kahan, D. M. (1996). What do alternative sanctions mean? 63 U. *Chicago Law Review, 591*, 603–604.

Kalakota, R., & Whinston, A. B. (1996). *Frontiers of electronic commerce*. New York: Addison-Wesley.

Katz, I. (2005, February 5). Suit against bank of America to highlight cybercriminal issues. *Knight Ridder Tribune Business News*, 1.

Kendall, N. (2009, August 1). What the cybercrime fraudsters get up to. *Times Online*. http://www.timesonline.co.uk/tol/news/uk/crime/article6735761.ece.

Kshetri, N. (2005, May/June). Hacking the odds. *Foreign Policy*, 93.

Kshetri, N. (2006). The simple economics of cybercrimes, *IEEE Security and Privacy, 4*(1), 33–39.

Lack, K. (2002). Why directors could end up behind bars quicker than the cyber criminal. *Credit Control, 23*(3), 4–9.

Larsen, E., & Lomi, A. (2002). Representing change: A system model of organizational inertia and capabilities as dynamic accumulation processes. *Simulation Model Practice and Theory, 10*(5), 271–296.

Marshall, A. (1890). *Principles of economics*. London: Macmillan.

Marshall, A. (1920). *Principles of economics* (8th ed.). London: Macmillan.

McCabe, S. (2000, April 24). Cyber-vandals: Is hacking a crime? *Junior Scholastic, 102*(17), 4–5.

McCord, E. S., Ratcliffe, J. H., Garcia, R. M., & Taylor, R. B. (2007). Nonresidential crime attractors and generators elevate perceived neighborhood crime and incivilities. *Journal of Research in Crime and Delinquency, 44*(3), 295–320.

McDonald, C. G., & Slawson, J., & Carlos, V. (2002, October). *Reputation in an internet auction market economic inquiry, 40*(4), 633–650.

Messmer, E. (2009, October 6). Malware flea market pays hackers to hijack PCs. *The Industry Standard*. http://www.thestandard.com/news/2009/10/06/malware-flea-market-pays-hackers-hijack-pcs. Accessed 21 October 2009.

Morton, F. S. (2006). Consumer benefit from use of the internet. *NBER Innovation Policy & the Economy, 6*(1), 67–90.

National Center for Policy Analysis. (2002). Crime and Punishment in Texas: Update. http://www.ncpa.org/pub/st/st202/st202c.html. Accessed 21 September 2006.

New Zealand Ministry of Justice. (2008). *Crime Prevention Unit Organised Crime: Organised Crime Strategy Developing a whole of government approach to combat organised crime*, March 2008–June 2009. http://www.justice.govt.nz/cpu/organised-crime/strategy.html. Accessed 21 September 2008.

Noda, T., & Collis, D. J. (2001). The evolution of intraindustry firm heterogeneity: Insights from a process study. *Academy of Management Journal, 44*(4), 897–925.

North, D. C. (1990). *Institutions, institutional change and economic performance.* Cambridge, UK: Cambridge University Press.

Orlans, H. (2002). Telecommunication crime. *Change, 34*(1), 8.

Poulsen, K. (2009, October 27). Cybercrooks trick Gawker into serving Malware-Laced Ad. *wired.com.* http://www.wired.com/threatlevel/2009/10/gawker/. Accessed 27 October 2009.

Property Rights & Competition. (2000). Institutions and order, 43–62.

Putnam, R. (2000). *Bowling alone.* New York: Touchstone Press.

Rogers, E. M. (1995). *Diffusion of innovation* (4th ed.). New York: Free Press.

Romer, P. M. (1986). Increasing return and long-run growth. *Journal of Political Economy, 94,* 1002–1037.

Rubenking, N. J. (2009, July 10). Top cybercrime fighters discuss their trade. *PC Magazine.com.*

Ruse, M. (1998). *Taking Darwin seriously; a naturalistic approach to philosophy.* Cambridge: Cambridge University Press.

Ruse, M., & Maienschein, J. (Eds.). (1999). *Biology and the foundation of ethics.* Cambridge: Cambridge University Press.

Sah, R. (1991). Social osmosis and patterns of crime. *Journal of Political Economy, 99*(6), 169–217.

Schuerman, L., & Kobrin, S. (1986). Community careers in crime. In A. J. Reiss, Jr., & M. Tonry (Eds.), *Communities and crime* (pp. 67–100). Chicago: University of Chicago Press.

Scott, R. (1995). *Institutions and organizations.* Thousand Oaks, CA: Sage.

Scott, R. (2001). *Institutions and organizations.* Thousand Oaks, CA: Sage.

Serio, J. D., & Gorkin, A. (2003). Changing lenses: Striving for sharper focus on the nature of the 'Russian Mafia' and its impact on the computer realm. *International Review of Law, Computers and Technology, 17*(2), 191–202.

Shubert, A. (2003, February 6). Taking a swipe at cyber card fraud. *CNN.com.* http://www.cnn.com/2003/WORLD/asiapcf/southeast/02/06/indonesia.fraud. Accessed 21 September 2006.

Skorodumova, O. (2004). Hackers as information space phenomenon. *Social Sciences, 35*(4), 105–113.

Smith, T. (2003, October 27). Technology; Brazil becomes a cybercrime lab. http://query.nytimes.com/gst/fullpage.html?res=9F02E3DA1131F934A15753C1A9659C8B63&sec=&spon=&pagewanted=2. Accessed 21 September 2006.

Strader, T. J., & Shaw, M. J. (1999). Consumer cost differences for traditional and ecommerce. *Internet Research, 9,* 82–92.

Sulaiman, H. (2007, October 15). Quest to fight cybercrime. *New Straits Times,* 13.

Swardson, A. (2000). Multi-nation conference confronts cybercrime; Officials warn virus attacks are virtually unpreventable. *The Washington Post,* A.18.

The Canadian Press. (2008, May 28). Police say banks not reporting cybercrime in effort to protect image. http://canadianpress.google.com/article/ALeqM5jr3niVbLuNtqPL5mrNxhvqw8naRA. Accessed 21 September 2008.

The Chronicle of Higher Education. (2007, January 5). We must educate young people about cybercrime before they start college. *Chronicle of Higher Education, 53*(18), B.29.

US Fed News Service, Including US State News. (2005, May 20). *Cracking down on cyber crime.* Washington, DC.

US Fed News Service, Including US State News. (2007, June 4). Sen. Biden: New FBI crime report should be a wake-up call to Bush administration.

Vallance, C. (2008, February 21). The battle against the botnet hordes. http://news.bbc.co.uk/1/hi/technology/7256501.stm. Accessed 21 September 2008.

Vardi, N. (2005, July 25). Chinese take out. *Forbes,* 54.

Voigt, K. (2009, June 21). Dangerous Internet search terms grow with cybercrime. *CNN.com.*

Walden, I. (2005). Crime and security in cyberspace. *Cambridge Review of International Affairs, 18*(1), 51–68.

Walker, C. (2004, June). Russian Mafia Extorts Gambling Websites. http://www.americanmafia. com/cgi/clickcount.pl?url=www.americanmafia.com/Feature_Articles_270.html. Accessed 27 October 2005.

Weisburd, D., Bushway, S., Lum, C., & Yang, S. M. (2004). Trajectories of crime at places: A longitudinal study of street segments in the city of Seattle. *Criminology, 42*(2), 283–320.

Williamson, O. E. (1975). *Markets and hierarchies: Analysis and antitrust implications*. New York: Free Press.

Williamson, O. E. (1985). *The economic institutions of capitalism*. New York: Free Press.

Wylie, I. (2007, December 26). Internet; Romania home base for EBay scammers; The auction website has dispatched its own cyber-sleuth to help police crack fraud rings. *Los Angeles Times*, C.1.

Zittrain, J. (2006). The generative internet. *Harvard Law Review, 119*(7), 1974–2040.

Chapter 5
Institutional Field Evolved Around Cybercrimes

"I only choose those people who are truly rich. I'm not comfortable using the money of poor people. I also don't want to use credit cards belonging to Indonesians. Those are a carder's ethics" (a carder in Indonesia, Antariksa, 2001, p. 16).
"Trust in Nigerian businessmen and princes" is among the "50 things that are being killed by the internet" (Telegraph.co.uk, 4 September 2009, Moore, 2009).

Abstract The growth of criminal enterprises in the cyberworld has been an issue of pressing concern to our society. Concepts and theory building are lacking on institutions from the standpoint of criminal entrepreneurship in the digital world. In an attempt to fill this void, this chapter proposes a framework for identifying clear contexts and attendant mechanisms associated with how institutions have interacted with cybercrimes. The underlying notion in this chapter is that the rules of the game offered by formal and informal institutions have favored cybercrimes more than most conventional crimes. The degree of institutional favor, which cybercrime-related entrepreneurs enjoyed before, however, is decreasing.

5.1 Introduction

It is apparent that, from the standpoint of the cybercrime industry, institutions have changed dramatically in the past few decades. There has been "historical and cultural shifts in practices, discourses and representations of hacking" (Best, 2003). In the 1960s, the term "hacker"[1] referred to a person able to solve technologically complex problems (Furnell, Dowland, & Sanders, 1999). As late as the 1980s, "hackers" were considered to be people with high level of computing skills. A complaint that was often heard in the law-enforcement community was that some hackers were "treated as media darlings" (Sandberg, 1995). Until the 1980s, there were a few laws to tackle hacking and cybercrimes. The Computer Fraud and Abuse Act, for instance, was one of the first laws developed to deal with cybercrimes (Table 5.1). The act was originally passed in 1984 to protect classified

N. Kshetri, *The Global Cybercrime Industry*, DOI 10.1007/978-3-642-11522-6_5, © Springer-Verlag Berlin Heidelberg 2010

information on government computers, which was broadened in 1986 to apply to "federal interest computers" (Davis, 2006).

In the past few decades, the fields of hacking and cybercrime have undergone political, social, and psychological metamorphosis. Cybercrime has been recognized as a mainstream crime. For instance, starting 2009, Gallup included identity theft as a category in its annual survey to study Americans' fear of being crime victims (Saad, 2009). Nowadays, hackers are often portrayed in the popular press

Table 5.1 Major events related to the evolution of cybercrime-related institutions

1973	Swedish Data Act of 1973 was enacted
1977	Senator Abe Ribicoff introduced the "Federal Computer Systems Protection Act of 1977". This was the first proposal for Federal computer crime legislation in the United States. The Bill was not adopted, but became the model legislation in state computer crime legislation[a]
1981	Interpol became the first international organization dealing with computer crimes
1981	Tracy Kidder's The Soul of a New Machine published
1982	Hollywood film Tron released
1983	The OECD appointed an expert committee to discuss computer-related crime
1983	Hollywood film Wargames released
1984	The Computer Fraud and Abuse Act was passed to protect classified information on government computers
1984	Steven Levy's "Hackers: Heroes of the Computer Revolution" published
1985	The CoE appointed an expert committee to discuss legal issues of computer crimes
1986	The Computer Fraud and Abuse Act was broadened to apply to "federal interest computers"
1989	The CoE recommendations addressing the need for new substantive laws criminalizing certain conduct committed through computer networks (Recommendation No. R. (89) 9)
Nov. 1989	Masters of Deception group attacked the Learning Link computer system operated by WNET, Channel 13, in New York
1990	The UN adopted a resolution on computer crime legislation at 8th UN Congress on the Prevention of Crime and the Treatment of Offenders in Havana, Cuba, in 1990
1992	Wurzburg conferences organized by the University of Wurzburg led to 29 national reports, and recommendations for the development of computer crime legislations
1994	The United Nations Manual on the Prevention and Control of Computer was developed
1995	Hollywood film Hackers released
1995	The CoE recommendations concerning problems of criminal procedure law related to IT
1996	The Computer Fraud and Abuse Act was replaced by the more general concept of "protected computer," making the statute more widely applicable to the private sector
1997	CoE Committee of Experts on Crime in Cyber-space was set up
1999	The first conviction under the NET Act
2000	A Philippino hacker launched the "Love Letter" virus
Mar. 2000	The US Department of Justice opened www.cybercrime.gov
Oct. 2001	The USA Patriot Act was enacted to expand the intelligence gathering and surveillance powers of law-enforcement and national security agencies

Table 5.1 (continued)

Nov. 2001	34 countries signed the CoE's Convention on cybercrime
2002	Cybercrime and cyber-terrorism became FBI's No. 3 priority
July 2002	The Gramm-Leach-Bliley Act of 1999 went into effect. It requires financial institutions to establish procedures for protecting personal information, including. Financial penalties and civil suits may result from the inadvertent disclosure of personal information[b]
Nov. 2002	Cybersecurity Enhancement Act of 2002 signed
Apr. 2004	Computer Software Privacy and Control Act signed
Nov. 2007	The Identity Theft Enforcement and Restitution Act of 2007 enacted
May 2009	US President Obama created a new White House office led by a Cybersecurity Coordinator
Oct. 2009	Gallup included identity theft in its annual survey conducted to study trends of Americans' fear of being crime victims[c]

[a]A brief history of computer crime legislation, http://www.cybercrimelaw.net/content/history.html
[b]http://www.allshredservices.com/faq/grammleachbliley.htm
[c]Saad (2009).

as "criminal, deviant and disorderly" (Best, 2003). Many sub-groups related to "hacker" are considered to be socially undesirable (Furnell et al., 1999). On the political front, many laws are enacted to deal with the rapidly growing cybercrimes. For instance, in 1996, the Computer Fraud and Abuse Act was replaced by the more general concept of "protected computer," making it widely applicable to the private sector (Table 5.1). Likewise, the US Patriot Act brought cyberattacks into the definition of terrorism with penalties of up to 20 years in prison. As of 2006, over 30 US states had laws that require businesses to report cybercrimes (Greenemeier, 2006).

How did the transformations occur in institutions related to hacking and cybercrime? Why is cybercrime rising despite the institutional transformations? These questions are not idiosyncratic to the cybercrimes, but pertain to an under-researched subject in institutional theory: What factors influence the legitimacy of a criminal activity? How do institutions related to such an activity change? It is important to note that an important and long-standing question in institutional research is how institutional change occurs (Greenwood, Suddaby, & Hinings, 2002). A related point is that "how existing logics and identities are dismantled and how actors adopt a new logic and identity" has been an under-researched aspect of institutional theory (Rao, Monin, & Durand, 2003). In this chapter, we seek to understand the loci of institutions related to cybercrimes in order to understand the growth of and institutional changes related to such crimes.

5.2 The Theoretical Framework: Institutional Field

The idea of institutional field can be very helpful in understanding institutions and institutional changes associated with cybercrimes. A field is "formed around the issues that become important to the interests and objectives of specific collectives of organizations" (Hoffman, 1999, p. 352). For a field formed around cybercrimes, these organizations include regulatory authorities, international organizations (e.g., WTO, The Council of Europe (CoU)), and software producers. The "content, rhetoric, and dialogue" among these constituents influence the nature of field formed around cybercrime (Hoffman, 1999, p. 355).

Institutional fields are "evolving" rather than "static" in nature (Hoffman, 1999, p. 352). Institutional theorists make an intriguing argument as to how a field evolves. A field is a dynamic system characterized by the entry and exit of various players and constituencies with competing interests and disparate purposes and a change in interaction patterns among them (Barnett & Carroll, 1993). As is the case of any "issue-based" field, these players continuously negotiate over issue interpretation and engage in institutional war leading to institutional evolution (Greenwood & Hinings, 1996).

Prior researchers have noted that fields evolve through three stages (Morrill, 2007, cf. Purdy & Gray, 2009). New logics are introduced and are drawn into debate in the innovation stage, which is the first stage of field evolution. In the second stage, mobilization, field development is characterized by a complex power dynamics. Institutional actors in this stage compete to validate and implement their logics. The final stage is the structuration stage, in which logics are translated into practices (Reay, Golden-Biddle, & GermAnn, 2006). In this stage, norms and structures are standardized and institutions deepen their taken-for-grantedness (Covaleski & Dirsmith, 1988; DiMaggio, 1991).

Prior research also indicates that institutional evolution entails transitions among the three institutional pillars—regulative, normative, and cognitive. Building a regulative/law pillar system is the first stage of field formation. It is followed by a formation of normative institutions (cybercrimes' assessment from ethical viewpoint) and then cognitive institutions ("culturally supported belief" related to cybercrimes) (Hoffman, 1999).

The formation of regulative pillar is characterized by the establishment of legal and regulatory infrastructures to deal with cybercrimes (Hoffman, 1999). The strength of this pillar also depends upon the state's administrative capacities and citizens' willingness to accept the established institutions. A normative institutional pillar is said to be established regarding cybercrime if such a crime is viewed as an ethically and socially inappropriate behavior. Likewise, a cognitive pillar related to cybercrime is established if there is a culturally supported belief that cybercrime is wrong.

In a discussion of institutional field around cybercrime the nature of social stigmatization (Blackwell, 2000; Grasmick & Bursik, 1990; Probasco, Clark, & Davis, 1995) deserves special attention. From the standpoint of stigmatization of cyber-criminals, to understand the roles of players and constituencies related to field formed around cybercrime, a central concept here is arbiter. Drawing on the conceptual foundation provided by theories of socially situated judgment (Bell & Tetlock, 1989; Kahneman, 2003; Tetlock, 2002), Wiesenfeld, Wurthmann, and Hambrick (2008) argue that arbiters' "constituent-minded sensemaking" influences stigmatization process. Wiesenfeld et al. (2008) have identified three categories of "arbiters"— social, legal, and economic. Social arbiters include members of the press, governance watchdog groups, academics, and activists. Legal arbiters are those who play role in enforcing rules and regulations. Economic arbiters make decisions about engaging in economic exchange with individuals.

Legal arbiters, who enforce rules, have stepped up campaign against cybercrimes. The Federal Trade Commission (FTC), the DOJ, and the Department of Homeland Security have taken measures to create public awareness of cybercrimes and to improve cyber readiness.

Social arbiters include members of the press, governance watchdog groups, academics, and activists. The media's anti-cybercrime sentiments are reflected in their negative discourses of criminal hackers (Best, 2003). Academics and activists have also pointed out that software vendors should not expect consumers to create their own security software and bear liability for cybercrimes (Ryan, 2003; Rustad & Koenig, 2005). Religious groups can also be considered as social arbiters. In June 2009, for instance, the Head Pastor of a Christian Centre in Ghana urged Pastors, and Christians in general, to declare war against cyber-fraud also known as "sakawa" (ghanabusinessnews.com, 2009). He made the call at a special prayer session, which was organized by the Church for the nation against the spread of cybercrime.

Economic arbiters make economic exchange-related decisions. In this regard, businesses are actively mobilizing discourses against technology and service providers to take anti-cybercrime measures. In 2006, a coalition of major brands such as Expedia and LendingTree expressed dissatisfaction with click fraud and pressured Google and Yahoo to be more accountable (Grow & Bush, 2005).

A field is a dynamic system characterized by the entry and exit of various members and constituencies with competing interests and disparate purposes and a change in interaction patterns among them (Barnett & Carroll, 1993). For a field formed around cybercrime, the members include criminal hacker (also known as black hat hackers), ethical hackers (or white hat hackers), regulatory authorities (e.g., the FBI), international organizations (e.g., Council of Europe and the G8 High Tech Crime Working Group), software manufacturers, and consumers. As is the case of any issue-based field, these field members continuously negotiate over issue interpretation and engage in institutional war, leading to institutional evolution (Barnett & Carroll, 1993; Hoffman, 1999). The "content, rhetoric, and dialogue" among the field members influence the nature of cybercrime and institutionalization of anti-cybercrime logics (Hoffman, 1999, p. 355).

Various members in an institutional field differ in their influence in shaping the field. The dominant field members, for instance, tend to be those with "greater formal authority, resources and discursive legitimacy" (Phillips, Lawrence, & Hardy, 2000, p. 33). A field member's degree of dominance is positively related to the member's influence in the development of the field's structures and practices (Phillips et al., 2000).

5.3 Institutional Field Change Mechanisms

To understand the changes in formal and informal constraints related to cyber-crime, it may be helpful to consider a set of institutions, including practices, understandings, and rules; as well as a network of related organizations (Tolbert & Zucker, 1983). In this regard, it is important to note that in looking at issues of institutional development and change from the standpoint of cybercrime, we are treating institutions as endogenous. Doing so, however, requires an understanding of other "higher" level existing institutions and exogenous parameters (Snidal, 1994, 1996). Snidal (1996, p. 131): "In the short run, given exogenous institutional and other constraints, actors maximize their outcomes both through their behavior and through the development of efficient endogenous institutions. In the longer term, exogenous institutional constraints are themselves subject to change. There may be efficiency gains in changing these erstwhile exogenous institutions as well as the corresponding endogenous institutions."

In prior theoretical and empirical research, scholars have identified mechanisms related to changes in institutional fields: "jolts" or exogenous shocks (Meyer, 1982; Meyer, Brooks, & Goes, 1990; Haveman, Russo, & Meyer, 2001; Meyer, Gaba, & Colwell, 2005), changes in organizational logics (Friedland & Alford, 1991; Leblebici, Salancik, Copay, & King, 1991; Haveman & Rao, 1997; Thornton & Ocasio, 1999), and gradual change in field structure (Clemens & Cook, 1999; Fligstein, 1991; Schneiberg, 2005).

5.3.1 Exogenous Shocks

According to Hoffman's (1999) model, evolution of an institutional pillar is associ-ated with and facilitated by initiating events or triggers also known as disruptive events. Disruptive events are also referred to as shocks (Fligstein, 1991), jolts (Meyer, 1982), or discontinuities (Lorange, Scott, & Ghoshal, 1986) and can overcome the effects of institutional inertia (White, 1992).

Disruptive events tend to create "disruptive uncertainty" and force organizations to adopt "unorthodox experiments" that differ drastically from established practice (Meyer, 1982). Preliminary evidence consistent with this proposition emerges from some governments' responses to cybercrimes. New forms of major cybercrimes have led to new laws as well as the creation of technical infrastructure for moni-toring and tracing (Katyal, 2001). According to Hannigan's (1995) typology, these disruptive events can be considered as catastrophes[2] in the cyberworld. For instance, in 2000, following hackers' attacks of several major websites, the US Congress con-sidered proposals to improve security (Morning Edition, 2000). In March 2000, the US Department of Justice (DOJ) opened the website: www.cybercrime.gov. The site provided measures to protect against hackers and to report cybercrimes (New York Times, 2000). Others materials featured on the website include DOJ reports and speeches, congressional testimony, efforts to protect infrastructures, and international efforts on that front (Larkin, 2000).

Similarly, following the September 11 attacks, the USA Patriot Act was enacted in 2001 to expand the intelligence gathering and surveillance powers of law-enforcement and national security agencies. As noted earlier, cybercrime and cyber-terrorism also became FBI's No. 3 priority since 2002.

Likewise, after a Philippino hacker launched the "Love Letter" virus in 2000, the Philippine Republic Act 8792 was enacted. The electronic commerce act laid out how "hacking or cracking" crimes should be punished in the country (Evans, 2000). Legal and administrative happenings also act as disruptive events (Hannigan, 1995). In 2007, New York State held advertisers responsible for using an agency distributing adware, which changed advertisers' adware policies.

5.3.2 Changes in Organizational Logics

In prior theoretical and empirical research, scholars have emphasized the coevolving nature of institutions and the organizational forms that embody them and found that changes in organizational logics lead to a change in a field's practices and conventions (Friedland & Alford, 1991; Leblebici et al., 1991; Haveman & Rao, 1997; Thornton & Ocasio, 1999). In a study of the thrift industry, Haveman and Rao (1997, p. 1614) found that creation of new organization and adoption of structures embodying norms, value, and beliefs lead to an expansion of institutional influences. Destruction of organizational infrastructures, on the other hand, is associated with the decline of institutions (Haveman & Rao, 1997).

There have been changes in organizational logics at various levels. First, consider government agencies. In 2006, the FBI and the US Postal Inspection Service realized that click fraud may have violated federal laws. There have also been changes in the logics of trade associations. In 2006, the Internet Advertising Bureau (IAB) launched the Click Measurement Working Group to create Click Measurement Guidelines including definition of a click, standard to measure and count clicks, and identify invalid clicks. Individual organizations have also changed their structures and practices. In 2006, Priceline stopped utilizing adware providers and adopted best practices related to Internet ads.

5.3.3 Gradual Change in Field Structure

Structure of an institutional field may change over time with the changes in rules and norms governing the field. Cybercrime-related institutions and related organizations have also undergone gradual changes. Observers have noted "historical and cultural shifts in practices, discourses and representations of hacking" (Best, 2003). In the 1960s, for instance, the term "hacker" referred to a person able to solve technologically complex problems (Furnell et al., 1999). As late as the 1980s, "hackers" were considered to be people with superior computing skills. A complaint that was often heard in the law-enforcement community was that some hackers were "treated as

media darlings" (Sandberg, 1995). As noted earlier, the media nowadays is mostly
against hackers. Many sub-groups related to "hacker" are considered to be socially
undesirable (Furnell et al., 1999).

The nature of gradual change in field structure can also be explained with the
entry and exit of field members and relative power and dominance of various
members in the field. In this regard, an issue that deserves mention relates to the
government agencies' increasing power and dominance through formal authority
and resources. Likewise, the entry of cybercrime-related supranational organizations such as Council of Europe and the G8 High Tech Crime Working Group has
a powerful impact on institutional fields formed around cybercrime at the national
level.

Regulative agencies' structures to fight cybercrime have also changed. In 1996,
the FBI established Computer Investigations and Infrastructure Threat Assessment
Center, which grew to 1,151 employees in 2007.

5.4 Institutional Evolution

Prior research indicates that institutional evolution entails a sequence of evolutionary development among the three institutional pillars—regulative, normative, and
cognitive. Building a regulative/law pillar system is often the first stage of field formation. According to Hoffman (1999), it is followed by the formation of normative
institutions (cybercrime as an ethically inappropriate behavior) (p. 363) and then
cognitive institutions ("culturally supported belief" against cybercrime) (p. 364).

5.4.1 Regulative Pillar Related to Cybercrime

Regulative institutions consist of regulatory bodies (such as the FBI) and existing
laws and rules related to cybercrimes. The formation of this pillar is characterized
by the establishment of legal and regulatory infrastructures to combat cybercrimes
(Hoffman, 1999). The strength of this pillar also depends upon the state's administrative capacities and citizens' willingness to accept the established regulative
institutions.

5.4.2 Normative and Cognitive Pillars Related to Cybercrime

Responses to external pressures are functions of a social construction. Normative
constraints discourage actions as "negative sanctions are anticipated if the actions
are carried out" (Galtung, 1958; p. 127). Galtung (1958, p. 127) distinguishes
two types of normative constraints facing a person (P). Institutionalized norms are
"norms from other members from the social system to P" and internalized norms are
"norms from P to himself" (p. 127). These norms can be expressed in the forms of
shame and embarrassment. Psychic costs associated with shame and embarrassment

reduces the propensity to commit a crime (Blackwell, 2000; Probasco et al., 1995). Shame is a "self-imposed sanction," which occurs when individuals violate their internalized norms (Grasmick & Bursik, 1990). Embarrassment, on the other hand, is related to a "socially imposed sanction" that occurs when actors violate norms that have been endorsed by others in the society (Probasco et al., 1995). Put differently, embarrassment is related to social stigmatization (Blackwell, 2000).

The formation of an anti-cybercrime institutional field requires the construction of new identities that redefine social, cognitive, and moral legitimacy related to cybercrime; frame actions in an anti-cybercrime manner; and facilitate the development of habits and practices consistent with an anti-cybercrime logic (Misangyi, Weaver, & Elms, 2008).

An anti-cybercrime normative pillar is said to be established if cybercrime is viewed as an ethically inappropriate behavior and institutional actors feel a sense of social obligation to act against cybercrimes. Likewise, an anti-cybercrime cognitive pillar is established if there is a culturally supported belief that cybercrime is wrong (Hoffman, 1999). Measures taken to build normative and cognitive pillars should affect both substance as well as symbolism related to cybercrime (Misangyi et al., 2008).

5.5 Institutional Field Formed Around Cybercrimes

5.5.1 The Formation of Regulative Pillar Around Cybercrime

A central concept here is related to dominant field members. The idea of the government in a country as a dominant field member can be very helpful in understanding the development of regulative institutions. Prior research indicates that powerful and dominant field members tend to be those with "greater formal authority, resources and discursive legitimacy" (Phillips et al., 2000, p. 33; Hardy & Phillips, 1998).

Formal authority is related to an institutional actor's "legitimately recognized right to make decisions" (Phillips et al., 2000, p. 33). In most cases, such power lies with the government (Hardy & Phillips, 1998). While new cybercrime laws have increased the government's formal authority in industrialized countries, many developing countries have no laws dealing with cybercrimes. In 2000, for instance, only about 45 nations in the world had laws recognizing and validating some forms of digital or electronic transactions (Kshetri & Dholakia, 2001). This means that even if governments in some developing countries want to fight against cybercrimes, a lack of regulatory framework means that they lack formal authority to do so.

Industrialized countries have also increased resources[3] devoted to fight cybercrimes. While some maintain that resources to fight cybercrimes are far from sufficient in industrialized countries, there has been a greater achievement in these countries than in developing countries. Many developing economies, on the other hand, lack resources to build anti-cybercrime institutions (Cuéllar, 2004). As one might expect, developing countries lack judges, lawyers, and other law-enforcement workforce, who understand cybercrimes.

Discursive legitimacy concerns speaking legitimately about issues and affected organizations (Phillips & Brown, 1993). Undoubtedly, increased cybercrimes in developed countries such as the United States has helped gain discursive legitimacy for agencies involved in anti-cybercrime efforts. To gain discursive legitimacy, www.cybercrime.gov, for instance, featured DOJ reports and speeches, congressional testimony, efforts to protect infrastructures, and international efforts on that front (Larkin, 2000). All this has to be contrasted with situations in developing countries, where governments lack discursive legitimacy to take actions against cybercrimes. Consider, for instance, piracy, a form of cybercrime. In developing countries, consumers perceive anti-piracy enforcement tools as supports to foreign software companies. The Taiwanese government's attempt to force students using pirated versions of Windows to pay up was perceived as a support to a foreign company rather than its own citizens (Kshetri, 2004). In sum, most governments in developing countries have been unable to fight cybercrimes due to the lack of resources, formal authority, and discursive legitimacy.

In sum, an increase in cybercrimes in a country leads to the development of stronger regulative institutions. A lower income country is thus likely to have thinner and more dysfunctional regulative institutions related to cybercrimes than a higher income country.

5.5.1.1 National and International Initiatives to Build Strong Regulative Institutions

Supranational institutions such as International Telecommunication Union (ITU) and the Council of Europe (CoU) are influencing individual countries to strengthen cybercrime-related regulative institutions. As of August 2009, 46 nations had signed the CoE Treaty and 26 of them ratified it (Chap. 1).

Many governments want to strengthen their countries' anti-cybercrime institutions. For instance, China is facing unprecedented political and trade pressures from Western governments to combat cybercrimes. Consequently, in contrast to the 1980s, China's central government leaders do not ignore or promote piracy and other forms of cybercrimes (Massey, 2006).

People's compliance and cooperation with regulatory requirements, however, are driven largely by their belief in the legitimacy and fairness of legal authority rather than the fear of remedial measures and sanctions (Balganesh, 2008). Hart (1961) referred this idea as the "critical reflexive attitude." For instance, consumers in Taiwan perceived the government's anti-piracy efforts unfair as they viewed the efforts as support to foreign software companies rather than its own citizens.

5.5.1.2 Higher Cybercrime Level Leading to Strong Regulative Institutions

An observation is that an increase in cybercrime victimization may strengthen anti-cybercrime regulative institutions through various institutional change mechanisms such as exogenous shocks (Meyer, 1982), changes in organizational logics (Friedland & Alford, 1991), and gradual change in institutions (Clemens & Cook, 1999). There are three interrelated reasons why a higher level of cybercrime victimization strengthens anti-cybercrime institutions. First, the government faces pressures to improve anti-cybercrime regulatory institutions and infrastructures. In the US, for instance, the Business Software Alliance (BSA) urged the Congress to enact legislation to "treat cybercrime as organized crime" and increase penalties (Natividad, 2008).

Second, a high-cybercrime level serves as a basis for the theorization process, which is an important stage in institutional change (Greenwood et al., 2002). Theorization provides rationales for the practices and thus increases the likelihood of acceptance of the practice (Strang & Meyer, 1993). Two key elements of theorization concern framing and justifying. Framing focuses on the need for change and justification is value of the proposed changes for concerned actors (Greenwood et al., 2002; Maguire, Hardy, & Lawrence, 2004). Businesses and governments may use increased cybercrime victimization as a basis for justifying actions to change established practices.

Regulators expanding their scope: Regulatory measures have been expanded in recent years in order to provide more comprehensive coverage of a diverse range of economic activities. Due to the increased concerns about cybercrimes, the Committee on Foreign Investment in the United States (CFIUS) regulations have been changed to protect the US company. According to new CFIUS regulations, a potential foreign acquirer of a US company needs to certify the cybersecurity protections that will be in place with respect to the acquired US company (Asner & Kleyna, 2009).

Finally, as noted in Chap. 1, when businesses are victimized, they are likely to help develop anti-cybercrime regulative institutions by pursuing cyber-criminals under the existing laws. For instance, in 2009, as allowed under the CAN-SPAM Act,[4] Facebook sought damages of over $7 billion from Sanford Wallace. A California federal judge awarded Facebook US $711 million (Claburn, 2009). Sanford Wallace also owed MySpace $234 million from another judgment in another suit.

5.5.1.3 Political Institutions' Built-In Biases Toward Manufacturers of Technologies

Drawing on political resource theory (Hicks, 1999), institutional politics theory (Amenta, 1998) and power constellations theory (Huber & Stephens, 2001), Jenkins, Leicht, and Wendt (2006) point to the possibility that "political institutions have built-in biases that systematically favor the interests of specific classes." State policy can be viewed as "the result of power relations in society mediated by political institutions" (Huber & Stephens, 2001, p. 13) or "a joint product of class forces and political institutions" (Jenkins et al., 2006). Commenting on the government's ability to develop capacity to fight crimes, Cuéllar (2004) notes: "building capacity may require regulatory enforcement and programs that are costly to certain interest groups" (p. 45). In this regard, one important aspect of cybercrime that renders it interesting is the fact that laws in industrialized countries do not require manufacturers of technologies to assume responsibility for the faults in their products (e.g., software flaws) (Bank, 2005). A *USA Today* article (2002) put the issue this way: "For decades, software makers have been protected from lawsuits as US courts have struggled with the task of defining something as abstract and fast-changing as computer code." The UK House of Lords' *Personal Internet Security* report published in 2007 stated: "The IT industry has not historically made security a priority" (IAM, 2007).

5.5.1.4 Arbiters and Institutional/Social Entrepreneurship

In recent years, different groups of arbiters are moving beyond cyber-criminals and are targeting groups that have enabled cybercrimes. Liability issues associated with network security have received considerable attention (Mead, 2004). For instance, the prospect of software vendor liability is gaining speed. Social arbiters such as watchdog groups, academics, and activists have pointed out that software vendors should bear liability for cybercrimes. Some experts argue that software vendors should not expect consumers to create their own security software (Ryan, 2003). Rustad and Koenig (2005) argued that software vendors should be liable to consumers for a new tort—the negligent enablement of cybercrime. Similarly, National Academy of Sciences (NAS) argued that companies producing insecure software should be punished and the congress should take actions on this front (Computer Fraud & Security, 2002). NAS wrote in a draft report on the nation's computer security systems after the September 11, 2001 attacks: "Policy makers should consider legislative responses to the failure of existing incentives to cause the market to respond adequately to the security challenge .... Possible options include steps that would increase the exposure of software and system vendors and system operators to liability for system breaches." Economic arbiters such as government and private sector CIOs, on the other hand, have suggested imposing sanctions on vendors whose software is breached (Miller, 2002).

The concepts of social entrepreneurship and institutional entrepreneurship can be helpful to understand the roles of these arbiters. Social entrepreneurs (e.g., NAS and academics) are individuals or private organizations, whose entrepreneurial behaviors are engaged in addressing social problems (Korosec & Berman, 2006; Wong & Tang, 2006/2007, p. 627). Institutional entrepreneurs "help establish market institutions in the process of their business activities" (Daokui Li, Feng, & Jiang, 2006, p. 358). DiMaggio (1988, p. 14) notes that "new institutions arise when organized actors with sufficient resources (institutional entrepreneurs) see in them an opportunity to realize interests that they value highly." They champion a model of social order and attempt to build new organizational fields to institutionalize that model (Bartley, 2007). Government and private sector CIOs in the above discussion can be considered as institutional entrepreneurs.

In response to pressures from social and institutional entrepreneurs, regulators have also taken some measures, at least symbolic, to make software vendors responsible for cybercrimes. The UK House of Lords' Personal Internet Security report published in 2007, for instance, called for "software vendors (to) make the development of more secure technologies their top design priority" (IAM, 2007).

5.5.2 The Formation of Normative Pillar Around Cybercrime

Condemnation of an act such as a cybercrime leads to internalization of norms against the act among the "condemners" and as well as the "condemned" (Kahan, 1996). From the society's point of view, whether victimization related to a crime "elicit a stigma or a sympathy effect may depend on the evaluator's characteristics" (Lyons, 2006). In this regard, social identity theory points to the possibility of ethnocentric bias (Hamner, 1992; Tajfel & Turner, 1986).

A central tenet of social identity theory is that ingroup victims and offenders are likely to be perceived sympathetically, while out-group victims and offenders may be stigmatized (Howard & Pike, 1986; Lyons, 2006). We extend this logic to argue that as more and more individuals and organizations experience cyberattacks and they belong to the ingroup of cybercrime victim, anti-cybercrime societal norms are likely to be stronger. On a more speculative basis, we can argue that Mitnick's hacking activities is more likely to be perceived in a negative way today compared to the mid-1990s.

A related point is that, the perceived social stigma associated with becoming a cybercrime victim may also reduce with an increase in cybercrime. Note that most Internet fraud victims are embarrassed to report that they have been victimized (Salu, 2004).

To illustrate this argument, we consider the transformation in cybercrime-related societal norms. Until the mid-1990s, cyber-criminals in the United States lacked social stigma. A US attorney argued that the public was impressed because cybercrime was viewed as "a clever crime" (Sandberg, 1995). For instance, in 1995, Kevin D. Mitnick was charged of breaking into corporate computers, stealing thousands of credit card records and software. He was a featured figure in a book and was regarded by his fans as a "legend," a "technology-wielding genius," and a "hero" (Sandberg, 1995). Nowadays, the media mostly portrays a negative image of cyber-crimes (Best, 2003; Furnell et al., 1999). Nowadays, cybercrimes' impacts are more clearly identified and understood. An Economist (2007) article notes: "As botnets evolve from simple vandalism to sophisticated criminality, people take them more seriously."

In the cyberworld, we expect that an increase in the rate of cybercrimes leads to an increase in the reporting of such crimes. It is also reasonable to expect that over time stigma associated with becoming a cybercrime victim will decrease and reporting of such a crime may increase. Gill and Gropp (1997) quote a computer-security expert: "there used to be an unspoken stigma about computer crime. For a company to prosecute computer theft was to publicly announce its vulnerabilities and invite copycats." Liebermann (2008) noted: "As companies report a greater number of these breaches, the perceived stigma of such a breach will lessen. Once companies accept that—just like all banks report armed robbery—all companies should report cyber breaches, investigations of such breaches will begin earlier and have greater success."

5.5.2.1 Glamour Associated with the "Hacker" Label

An issue that deserves mention relates to the glamour associated with the "hacker" label. As noted above, as late as the 1980s, "hackers" were considered to be people with high level of computing skills. Following Garvin's (1987) "unstated analogy," we can argue that individuals perceive the image of hacking activities "today" as similar to the image "yesterday." This institutional inertia effect has increased the attractiveness of hacking activities in general.

Many teens are still attracted by the glamour surrounding the "hacker" label. A major problem is related to youths' inability to distinguish the boundary between white hat hacking and criminal hacking (Rao, Monin, & Durand, 2005). Organized crime groups have recruited young people in cybercrime enterprises (BBC news, 2006). According to a March 2007 *McAfee Virtual Criminology Report* produced with the United States and European high-tech crime units, 88% of computer science students at a US university admitted committing an illegal act online. David Marcus, security research and communications manager with McAfee observed: "They watch for bright kids and they start them on small tasks, like 'Find me 100 passwords and I'll give you 1,000 rubles' " (Sullivan, 2007). Another McAfee analyst noted that Crime gangs are recruiting and training teenagers as young as 14 for cybercrimes (Personal Computer World, 2007).

A final issue that deserves mention relates to potential social benefit associated with white hat hacking. It is argued that hacking may also generate social benefit by exposing security flaws (Best, 2003). Most obviously, these types of hacking activities tend to be honored rather than being stigmatized. To take one example, 'Back Orifice' released by the hacker group Cult of the Dead Cow (cDc) was intended to exploit vulnerabilities in Microsoft's Windows 95 and 98 (Best, 2003). Similarly, L0pht created L0phtCrack, which illustrated a flaw in Windows NT (Thomas, 2002).

5.5.2.2 The Hollywood Effect

Many youths adopt their role models from Hollywood (Welsch, 1998).[5] Many hackers have found their role models in cyberpunk sci-fi stories and especially, Hollywood movies have helped shape the cultural image of hacking (Brandt, 2001). The 1982 movie, *Tron*, portrayed "triumph of individual (hacker) good over corporate evil" (Brandt, 2001). Speaking of *WarGames*, Christopher Null (2003) notes: "[the movie] sparked an almost inconceivable interest in computer hacking among our juvenile intelligencia (I was one of them), and the movie's effect on Hollywood and the American consciousness can still be seen today." Likewise, the theme of *Real Genius* (1985) was that hackers are young geniuses, who understand and respect technology better than the adults who create it (Brandt, 2001).

Beginning the 1990s, however, digital crimes increased rapidly. Accordingly, in the latter half of the 1990s, there were several widely publicized movies, in which hacker engaged in criminal activities. Hackers were no longer a harmless character (Brandt, 2001). The *Hackers* (1995) was the first movie to focus solely on the hacker community. The film portrayed hacker as a "quintessentially teenage miscreant" (Levi, 2001, pp. 46–47). In the movie, teenage hackers are engaged in criminal hacking activities, who, in an attempt to extort money, threaten to release a destructive virus (Brandt, 2001). Likewise, in *Goldeneye* (1995), a hacker in Siberia helps the villains steal a high-tech helicopter and a satellite weapon, with capability to disrupt networks located in hundreds of miles away (Brandt, 2001).

Based on above discussion, we can thus argue that anti-cybercrime societal norms are stronger in a society with a higher concentration of cybercrimes than in one with a lower concentration of cybercrimes.

5.5.3 The Formation of Cognitive Pillar Around Cybercrime

Cognitive institutions are associated with culture (Jepperson, 1991). In most cases, they are based on subconsciously accepted rules and customs as well as some taken-for-granted cultural account of cybercrime-related activities (Berger & Luckmann, 1967). Anti-cybercrime cognitive institutions are also associated with consumers' cultural resources related to behaviors, dispositions, knowledge, and habits internalized through socialization (Bourdieu, 1986).

The real question is how anti-cybercrime habits and practices develop among organizations and Internet users. Note that anti-cybercrime practices include staying away from cybercrime as well as helping to combat cybercrimes. As noted earlier, most people using computer networks unethically do not perceive ethical implications of their actions (Kallman & Grillo, 1996). Consider, for instance, piracy, a form of cybercrime. It should be noted that software sharing was more common in the United States when computers were rare and found mostly in universities (Gallaway & Kinnear, 2004). There is some evidence that parents, and even teachers, advocate certain computer crimes, particularly software piracy among students (Bowker, 2000). The Chronicle of Higher Education (2007) noted: "We continue to seek technological, legislative, and law-enforcement solutions to what is largely an educational problem." For some cybercrime victims, it also takes some time to realize that they have been victims (Wall, 1998; Richtel, 1999).

Different theoretical contributions and various empirical studies have led to the accepted view that when institutional rules and norms are broadly diffused and supported, organizations are more likely to acquiesce to these pressures because their social validity is less likely to be questioned (Knoke, 1982; Oliver, 1991; Tolbert & Zucker, 1983). For instance, Knoke (1982) found that one of the best predictors of a municipality's adoption of reforms was the proportion of other municipalities that had adopted such reforms. Likewise, Tolbert and Zucker's (1983) study indicated that the degree of diffusion of civil service policies and programs was positively related to the probability of adoption by a firm that had not yet adopted such policies and programs. We extend this logic to argue that increased Internet penetration and consumers' and businesses' longer experiences facilitate the development of habits and practices consistent with an anti-cybercrime logic. To take one example, in 2005, Priceline.com started working on a draft of the company's adware policy (Heun, 2005). Likewise, more experienced users are likely to be more capable to realize that they are victimized.

5.5.3.1 The Novelty Factor

A US attorney argued that a cybercrime is "a clever crime" and "everyone's impressed" (Sandberg, 1995). The 1995 arrest of Kevin D. Mitnick, who was charged of cracking dozens of corporate computers, stealing thousands of credit card records and software, provides a remarkable example of how the society perceives such crimes. The public handled it as a "heroic act" or "a funny story" (Zombori, 2001). He was a featured figure in a book and was regarded by his fans as a "legend," a "technology-wielding genius" and a "hero" (Sandberg, 1995; New York Times, 1995). More broadly, American society has been very fond of clever outlaws (Sandberg, 1995).

Reflective pieces from the popular press and academic articles have illustrated how different forms of cybercrimes lack stigma. It is, for instance, argued that there is no public and social stigma if an operator of an online gambling is caught. Clark (1998) observes: "in fact the opposite is often the case." Likewise some analysts observe that "Internet gambling [lacks] ... the social stigma of gambling" (The Washington Post, 1998). Other similar examples have been noted in Chap. 2. The real issue thus concerns a lack of social stigma in cybercrimes.

5.6 Concluding Comments

In this chapter, we examined the nature institutional legitimacy for cyber-criminals. This matters not only for theoretical reasons, but also for practical ones. Hacking and cybercrime are going through a rapid transition phase. In the past two decade, most industrialized countries have enacted many laws to deal with cybercrimes and have developed other regulatory infrastructures. Yet, notwithstanding the accomplishments on the regulative front, normative and cognitive institutions related to cybercrime have been relatively slow to change. Informal institutions inherited from the past have helped the growth of this industry. For instance, traditionally cybercrime victims were stigmatized and cyber-criminals were honored. A related point is that while hackers share the things they find, attack victims are embarrassed to publicize their vulnerabilities and fear that it would aid other attackers (Paller, 1998).

They thus tend to hide such information. There is, however, some indication that this situation is changing.

Regulators in industrialized countries have a plenty of wind in their sails. Due to institutional inertia, the seriousness of cybercrimes and their far-reaching influence seem to be underrecognized in the political community. Well coordinated, well funded campaigns are thus needed to combat cybercrimes. By well coordinated, we mean a better international, inter-governmental agency, and government–business collaborations and coordination to fight cybercrimes. It is also necessary to increases resources and funding to fight cybercrimes in proportion to the impact of such crimes.

The novelty effect of hacking is expected to decline with a higher level of cybercrime in a society and the public's longer experience with the Internet (Coates & Humphreys, 2008). Likewise, anti-cybercrime codes, policies, principles, standards, and procedures are likely to develop over time. The example of piracy helps explain the processes that underlie the gradual development of anti-cybercrime cognitive institutions. It should be noted that software sharing was more common in the United States when computers were rare and found mostly in universities (Gallaway & Kinnear, 2004). Nowadays, public awareness toward intellectual property protection has increased. In sum, anti-cybercrime normative and cognitive institutions are likely to be stronger in a society that has more experienced consumers and businesses than in one with less experienced consumers and businesses.

We discussed various examples of exogenous shocks. Some analysts, however, believe that these external shocks have not been big enough to lead to the development of strong anti-cybercrime institutions. In 2003, Mike McConnell, a former director of the US National Security Agency, noted that until "there is a cyber 9/11," or "without something that serves as a forcing issue," governments and the private sector would not be prepared for attack (Cant, 2003).

Finally, in some developing economies, efforts to develop regulative institutions have been mainly directed toward protecting the ruling regimes' interests instead of ensuring the security of the country and its citizens. In Pakistan, for instance, the Interior Ministry announced in July 2009 that acts such as mocking the president via text messages, e-mail, or blogs may face prison sentences of up to 14 years under a new Cybercrimes Act (Ahmed, 2009). Likewise, in China, about 30,000–40,000 cyber police "patrol" the Internet including chat rooms and Weblogs, who also provide viewpoints that are favorable to the Communist Party of China (CPC) (Cannici, 2009; Kshetri, 2008).

Notes

1. It is important to note that most cybercrimes are associated with hacking.
2. Hannigan (1995, p. 64) identified three types of disruptive events: milestones; catastrophes; and legal/administrative happenings.
3. Resources are tangible (economic/financial, human) and intangible (cultural, social, symbolic) (Misangyi et al., 2008). We, however, deal with only tangible resources in this chapter.

4. The CAN-SPAM Act is a law that "sets the rules for commercial email, establishes requirements for commercial messages, gives recipients the right to have … stop emailing them, and spells out tough penalties for violations" (ftc.gov, 2009).
5. Welsch (1998) observes: "One gangster compares himself to Jesse James and Al Capone by turns; another comments that he likes it when the movies make the mob boss 'good looking' ".

References

Ahmed, I. (2009). Zardari's popularity sags – Will it undermine Pakistan's fight with Taliban? *Christian Science Monitor.* http://www.csmonitor.com/2009/0909/p06s01-wosc.html. Accessed 30 October 2009.

Amenta, E. (1998). *Bold relief.* Princeton, NJ: Princeton University Press.

Antariksa. (2001, July). I am a thief, not a hacker: Indonesia's electronic underground. *Latitudes Magazine,* 12–17.

Asner, M. A., & Kleyna, M. (2009). The new white house cyber czar. *Computer & Internet Lawyer, 26*(7), 1–4.

Balganesh, S. (2008). Demystifying the right to exclude: Of property, inviolability, and automatic injunctions. *Harvard Journal of Law and Public Policy, 31*(2), 593–661.

Bank, D. (2005, February 24). Companies seek to hold software makers liable for flaws. *Wall Street Journal,* B.1.

Barnett, W. P., & Carroll, G. R. (1993). How institutional constraints affected the organization of early US telephonies. *Journal of Law, Economics and Organization, 9,* 98–126.

Bartley, T. (2007). How foundations shape social movements: The construction of an organizational field and the rise of forest certification. *Social Problems, 54*(3), 229–256.

BBC News. (2006, December 8). Criminals 'target tech students'. http://news.bbc.co.uk/2/hi/technology/6220416.stm. Accessed 1 September 2009.

Bell, N., & Tetlock, P. E. (1989). The intuitive politician and the assignment of blame in organizations. In R. A. Giacalone & P. Rosenfeld (Eds.), *Impression management in the organization* (pp. 105–124). Hillsdale, NJ: Lawrence Erlbaum Associates.

Berger, P. L., & Luckmann, T. (1967). *The social construction of reality: A treatise in the sociology of knowledge.* New York: Doubleday.

Best, K. (2003). The Hacker's challenge: Active access to information, visceral democracy and discursive practice. *Social Semiotics, 13*(3), 263–282.

Blackwell, B. S. (2000). Perceived sanction threats, gender, and crime: A test and elaboration of power-control theory, criminology. *Beverly Hills, 38*(2), 439–489.

Bourdieu, P. (1986). The forms of capital. In J. Richardson (Ed.), *Handbook of theory and research for the sociology of education* (pp. 241–258). London: Greenwood Press.

Bowker, A. L. (2000). The advent of the computer delinquent. *FBI Law Enforcement, 69*(12), 7–11.

Brandt, A. (2001). Hacking Hollywood. http://pcworld.about.com/news/Apr042001id45804.htm. Accessed 1 September 2005.

Cannici, Jr., W. J. (2009). The global online freedom act: combating american businesses that facilitate internet censorship in China. *Journal of Internet Law, 12*(11), 3–17.

Cant, S. (2003, April 22). 'Cyber 9/11' risk warning. *The Sydney Morning Herald.* http://www.smh.com.au/articles/2003/04/21/1050777200225.html. Accessed 1 September 2009.

Claburn, T. (2009, October 30). Facebook wins $711 million from spammer. *Information Week.* http://www.informationweek.com/news/global-cio/security/showArticle.jhtml?articleID=221400140. Accessed 31 October 2009.

Clark, B. (1998). *Techno gambling: Stepping outside the cyber-gambling square.* Paper presented at the conference Gambling, Technology and Society: Regulatory Challenges for the 21st Century, convened by the Australian Institute of Criminology in conjunction with the Australian Institute for Gambling Research, Sydney.

Clemens, E., & Cook, J. (1999). Politics and institutionalism: Explaining durability and change. *Annual Review of Sociology, 25*, 441–466.

Coates, D., & Humphreys, B. R. (2008). Novelty effects of new facilities on attendance at professional sporting events. *Contemporary Economic Policy, 23*(3), 436–455.

Computer Fraud & Security. (2002). News: Should software vendors be responsible for security vulnerabilities? 2002(2), 4–5.

Covaleski, M., & Dirsmith, M. (1988). An institutional perspective on the rise, social transformation, and fall of a university budget category. *Administrative Science Quarterly, 33*, 562–587.

Cuéllar, M. (2004). The mismatch between state power and state capacity in transnational law enforcement. *Berkeley Journal of International Law, 22*(1), 15–58.

Daokui Li, D., Feng, J., & Jiang, H. (2006). Institutional entrepreneurs. *American Economic Review, 96*(2), 358–362.

Davis, J. B. (2006). Cybercrime fighters. *ABA Journal, 89*, 36.

DiMaggio, P. J. (1988). Interest and agency in institutional theory. In L. G. Zucker (Ed.), *Institutional patterns and organizations: Culture and environment*, (pp. 3–22). Cambridge, MA: Ballinger.

DiMaggio, P. (1991). Constructing an organizational field as a professional project: U.S. art museums, 1920–1940. In W. W. Powell & P. J. DiMaggio (Eds.), *The new institutionalism in organizational analysis* (pp. 267–292). Chicago: University of Chicago Press.

Economist.com. (2007, August 30). Global Agenda. A walk on the dark side. *Europeview*, 1.

Evans, J. (2000). Cyber-crime laws emerge, but slowly. http://archives.cnn.com/2000/TECH/computing/07/05/cyber.laws.idg. Accessed 1 September 2005.

Fligstein, N. (1991). The structural transformation of American industry: An institutional account of the causes of diversification in the largest firms: 1919–1979. In W. Powell & P. DiMaggio (Eds.), *The new institutionalism in organizational analysis* (pp. 311–336). Chicago: University of Chicago Press.

Friedland, R., & Alford, R. R. (1991). Bringing society back in: Symbols, practices, and institutional contradictions. In W. W. Powell & P. J. DiMaggio (Eds.), *The new institutionalism in organizational analysis* (pp. 232–263). Chicago: University of Chicago Press.

ftc.gov. (2009, September). Facts for business. http://www.ftc.gov/bcp/edu/pubs/business/ecommerce/bus61.shtm. Accessed 31 October 2009.

Furnell, S. M., Dowland, P. S., & Sanders, P. W. (1999). Dissecting the "Hacker Manifesto". *Information Management & Computer Security, 7*(2), 69–75.

Gallaway, T., & Kinnear, D. (2004). Open source software, the wrongs of copyright, and the rise of technology. *Journal of Economic Issues, 38*(2), 467–474.

Galtung, J. (1958). The social functions of a prison. *Social Problems, 6*, 127–140.

Garvin, D. A. (1987). Competing on the eight dimensions of quality. *Harvard Business Review, 65*, 101–109.

ghanabusinessnews.com. (2009). Church prays against cyber crime in Ghana. http://ghanabusinessnews.com/2009/06/01/church-prays-against-cyber-crime-in-ghana. Accessed 1 September 2009.

Gill, M. S., & Gropp, G. (1997). Cybercops take a byte out of computer crime. *Smithsonian, 28*(2), 114–124.

Grasmick, H. G., & Bursik, J. R. (1990). Conscience, significant others, and rational choice: Extending the deterrence model. *Law and Society Review, 24*, 837–862.

Greenemeier, L. (2006). New from cybercrooks: Fake chrome, pump-and-dump. *InformationWeek, 1112*, 26.

Greenwood, R., & Hinings, C. R. (1996). Understanding radical organizational change: Bringing together the old and the new institutionalism. *Academy of Management Review, 21*, 1022–1054.

Greenwood, R., Suddaby, R., & Hinings, C. R. (2002). Theorizing change: The role of professional associations in the transformation of institutionalized fields. *Academy of Management Journal, 45*(1), 58–80.

Grow, B., & Bush, J. (2005, May 30). Hacker hunters. *Business Week*.

Hamner, K. M. (1992). Gay-Bashing: A social identity analysis of violence against lesbians and gay men. In G. M. Herek & K. Berrill (Eds.), *Hate crimes: Confronting violence against lesbians and gay men* (pp. 179–190). Newbury Park, CA: Sage.

Hannigan, J. (1995). *Environmental sociology*. New York: Routledge.

Hardy, C., & Phillips, N. (1998). Strategies of engagement: Lessons from the critical examination of collaboration and conflict in an organizational domain. *Organization Science, 9*(2), 217–230.

Hart, H. L. A. (1961). *The concept of law*. Oxford: Clarendon Press.

Haveman, H. A., & Rao, H. (1997). Structuring a theory of moral sentiments. *American Journal of Sociology, 102*, 1606–1651.

Haveman, H. A., Russo, M. V., & Meyer, A. D. (2001). Organizational environments in flux: The impact of regulatory punctuations on organizational domains, CEO succession, and performance. *Organization Science, 12*, 253–273.

Heun, C. T. (2005). Can spyware ever come in from the cold? *InformationWeek, 1061*, 70–71.

Hicks, A. (1999). *Social democracy and welfare capitalism*. Ithaca: Cornell University Press.

Hoffman, A. J. (1999). Institutional evolution and change: Environmentalism and the US chemical industry. *Academy of Management Journal, 42*(4), 351–371.

Howard, J. A., & Pike, K. C. (1986). Ideological investment in cognitive processing: The influence of social statuses on attribution. *Social Psychology, 49*, 154–167.

Huber, E., & Stephens, J. D. (2001). *Development and crisis of the welfare state*. Chicago: University of Chicago Press.

Identity and Access Management (IAM). (2007). Software Quality: The UK Report on Internet Security. http://community.ca.com/blogs/iam/archive/2007/08/14/software-quality-the-uk-report-on-internet-security.aspx. Accessed 1 September 2008.

Jenkins, J. C., Leicht, K. T., & Wendt, H. (2006). Class Forces, Political Institutions, and State Intervention: Subnational Economic Development Policy in the United States, 1971–1990. *The American Journal of Sociology, 111*(4), 1122–1182.

Jepperson, R. (1991). Institutions, institutional effects, and institutionalism. In Powell, W. W. & DiMaggio, P. J. (Eds.), *The new institutionalism in organizational analysis* (pp.143–163). Chicago, IL: University of Chicago Press.

Kahan, D. M. (1996). What do alternative sanctions mean? 63 U. *Chicago Law Review, 591*, 603–604.

Kahneman, D. (2003). A perspective on judgment and choice: Mapping bounded rationality. *American Psychologist, 58*, 697–720.

Kallman, E. A., & Grillo, J. P. (1996). *Ethical decision making and information technology*, 2e. New York: McGraw Hill.

Katyal, N. K. (2001). Criminal law in cyberspace. *University of Pennsylvania Law Review, 149*(4), 1003–1114.

Knoke, D. (1982). The spread of municipal reform: Temporal, spatial, and social dynamics. *American Journal of Sociology, 87*(6), 1314–1339.

Korosec, R. L., & Berman, E. M. (2006). Municipal support for social entrepreneurship. *Public Administration Review, 66*(3), 448–462.

Kshetri, N. (2004). Economics of linux adoption in developing countries. *IEEE Software, 21*(1), 74–81.

Kshetri, N. (2008). *The rapidly transforming Chinese high technology industry and market: Institutions, ingredients, mechanisms and modus Operandi*, Caas Business School, City of London and Chandos Publishing (Oxford).

Kshetri, N., & Dholakia, N. (2001, August). *Impact of cultural and political factors on the adoption of digital signatures in Asia*. Proceedings of the Americas' conference on Information System (AMCIS), Boston.

Larkin, M. (2000). Websites in brief. *The Lancet, 355*(9216), 1735.

Leblebici, H., Salancik, G. R., Copay, A., & King, T. (1991). Institutional change and the transformation of interorganizational fields: An organizational history of the US radio broadcasting industry. *Administrative Science Quarterly, 36*, 333–363.

Levi, P. (2001). Between the risk and the reality falls the shadow: Evidence and urban legends in computer fraud. In D. Wall (Ed.), *Crime and the internet*. London, England: Routledge.

Liebermann, E. (2008). A collective crackdown on cybercrime. http://www.internetevolution.com/author.asp?section_id=490&doc_id=144804&. Accessed 1 September 2009.

Lorange, P., Scott, M. M., & Ghoshal, S. (1986). *Strategic control systems*. St. Paul: West.

Lyons, C. J. (2006). Stigma or sympathy? Attributions of fault to hate crime victims and offenders. *Social Psychology Quarterly, 69*(1), 39–60.

Maguire, S., Hardy, C., & Lawrence, T. B. (2004). Institutional entrepreneurship in emerging fields: HIV/AIDS treatment advocacy in Canada. *Academy of Management Journal, 47*(5), 657–679.

Massey, J. A. (2006). The emperor is far away: China's enforcement of intellectual property rights protection, 1986–2006, *Chicago Journal of International Law, 7*(1), 231–237.

Mead, N. R. (2004). Who is liable for insecure systems? *Computer, 37*(7), 27–34.

Meyer, A. D., Brooks, G. R., & Goes, J. B. (1990). Environmental jolts and industry revolutions: Organizational responses to discontinuous change. *Strategic Management Journal, 11*, 93–110.

Meyer, A. (1982). Adapting to environmental jolts. *Administrative Science Quarterly, 27*, 515–537.

Meyer, A. D., Gaba, V., & Colwell, K. A. (2005). Organizing far from equilibrium: Nonlinear change in organizational fields. *Organization Science, 16*, 456–473.

Miller, H. (2002). Penalizing vendors brings consequences. *Network World*. http://www.networkworld.com/columnists/2002/0422faceoffno.html. Accessed 1 September 2003.

Misangyi, V. F., Weaver, G. R., & Elms, H. (2008). Ending corruption: The interplay among institutional logics, resources, and institutional entrepreneurs. *Academy of Management Review, 33*(3), 750–770.

Moore, M. (2009, September 4). 50 things that are being killed by the internet. *Telegraph. co.uk*. http://www.telegraph.co.uk/technology/6133903/50-things-that-are-being-killed-by-the-internet.html. Accessed 27 October 2009.

Morning Edition. (2000). Profile: Government claims that they lack appropriate resources to fight cybercrime. *Morning Edition*, 1.

Natividad, K. F. (2008). Stepping it up and taking it to the streets: Changing civil and criminal copyright enforcement tactics. *Berkeley Technology Law Journal, 2008 Annual Review, 23*(1), 469–501.

New York Times. (1995, July 2). Hacker is said to agree to a plea bargain, p. I22, http://www.nytimes.com/1995/07/02/us/hacker-is-said-to-agree-to-a-plea-bargain.html. Accessed 31 October 2009.

New York Times. (2000, March 14). New federal web site seeks to counter hackers, A19. http://www.nytimes.com/2000/03/14/us/national-news-briefs-new-federal-web-site-seeks-to-counter-hackers.html. Accessed 31 October 2009.

Null, C. (2003). WarGames, film review by Christopher Null – 2003 Filmcritic.com. http://www.toptenreviews.com/scripts/eframe/url.htm?u=http://www.filmcritic.com/misc/emporium.nsf/ddb5490109a79f598625623d0015f1e4/137bf7e25ae567f188256de900147c08?OpenDocument. Accessed 1 September 2004.

Oliver, C. (1991). Strategic responses to institutional processes. *Academy of Management Review, 16*, 145–179.

Paller, A. (1998). CyberCrime come to Washington. *Government Executive, 30*(9), 59–63.

Personal Computer World. (2007). Criminals Recruiting Students for Cyber-Crime.

Phillips, N., & Brown, J. (1993). Analyzing communication in and around organizations: A critical hermeneutic approach. *The Academy of Management Journal, 36*(6), 1547–1576.

Phillips, N., Lawrence, T. B., & Hardy, C. (2000). Inter-organizational collaboration and the dynamics of institutional fields. *Journal of Management Studies, 37*(1), 23–43.

Probasco, J., Clark, R., & Davis, W. L. (1995). A human capital perspective on criminal careers. *Journal of Applied Business Research, 11*(3), 58–64.

Purdy, J. M., & Gray, B. (2009) Conflicting logics, mechanisms of diffusion, and multilevel dynamics in emerging institutional fields. *Academy of Management Journal, 52*(2), 355–380.

Rao, H., Monin, P., & Durand, R. (2003). Institutional change in Toque Ville: Nouvelle Cuisine as an identity movement in French gastronomy. *American Journal of Sociology, 108*(4), 795–843.

Rao, H., Monin, P., & Durand, R. (2005). Border crossing: Bricolage and the erosion of categorical boundaries in French gastronomy. *American Sociological Review, 70*(6), 968–992.

Reay, R., Golden-Biddle, K., & GermAnn, K. (2006). Legitimizing a new role: Small wins and microprocesses of change. *Academy of Management Journal, 49*, 977–998.

Richtel, M. (1999, June 2). Federal cybercrime unit hunts for hackers. *New York Times*, A16.

Rustad, M. L., & Koenig, T. H. (2005). The tort of negligent enablement of cybercrime. *Berkeley Technology Law Journal, 20*(4), 1553–1611.

Ryan, D. J. (2003). Two views on security software liability: Let the legal system decide. *IEEE Security & Privacy*, 70–72.

Saad, L. (2009, October 16). Two in three Americans worry about identity theft. *Gallup*. http://www.gallup.com/poll/123713/Two-in-Three-Americans-Worry-About-Identity-Theft.aspx. Accessed 16 October 2009.

Salu, A. O. (2004). Online crimes and advance fee fraud in nigeria – Are available legal remedies adequate? *Journal of Money Laundering Control, 8*(2), 159–167.

Sandberg, J. (1995, February 27). On-line: Immorality play: Acclaiming hackers as heroes. *Wall Street Journal*, B1.

Schneiberg, M. (2005). Combining new institutionalisms: Explaining institutional change in American property insurance. *Sociological Forum, 20*, 93–137.

Snidal, D. (1994). The politics of scope: Endogenous actors, heterogeneity and institutions. *Journal of Theoretical Politics, 6*(4), 449–472.

Snidal, D. (1996). Political economy and international institutions. *International Review of Law and Economics, 16*(1), 121–137.

Strang, D., & Meyer, J. (1993). Institutional conditions for diffusion. *Theory and Society, 22*, 487–511.

Sullivan, B. (2007, April 10). Who's behind criminal bot networks? http://redtape.msnbc.com/2007/04/whos_behind_cri.html. Accessed 1 September 2008.

Tajfel, H., & Turner, J. C. (1986). The social identity theory of intergroup behavior. In S. Worchel & W. G. Austin (Eds.), *Psychology of intergroup relations* (pp. 7–24). Chicago, IL: Nelson-Hall.

Tetlock, P. E. (2002). Social functionalist frameworks for judgment and choice: Intuitive politicians, theologians and prosecutors. *Psychological Review, 109*, 451–471.

The Chronicle of Higher Education. (2007, January 5). We must educate young people about cybercrime before they start college. *53*(18), B.29.

The Washington Post. (1998, August 17). Internet gambling: A bad bet, A.18.

Thomas, D. (2002). *Hacker culture*. Minneapolis, MN: University of Minnesota Press.

Thornton, P. H., & Ocasio, W. (1999). Institutional logics and the historical contingency of power in organizations: Executive succession in the higher education publishing industry, 1958–1990. *American Journal of Sociology, 105*, 801–843.

Tolbert, P. S., & Zucker, L. G. (1983). Institutional Sources of Change in the Formal Structure of Organizations: The Diffusion of Civil Service Reform, 1880–1935. *Administrative Science Quarterly, 28*, 22–39.

USA Today. (2002). Microsoft Glitches Prompt Liability Concerns. http://www.usatoday.com/tech/news/2002/06/17/microsoft-security.htm.

Wall, D. S. (1998). Catching cybercriminals: Policing the internet. *International Review of Law, 12*(2), 201–218.

Welsch, T. (1998). Killing them with tap shoes: Violent performance in The Cotton Club. *Journal of Popular Film & Television, 25*(4), 162–171.

White, H. (1992). *Identity and control: A structural theory of social interaction.* Princeton, NJ: Princeton University Press.

Wiesenfeld, B. M., Wurthmann, K. A., & Hambrick, D. C. (2008). The stigmatization and devaluation of elites associated with corporate failures: A process model. *Academy of Management Review, 33*(1), 231–251.

Wong, L., & Tang, J. (2006/2007). Dilemmas confronting social entrepreneurs: Care homes for elderly people in Chinese cities. *Pac Aff, 79*(4), 623–640.

Zombori, G. (2001). *e + Finance + Crime: A Report on Cyber-Crime and Money Laundering,* Study of Organized Crime and Corruption, Osgoode Hall Law School, York University, Toronto, Ontario, Canada, 5 January. http://www.yorku.ca/nathanson/Publications/e.htm.

Chapter 6
Information and Communications Technologies, Cyberattacks, and Strategic Asymmetry

Criminals, for their part, are motivated by greed. Few leaders of the cyber-organized crime world would hesitate to sell their capabilities to a terrorist loaded with hard currency. That, combined with the ever-growing terrorist awareness of cyber vulnerabilities, makes this set of scenarios not just highly likely, but close to inevitable (Bucci & Steven, 2009).

"If you're able to take down part of the electrical grid, pretty much everything else fails . . .. You're not back in the 1970s; you're back in the 1870s." James Woolsey, former director of the US Central Intelligence Agency (cf. Maltz, 2009).

Abstract In the history of warfare, there are a number of examples of strategic uses of asymmetric technologies. Consistent with history and theory, individuals, organizations, and nations have spotted opportunities to employ information and communications technologies to gain and exploit asymmetric advantages and to counter asymmetric weaknesses. This chapter discusses various asymmetries associated with institutions, nations, and organizations that influence the ICT-security nexus. Regulative, normative, and cognitive institutions in a country provide various mechanisms that affect the nature of positive and negative asymmetries. Nations and organizations also differ in terms of their capability to assimilate ICT tools to gain positive asymmetries and deal with vulnerabilities of negative asymmetries.

6.1 Introduction

Information and communications technologies (ICTs) have fundamentally changed the equations related to security functions of nations, organizations, and individuals (e.g., English, 2005; Metz, 2001; Zhou, 2005). The vulnerability to threat as well as the capability to strategically deploy ICTs varies across entities. The characteristics of organizations, nations, and institutions superimpose in a unique interaction with ICTs' nature that influence the ICT-security nexus.

N. Kshetri, *The Global Cybercrime Industry*, DOI 10.1007/978-3-642-11522-6_6,   119
© Springer-Verlag Berlin Heidelberg 2010

This chapter explores the nature of ICT-related asymmetries (see Table 6.1 for definitions of terms) from the perspective of national, organizational, and individual security. Asymmetry created by ICTs (more broadly: technologies) is among six forms of asymmetry identified by Metz and Johnson (2001). Nations and organizations can exploit asymmetric advantages by strategically employing ICTs in war against enemies (e.g., cyberattacks) as well as by using ICTs in facilitating other functions contributing to attack and defense such as communications, detection of threats from enemies, gathering intelligence. For instance, it was reported that in

Table 6.1 Explanation of major terms used in the chapter

Term	Explanation
Encryption technologies	These technologies transform text or data into a coded form that is close to impossible to read without the key to decode the message. This scrambling of the message is done by using a mathematical formula
ICTs[a]	These include telecommunications as well as digital technologies such as telephony, cable, satellite, radio, computers, information networks, and software
Negative asymmetry[b]	A difference an adversary is likely to use to exploit a weakness or vulnerability
National security	"Measures taken by a state to ensure its survival and safety". "Includes the deterrence of attack, from within and without, as well as the protection and well-being of citizens"[c]
Positive asymmetry[b]	Capitalizing on differences to gain an advantage.
Steganography[d]	A technique that allows hiding messages within pictures, music, and other media. Steganography can be used with or without encryption. It is, however, of limited use without encryption
Symmetric advantage[b]	The advantage that can result from matching the opponent in terms of strategic resources
Strategic asymmetry[b]	Employing "some sort of differences to gain an advantage over an adversary." It could be real as well as perceived
The Gramm-Leach-Bliley Act[e]	The Gramm-Leach-Bliley Act of 1999 went into effect in July 2002. It mandates that all financial institutions establish procedures for protecting personal information, including the protection of discarded information. Financial penalties and civil suits may result from the inadvertent disclosure of personal information
The USA Patriot Act[f]	The USA Patriot Act was enacted on October 26, 2001 to expand the intelligence gathering and surveillance powers of law-enforcement and national security agencies

[a]See "Glossary of Terms," http://cyber.law.harvard.edu/readinessguide/glossary.html (accessed 16 October 2009).
[b]Metz (2001) and Metz and Johnson (2001).
[c]See http://en.wikipedia.org/wiki/National_security (accessed 16 October 2009).
[d]Maney (2001) and Hernandez, Sierra, and Ribagorda (2004).
[e]http://www.allshredservices.com/faq/grammleachbliley.htm
[f]Young (2004).

the planning phase of the Mumbai attacks in 2008 in India, the attackers were using VoIP for communications (Aggarwal, 2009). The Internet as well as non-Internet ICTs such as wireless telephony, satellite TV, satellite phones, and supercomputers can be employed in the management of asymmetries (see Table 6.2).

In the history of warfare, there are several examples of strategic uses of asymmetric technologies that have provided "a decisive advantage over an opponent in combat" (Rosenberger, 2005). The Maxim Machine-Gun adopted by the British Army in 1889 is a good example of an asymmetric technology. A Maxim gun could fire 500 rounds per minute—equivalent to that of 100 rifles at that time. In the 1893–1894 Matabele war, 50 British soldiers with just four Maxim guns fought off 5,000 Matabele warriors (spartacus UD). Similarly, asymmetric technologies used by the US Army include cruise missiles, laser-guided bombs, satellite reconnaissance systems, high-altitude reconnaissance aircraft, and unmanned aerial vehicles (Rosenberger, 2005).

The example of a strategic disruption of the enemy's communications technology goes back at least to the mid-19th century in the American Civil War. On October 4, 1862, for example, a landing party from Thomas Freeborn, a steamer acquired by the Union Navy, cut the telegraph lines stretching from Occoquan and Fredericksburg to Richmond, Virginia (The Economist, 2008a). Likewise, in the Russo-Japanese War of 1904–1905, the Russian navy used radio jamming to block and frustrate the Japanese Military's communications.

Consistent with history and theory, organizations and nations have spotted opportunities to employ ICTs to gain and exploit asymmetric advantages and to counter asymmetric weaknesses. For instance, in the Iraq War, powerful ICT tools such as *Analyst's Notebook* allowed US investigators to convert huge amount of data into actionable intelligence. The intelligence helped to track the wanted Iraqis. *Analyst's*

Table 6.2 A classification of strategic asymmetry by type of ICTs and type of deployment: Some examples

		Type of deployment	
		Direct use in war	Facilitating functions contributing to attack and defense
Type of ICTs	Internet	• Cyberattacks on critical infrastructures	• Communications (e.g., Al Qaeda's encrypted e-mails; the attackers in the Mumbai attacks in 2008 used VoIP for their planning and communications) • Detection of threats from enemies (smart containers in US customs)
	Non-Internet ICTs	• Use of satellite phones to coordinate war plans (e.g., by Al Qaeda)	• Use of supercomputers to model nuclear explosions and to simulate the forces acting on a missile

Notebook also helped to trace the creator of "love bug" computer virus of 2000 (Yousafzai & Hirsh, 2004). The US military and intelligence officials are using the same technology to track Al Qaeda's network. Al Qaeda's network, on the other hand, has been reportedly using symmetric and asymmetric technologies[1] including satellite phones, the Internet, and advanced encryption methods to recruit followers; raise money; formulate plans and operations; and to communicate securely (see Box 6.1).

Box 6.1 Al Qaeda's Amazingly Advanced Internet Network

Experts believe critical US infrastructures such as energy, transportation, water, and telecomm are highly susceptible to Al Qaeda's cyberattacks. In the early 2004, Dan Verton, a former intelligence officer, told a Senate subcommittee that one of the goals of Al Qaeda is to overthrow the US economy by penetrating the computer networks of major companies. Although no cyberattack has yet been traced to Al Qaeda, this outfit's network use has been amazingly sophisticated.

Family influence played an important role in Osama bin Laden's fascination with modern technologies (Coll, 2008; *The Economist,* 2008b). A July 1999 article published *in Christian Science Monitor* reported that Al Qaeda's Egyptian members helped establish a secure communications network based on the Internet, e-mail, and electronic bulletin boards for its members to exchange information. According to an article published *in San Francisco Chronicle* on October 6, 2001, Al Qaeda has recruited talented software engineers to achieve its Internet ambition. It is reported that Al Qaeda followers are acquiring skills in operating computers, and Internet connections though satellite (Nance, 2008).

Al Qaeda has been among the earliest adopters of encryption technologies, which employ mathematical formulae to scramble data for secure transmission of information on the Internet. According to the former CIA director George Tenet, these technologies have enabled the organization to formulate plans, strategies, and operations; to recruit followers; spread the network; and to raise fund.

US officials have reported that Bin Laden followers got encryption trainings at camps in Afghanistan and Sudan. A convicted conceiver of the 1993 World Trade Center bombing, for instance, used encryption software to hide the details of his plans to destroy 11 US airliners. Similarly, a suspect in the bombings of US embassies in Kenya and Tanzania in 1998 reportedly sent encrypted e-mails to several recipients. Investigators believe that encryption might have played a key role in the September 11, 2001 attack in the United States.

Al Qaeda's integration of encryption with advanced applications such as steganography has been a real challenge to US counterterrorism officials. The use of steganography software file has helped them hide plaintext messages within a wide range of media such as pictures, music, MP3 files, sports chat rooms, and pornographic bulletin boards. Most impressive of all, Al Qaeda has created "self-starting jihad," an Internet-based campaign to inspire and educate its followers (Nance, 2008). Michael (2009, p. 147) observed: "The Internet is an integral part of al-Qaeda's strategy."

6.2 Strategic Asymmetry and ICTs

True examples of strategic asymmetry are arguably very rare. Experts say that strategic asymmetries are created by combining technological, operational, as well as tactical innovations (Meigs, 2003). Metz and Johnson (2001) have identified six forms of asymmetry: method, technology, will, morale, organization, and patience.

From a terrorist organization's standpoint, cyber-terrorism has some advantages over physical methods. First, cyber-terrorism can be conducted remotely and anonymously. Unlike in the traditional warfare, it is almost impossible to identify the attacker in the IT warfare. Second, cyber-terrorism is cheaper to carry out as it does not require the handling of explosives or a suicide mission. Finally, due to the novelty, journalists and the public are likely to be fascinated by computer attacks. Cyber-terrorism may thus perform better in attracting media coverage than conventional warfare (Denning, p. 281).

At the same time, compared to physical warfare, cyber-terrorism is less effective in some aspects. Note that terrorists want to maximize damages (Harvard Law Review, 2006). Complexity of networks and systems means that it may be harder to control cyberattacks once they are launched. It is also hard to achieve the level of damage that is desired. Since there is no injury, death, or physical harm, cyber-terrorism do not create strong emotional appeal and drama (Denning, 2003, p. 282). Finally, as long as terrorists see their existing techniques are working, they may be unwilling to try new methods such as cyberattacks (Hoo, Goodman, & Greenberg, 1997).

To maximize positive asymmetries and to minimize vulnerabilities of negative asymmetries, the category of asymmetric strategic means should be such that the adversary cannot effectively counter. This is especially important for asymmetries that are deliberately created than those that arise by default.

At this point, it must be emphasized that only "desperate antagonists" depend solely on ICT-created or other types of asymmetric methods (Metz, 2001). Military theorists and empiricists have presented evidence which indicates that integrated approaches that appropriately combine symmetric and asymmetric methods are more likely to give intended results and to defeat adversaries (Metz, 2001). In particular, given the limitations of ICTs, approaches that combine non-ICT and ICT tools are more effective. For this reason, defense analysts argue that large and powerful nations such as China and Russia pose the most severe threats to the United States because of their technology advanced research (Bridis, 2001) as well as capabilities to combine ICTs with non-ICT resources. It is argued that a cyberattack coordinated with physical attacks could compound the fallout by "disrupting communications, distracting the government response, and exacerbating the psychological damage from terrorism" (Harvard Law Review, 2006).

Before proceeding further, it is important to understand the concepts of positive and negative asymmetries associated with ICTs. ICT deployments by terrorist groups, nations, and individuals involve some forms of positive and negative asymmetries. Positive asymmetry entails capitalizing on differences to gain an advantage.[1] For instance, the US military combines training and leadership (non-ICT resources) with ICTs to gain and sustain its superiority (Metz, 2001). In the war in Afghanistan, special operations forces downloaded real-time video of Al Qaeda and Taliban forces, used GPS to mark the exact locations, and employed LASERS to bring smart bombs directly onto their positions.

Similarly, according to the US-China Economic and Security Review Commission report, Chinese military strategists have written openly about exploiting the vulnerabilities associated with the US military's reliance on ICTs and traditional infrastructure used to conduct operations (GAO Reports June 22, 2007). According to Al Santoli, editor of the *China Reform Monitor*, senior colonels of the Chinese military Qiao Liang and Wang Xiangsui (1999) in their book, *Unrestricted Warfare*, have argued that since China's People's Liberation Army (PLA) lacks resources to compete with the United States in conventional weapons, it should focus on the "development of new information and cyber war technologies and viruses to neutralize or erode an enemy's political, economic and military information and command and control infrastructures" (cf. Waller, 2000). The authors have urged on the development of a means of challenging the United States through asymmetry rather than matching the United States in terms of all types of resources (Waller, 2000). Some analysts suspect that the Chinese government has been using cyberattacks to break into the US Defense Department's and other US agencies' computers, which is code-named Titan Rain by federal investigators (Jesdanun, 2008). Speaking of cyberattacks originated from China and its growing cyberwarfare capabilities, David Sedney, US deputy assistant secretary of defense for East Asia noted: "the techniques that are used, the way these intrusions are conducted, are certainly very consistent with what you would need if you were going to actually carry out cyberwarfare, and the kinds of activities that are carried out are consistent with a lot of writings we see from Chinese military and Chinese military theorists" (World Tribune, 2008).

The United States considers cyberwarfare as one of the major asymmetric threats (Blank, 2004). Estimate suggested that 100–120 countries in the world are planning infowar capabilities and developing cyberattack strategies (Swartz, 2007;

Robertson, 2007). In response, US Defense Secretary Robert Gates initiated the creation of a new military cyber-command, which defends the Pentagon's networks and conducts cyberwarfare (Harris, 2009).

The US National Security Agency and some US observers believe that countries like China, Iran, Russia, and North Korea have developed computer attack capabilities, trained hackers in Internet warfare, and are systematically probing the computer networks in the United States to find weaknesses that can be exploited (Bickers, 2001; Lenzner & Vardi, 2004). Although most are currently only testing cyberattack tools to determine the risks involved, experts argue that serious international cyberattacks may occur in the future (Robertson, 2007). Some analysts observe that cyberattacks on the United States by China have been "frequent and aggressive" (Reid, 2007). It is suggested that there may be over 60,000 cyber-war fighters in China's PLA (Bronk, 2009). Likewise, it is estimated that North Korea has a cyber-military unit, which employs about 1,000 skilled hackers (Sudworth, 2009). The US Central Intelligence Agency has also identified two terrorist organizations that possess the capability and have the greatest possibility to use cyberattacks against the US infrastructures (GAO Reports June 22, 2007).

Not only nations and terrorists but also individuals are employing modern ICTs strategically to gain asymmetric advantages. In 2003, a Pakistani medical transcriber working for a US-based medical centre threatened to post confidential voice files and patient records on the Internet if her pay was not increased. In this example, the transcriber took advantages of the differences in normative institutions (e.g., the medical center's obligation to maintain patients' privacy in the United States) and regulative institutions (e.g., a potential threat of lawsuit for failing to protect patients' information).

Negative asymmetry involves "an opponent's threat to one's vulnerabilities" (Metz, 2001). It is important to note that vulnerability has two dimensions: objective and subjective (Busetta & Milito, 2009; Zombori, 2001). The objective vulnerability is related to political, social, economic, and demographic characteristics of an entity that determine the vulnerability to cyberattacks. The subjective vulnerability refers to an entity's self-perception related to the risk of becoming a cyberattack victim. It is also important to note that an individual's or an organization's vulnerability is determined by the personal or organizational characteristics as well as the contexts provided by "higher" level institutions and exogenous parameters (Busetta & Milito, 2009; Snidal, 1994, 1996).

Organizations and nations are employing ICTs strategically to minimize vulnerabilities associated with negative asymmetry. For instance, Al Qaeda reportedly uses powerful encryption technologies to support its operations. According to a *USA Today* article (Maney, 2001), Al Qaeda is also using more advanced and sophisticated technologies such as steganography to hide messages within pictures, music, and other media. A plaintext message with or without encryption is hidden in a picture or MP3 file using a steganography software file. These technologies have helped Al Qaeda members to communicate without a major risk of being caught by US counterterrorism organizations. Similarly, a suspect in the bombings of the

US embassies in Kenya and Tanzania in 1998 reportedly sent encrypted e-mails under various names (Kelley, 2001). Likewise, a convicted mastermind of the World Trade Center bombing in 1993 used encryption software to hide details of his plan to destroy 11 US airliners. To take yet another example of ICTs' use to minimize vulnerabilities associated with negative asymmetry, consider the Israeli Defense Force's attack into Gaza in the early 2009. Israeli networks experienced a massive distributed DoS attacks (Bucci & Steven, 2009).

6.3 Institutional and Organizational Factors Linked with Positive and Negative Asymmetries

Table 6.3 summarizes how institutional and organizational factors may be linked with positive and negative asymmetries associated with ICTs. The relationships are expressed in terms of dependent and independent variables. In the first two relations, potential positive and negative asymmetries created by business models are dependent variables and regulative legitimacy to such models is an independent variable. In the last six relations, positive and negative asymmetries are dependent variables and constructs, which are related to institutional and organizational factors as independent variables. As indicated in Table 6.3 some of the relations are specific to certain deploying units such as a government and a criminal group. Table 6.4 explains these relationships in more details with some examples.

Table 6.3 How institutional and organizational factors linked with positive and negative asymmetries

	Construct	Positive(+)/negative(−) asymmetry created by ICTs	Measures to deal with vulnerability to negative asymmetry
1	Lack of regulative legitimacy to business model (DV)	Government/citizen (−) (IV)	
2	Lack of regulative legitimacy to business model (DV)	A nation's adversary (+) (IV)	
3	Lack of strong rules of law (IV)	Cyber-criminal (+) (DV)	
4	Strength of normative legitimacy (IV)	(+) DV	(+) DV
5	Perception of ICT-related security threats (IV)	Governments (+) (DV)	Governments (+) (DV)
6	Economic development of a nation (IV)	Governments (+) (DV)	(+) (DV)
7	Higher dependence on digital technologies (IV)	(−) (DV)	
8	Anonymity functions (IV)	(+) (DV)	

Note: IV, independent variable; DV, dependent variable.

Table 6.4 Some sources of ICT-led asymmetries

Source of asymmetry	Explanation	Remarks/examples
Institutions		
Regulatory	• Strength of the rule of laws • Laws to minimize vulnerability to negative asymmetries • Laws directed toward minimizing symmetric advantages of adversaries	• The lack of laws against cyberattacks and the lack of existence of enforcement mechanisms increase positive asymmetries of cyber-criminals • The Patriot act in the United States and China's regulation regarding encryption software • Laws dealing with the export of encryption products (also COCOM restriction)
Normative	• Social obligations • Professional obligations	• ACLU in the US • Honker Union (Red Hackers) of China
Cognitive	• Perception of threat • Perception of adversaries' capability	• China's interpretation of military security associated with ICT import • Chinese military's interpretation of US Army's ability to assimilate ICTs in warfare
Adopting/deploying units		
Capability and rank effect	• Some adopting units are better able to assimilate ICTs than other	• Japan has planned to introduce passports with chips containing biometrics. Developing countries are less capable to take such measures
Vulnerability to attack	• Computer networks of some organizations are more vulnerable to attack	• Financial agencies, online casinos, and e-commerce websites are more likely to be attacked
Compatibility with ICTs	• Some business models are more compatible with ICTs' nature	• Al Quaeda's secure e-mail communications

6.3.1 Institutions, ICTs, and National Security

Institutionalists have recognized that success of an innovation to perform a particular function (e.g., defense and attack) is tightly linked to the context provided by institutions (Storper & Walker, 1989; Sabel & Zeitlin, 1997). Various asymmetries to a unit arise by default because of the nature of the institutions in which the unit is embedded. In particular, institutions in a country influence the equation of national choice in terms of priority and combinations of technologies employed to defend the people and to attack enemies.

In Chap. 3, we discussed Scott's (1995, 2001) three broad categories of institutions—regulative, cognitive, and normative (see Table 6.4). These components influence institutional preference for employing ICTs to create positive and negative asymmetries. Each set has corresponding legitimacy concerns. Let's take a look at each of the components in turn.

6.3.1.1 Regulative Institutions

First, there are international differences in terms of laws to minimize vulnerability to several forms of negative asymmetries. The US government, for instance, requires commercial banks to secure their networks. The *Patriot Act* and the *Gramm Leach Bliley (GLB) Act* (Table 6.1) require new security measures including customer identification and privacy protection. Notwithstanding the existence of similar regulations for a long time, the *Patriot Act* reflected a change in the banking landscape. These laws are expected to enhance domestic security against terrorism.

To take another example, China's regulation requires companies to reveal the type of encryption software they use for protecting confidential information sent over the Internet, as well as the name, phone number, and e-mail address of every employee using such software. To take yet another example, following September 11, 2001 attacks, the United States has enacted legislations that have resulted in increased electronic surveillance and the ability of Federal agencies to intercept Internet traffic.

Corporations are also facing regulatory pressures to change their business models so as to minimize real and perceived vulnerabilities of negative asymmetry. For instance, Microsoft was forced to open Windows XP, Windows 2000, and other systems programs to government technical security experts of several countries including those of Russia, Britain, the United States, and China.

Second, nations across the world differ in terms of laws directed toward maintaining positive asymmetries. For instance, until the late1990s, the US government did not allow domestic companies to export encryption products with keys of more than 40 bits. Feeling pressure from domestic technology companies, the Clinton Administration, however, allowed exports of 56-bit products and even stronger ones with government permission. Many terrorist groups, nevertheless, can buy encryption software in countries that lack such laws. For instance, encryption devices that Al Qaeda network reportedly uses are commercially available in several countries.

Some laws are directed toward specific sources of threat. In the 1980s, national security concerns from the United States and its allies in the form of a Coordinating Committee for Multilateral Export Security (COCOM), for instance, put restriction on high-technology exports to countries such as China and Soviet Union. Before 1996, China had been denied access to high-performance computers. Despite the disbandment of COCOM in 1994, the US law still restricts the sales of computers that exceed specified performance limits.

Powerful supercomputers can be used to model nuclear explosions and can simulate the forces acting on a missile from launch to impact. These supercomputers thus enable nations to develop nuclear weapons without explosive testing. The United States was concerned that access to powerful supercomputer would allow China, Soviet Union, and their allies to gain and combine symmetric and asymmetric methods. Before 1996, China experienced a series of failures in its attempt to launch satellites. Following COCOM disbandment, China was able to acquire over 600 high-performance computers from US companies during 1996–1998, with the approval of the Department of Commerce.

Third, nations across the world differ in terms of regulative institutions that help to create positive asymmetry and deal with negative asymmetry. Although criminals in general are emboldened if laws are weak, a much higher degree of jurisdictional arbitrage is available in digital crimes. Many developing economies have no laws prohibiting such crimes. Some nations that have enacted laws against computer crimes, on the other hand, lack enforcement mechanisms.

Likewise, too weak state (Varese, 2002), inefficient police, and weak cybercrime laws (Onlinecasinonews.com, 2004) have provided a fertile ground for Russian Mafia's digital world. In 2000, three alleged members of the Russia-based HangUp Team, which released Berbew and Webber viruses in 2003, were arrested for attacking two local computer networks, but were released with suspended sentences (Grow & Bush, 2005). Experts also argue that law-enforcement officials in countries like China and Russia do not take major actions against hackers attacking international websites and are more interested in protecting national security (Blau, 2004; Vardi, 2005). Weak rule of laws bolsters the morale of criminals or produces morale asymmetry (Metz & Johnson, 2001).

6.3.1.2 Normative Institutions

Normative institutions are concerned with procedural legitimacy and require individuals and organizations to embrace socially accepted norms and behaviors. National governments and terrorist organizations differ on acceptable norms and behaviors. Pointing out vulnerabilities of unprotected wireless networks in hospitals, for instance, Verton (2003) illustrates how a terrorist sitting in a car in a hospital parking lot can change medical records (e.g., information about blood type) resulting in patients receiving wrong blood types. National governments, on the other hand, are less likely to prescribe such behavior toward civilians.

As we discussed earlier, normative institutions represent obligations and norms in different sections of societies. In some cases, organizations are likely to face several dimensions of obligatory and prescriptive pressures (e.g., from customers, special interest groups, governments, etc.) that are contradictory in nature. For instance, consider the deployment of biometrics technologies. Commercial banks in the United States are experiencing the powerful emotional impact following the incident of September 11, 2001. They do not want to be branded as Al Qaeda's bank (McGeer, 2002). Deployment of biometric technologies can minimize the possibility of banking transactions with terrorists. Investment in biometric thus reduce bank's vulnerabilities associated with negative asymmetry.

At the same time, obligations to protect privacy have hindered the deployment of biometric technologies in these banks. The United States and European countries, for instance, have different views on privacy protection. In the United States, it is argued that identification systems based on face-recognition technology pose civil liberty threats (Johnson, 2004). The US banks feel more obligated to protect personal privacy of their patrons than their European counterparts. For this reason, US banks are slower to adopt biometric products in a range of services. Most European Union (EU) nations, on the other hand, have included biometric fingerprints in national drivers' licenses.

In 2003, 14 US states had bills related to biometrics, but many of them were not passed because of privacy concerns. As discussed above, non-profit organizations can use social obligation requirements to induce certain behavior. In the US, the lobbying and efforts of organizations like the *American Civil Liberties Union* (ACLU) played key roles in the failure of the bills.[2]

Professional organizations such as the Honker Union of China (or the Red Hackers)[3] also provide normative legitimacy to web attacks. For instance, consider Red Hackers' reaction to accidental bombing of the Embassy of the People's Republic of China in Belgrade, Yugoslavia on May 7, 1999 by a US warplane.

6.3.1.3 Cognitive Institutions

Cognitive institutions are associated with culturally supported habits and exert subtle influences on ICT deployment for proactive security, defense, and protection efforts. Political elites of some nations have realized that they have militarily fallen behind and are employing the Internet to create strategic asymmetry. Russian political and military leaders think that they are losing the cyber-space war to the US during 1991–2001, Moscow circulated among the members of the UN Security Council drafts of a possible arms-control treaty for cyber-space (Adams, 2001).

In addition, Chinese government also suspects that it is under cyberattack from the United States. There has been a deep-rooted perception among Chinese policy makers that Microsoft and the US government spy on Chinese computer users through secret "back doors" in Microsoft products. Computer hardware and software imported from the United States and its allies are subject to detailed inspection. Chinese technicians take control of such goods and either resist or closely monitor if Western experts install them (Adams, 2001). Chinese cryptographers reportedly found an "NSA Key" in Microsoft products, which was interpreted as the National Security Agency. The key allegedly provided the US government back-door access to Microsoft Windows 95, 98, N-T4, and 2000. Although Microsoft denied such allegation and even issued a patch to fix the problem, the Chinese government has not been convinced.

As mentioned earlier, cognitive institutions influence the way people view the reality that surrounds them and the frames through which they make meanings. For instance, consider Chinese military's assessment of US military's capability to assimilate ICTs in warfare. The authors of *Unrestricted Warfare*, for example, have observed that the US Army is too focused on "weapons whose immediate goal is to kill and destroy" and may not be well-equipped in assimilating ICTs in the warfare (Waller, 2000).

6.3.2 Ability to Create Positive Asymmetry and Minimize Vulnerabilities of Negative Asymmetry

Nations and organizations differ in terms of their capability to deploy ICTs to create positive asymmetry and minimize vulnerabilities of negative asymmetry (see Table 6.4).

6.3.2.1 The Rank Effect

ICT deployment for national security tends to diffuse from more advanced to less advanced nations. This is known as the *rank effect* (Gotz, 1999). For instance, currently deployment of anti-fraud technologies is limited to a small elite group of businesses.

The US military officials are seeking to enhance the country's cyberwarfare capabilities. To do so, they are looking beyond defending the Internet and are developing ways to launch virtual attacks on enemies. Lt. Gen. Robert J. Elder Jr., the head of the Air Force's cyberoperations command noted that initial uses are likely to be in "diverting or killing data packets that threaten the nation's systems" (Jesdanun, 2008).

Similarly Japan introduced passports with chips containing biometrics information in 2005 and also is assessing whether to make use of such technology to screen foreign visitors. In the United States, there are a number of automated entry systems to address a wide range of immigration situations, such as vehicular or pedestrian traffic along the Canadian and Mexican borders, or arrivals at international airports (Baron, 1997).

Whereas industrialized countries are rapidly adopting ICTs to create positive asymmetries and to counter asymmetric threats, most developing countries are characterized by lack of resources and inefficient institutions, which hamper the deployment of such measures. Consider, for instance, strategic uses of ICTs in customs organizations to detect and respond to national security threats. To minimize container-oriented terror events, some developed countries have transformed their customs organizations (Lane, 2005). One such example is the deployment of smart containers that use electronic seals, sensors, and GPS systems to record containers' movements. These technologies alert law-enforcement authorities in case of suspicious activities (Gillis & McHugh, 2002, p. 33). The Smart and Secure Tradelanes Pilot Program already employs smart containers using radio frequency identification devices (RFID), GPS, electronic seals, and other Internet-based technologies[4] (McHugh & Damas, 2002). Although some developing economies such as China and Peru are modernizing their customs infrastructure (Lane, 2005), most are far from ready to deploy advanced ICTs in their customs organizations.

Developing countries' lack of resources to enforce laws also hampers their ability to create ICT-related positive asymmetries and deal with negative asymmetries. For instance, according to laws enacted in Pakistan in the early 2000s, Internet cafés were required to check their clients' identity cards (Fisher, 2002) and Internet users were not allowed to use encryption technology. Nonetheless, these laws had been largely ignored (World IT Report, 2003).

Beyond all that small, less developed countries are less likely to be included in international cybercrime efforts. For instance, as of 2007, to address problems related to international jurisdiction, investigation, and prosecution, the US Department of Justice (DOJ) and the US State Department had agreements with about 40 nations through the G-8 High Tech Crime Working Group (United States Government Accountability Office, 2007). This means that the United States did not have such agreements with about 180 countries by that time.

6.3.2.2 Degree of Dependence on Digital Technologies

Adopting and deploying units also differ in terms of the degree of vulnerability of negative asymmetries. Businesses with a high dependence on digital technologies— such as online casinos, banks, and e-commerce hubs—are the most likely to fall victim to cyberattacks (Kshetri, 2005). A high dependence on digital technologies is a weakness that adversaries can exploit. Garner (1997, p. 1) observed

> Perhaps nowhere is our vulnerability to asymmetric technologies greater than in our relentless pursuit of information superiority. Our vulnerability lies in the realization that the more proficient we become at collecting, processing, displaying and disseminating relevant, accurate information to aid decision makers, the more dependent we become on that capability and therefore the more lucrative a target. (cf. Thomas, 1999)

To some extent, rank effect discussed in the previous section also holds true for vulnerabilities to threat. Cyberattacks, for instance, are more likely to be targeted to developed countries with large networks such as the United States than developing countries. Libicki (2009, p. 70) observed: "The US economy and society are heavily networked; so is its military. The attacker, by contrast, may have no targets of consequence, either because it is not particularly digitized, because its digital assets are not networked to the outside world, or because such assets are not terribly important to its government." Likewise, Dan Verton, the author of *Black Ice: The Invisible Threat of Cyberterrorism* told a Senate subcommittee in the early 2004 that one of the goals of Al Qaeda is "to topple the US economy by breaking encryption algorithms and infiltrating the technological systems of major corporations."

6.3.2.3 Compatibility with ICTs

The experience and business models of some organizations are more compatible (Rogers, 1983, 1995) with modern ICTs and for this reason they are more likely to benefit from digital technology. Because of the anonymity features of modern ICT tools such as the Internet, it is almost impossible to identify the attacker in ICT warfare. The encryption technology has further reinforced the effect. Thanks to ICTs' anonymity, some sources of malicious activities have been able to enjoy a higher degree of positive asymmetry. Victims may not know whether an attacker is a teenager, a terrorist group, a rival company, or a foreign government. For instance, in 2000, a hacker reportedly accessed software blueprints at Microsoft. Detectives believed the hacker used software from Asia and transferred data to an anonymous e-mail account in Russia (Bridis, 2001). In the Storm Cloud case,[5] US officials were not able to identify with certainty whether the source was a foreign government or a hacking group (Bridis, 2001). To take another example, in the late 2003 and early 2004, the FBI and National Hi-Tech Crime units discovered that computer hackers employed by Russian mafia launched a DOS attack on Worldpay[6] System that affected thousands of online casinos.

The online anonymous communication environment has also provided terrorists with opportunities to escape from laws, social obligations, and taboos; and express whatever they want. In this way, terrorists are using the Internet to tell their "story" directly to the public thus bypassing traditional media. To take an example, Al Qaeda transmitted videos of *Wall Street Journal* reporter Daniel Pearl's execution on the Internet (Hirsh, 2002).

There have also been instances of the uses of encryption software for controversial and illegal purposes. In 1996, a European Commission Communication identified some areas of risk in using encryption on the Internet, including national security risks (e.g., instructions on making bombs, illegal drug production, etc.) (Price, 1999).

The anonymity feature of ICTs, however, is a double-edged sword. The Internet's anonymity has made it possible for law-enforcement authorities to track and capture some sources of malicious activities. According to a June 2001 indictment by a US federal grand jury, two Russian hackers allegedly broke into computer systems of US banks and e-commerce sites in 10 states; stole thousands of credit card numbers and threatened the victim firms that they would not stop unless they were hired as security consultants. The anonymity feature also allowed US FBI agents to pretend as executives of an e-commerce company. They brought the hackers to the United States for job interviews and arrested (Stone, 2001).

6.4 Concluding Comments

This chapter has shed some lights on positive and negative asymmetries associated with ICTs. Such asymmetries are functions of characteristics of nations, organizations, individuals, and institutions. Libicki (2009, p. 70) observes: "Perfectly symmetric warfare does not exist, particularly when the United States is involved. Yet cyberwarfare may be more asymmetric than most."

Experts say that cyber-terrorism, which can be considered as "the marriage of terrorism and cyberspace" has been relatively absent in the world (Gabrys, 2002). Although negative asymmetries created by ICTs cannot be completely eliminated, they can, at least, be lessened (Metz, 2001). The world will be more secure if measures are taken at various levels to minimize vulnerabilities associated with negative asymmetries. These asymmetries are related to direct or first degree threats ranging from simple viruses to sophisticated cyber-terrorism, and indirect or second degree threats such as use of ICTs for secure communication by terrorists.

Finally, international competitiveness of a nation in the digital age is a function of its capability to ensure national security. Various sources of positive and negative asymmetries discussed in this chapter provide insight into the ICT-national security nexus.

Notes

1. Nemets and Torda (2001) report that Russian organized crime groups were supplying nuclear, biological, and chemical warfare technologies as well as other sophisticated asymmetric technologies to Al Qaeda in exchange of Afghan heroin.
2. See Bank Technology News (2003). Security: Biometrics takes hold overseas: Significant hurdles remain to adoption in the US 16(12) (December): 10.
3. The "Red Hacker Alliance" is arguably the largest and earliest hacking group in China. An estimate suggested that it had 20,000 hackers in 2005, which has about 80,000 registered members at the peak (crime-research.org, 2005).
4. Also see "Material handling news article" http://www.mhmonline.com/nID/2957/MHM/viewStory.asp.
5. The "Storm Cloud" is a US spy investigation case. During 1998–2000, hackers that were traced back to Russia allegedly downloaded a huge mass of sensitive data that included one colonel's entire e-mail inbox and hacked the US Defense Department computers, among others (Bridis, 2001).
6. Online casinos rely on Worldpay to process customer's transactions and pay off gamblers (Walker, 2004).

References

Adams, J. (2001, May/June). Virtual defense. *Foreign Affairs, 98–112.*

Aggarwal, V. (2009, August 3). Lead: Cyber crime's rampant. *Express Computer.* http://www.expresscomputeronline.com/20090803/market01.shtml. (Accessed 22 October 2009).

Baron, W. R. (1997, Spring). Volpe engineers use biometrics to help ease border crush. *Volpe Journal,* available at: http://www.volpe.dot.gov/infosrc/journal/spring97/biomet.html (Accessed 22 October 2009).

Bickers, C. (2001, August 16). Combat on the Web. *Far Eastern Economic Review, 30–33.*

Blank, S. (2004). Rethinking the concept of asymmetric threats in US strategy. *Comparative Strategy, 23*(4/5), 343–367.

Blau, J. (2004, May 26). Russia – A happy haven for hackers. http://www.computerweekly.com/Article130839.htm

Bridis, T. (2001, June 27). E-Espionage rekindles cold-war tensions – US tries to identify hackers; millions of documents are stolen. *Wall Street Journal, A.18.*

Bronk, C. (2009). Time to move toward a more secure cyberspace. *World Politics Review.* http://www.worldpoliticsreview.com/article.aspx?id=4194

Bucci, C., & Steven, P. (2009). A most dangerous link. *US Naval Institute Proceedings, 135*(10), 38–42.

Busetta, A., & Milito, A. M. (2009). Socio-demographic vulnerability: The condition of Italian young people. *Social Indicators Research.* DOI 10.1007/s11205-009-9507-9.

Coll, S. (2008). *The Bin Ladens: An Arabian family in the American century.* New York: The Penguin Press.

crime-research.org. (2005, May 3). Red Hackers come back! http://www.crime-research.org/news/03.05.2005/1199. (Accessed 22 October 2007).

Denning, D. E. (2003). Chapter eight: Activism, hacktivism, and cyberterrorism: The internet as a tool for influencing foreign policy. In J. Arquilla & D. Ronfeldt (Eds.), *Networks and netwars: The future of terror, crime, and militancy*. Rand Corporation Monograph/Report MR-1382. http://www.rand.org/pubs/monograph_reports/MR1382/index.html. (Accessed 22 October 2008).

The Economist. (2008a, December 8). Marching off to cyberwar. *389*(8609), 20.

The Economist. (2008b). Between Allah and America. *387*(8575), 92–93.

English, L. P. (2005). Information quality: Critical ingredient for national security. *Journal of Database Management, 16*(1), 18–32.

Fisher, I. (2002, August 1). Cybercafe crackdown may trip up leering boys. *New York Times*.

Gabrys, E. (2002). The international dimensions of cyber-crime, Part 1. *Information Systems Security, 11*(4), 21–32.

GAO Reports. (2007, June 22). *Public and private entities face challenges in addressing cyber threats*. RPT-number: GAO-07-705.

Garner, J. M. (1997, March). Asymmetric niche warfare. *Phalanx*, 1.

Gillis, C., & McHugh, M. (2002, February). Bonner proposes 'smart box'. *American Shipper*, 33.

Gotz, G. (1999). Monopolistic competition and the diffusion of new technology. *The Rand Journal of Economics, 30*(4), 679–693.

Grow, B., & Bush, J. (2005, May 30). Hacker hunters. *Business Week*.

Harris, C. (2009, October 6). Making cyber-security a national priority. *Government Technology Magazine*. http://www.govtech.com/dc/articles/714308. (Accessed 22 October 2009).

Harvard Law Review. (2006, June). Note: Immunizing the Internet, Or: How I learned to stop worrying and love the worm, *119*, 2442.

Hernandez, J. C., Sierra, J. M., & Ribagorda, A. (2004). Beware of the security software. *Information Systems Security, 12*(6), 39–45.

Hirsh, M. (2002). Bush and the world. *Foreign Affairs, 81*(5), 18–44.

Hoo, K. S., Goodman, S., & Greenberg, L. (1997). Information technology and the terrorist threat. *Survival, 39*(3), 135–155.

Jesdanun, A. (2008, April 6). US cyberwarfare prep includes offense. http://news.yahoo.com/s/ap/20080406/ap_on_hi_te/cyberwarfare. (Accessed 22 October 2009).

Johnson, M. L. (2004, April). Biometrics and the threat to civil liberties. *Computer*, 90–93.

Kelley, J. (2001, February 5). Terror Groups Hide Behind Web Encryption, USA Today, http://www.usatoday.com/tech/news/2001-02-05-binladen.htm. Accessed 20 March 2010.

Kshetri, N. (2005, May/June). Hacking the odds. *Foreign Policy*, 93.

Lane, M. (2005, February 2005). Customs reform and trade facilitation: An entrée to the global marketplace. *USAID*. http://tcb-fastrade.com/downloads/IP_Customs_Reform_S.pdf. (Accessed 22 October 2006).

Lenzner, R., & Vardi, N. (2004, September 20). The next threat. *Forbes*, 70.

Liang, Q., & Xiangsui, W. (1999, February). *Unrestricted warfare*. Beijing: PLA Literature and Arts Publishing House. http://www.terrorism.com/documents/TRC-Analysis/unrestricted.pdf. (Accessed 22 October 2004).

Libicki, M. C. (2009). Cyberdeterrence and cyberWar, a report prepared for the United States Air Force. *The RAND Corporation*. http://www.rand.org/pubs/monographs/2009/RAND_MG877.pdf. Accessed 27 October 2009.

Maltz, M. (2009,October 21). Turning power lines into battle lines. *The National Post*. http://network.nationalpost.com/np/blogs/fullcomment/archive/2009/10/21/milton-maltz-turning-power-lines-into-battle-lines.aspx (Accessed 22 October 2009).

Maney, K. (2001). Osama's messages could be hiding in plain sight. *USA Today*, B6.

McGeer, B. (2002). Security: Bankers fight a new battle it adjustments, purchases Part of Patriot Act. *Bank Technology News*, 15(11), 1.

McHugh, M., & Damas, P. (2002, November). Mega-port groups back security pilot. *American Shipper*, 14–18.

Meigs, M. C. (2003). Unorthodox thoughts about asymmetric warfare. *Parameters, 33*(2), 4–18.

Metz, S. (2001, July–August). Strategic asymmetry. *Military Review, 81*(4), 23–31.

Metz, S., & Johnson, D. V., II. (2001, January). *Asymmetry and US military strategy: Definition, background, and strategic concepts.* Carlisle Barracks, PA: US Army War College, Strategic Studies Institute.

Michael, G. (2009). Adam Gadahn and Al-Qaeda's internet strategy. *Middle East Policy, 16*(3), 135–152.

Nance, M. (2008, May/June). How (not) to spot a terrorist. *Foreign Policy, 166*, 74–76.

Nemets, A., & Torda, T. (2001, November 9). Interesting cards up Putin's sleeve: Russian sponsorship of international terrorism. *newsmax.com.* http://www.newsmax.com/archives/articles/2001/11/9/143709.shtml. (Accessed 22 October 2009).

Onlinecasinonews.com. (2004, February 3). Mob's extortion attempt on Internet bookies. http://www.onlinecasinonews.com/ocnv2_1/article/article.asp?id=4748. (Accessed 22 October 2005).

Price, S. A. (1999). Understanding contemporary cryptography and its wider impact upon the general law. *International Review of Law, Computers & Technology, 13*(2), 95–126.

Reid, T. (2007). China's cyber army is preparing to march on America, says Pentagon. http://technology.timesonline.co.uk/tol/news/tech_and_web/the_web/article2409865.ece. (Accessed 22 October 2008).

Robertson, J. (2007, November 30). China disputes report calling it a key cyber warfare instigator. *The Age,* http://news.theage.com.au/technology/china-disputes-report-calling-it-a-key-cyber-warfare-instigator-20071130-1dwx.html. Accessed 20 March 2010.

Rogers, E. M. (1983). *The diffusion of innovations* (3rd ed.). New York: Free Press.

Rogers, E. M. (1995). *The diffusion of innovations* (4th ed.). New York: Free Press.

Rosenberger, J. D. (2005). The inherent vulnerabilities of technology. *The Wargames Directory.* http://www.wargamesdirectory.com/html/articles/Various/technology.asp. (Accessed 22 October 2006).

Sabel, C., & Zeitlin, J. (eds.) (1997). *World of possibilities: Flexibility and mass production in western industrialization.* New York: Cambridge University Press.

Scott, W. R. (1995). *Institutions and organizations.* Thousand Oaks, CA: Sage.

Scott, W. R. (2001). *Institutions and organizations.* Thousand Oaks, CA: Sage.

Snidal, D. (1994). The politics of scope: Endogenous actors, heterogeneity and institutions. *Journal of Theoretical Politics, 6*(4), 449–472.

Snidal, D. (1996). Political economy and international institutions. *International Review of Law and Economics, 16*(1), 121–137.

Spartacus (UD) Spartacus educational, http://www.spartacus.schoolnet.co.uk/FWWmaximgun.htm. Accessed 22 October 2009.

Stone, B. (2001, July 16). Busting the web bandits. *Newsweek*, 55.

Storper, M., & Walker, R. (1989). *The capitalist imperative: Territory, technology and industrial growth.* London: Basil Blackwell.

Swartz, J. (2007, March 12). Chinese hackers seek US access; Attacks highlight weaknesses in Internet security. *USA Today*, 3B.

Sudworth, J. (2009). New 'cyber attacks' hit S Korea. *BBC News.* http://news.bbc.co.uk/2/hi/asia-pacific/8142282.stm. (Accessed 22 October 2009).

Thomas, T. L. (1999, September–October). Infosphere threats. *Military Review.* Posted on: Foreign Military Studies Office. http://fmso.leavenworth.army.mil/fmsopubs/issues/infosphere/infosphere.htm. (Accessed 22 October 2005).

United States Government Accountability Office. (2007). Cybercrime: Public and Private Entities Face Challenges in Addressing Cyber Threats: GAO-07-705, June. http://www.gao.gov/htext/d07705.html. (Accessed 22 October 2008).

Vardi, N. (2005, July 25). Chinese take out. *Forbes*, 54.

Varese, F. (2002). *The Russian Mafia: Private protection in a new market economy.* New York: Oxford University Press.

Verton, D. (2003). *Black ice: The invisible threat of cyberterrorism.* New York: McGraw-Hill/Osborne.

Walker, C. (2004, June). Russian Mafia Extorts Gambling Websites. http://www.americanmafia.com/cgi/clickcount.pl?url=www.americanmafia.com/Feature_Articles_270.html. (Accessed 22 October 2005).

Waller, J. M. (2000, February 28). PLA revises the art of war. *Insight on the News, 21–23.*

World IT Report. (2003, February 3). Pakistan faces difficulties to block porn sites.

World Tribune. (2008). Pentagon official: China may already be at cyberwar with US March 13. http://www.worldtribune.com/worldtribune/WTARC/2008/ea_china_03_13.asp. (Accessed 22 October 2009).

Young, J. (2004). BC attempts to regulate international outsourcing of personal information. *Deeth Williams Wall LLP.* http://www.dww.com/articles/bcpatriot_amendments.htm. (Accessed 22 October 2005).

Yousafzai, S., & Hirsh, M. (2004). The harder hunt for Bin Laden. *Newsweek*, December 29, 2003/January 5, 2004, 58.

Zhou, L. (2005). Special Issue: Database technology for enhancing national security. *Journal of Database Management, 16*(1), I–III.

Zombori, G. (2001, January 5). *e + Finance + Crime: A report on cyber-crime and money laundering.* Study of Organized Crime and Corruption, Osgoode Hall Law School, York University, Toronto, Ontario, Canada. http://www.yorku.ca/nathanson/Publications/e.htm. (Accessed 22 October 2009).

Chapter 7
Global Heterogeneity in the Pattern of the Cybercrime Industry

Why should an Indonesian get arrested for damaging [an] American business? (an Indonesian hacker, cf. Shubert, 2003).
"We are ready to devote anything to our motherland, including our lives," message left by Chinese hackers on several American websites in a 2001 cyber war with American hackers (cf. Smith, 2001).

Abstract This chapter draws upon literatures on psychology, economics, international relation, and warfare to propose a framework to explain international heterogeneity in cybercrimes. We found that countries across the world differ in terms of regulative, normative, and cognitive legitimacy to different types of web attacks. Cyber-wars and crimes are also functions of the stocks of hacking skills relative to the availability of economic opportunities. An attacking unit's selection criteria for the target network include symbolic significance and criticalness, degree of digitization of values, and weakness in defense mechanisms.

7.1 Introduction

Information and communications technologies (ICTs) have drastically increased the porosity among national borders and contributed to the growth of transnational organized crimes and an illicit global economy (Etges & Sutcliffe, 2008; Naím, 2005; Rosenau, 1995; Serio & Gorkin, 2003). The increased porosity and anonymity of the Internet have superimposed in a complex interaction that has enabled criminal and violent groups, transnational terrorist organizations, and companies engaged in espionage to expand their operations globally. Government-backed cyberwarfare in some countries (Comité Européen Des Assurances, 2004) and maverick hackers testing their skills have further threatened the security of the digital world. Commenting on a rapid rise of cybercrimes, McAfee analyst Greg Day notes, "Blackmail, money motivation and new opportunities cross international borders" (Muncaster, 2006). Hi-tech and cybercrimes are among Interpol's top six priorities

N. Kshetri, *The Global Cybercrime Industry*, DOI 10.1007/978-3-642-11522-6_7,
© Springer-Verlag Berlin Heidelberg 2010

(drugs and criminal organizations, tracking fugitives, public safety and terrorism, trafficking of human beings, and corruption are the other five) (Interpol, 2007).

Steffensmeier and Ulmer (2006) note, "the concept of criminal entrepreneurship ... implies that some groups are better endowed to exploit opportunities for illegal gain, whereas other groups may be weakly positioned to do so." Extending this line of reasoning at the institutional level, we can argue that institutions in some societies are likely to provide better payoffs and less political risk to cyber-criminals than others.

7.2 The Global Digital Security Threat: A Brief Survey

A large proportion of cyberattacks are international in scope (Tables 7.1 and 7.2). According to a report released by the FBI in January 2006, the agency tracked cyberattacks targeting the United States from 36 different countries (Regan, 2006). A 2002 survey of Australian firms indicated that 24% respondents perceived foreign governments as sources of attacks and 30% perceived foreign companies as such sources (Deloitte Touche Tohmatsu, 2002). In October 2009, largest Australian

Table 7.1 Top cybercrime sources (2002–2004)

Countries from which most online fraud originates[a]	Rank of countries according to percent of orders that US sites declared as fraudulent[b]	Rate of attacks per 10,000 Internet users (first-half 2004)[c]	Number of attacks per 10,000 Internet users (first-half 2002)[d]	Percent of total attacks (first-half 2002)[d]
Ukraine	Former Yugoslavia	Latvia	Kuwait (50.8)	USA (40)
Indonesia	Nigeria	Macau	Israel (33.1)	Germany (7.6)
Former Yugoslavia	Romania	Israel	Iran (30.8)	South Korea (7.4)
Lithuania	Pakistan	Australia	Peru (24.5)	China (6.9)
Egypt	Indonesia	Finland	Chile (24.4)	France (5.2)
Romania	Macedonia	Egypt	Nigeria (23.4)	Canada (3.0)
Bulgaria	Bulgaria	Turkey	Morocco (22.3)	Italy (2.7)
Turkey	Ukraine	Spain	Hong Kong (22.1)	Taiwan (2.4)
Russia	Lebanon	Canada	Puerto Rico (20.8)	UK (2.1)
Pakistan	Lithuania	Nigeria	France (19.9)	Japan (2.1)
Malaysia			Argentina (19.3)	
Israel			Belgium (17.6)	
			Romania (16.5)	

[a]International Fraud Watch (Online Fraud Stats http://www.ocalasmostwanted.com/online_fraud_stats.htm).
[b]Merchant Risk Council (Sullivan, 2004).
[c]Symantec (2004, p. 17).
[d]Riptech (2002).

Table 7.2 Top cybercrime sources (2007)

Top infection program creating countries in (2007)[a]	Top ten malware-hosting countries in (2007)[b]	Malicious activity per broadband user (second-half of 2007)[c]	Top ten countries for spam origin (second-half of 2007)[c]	Top countries hosting phishing websites (second-half of 2007)[c]	Top countries by perpetrators based on complaints made to I3C (second-half of 2007)[d]
The United States (35%)	China (51.4%)	Peru (9%)	The United States (40%)	The United States (66%)	The United States (63.2%)
China (30%)	The United States (23.4%)	The United States (7%)	The United Kingdom (5%)	China (14%)	The United Kingdom (15.3%)
Brazil (14.2%)	Russia (9.6%)	Poland (6%)	Russia (4%)	Romania (5%)	Nigeria (5.7%)
Russia (4.1%)	Ukraine (3.0%)	Argentina (6%)	China (4%)	Guam (5%)	Canada (5.6%)
Sweden (3.8%)	Germany (2.3%)	Israel (6%)	Poland (3%)	France (5%)	Romania (1.5%)
Ukraine (3.4%)	Poland (0.9%)	India (5%)	Taiwan (3%)	German (1%)	Italy (1.3%)
The United Kingdom and India Combined (1.3%)[e]	The United Kingdom (0.7%)	Taiwan (5%)	Japan (3%)	Italy (1%)	Spain (0.9%)
Germany (1%)	France (0.7%)	Chile (5%)	Germany (3%)	Canada (1%)	South Africa (0.9%)
	Canada (0.7%)	Canada (5%)	South Korea (3%)	Sweden (1%)	Russia (0.8%)
	Netherlands (0.7%)	Sweden (4%)	Spain (2%)	Netherlands (1%)	Ghana (0.7%)

[a]Greenberg (2007).
[b]sophos.com (2008).
[c]Symantec Internet Security Threat Report Vol. XIII, 2008.
[d]Internet Crime Complaint Center (2007) 2007 Internet Crime Report, http://www.ic3.gov/media/annualreport/2007_IC3Report.pdf
[e]Sophos' list. Both countries use British English. Sophos researchers could not be separate the countries but thought that the majority of that criminal activity came from the UK.

banks' representatives told a senate inquiry into cybercrime that 70% of phishing attacks to their customers originated outside Australia (Winterford, 2009).

The United States is the No. 1 country in terms of source as well as targets for web attacks. According to a *Foreign Policy* article (March/April, 2008), 61% of the world's DoS attacks targeted US-based computers. Likewise, one estimate suggested that 66.1% of Internet frauds occur in the United States (Datamonitor, 2009). Many cyber-criminals targeting US businesses and consumers operate outside of US jurisdiction (Grow & Bush, 2005; Hahn & Layne-Farrar, 2006).

The US share in the global cybercrime industry is decreasing rapidly. The proportion of attacks originated from the United States dropped from 58% in the second-half of 2003 to 37% in the first-half of 2004 (Symantec, 2004).

As noted in Chap. 1, a large number of cybercrimes result from international collaborations. A hacker accused of pirating DirecTV and EchoStar signals in Florida told law-enforcement authorities that he had received request from Afghanistan to provide hacking services (Lieberman, 2003). In the same vein, ShadowCrew, the international clearinghouse for stolen credit cards and identity documents, whose masterminds were arrested in the United States in the mid-2005, had 4,000 members in a number of countries including Bulgaria, Canada, Poland, Sweden, and the United States (Grow & Bush, 2005). Mohammad Khairuddin Abdullah, Malaysia's HeiTech Padu Berhad's director noted that Russian mafia and Japanese Yakuza have financially sponsored the country's cyber-criminals (Ismail, 2008).

Tables 7.1 and 7.2 rank the world's top nations in terms of cyberattacks and frauds on the Internet. One estimate suggests that in 2003, less than 1% of computer attacks originate in countries that the United States considers "breeding grounds for terrorists" (The Economist, 2003). Another estimate suggests that 60% of fraudulent transactions originate from just 15 nations (Table 7.1).

7.3 Pattern of the Global Cyber-War and Crime: A Proposed Model

Our proposed model on the pattern of global cyberattacks is presented in Fig. 7.1. Although the model entails different levels of analysis, it helps us understand the mechanisms connecting sources and targets. In this section, we briefly discuss building blocks of the model.

7.3.1 Characteristics of the Source Nation

7.3.1.1 Regulative Institutions: Strength of the Rule of Law

An issue that deserves mention relates to regulatory arbitrage. Economies worldwide vary greatly in terms of the legal systems related to cybercrimes. Moreover, legal systems take long time to change (Dempsey, 2008).

Prior research indicates that criminals avoid prosecution by using "clever regulatory arbitrage" (Levi, 2002, p. 905). Cyberattacks have tremendously benefited from

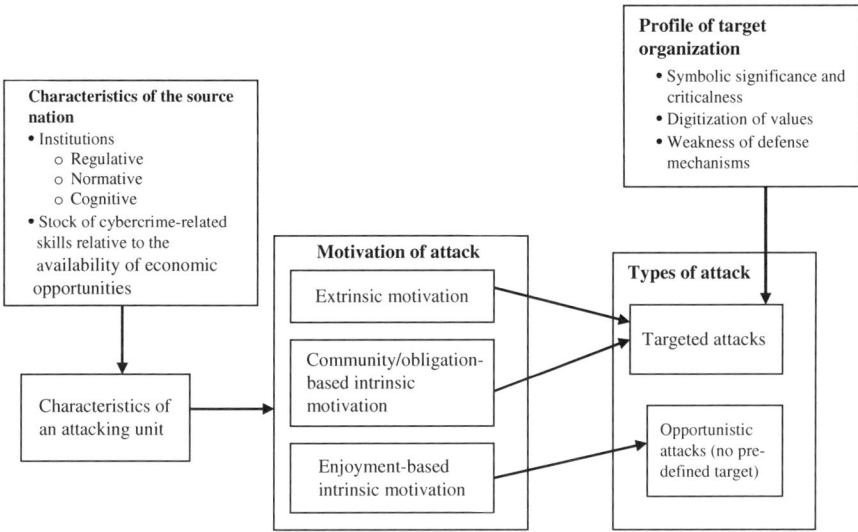

Fig. 7.1 Understanding the pattern of the global cyberattacks: a proposed framework

jurisdictional arbitrage. The lack of a strong rule of law is associated with the origination of cyberattacks (see Boxes 7.1 and 7.2). Not surprisingly, many organized cybercrimes are initiated from countries that have few or no laws directed against cybercrimes and little capacity and willingness to enforce existing laws (Grow & Bush, 2005; Williams, 2001; see Tables 7.1 and 7.2).

Box 7.1 Internet-led Globalization of Russian Organized Crime Group

The Internet can play a critical role in enhancing an organization's market reach and operational efficiency (Porter, 2001). Some organizations are more compatible (Rogers, 1983) with the Internet and hence are more likely to benefit from the increased reach and efficiency created by the digital technology. In particular, Mafia's work style and prior work experience seem to be compatible with the Internet.

The Mafia and the Internet

According to Diego Oambetta, the Mafia is a profit-focused firm selling private protection (1988, 130). Legal as well as illegal businesses in Russia were required to buy the dispute—resolution and contract-enforcement "services" of the mafia and to pay fees to protect their business and even to remain alive (Handelman, 1999; Varese, 2002). With rapid digitization of values and organizations' increased dependence on digital technology worldwide, mafia groups have realized huge financial potential of the Internet. In recent years, the Russian Mafia has developed expertise in cybercrime (Giannangeli, 2008).

Mafia groups have developed digital versions of bombings, murders, kidnappings, and hijackings. They carefully plan attacks in terms of the target, the time, and the amount of extortion. In most cases, they demand much less than the costs to repair a broken site (Walker, 2004). Many firms choose to comply with hackers' demand rather than taking the risk of attack and losing all customers and profits in one massive attack. The FBI found that in many cases extortions were paid off. For instance, online sports books, BETWWTS, reportedly paid Mafia extortionists thousands of dollars (Walker, 2004). Internet betting sites, financial institutions, and e-commerce firms are the red hot targets.

Hackers that attacked Internet betting sites before American football's Super Bowl in January 2004 were based in Eastern Europe and Russia (Onlinecasinonews.com, 2004). Online gambling websites are targeted due to the time-specific nature of services (Walker, 2004). In the late 2003 and early 2004, the FBI and National Hi-Tech Crime units discovered that computer hackers employed by Russian mafia launched a DOS attack[4] on Worldpay[5] System that affected thousands of online casinos.

Similarly, in January 2000, an unknown Russian hacker stole 300,000 credit card numbers from CD Universe and distributed 25,000 of them on a website after the US retailer refused to pay a $100,000 ransom (CNN.Com, 2000). The hacker claimed that he used some of the credit card numbers to get money. In 2001, FBI reported that 40 businesses in 20 US states were hit by hacker rings working in Russia and the Ukraine, and that more than a million credit card numbers had been stolen (Gomes & Bridis, 2001). The hacker issued blackmail threats, some of which exceeded $100,000 (Forensic Accounting Review and Computer Security Digest, 2001; Kshetri, 2005). FBI officials said many more companies might have been attacked without reporting the matter to authorities.

The Cybercrime Workforce

Russia has a highly educated workforce, programming skills, and a hacking friendly environment. Unavailability of other economic opportunities has forced educated computer wizards to work in the electronic underground. A self-described hacker from Moscow confessed to reporters, "Hacking is one of the few good jobs left here" (Walker, 2004). Specialized training schools teach hacking skills. Russian hackers perform sophisticated attacks with limited computer power and inexpensive software. Eighty-two percent of respondents participating in a worldwide poll conducted on a hacker-oriented website indicated that Russia had the world's best computer hackers. Only 5% of the respondents believed that American hackers were the best[6] (Walker, 2004).

Formal Institutions and Cybercrimes

The fragile property rights, too weak state (Varese, 2002), inefficient police, and weak cybercrime laws (Onlinecasinonews.com, 2004) have provided a fertile ground for Mafia's digital world. Although it is illegal under Russian law to hack into computer systems, few cases are prosecuted (Lorek, 2001). The police said most hackers are young and educated, work independently, and do not fit police profiles of criminals (Newpaper.asia1.com.sg, 2004).

Although Russia has signed an agreement to help the United States in investigating some crimes and computer crimes are not among them. In 2001, the US Department of Justice requested the assistance from Russian authorities, but there was no response (Lemos, 2001).

Box 7.2 Indonesia's Electronic Underground

Pervasive Credit Card Fraud in Indonesia

Credit card fraud has been pervasive in Indonesia. Estimates suggested that over 20% of Internet credit card transactions in Indonesia were fraudulent (Tedjasukmana, 2002), which were valued at $6 million a year in the early 2000s (Darmosumarto, 2003). Indonesian police also believed that the 2002 terrorist bombings in Bali were financed through online credit card fraud (GAO Reports June 22, 2007).

Users of stolen credit card information (known as carders) buy a wide range of items on the Internet from foreign countries. Warnets, the Indonesian Internet cafes, are a popular means of accessing the Internet for those who do not have home connections. In order to attract customers, many Warnets reportedly provide files with a list of credit card numbers as a special service (de Kloet, 2002). Although some frauds are detected, there are instances of success. For example, a carder ordered a Harley Davidson motorcycle on the Internet and was able to receive it. The motorcycle was delivered to the carder after he bribed government officials (de Kloet, 2002).

An annual survey of *CyberSource Corp.* released in 2006 ranked Indonesia as the world's third riskiest country for online transactions, only behind

Nigeria and China (Lindenmayer, 2006). Indonesia has been consistently rated among the top nations in terms of fraudulent activities on the Internet (Table 7.1). The US online merchants consider Indonesia as one of the high-risk countries and block orders from the country (Richmond, 2003). Indonesia was banned for some time from e-Bay auctions after a carder manipulated sellers under a false identity and card number (Lim, 2001).

Cognitive Acceptance of Cyber-Fraud

Many Indonesian hackers feel that cyber-fraud is wrong but acceptable, especially if the credit card owner is rich and not an Indonesian. A carder[7] reportedly said, "Yes, it's wrong but it really only hurts other rich countries that were dumb enough to let us. Why should an Indonesian get arrested for damaging American business?" (Shubert, 2003). Another carder said, "I only choose those people who are truly rich. I'm not comfortable using the money of poor people. I also don't want to use credit cards belonging to Indonesians. Those are a carder's ethics" (Antariksa, 2001, p. 16).

Weak Regulative Institutions to Fight Cybercrimes

Indonesian police say they lack expertise and resources to fight against cybercrimes (Tedjasukmana, 2002). Moreover, due to a lack of cybercrime laws, Indonesian police use a 'red book,' a manual to conduct credit card investigations available since 1997, to handle Internet credit card fraud (Darmosumarto, 2003). The lack of resources such as manpower, equipment, and funding has been a serious problem. Only 15% of reported incidents are actually investigated (Shubert, 2003). Indonesia's Information Technology Sub-Directorate of the Directorate of Special Crimes of the National Police Headquarters had only one dial-up connection in 2002.

In 2003, the Indonesian government submitted to the parliament a draft Cyber Law on information technology, electronic transactions, and freedom of information on the Internet. Progress on the law, however, has been slow (The Economist Intelligence Unit Limited, 2008). A special committee was formed to evaluate the law in November 2004. The bill was resubmitted in July 2005. In March 2008, the parliament finally approved the proposed draft Cyber Law (Handayani, 2008).

Regulative institutions dealing with cybercrimes are non-existent at worst and thin at best in developing countries. Many developing economies lack regulative framework to fight cybercrimes. For instance, as of the mid-2009, Asian economies such as Laos Cambodia and Vietnam had no cybercrime laws (Kirk, 2009). Likewise, as of September 2009, some countries in Africa and the Middle East such as Iraq, Morocco, Tunisia, and Egypt did not have such legislations (Ryan, 2009).

Many developing economies such as those in Eastern Europe and Russia have weak cybercrime laws and a lack of enforcement mechanisms, which have provided a fertile ground for computer crimes (see Box 7.1 for Russia). Many activities that are considered illegal in the United States and Western Europe have not been outlawed in these countries.

The Russian Business Network (RBN) reportedly sold website hosting services to cyber-criminal. Krebs (2007) quoted an analyst with Kaspersky Lab, a Russian anti-virus and computer security firm: "They make money on the services they provide … the illegal activities are all carried out by groups that buy hosting services ….RBN, … does not violate the law. From a legal point of view, they are clean." According to the Serious Organised Crime Agency (Soca), the RBN allegedly bribed local police, judges, and government officials (cf. Leyden, 2009). An *Economist.com* article (2007) noted

> Despite the attention it is receiving from Western law enforcement agencies, RBN is not on the run. Its users are becoming more sophisticated, moving for example from simple phishing (using fake e-mails) to malware known as "trojans" that sit inside a victim's computer collecting passwords and other sensitive information and sending them to their criminal masters.

David Pérez, a consultant to Spanish banks, noted that among about hundred illegal servers, he identified, he could break into only three because many were located in Russia. The problem was further compounded as server administrators were often in yet another country (Sutherland, 2008).

A related point is that in most cases, it is difficult to decide which jurisdiction should rule on a cybercrime case. Once jurisdiction is determined, extradition may prove to be a challenge of another magnitude. For instance, to extradite from a county, the US law requires the existence of an extradition treaty with the country. In addition, the treaty must either list the specific crimes covered by it, or require dual criminality, that is, the US law is recognized in the country (Godoy, 2000). There has been an absence of international agreement on what constitutes a cyber-criminal activity (Jewkes & Andrews, 2005). The United States has signed Mutual Legal Assistance Treaties with only a few nations (Katyal, 2001). As of 2000, the United States had about 100 extradition treaties (Gabrys, 2002).

In some countries, it is unconstitutional to extradite citizens even if they are engaged in criminal activities. For instance, according to article 25 of the Constitution of Ukraine, a citizen of the country "cannot be expelled from Ukraine or extradited to other state" (ohchr.org, 2007).

If a country does not outlaw a computer crime, the dual criminality doctrine prevents extradition (Katyal, 2001). Perhaps the best example of this is the 1992 Swiss hackers' attack on the San Diego Supercomputer center. The Swiss government did not cooperate with US authorities because of dual criminality issues (Katyal, 2001;

Cronin, 2001). In some cases, local members of the judiciary and civil officers with power to administer and enforce law may lack knowledge about cybercrime (GAO Reports June 22, 2007). Since most countries lack comprehensive cybercrime laws, it complicates the extradition of a suspected cyber-criminal to the United States (Gabrys, 2002). Moreover, without federal assistance, state and local officials may not be able to extradite persons from other nations (GAO Reports June 22, 2007). The above discussion indicates that regulatory arbitrage is likely to be higher in cybercrimes compared to most conventional crimes.

That being said, it is also the case that some encouraging signs have emerged in recent years to suggest an improving international collaborations on cybercrimes. For instance, the US FBI also announced in May 2009 that it would permanently base a computer crime expert in Estonia to help fight international threats against computer systems (Associated Press Worldstream, May 11, 2009).

Interpol played a critical role to catch a member of Cyber Lords in Japan. The US federal agents have partnered closely with their counterparts in countries such as Egypt, Romania, Turkey, and Germany. As of 2003, 60 Romanian hackers were arrested in joint operations involving the FBI, Secret Service, Scotland Yard, the US Postal Inspection Service, and a number of European police agencies (Romania Gateway, 2003). As of 2008, Romania's national police and the FBI arrested 90 Romanians engaged in cybercrime activities. Likewise, Russian agents were trained in the United States (Swartz, 2008). In July 2004, collaboration between British and Russian police led to the arrest of the members of an online extortion ring accused of blackmailing online sports betting websites that cost British companies $120 million (sophos.com, 2004). In October 2009, law-enforcement agencies in the United States and Egypt charged 100 people engaged in a phishing operation, who stole over $1.5 million from Bank of America and Well Fargo customers (Goodin, 2009). Fifty-three were from the US states of California, Nevada, and North Carolina and 47 were from Egypt.

In most cybercrimes, offenders and victims live in different jurisdiction. Industrialized countries have resources and a high-victimization level forced them to develop anti-cybercrime institutions. As noted above, many developing countries lack these conditions. Inter-jurisdictional collaborations and cooperation among law-enforcement agencies are "notoriously slow and bureaucratic" (Walden, 2005).

We would further argue that the issue here is not one of the existence of cyber-crime laws,[1] but of enforcement mechanisms. Indeed, many developing economies have enacted cybercrime laws. In 2006, the United Arab Emirates (UAE) became the first country in North Africa and the Middle East to pass legislation on cybercrime and cyber-terrorism (Cybercrime Law, 2009; Ryan, 2009). Saudi Arabia followed the UAE in the same year (itp.net, 2006). Many of the 46 nations that had signed the CoE Treaty as of August 2009 are developing economies (COE, 2009). Diffusion patterns of cybercrime-related laws in some non-CoE developing economies are presented in Table 7.3.

A Saudi official noted that while cybercrime laws in Saudi Arabia offers basic legal measures, they lack details of technical and procedural measures required to prosecute cyber-criminals (Pinaroc, 2009). ITU secretary general Hamadoun Touré

Table 7.3 Diffusion of cybercrime-related laws in non-COE developing economies

Country	Status of cybercrime legislation
Botswana	October 2007: The cybercrime and computer-related Crimes Bill published in Government Gazette[a]
	December 2007: Parliament adopted the Bill with amendments by Minister of Communications
Gambia	October 2008: A draft Information and Communications Bill 2008, including computer misuse and cybercrime issues introduced[b]
India	October 2000: Information Technology Act, 2000 came into force
	December 2008: Information Technology (Amendment) Bill 2008 passed by Indian Parliament[c].
	February 2009: The IT (Amendment) Act 2008 received the assent of the President[c]
	October 2009: The IT (Amendment) Act 2008 came into force[d]
Indonesia	July 2005: The Electronic Transaction and Information Law submitted to the House[b]
	March 2008: The parliament approved the proposed draft Cyber Law[e]
Kenya	January 2009: The Kenya Communications (Amendment) Act passed by the Parliament and signed into law by the President[b]
Macao	June 2009: A cybercrime bill drafted by the Macao Special Administrative Region (SAR) government was passed by local Legislative Assembly[f]
Malaysia	1997: Computer Crime Act 1997 introduced[g]
Nigeria	2005: Computer security and critical information infrastructure protection bill 2005 (Sb254) introduced to the National Assembly[b]
Pakistan	January 2007: A cybercrime Bill titled the Prevention of Electronic Crimes Bill 2006 has been adopted by the Federal Cabinet.[b] The President issued a decree, which made cybercrime "punishable with death or imprisonment with heavy fines"
Saudi Arabia	*October 2006: The Shariah Council* passed the first legislation to address electronic crime[h]
South Africa	July 2002: The Electronic Communications and Transactions Act, passed in 2002, has so far failed to prevent the proliferation (Assented)[i]
Thailand	July 2007: The Computer Crime Act took effect
The Philippines	2005: The government submitted an anti-cybercrime draft bill (not passed by Congress until April 2008)[j]
Uganda	June 2008: Draft electronic laws approved by Cabinet[k]
United Arab Emirates	February 2006: Cyber-Crime Law No. 2 issued by the President[b]
Zambia	August 2004: Parliament passed The Computer Misuse and Crimes law[l]

[a] Motlogelwa (2007).
[b] Cybercrime Law (2009).
[c] alertindian.com (2009).
[d] Business Standard (2009).
[e] Handayani (2008).
[f] chinadaily.com.cn (2009).
[g] bernama.com (2007).
[h] itp.net (2006).
[i] Government Gazette (2002).
[j] Yeo (2008).
[k] Kisambira (2008).
[l] ITU (2008).
[m] Khan (2008).

noted, "It [a global coalition] needs an organisational structure with a well-equipped cyber response team, all trained to similar levels across the globe – otherwise cyber-criminals will locate themselves at the weakest point" (Bailey, 2009). Jurisdictional arbitrage is thus more than a matter of the existence of cybercrime laws and their enforcement.

7.3.1.2 Normative Institutions: Social Justifiability of Cybercrimes

Cybercrimes are more justifiable in some societies compared to others. Similarly, many Indonesian hackers feel that cyber-fraud is wrong, but acceptable if the victim is from a developed country (see Box 7.2). The above cybercrime behaviors can be reasonably explained by focusing on "higher" level existing institutions and exogenous parameters (Snidal, 1994, 1996). The hackers' views and perceptions, for instance, are similar to those of some historians and economists who argue that in the current global trading order, rich countries have exploited the developing world (Bemis, 1957; Bales, 1999; Buzzanco, 1999). Buzzanco (1999), for instance, argues that during the Cold War, the United States established a "hegemonic" trading order and imposed a global market that took advantage of the rest of the world to increase American companies' profit. This notion seems to be implicit in the arguments of many developing world-based hackers and computer criminals that are targeting industrialized world-based businesses and consumers.

7.3.1.3 Cognitive Institutions: Ideology

Ideology is defined as the taken-for-granted assumptions, beliefs and value systems shared collectively by social groups (Simpson, 1993). The American Heritage Dictionary, third edition, defines ideology as "the body of ideas reflecting the social needs and aspirations of an individual, a group, a class, or a culture." Ideology is an important component of cognitive institutions that energizes the behavior of many computer hackers. A number of cyberattacks are linked with fights for ideology. Ideological hackers attack websites to further political purposes. Such hackings can be mapped with obligation/community-based intrinsic motivations (Deci & Ryan, 1985; Lindenberg, 2001).

Prior researchers have also noted the important role of the community-based clan control to fight crimes (Chua, Huang, Wareham, & Robey, 2007). Community-based and formal control mechanisms, however, complement, contradict, oppose, or support each other (Chua et al., 2007). While some ideological hackers express nationalistic longings (see next section and Box 7.3) by acting up in line with the government (de Kloet, 2002), others act against their own nation or state. Prior researchers have recognized that communities may sanction breaking laws that are perceived as discriminatory or oppressive (Kane, 2002).For instance, in the mid-2001, Cyberjihad, a group of hackers in Indonesia attacked the website of the Indonesian police to force them to free a militant Muslim leader (Antariksa, 2001, p. 15). Similarly, in October 2001, a hacker in China replaced a Chinese government website with pornographic contents (de Kloet, 2002). In addition to nationalism and religion, hackers' interests are also framed by fight against global capitalism (de Kloet, 2002). Such hackers are likely to attack networks of big multinationals.

Box 7.3 Internet as a Medium to Express Nationalistic and Patriotic Longings

Some scholars suggest that the Internet disconnects citizens from public life, while other studies have found that it provides a venue for public participation (Weber, Loumakis, & Bergman, 2003). According to the latter camp, the Internet arguably is an important new venue for stimulating civic participation and engagement. In particular, the Internet has facilitated the expression of nationalistic and patriotic longings.

The Chinese Nationalism

The Chinese nationalism and patriotism are the focus of this case. China's transition to market economy has followed a trajectory significantly different from those of Eastern Europe and the Soviet Union. While Russia followed the Western prescriptions, China has successfully blended nationalism with Marxism (Shlapentokh, 2002).

Before proceeding further, let's briefly review Chinese and American versions of nationalism and patriotism. Pei (2003) has identified several dimensions of nationalism. Consider two of them: source and bases. In terms of source, he argues that some nationalism are product of grass-root voluntarism (as US nationalism) while others are fostered by government elites and promoted by the apparatus of the state (police, military, state-run media). Chinese nationalism is viewed as state sponsored and an attempt to fill an "ideological vacuum" left by the weakening socialism (Oksenberg, 1987; Christensen, 1996; Sautman, 2001).

In terms of bases, Pei distinguishes nationalism related to universalistic ideals (democracy, rule of law, free marketplace) and institutions from that based on ethnicity, religion, language, and geography. China falls in the latter category. In China, the state arguably bolsters its legitimacy through invoking a deep sense of "Chineseness" among citizens (Ong, 1997; Barme, 1999; Hansen, 1999). Sautman (2001) has documented how China has adapted a body of complex scholarship to invoke a deep sense of "Chineseness." In a review of literature, Sautman (2001) concludes, "Nowhere is this more pronounced than in China, where these disciplines [Archaeology and paleoanthropology[8]] provide the conceptual warp and woof of China's 'racial' nationalism."

Chinese Hackers' Patriotic and Nationalistic Longings

Chinese hackers have expressed patriotic and nationalistic longings in several cyber-wars. In August 1999, Web defacements led to a cyber-war between Chinese and Taiwanese hackers. Initially, Chinese hackers defaced several Taiwanese websites with pro-China messages and said that Taiwan was and would always be a part of China (Denning, 2000). Chinese have also fought cyber-wars with Indonesians and Japanese (de Kloet, 2002).

The United States–China cyber-wars are particularly telling. In September 1999, following the accidental bombing of the Chinese Embassy in Belgrade, a group of hackers that identified itself as Level Seven Crew, defaced the website of the US embassy in China and replaced the home page with racist and anti-government slogans (Denning, 2000). Following the collision of a US surveillance plane and a Chinese fighter in 2001, a Chinese hacking group publicly released its plans for a "Net War," which was planned to continue until the anniversary of the bombing in Belgrade (May 7). In response, hacking groups from the United States, Brazil, and Europe attacked Chinese websites. According to a NewMax.com Wires article, Chinese hackers attacked about 1,100 US sites while American hackers broke into 1,600 Chinese sites (NewMax.com Wires, 2001). Similarly, after the collision of a Chinese fighter jet with a US surveillance plane in April 2001, Chinese hacking group attacked hundreds of US websites including that of the White House (Bridis, 2001).

A comparative study between mailings of Chinese and Americans indicated that fierce feelings of nationalist fervor had fuelled both camps (Kluver, 2001, p. 7). On several American websites, Chinese hackers left the following message, "We are ready to devote anything to our motherland, including our lives" (Smith, 2001). The Chinese hackers involved in the attacks argued that they were patriotic and thus did not do anything wrong. Patriotism and nationalism have thus provided cognitive legitimacy of these hackers' activities.

Hackings by Islamic activists are also interesting examples of ideological cyber-attacks. Except for occasional India–Pakistan and Israel–Palestine cyber-wars, hacking by Islamist activists was insignificant before September 11, 2001. *mi2g Intelligence Unit* reported increasing Islamist hacking, the targets being networks of the United States, Britain, Australia, and other coalition partners as well as domestic networks of Russia, Turkey, Indonesia, Pakistan, Saudi Arabia, Morocco, and Kuwait.

Another example of ideological hacking is the *Milworm* group's attack the website of India's Bhabha Atomic Research Center (BARC) (Chap. 3). Similarly, in South Korea, 58 Internet servers were attacked by a Japanese student in November 2003 to protest the war in Iraq (Duk-kun, 2003).

Nationalism and Patriotism

Nationalism and patriotism[2,3] can be considered as conceptual subsets of ideology. These are universally accepted as vital elements of state strength (Alagappa, 1995, 26–27). Salmon (1995) argues that "patriotism or attachment to one's country often leads to actions and attitudes which are disinterested or self-sacrificing, help solve free-riding problems" (p. 296).

We can find many instances of hackings linked to nationalism and patriotism. To take an example, in the early 1990s, a group of Portuguese hackers named TOXYN infiltrated a number of Indonesian government websites to fight against the occupation of East Timor (de Kloet, 2002). Indonesian hackers responded by attacking Portuguese servers that hosted the East Timor movement (Antariksa, 2001).

To take another example, in 1997, cyberattacks occurred in Sri Lanka in support of the Tamil Tiger separatists. The strike was intended to disrupt government communications by overloading Sri Lankan embassies with millions of e-mails (Havely, 2000). To take yet another example, in 1998, Indian army's website on Kashmir was "hijacked" by supporters of Pakistan's claim to the disputed territory, who plastered the site with their own political slogans (Havely, 2000). In response, in July 2001, the website of the Pakistan-based militant outfit Lashkar-e-Tayiba was attacked by a hacker who called himself "*True Indian*" (Peer, 2001). It was in response to attacks of G-force, a Pakistani hacker group, to the Indian Ministry of External Affairs' websites.

Interestingly, Israel–Palestine tensions have a powerful virtual dimension. From October 2000 to January 2001, escalation in Israel–Palestine tensions resulted in attacks on 250 websites, which included networks of foreign companies and groups outside the Middle East (Adams, 2001).

Nationalism and patriotism were dominant codes of appeal in the United States–China cyber-wars of April–May 2001 (Box 7.3). Quoting a security engineer from Guangdong Province of China, *Netease* reported the daily number of attacks increased by over 20 times the average during April–May 2001. Analyzing the United States–China cyber-wars, Kluver (2001, p. 8) concluded that "the technological optimism which sees in the Internet the end of nationalism and parochialism is an unrealistic understanding of how the Internet functions as a medium for human interaction."

7.3.1.4 Stock of Cybercrime Skills Relative to the Availability of Economic Opportunities

Unlike conventional crimes against persons or property such as rape, burglary, and murder, cybercrimes are very skill-intensive. Stock of hacking skills is thus a prerequisite to online crimes. Whereas minimal skill is needed for opportunistic attacks, targeted attacks require more sophisticated skills.

As discussed in Chap. 2, crime rates are tightly linked to the lack of economic opportunities. Also addressed in much empirical study are linkages of crime and other deviant behaviors with people living in poverty (Oxoby, 2004). The combination of over-educated and under-employed computer experts has made Russia and some Eastern European countries fertile ground for hackers. In these counties, there are a large number of students good at mathematics, physics, and computer science, but having difficulties to find jobs (Blau, 2004). A financial crash in 1998 left many computer programmers unemployed, worsening the situation. A self-described hacker from Moscow told reporters, "Hacking is one of the few good jobs left here" (Walker, 2004). Regarding computer attacks originating from Romania, the US-based Internet Fraud Complaint Center, run by the FBI and the National White Collar Crime Center has reported: "Frustrated with the employment possibilities offered in Romania, some of the world's most talented computer students are exploiting their talents online" (Romania Gateway, 2003). On the other hand, the primary reason behind India's low-cybercrime profile is the existence of a well-developed legitimate IT industry in the country (Greenberg, 2007).

A large number of extortion-related cyberattacks originate from Eastern Europe and Russia (see Box 7.1). Hackers in these economies possess capability to do very sophisticated attacks with limited computer power (Walker, 2004). It can be attributed to Russia's highly educated workforce and programming skills (newpaper.asia1.com.sg, 2004). Russian hackers have a deep understanding of networks and know how to "get in and out without a trace" (Walker, 2004). Consider the US National Security Agency-backed "hacking" competition of June 2009. Four thousand two hundred programmers from all over the world participated in algorithm coding and other contests. Of the finalists in the competitions, 20 were from China, 10 were from Russia, and only 2 were from the US (Cetron & Davies, 2009).

7.3.2 Profile of Target Organization

7.3.2.1 Symbolic Significance and Criticalness

The ideal targets for terrorists of September 11, 2001 were the World Trade Center's Twin Towers, the White House, and the Pentagon, the ones with tremendous symbolic significance (Coates, 2002). One can draw a parallel—or an analogy—to what is seen in cyberattacks. Hackers similarly have ideal targets. Attacks initiated by terrorists are likely to be targeted against decisive and critical infrastructure systems such as telecommunications, the supply of gas, oil, and fuel (Comité Européen Des Assurances, 2004).

Following the collision of an American spy plane and a Chinese jet in April 2001, Chinese and US hackers attacked each other's websites. Each camp selected websites that had symbolic values. In the United States, the White House's site was shut down for many hours; there was a virus attack against computers at the California Department of Justice; and Ohio's Bellaire School District site played the Chinese national anthem displaying Chinese flag (Smith, 2001). In China, sina.com, one of the most popular portals; the website of Xinhua news agency; and those of local governments were attacked (The Happy Hacker, 2001). Speaking of challenges facing the US Defense Department, Robert Lentz, deputy assistant Defense secretary for information and identity assurance, noted that the Pentagon "is the number-one target" for cyberattacks (Campbell, 2008).

7.3.2.2   Digitization of Value and Target Attractiveness

As to the target attractiveness (Chap. 2), it is worth noting that crimes target sources of value, and for this reason, digitization of value is tightly linked with digitization of crime. Regarding the devastating impact of the 2007 cyberattacks against Estonia, it is important to note that, by 2007, Estonia had implemented various high-profile, e-government projects. For instance, 90% of banking services, and parliamentary elections, were conducted online (BBC News, 2007).

Cybercrimes' impacts are clearly skewed towards rich economies, large companies, and high-income people. As noted earlier, the United States is the world's No. 1 cybercrime target. Analysts suggest that the Gulf region's oil-fueled prosperity has made the region attractive cybercrime target. In the Gulf Cooperation Councils (GCC) economies, for instance, in the first 9 months of 2009, there were over 769,000 instances of "compromised systems breakdown" in Saudi Arabia, 248,000 in the UAE, 95,000 in Kuwait, 60,000 in Bahrain, and 37,000 in Oman (Gulf Daily News, 2009).

Large companies have larger networks, which offer more targets to hackers. A survey of Riptech indicated that attackers are more likely to launch targeted attacks against larger companies than smaller. A survey conducted among Australian firms indicated that average looses of a cybercrime were A $360 small businesses, A $2,757 medium businesses, and A $17,578 for large businesses (Andrews, 2009).

A study indicated that high-income earners (more than £50,000 a year) in the United Kingdom are 3–5 times more likely to become victims of identity fraud than the average UK resident (Heera, 2008; cf. Rush, Chris Erika, & Puay, 2009). Likewise, in Bangladesh, businesspersons, contractors, and wealthy people have been targets of extortion activities that use cellphones with unregistered subscriber identity module (SIM) cards (The New Nation, 2009).

Businesses with a high dependence on digital technologies—including online casinos, banks, and e-commerce hubs—are more likely to be the target for extrinsically motivated hackers. For instance, estimates suggest that a few hours downtime on Super Bowl weekend cost online casinos up to $1 million (onlinecasinonews.com, 2004). According to IDC, over 60% of computer hacks targeted financial institutions in 2003 (Swartz, 2004). Similarly, in the first-half of 2004, 16% of e-commerce attacks were targeted compared to 4% in 2003 (Symantec, 2004).

7.3.2.3   Weakness of Defense Mechanisms

Weakness of defense mechanism co-varies positively with the likelihood of an attack (Glaeser & Sacerdote, 1999). In this regard, it is important to note that computer systems contain many flaws. Such flaws can be attributed to factors such as complexity, rapid change in the software industry, and a lack of penalties for companies that develop flawed software (Mann, 2002). Hackers in most cases take advantage of these flaws. It is important to note that hundreds of millions of computers that are connected to the Internet have security holes. While many of them are easily fixable, many are undiscovered. Due to weak defenses of most computer networks, it is also difficult to track origins of cyberattacks (Kong and Swartz, 2000).

7.4 Concluding Comments

This chapter has contributed to the conceptual and empirical understanding of global cyber-wars and crimes. The analyses of this chapter indicated that the nature of the source of a web attack is a function of the nature of regulative, normative, and cognitive legitimacy to the attacking unit; and stocks of hacking skills relative to the availability of economic opportunities. An attacking unit's selection criteria for the target include symbolic significance and degree of digitization of values. Extrinsically motivated hackers are likely to attack the networks with high degree of digitization of values. These include financial institutions, e-commerce hubs, and online casinos. Intrinsically motivated hackers' targeted attacks, on the other hand, are directed towards organizations that with symbolic significance and criticalness. These include websites of government, critical infrastructures, and also some companies that are perceived as national symbol. Different motivations of hackers, source characteristics, and target country characteristics lead to different likelihoods of attacks on different organizations. Put differently, an independent variable may have different coefficients in regressions with attacks on different organizations as dependent variables.

Nations across the world differ widely on key elements represented by Fig. 7.1 and hence on domestic/foreign composition of sources and targets of cyberattacks as well as attackers' motivations. For instance, societies that have weak or no cybercrime laws and where socio-cultural practices provide some degree of legitimacy to such crimes are likely to provide fertile ground for these crimes. To illustrate from the US perspective, in Table 7.4, we have classified targeted cyberattacks impacting the US by national border in terms of target and source.

For industrialized economies, the battle against cybercrime is about more than just developing capacity on the home front. Important technological issues crossing national borders can be better dealt with at policy levels (Skolnikoff, 1989). International collaborations are, however, lacking with law-enforcement agencies in some of the top cybercrime sources. For instance, it is reported that government officials in Nigeria claimed that they were ignorant of Internet crimes originated from Nigeria and some labeled it as Western propaganda (Lawal, 2006). In general, a lack of legal infrastructures and enforcement mechanisms in developing countries has increased the jurisdictional arbitrage (Table 7.5).

When law-enforcement agencies in developing economies are genuinely engaged in fighting cybercrime activities targeting foreign countries, the likelihood of them controlling such activities is much greater than when a foreign government simply imposes them to do so. From the US standpoint, it is worth noting that the United

Table 7.4 Classification of targeted cyberattacks by national border: an illustration from the US perspective

		Target	
		Domestic	Foreign
Source	Domestic	[1] • Former and current employees • Domestic customers • Domestic competitors • Domestic hackers • Domestic organized criminal groups (e.g., the "Phonemasters")	[3] • US cyber scammers attacking foreign websites (e.g., ShadowCrew) • Patriotic/nationalistic hackers (e.g., those attacking Chinese websites) • Other ideological hackers (e.g., those attacking India's Bhabha Atomic Research Center)
	Foreign	[2] • Foreign competitors • Foreign customers targeting US companies • Foreign cyber scammers targeting US companies/Internet users • Foreign organized criminal groups (e.g., Russian online extortionists) targeting US companies • Foreign government agencies (e.g., the government of Burma sending virus-attached e-mails to its critics residing in the US) • Foreign patriotic/nationalistic hackers (e.g., Chinese attacking US websites) • Foreign terrorists (e.g., request from Afghanistan to provide hacking services)	[4] • Attack on US-based MNCs' foreign websites • Attack on the websites of US diplomatic offices (e.g., The China-based Level Seven Crew's attack on the website of the US embassy in China)

States is facing an image problem in many countries that are among the top cyber-crime sources (Tables 7.1 and 7.2): According to the 2009 Pew Global Attitudes Survey conducted by the Washington, DC-based Pew Research Center, only 14% Turkish, 16% Pakistanis, 27% of Egyptians, 38% Argentinanians, 44% of Russians, and 47% of Chinese have a favorable view of the United States (Pew Research Center, 2009). Likewise, a survey conducted by the BBC and the University of Maryland in April 2008 found that people in 23 countries viewed US influence in the world more negatively than that of North Korea (Debusmann, 2008).

One view is that, the US foreign policy would be drastically different in Obama's administration, which is likely to lead to a more positive image of the US worldwide (Debusmann, 2008). The opposite argument is that there really are no fundamental

Table 7.5 Measuring the cybersafety environment

Stage of cybersafety	Institutional indicators	Business-related indicators
Number of attacks per 1,000 Internet users	Existence of laws that require appropriate defense mechanisms (+)	Proportion of revenue spent in network security (+)
Proportion of cyberattacks that are targeted	Existence of laws that require reporting cybercrime (+)	Degree of compliance with cyber-criminals' demands (e.g., extortion money paid annually) (–)
	Proportion of reported crimes that are investigated (+)	Willingness of cybercrime victims to report crimes (+)
	Proportion of reported crimes that lead to arrest (+)	
	Proportion of reported crimes that lead to conviction (+)	
	Severity of punishment for convicted cyber-criminals (+)	
	Existence of social norms that justify cyberattacks (–)	

Note: +: positive contribution to cybersafety; –: negative contribution to cybersafety.

differences in the foreign policy approaches of the new and the old government. Arguing that Obama's approach is likely to be "surprisingly similar" to George W. Bush, Posner (2009) notes: "The United States—under the leadership of both the Republican and Democratic parties—has taken a fairly consistent approach to international law over the decades, one that involves building legal regimes that serve US interests and tearing down those that do not." If this view is substantially correct, it seems clear that the cybercrime fighting efforts of the United States are likely to face serious difficulties in some of the top cybercrime sources.

Notes

1. For instance, the law enacted in Romania in 2003 punishes convicts with up to 15 years in prison (Romania Gateway, 2003).
2. Before proceeding further, it is important to review definitional issues and difference in the meanings of the two terms. One school of thought maintains that "there is a distinction, but no real difference" between patriotism and nationalism (Pei, 2003). According to this school, patriotism is related with "allegiance to one's country" and nationalism as "sentiments of ethno-national superiority" (Pei, 2003). Brown (1999) considers patriotism as identification with territory whereas nationalism as identification with the group. We use the terms nationalism and patriotism interchangeably.
3. There are some studies that have compared the impacts of nationalism and patriotism on consumer behavior. In a comparative study of the impact of patriotism, nationalism on consumer ethnocentrism in Turkey and the Czech Republic, Balabanis, Diamantopoulos, Mueller, and Melewar (2001) found that the impact of patriotism and nationalism on consumer ethnocentrism is not consistent across the two countries. Consumer ethnocentrism in Turkey is fueled by patriotism, and in the Czech Republic by nationalism.

4. There are two categories of DoS attacks: Operating System (OS) attacks, and Network attacks. OS attacks entail discovering holes in the security of the OS and bringing down the system. Network attacks disconnect a network from the Internet services provider (ISP). The attackers use mis-configured networks to perform such attacks (See "Help! I am being DoS'ed" at http://www.irc-junkie.org/content/a-DoS.php). Accessed 27 October 2004.

5. Online casinos rely on Worldpay to process customer's transactions and pay off gamblers (Walker, 2004).

6. "Russia's Hackers: Notorious or Desperate?" CNN.com. November 20, 2000. http://www.cnn.com/2000/TECH/computing/11/20/russia.hackers.ap/index.html (Accessed 27 October 2004).

7. A carder is a person who uses stolen credit card information to buy items online.

8. Archaeology is the study of ancient societies and cultures. Paleoanthropology is the study of the human fossil record.

References

Adams, J. (2001, May/June). Virtual defense. *Foreign Affairs*, 98–112.

Alagappa, M. (1995). *Political legitimacy in Southeast Asia*. Stanford, CA: Stanford University Press.

alertindian.com. (2009). Cyber crime laws in India. http://www.alertindian.com/node/5. Accessed 27 October 2009.

Andrews, L. (2009, June 9). Online scams go unreported and unpunished. *Cybercriminals Beating the Law Canberra Times* (Australia) SECTION: A; 5.

Antariksa. (2001, July). I am a thief, not a hacker: Indonesia's electronic underground. *Latitudes Magazine*, 12–17.

Associated Press Worldstream. (2009). FBI to station cybercrime expert in Estonia.

Bailey, D. (2009, September 30). ITU pledges to fight global cybercrime, *Computing*. http://www.computing.co.uk/computing/analysis/2250377/q-international. Accessed 27 October 2009.

Balabanis, G., Diamantopoulos, A., Mueller, R. D., & Melewar, T. C. (2001). The impact of nationalism, patriotism and internationalism on consumer ethnocentric tendencies. *Journal of International Business Studies, 32*(1), 157–175.

Bales, K. (1999). *Disposable people: New slavery in the global economy*. Berkeley, CA: University of California Press.

Barme, G. (1999). *In the red: On contemporary Chinese culture*. New York: Columbia University Press.

BBC News. (2007) Estonia hit by 'Moscow cyber war'. http://news.bbc.eo.uk/2/hi/europe/6665145.stm. Accessed 27 October 2009.

Bemis, S. F. (1957). *The diplomacy of the American revolution*. Bloomington, IN: Indiana University Press.

bernama.com. (2007). Malaysia Should Focus More On Enforcing Cyber Law, Says Microsoft, December 12, 2007. http://www.bernama.com/kpdnhep/news.php?id=302117&lang=en. Accessed 27 October 2009.

Blau, J. (2004, May 28). Viruses: From Russia, with love? *IDG News Service*. http://www.pcworld.com/news/article/0,aid,116304,00.asp. Accessed 27 October 2006.

Bridis, T. (2001). E-Espionage rekindles cold-war tensions – US Tries to identify hackers; millions of documents are stolen. *Wall Street Journal*, A.18.

Brown, L. C. (1999). The multiple identities of the Middle East. *Foreign Affairs, 78*(6), 158–159.

Business Standard. (2009). Amended IT Act to prevent cyber crime comes into effect, October 27, 2009. http://www.business-standard.com/india/news/amended-it-act-to-prevent-cyber-crime-comes-into-effect/21/19/76884/on. Accessed 11 April 2010.

Buzzanco, R. (1999). What happened to the new left? Toward a radical reading of American foreign relations. *Diplomatic History*, 575–608.

Campbell, D. (2008, April 1). Lentz: Content-centricity key to DOD communications. *Government Computer News.* http://gcn.com/articles/2008/04/01/lentz-contentcentricity-key-to-dod-communications.aspx.

Cetron, M. J., & Davies, O. (2009). Ten Critical Trends for Cybersecurity. *Futurist, 43*(5), 40–49.

chinadaily.com.cn. (2009). Macao passes cyber-crime bill, 2009-06-25. http://www.chinadaily.com.cn/china/2009-06/25/content_8324247.htm. Accessed 27 October 2009.

Christensen, T. (1996). Chinese Realpolitik. *Foreign Affairs, 75*(5), 37–52.

Chua, C., Huang, E., Wareham, J, & Robey, D. (2007). The role of online trading communities in managing internet auction fraud. *MIS Quarterly, 31*(4), 759–781.

CNN.Com. (2000, January 10). Rebuffed Internet extortionist posts stolen credit card data. http://cnn.com/2000/TECH/computing/01/10/credit.card.crack.2/index.html. Accessed 27 October 2005.

Coates, J. F. (2002). What's next? Foreseeable terrorist acts. *The Futurist,* 36(5), 23–26.

COE. (2009). Convention on Cybercrime: CETS No.:185. http://conventions.coe.int/Treaty/Commun/ChercheSig.asp?NT=185&CM=&DF=&CL=ENG. Accessed 27 October 2009.

Comité Européen Des Assurances. (2004, February). Terrorist Acts Against Computer Installations and the Role of the Internet in the Context of International Terrorism Property Insurance Committee, *IT Risks Insurance Sub-committee.* http://www.cea.assur.org/cea/v1.1/actu/pdf/uk/annexe180.pdf. Accessed 27 October 2006.

Cronin, B. (2001). Information warfare: Peering inside Pandora's postmodern box. *Library Review, 50*(6), 279–295.

Cybercrime Law. (2009). News. http://www.cybercrimelaw.net.

Darmosumarto, S. (2003, December 8). Battle on Internet credit card fraud still long. *The Jakarta Post.* http://www.crime-research.org/news/2003/12/Mess0802.html. Accessed 27 October 2006.

Datamonitor. (2009, July). eBay, Inc. *SWOT Analysis,* 1–9.

de Kloet, J. (2002). Digitisation and its Asian discontents: The Internet, politics and hacking in china and Indonesia. *First Monday,* 7(9). http://firstmonday.org/issues/issue7_9/kloet/index.html. Accessed 1 October 2005.

Debusmann, B. (2008, November 13). Obama and a makeover for the 'ugly American'. http://www.nytimes.com/2008/11/13/world/americas/13iht-letter.1.17790862.html. Accessed 27 October 2009.

Deci, E. L, & Ryan, R. M. (1985). *Intrinsic motivation and self-determination in human behavior.* New York, NY: Plenum Press.

Deloitte Touche Tohmatsu. (2002). *Australian computer crime and security survey.* http://www.4law.co.il/346.pdf. Accessed 27 October 2005.

Dempsey, P. J. (2008). Unprepared to fight worldwide cyber crime. http://www.internetevolution.com/author.asp?section_id=593&doc_id=147027&piddl_msgid=154774#msg_154774. Accessed 27 October 2009.

Denning, D. E. (2000). Hacktivism: An emerging threat to diplomacy. *American Foreign Service Association.* www.afsa.org/fsj/sept00/Denning.cfm. Accessed 27 October 2004.

Duk-kun, B. (2003, November 19). Largest Internet hacking ring uncovered. *The Korea Times.*

Etges, R., & Sutcliffe, E. (2008). An overview of transnational organized cyber crime. *Information Security Journal: A Global Perspective, 17*(2), 87–94.

Foreign Policy. (2005, March/April). Caught in the net: Australian teens, 92.

Forensic Accounting Review and Computer Security Digest. (2001). FBI warns of Russian hackers stealing US credit-card data. *17*(8), 2.

Gabrys, E. (2002). The international dimensions of cyber-crime, Part 1. *Information Systems Security, 11*(4), 21–32.

GAO Reports. (2007). *Public and private entities face challenges in addressing cyber threats.* RPT-Number: GAO-07-705.

Giannangeli, M. (2008, June 8). Are we ready for Russian Mafia's crime revolution? *Sunday Express,* Scottish Edition, 4.

Glaeser, E. L., & Sacerdote, B. (1999). Why is there more crime in cities? *The Journal of Political Economy, 107*(6), Part 2, S225–S258.

Godoy, J. (2000). Computers and International Criminal Law: High Tech Crimes and Criminals. *New England International and Comparative Law Annual*, 6. http://www.nesl.edu/intljournal/vol6indx.cfm. Accessed 27 October 2005.

Gomes, L., & Bridis, T. (2001, March 9). FBI warns of Russian hackers stealing credit-card data from US computers. *Wall Street Journal*, A.4.

Goodin, D. (2009, October 8). Feds net 100 phishers in biggest cybercrime case ever. http://www.theregister.co.uk/2009/10/08/100_phishers_netted. Accessed 27 October 2009.

Government Gazette. (2002, August 2). Act No. 25, 2002 Electronic Communications and Transactions Act, 2002, Government Gazette. http://web.uct.ac.za/depts/shiplaw/fulltext/electcomsact.pdf. Accessed 27 October 2006.

Greenberg, A. (2007). The top countries for cybercrime. *Forbes.com*. http://www.forbes.com/2007/07/13/cybercrime-world-regions-tech-cx_ag_0716cybercrime.html. Accessed 27 October 2008.

Grow, B., & Bush, J. (2005, May 30). Hacker hunters. *Business Week*, 2005.

Gulf Daily News. (2009, October 23). Cyber crime alert. *gulf-daily-news.com*. http://www.gulf-daily-news.com/NewsDetails.aspx?storyid=262426. Accessed 23 October 2009.

Hahn, R.W., & Layne-Farrar, A. (2006). The law and economics of software security. *Harvard Journal of Law and Public Policy, 30*(1), 283–353.

Handayani, R. (2008, June 13). Indonesia: Introducing the first Indonesian Cyber law. http://asia.legalbusinessonline.com/regional-updates/25196/details.aspx. Accessed 27 October 2009.

Handelman, S. (1999, September 20). Russia's rule by racketeers. *Wall Street Journal*, A.28.

Hansen, M. (1999). *Lessons in being Chinese: Minority education and ethnic identity in Southwest China*. Seattle: University of Washington Press.

Havely, J. (2000, February 16). Online's when states go to cyber-war. *BBC News*.

Heera, S. (2008). Directors of larger dealerships at significant risk of identity theft, warns Experian, New Release. *Experian.com*. http://press.experian.com/documents/showdoc.cfm. Accessed 27 October 2009.

Interpol. (2007). INTERPOL's six priority crime areas. http://www.interpol.int. Accessed 27 October 2008.

Ismail, I. (2008, February 18). Understanding cybercriminals. *New Straits Times* (Malaysia), 12.

itp.net. (2006, October 15). Saudi passes cybercrime laws. http://www.itp.net/487865. Accessed 27 October 2009.

ITU. (2008). ITU Regional Cybersecurity Forum 2008 Lusaka, Zambia, Meeting Report: ITU Regional Cybersecurity Forum for Eastern and Southern Africa, Lusaka, Zambia, 25–28 August 2008, 29 August 2008. http://www.itu.int/ITU-D/cyb/events/2008/lusaka/docs/lusaka-cybersecurity-forum-report-aug-08.pdf. Accessed 27 October 2009.

Jewkes, Y., & Andrews, C. (2005). Policing the filth: The problems of investigating online child pornography in England and Wales. *Policing & Society, 15*(1), 42–62.

Kane, R. J. (2002). The social ecology of police misconduct. *Criminology, 40*(4), 867–896.

Katyal, N. K. (2001). Criminal law in cyberspace. *University of Pennsylvania Law Review, 149*(4), 1003–1114.

Khan, M. I. (2008). Pakistan unveils cybercrime laws, 7 November 2008. http://news.bbc.co.uk/2/hi/7714714.stm. Accessed 27 October 2009.

Kirk, J. (2009, March 11). Countries move forward on cybercrime treaty. *PC World*. http://www.pcworld.com/article/161067/countries_move_forward_on_cybercrime_treaty.html. Accessed 27 October 2009.

Kisambira, E. (2008, October, 6). Uganda cyber laws going to parliament. http://www.networkworld.com/news/2008/100608-uganda-cyber-laws-going-to.html. Accessed 27 October 2009.

Kluver, R. (2001). New media and the end of nationalism: China and the US in a war of words. *Mots Pluriels*. www.arts.uwa.edu.au/MotsPluriels/MP1801ak.html. Accessed 27 October 2009.

Kong, D., & Swartz, J. (2000, September 27). Experts see rash of hack attacks coming recent costly hits show 'more brazen' criminals preying on companies. *USA Today*, 01.B.

Krebs, B. (2007, October 13). Taking on the Russian Business Network. http://blog. washingtonpost.com/securityfix/2007/10/taking_on_the_russian_business.html. Accessed 27 October 2009.

Kshetri, N. (2005, May/June). Hacking the odds. *Foreign Policy*, 93.

Lawal, L. (2006, May 22). Online scams create "Yahoo! millionaires": In Lagos, where scamming is an art, the quickest way to wealth for the cyber-generation runs through a computer screen. *Fortune*. http://money.cnn.com/magazines/fortune/fortune_archive/2006/05/29/ 8378124/. Accessed 27 October 2009.

Lemos, R. (2001, May 1). FBI "hack" raises global security concerns. *CNet News*. http:// news.com.com/2100-1001-950719.html

Levi, M. (2002). The organization of serious crimes. *The Oxford Handbook of Criminology* (pp. 878–913). Oxford: Oxford University Press.

Leyden, J. (2009, October 22). FBI and SOCA plot cybercrime smackdown. *The Register*. http://www.theregister.co.uk/2009/10/22/soca_fbi_cybercrime_strategy/ Accessed 27 October 2009.

Lieberman, D. (2003). Feds enlist hacker to foil piracy rings; Plea agreement includes help in satellite TV cases. *USA Today*, January 10, B.01.

Lim, M. (2001). *From real to virtual (and back again): Civil society, public sphere, and the Internet in Indonesia*. Paper presented at Internet political economy forum conference, Singapore.

Lindenberg, S. (2001). Intrinsic motivation in a new light. *Kyklos, 54*(2/3), 317–342.

Lindenmayer, I. (2006). *Online American Banker, 171*(18), 6.

Lorek, L. (2001). Russian Mafia net threat. *Interactive Week*, 11.

Mann, C. C. (2002, July–August). Why software is so bad. *Technical Review*, 33. http://www. technologyreview.com/InfoTech/wtr12887,300,p1.html. Accessed 27 October 2005.

Motlogelwa, T. (2007, October 5). Cyber crime law gets teeth. http://www.mmegi.bw/index. php?sid=1&aid=30&dir=2007/October/Friday5. Accessed 27 October 2009.

Muncaster, P. (2006, December 11). Organised crime gangs lure IT graduates. *IT Week*, http://www.businessgreen.com/itweek/news/2170640/organised-crime-gangs-lure. Accessed 18 March 2010.

Naím, M. (2005). *Illicit: How smugglers, traffickers, and copycats are hijacking the global economy*. New York: Doubleday.

NewMax.com Wires. (2001, May 21). Chinese hackers may be rallying forces. http://archive. newsmax.com/archives/articles/2001/5/22/84452.shtml. Accessed 27 October 2005.

newpaper.asia1.com.sg. (2004, August 3). Hackers – The new breed of gangsters. http://newpaper. asia1.com.sg/top/story/0,4136,69503-1-1098892740,00.html. Accessed 27 October 2005.

ohchr.org (2007, April) Report by the Kharkiv Human Rights Protection Group about Ukraine's compliance with the Convention against Torture and Other Cruel, Inhuman or Degrading Treatment or Punishment. http://www2.ohchr.org/english/bodies/cat/docs/ngos/khrpg.doc Accessed 27 October 2009.

Oksenberg, M. (1987). China's confident nationalism. *Foreign Affairs, 65*(3), 501–523.

Ong, A. (1997). Chinese modernities: Narratives of nation and of capitalism. In A. Ong & D. Nonini (Eds.), *Underground empires: The cultural politics of modern Chinese transformation*. New York: Routledge.

Onlinecasinonews.com. (2004, February 3). Mob's extortion attempt on Internet bookies. http:// www.onlinecasinonews.com/ocnv2_1/article/article.asp?id=4748. Accessed 27 October 2005.

Oxoby, R. J. (2004). Cognitive dissonance, status and growth of the underclass. *Economic Journal, 114*(498), 727–749.

Peer, B. (2001, July 10). Lashkar web site hacked. http://www.rediff.com/news/2001/jul/ 10hack1.htm. Accessed 27 October 2005.

Pei, M. (2003). The paradoxes of American nationalism. *Foreign Policy, 136*, 30–37.

Pew Research Center. (2009). Opinion of the United States. http://pewglobal.org/database/?indicator=1&mode=chart. Accessed 27 October 2009.

Pinaroc, J. D. (2009, October 14). Saudi faces tough time with cybercrimes. *ZDNet Asia*. http://www.zdnetasia.com/news/security/0,39044215,62058637,00.htm. Accessed 27 October 2009.

Porter, M. E. (2001). Strategy and the Internet. *Harvard Business Review, 79*(3), 63–78.

Posner, E. (2009). Think again: International law: Governments respect international law only when it suits their national interests. Don't expect that to change any time soon.

Regan, K. (2006) FBI: Cybercrime causes financial pain for many businesses. *TechNewsWorld*. http://www.technewsworld.com/story/48417.html. Accessed 27 October 2008.

Richmond, R. (2003, January 27). Selling strategies – Scammed! Web merchants use new tools to keep buyers from ripping them off. *Wall Street Journal*, R.6.

Riptech. (2002, July). *Riptech internet security threat report* (Vol. II). http://www.4law.co.il/276.pdf. Accessed 27 October 2005.

Rogers, E. M. (1983). *The diffusion of innovations* (3rd ed.). New York: Free Press.

Romania Gateway. (2003, October 24). Romania emerges as nexus of cybercrime. http://rogateway.ro/node/185929/comnews/item?item_id=223937. Accessed 27 October 2006.

Rosenau, J. N. (1995). Security in a turbulent world. *Current History, 94*(592), 193–200.

Rush, H., Chris, S., Erika, K. M., & Puay, T. (2009). Crime online: Cybercrime and illegal innovation. Research report: July 2009, CENTRIM, University of Brighton. http://eprints.brighton.ac.uk/5800/01/Crime_Online.pdf. Accessed 27 October 2009.

Ryan, Y. (2009). Algerian bloggers feel threatened by proposed law. http://www.nytimes.com/2009/09/21/technology/21iht-censor.html, September 21, 2009. Accessed 27 October 2009.

Salmon, P. (1995). Nations competing against themselves: An interpretation of European integration. In A. Breton, G. Galeotti, P. Salmon, & R. Wintrobe (Eds.), *Nationalism and rationality*. Cambridge: Cambridge University Press.

Sautman, B. (2001). Peking man and the politics of paleoanthropological nationalism in China. *The Journal of Asian Studies, 60*(1), 95–124.

Serio, J. D., & Gorkin, A. (2003). Changing lenses: Striving for sharper focus on the nature of the 'Russian Mafia' and its impact on the computer realm. *International Review of Law, Computers and Technology, 17*(2), 191–202.

Shlapentokh, D. (2002). Post-Mao China: An alternative to 'The end of history'? Communist and Post – Communist Studies. *Kidlington, 35*(3), 237.

Shubert, A. (2003, February 6). Taking a swipe at cyber card fraud. *CNN.com*. http://www.cnn.com/2003/WORLD/asiapcf/southeast/02/06/indonesia.fraud. Accessed 27 October 2006.

Simpson, P. (1993). *Language, ideology and point of view*. London/New York: Routledge.

Skolnikoff, E. B. (1989). Technology and the world tomorrow. *Current History, 88*(534), 5–13.

Smith, C. S. (2001, May 13). The first world hacker war. *New York Times*, 4.2.

Snidal, D. (1994). The politics of scope: Endogenous actors, heterogeneity and institutions. *Journal of Theoretical Politics, 6*(4), 449–472.

Snidal, D. (1996). Political economy and international institutions. *International Review of Law and Economics, 16*(1), 121–137.

sophos.com. (2004, July 23). Police crack suspected online extortion ring. *Sophos reports*. http://www.sophos.com/virusinfo/articles/extortion.html.

sophos.com. (2008, July 23). Police crack suspected online extortion ring. *Sophos reports*. http://www.sophos.com/virusinfo/articles/extortion.html. Accessed 27 October 2009.

Steffensmeier, D., & Ulmer, J. T. (2006). Black and white control of numbers gambling: A cultural assets-social capital view. *American Sociological Review, 71*(1), 123–157.

Sullivan, B. (2004, April 1). Foreign fraud hits US e-commerce firms hard. *MSNBC*. http://www.msnbc.msn.com/id/4648378. Accessed 27 October 2005.

Sutherland, B. (2008). The rise of black market data; Criminals who steal personal data often don't exploit it. Instead, they put it up for sale on one of the many vibrant online markets. *Newsweek, 152*(24) (International ed.).

Swartz, J. (2004, October 21). Crooks slither into Net's shady nooks and crannies crime explodes as legions of strong-arm thugs, sneaky thieves log on. *USA Today*. www.usatoday.com/printedition/money/20041021/cybercrimecover.art.htm. Accessed 2 October 2005.

Swartz, J. (2008, November 17). Hackers, phishers can't get away with it like they used to, *USA Today*, http://www.usatoday.com/money/industries/technology/2008-11-16-hackers-phisher-crime-fbi_N.htm. Accessed 18 March 2010.

Symantec. (2004). *Symantec internet security threat report* (Vol. VI). http://www.4law.co.il/L138.pdf. Accessed 2 October 2005.

Tedjasukmana, J. (2002, September 23). The no-payment plan: Thousands of young Indonesians commit cyberfraud for fun and profit. http://www.time.com/time/globalbusiness/article/0,9171,1101020923-351237,00.html. Accessed 27 October 2005.

The Economist Intelligence Unit Limited. (2008). Country Commerce, Indonesia, 77–81. www.eiu.com. Accessed 27 October 2009.

The Economist. (2003, November 29). Special report: Fighting the worms of mass destruction – Internet security, 101.

The Happy Hacker. (2001).The US/China cyberwar of April/May 2001. http://www.happyhacker.org/news/china.shtml. Accessed 27 October 2005.

The New Nation. (2009, October 5). Cell phone crime rise: Extortions go on unabated, Internet Edition. http://nation.ittefaq.com/issues/2009/10/05/news0827.htm. Accessed 27 October 2009.

Varese, F. (2002). *The Russian Mafia: Private protection in a new market economy*. New York: Oxford University Press.

Walden, I. (2005). Crime and security in cyberspace. *Cambridge Review of International Affairs, 18*(1), 51–68.

Walker, C. (2004, June). Russian Mafia Extorts Gambling Websites. http://www.americanmafia.com/cgi/clickcount.pl?url=www.americanmafia.com/Feature_Articles_270.html. Accessed 27 October 2005.

Weber, L. M., Loumakis, A., & Bergman, J. (2003). Who participates and why?: An analysis of citizens on the Internet and the mass public. *Social Science Computer Review, 21*(1), 26–42.

Williams, P. (2001, August 13). Organized Crime and Cybercrime: Synergies, Trends, and Responses. Office of International Information Programs, US Department of State. http://usinfo.state.gov. Accessed 27 October 2005.

Winterford, B. (2009, October 12). Banks report 70 percent of phishing attacks hosted offshore. *IT News.* http://www.itnews.com.au/News/158011,banks-report-70-percent-of-phishing-attacks-hosted-offshore.aspx. Accessed 27 October 2009.

Yeo, V. (2008, April 15). Asia hindered by lack of cybercrime laws. http://www.businessweek.com/globalbiz/content/apr2008/gb20080415_220378.htm?chan=top+news_top+news+index_global+business. Accessed 27 October 2009.

Chapter 8
Structure of Cybercrime in Developing Economies

At the moment, cybercriminals see Africa as a safe haven to operate illegally with impunity (Hamadoun Toure, secretary-general of the ITU, cf. Africa News, 2007).
"Even in 2001, I was meeting judges who thought cyber-crime was someone stealing a computer" (eBay's Albena Spasova, who worked in promoting law reform in Moldova and Bulgaria, cf. Wylie, 2007).

Abstract Cybercrime's footprints across the developing world are getting bigger. In this chapter, we examine the structure of cybercrimes in developing economies. Specifically, we analyze economic and institutional factors facing cyber-criminals and potential victims in the developing world. The findings indicate that formal institutions related to cybercrimes are thin and dysfunctional in a developing economy; a cyber-criminal is less likely to be stigmatized in a developing economy than in a developed economy; and organizations' and individuals' technological and behavioral defense mechanisms are likely to be weaker in a developing economy than in a developed economy.

8.1 Introduction

With the Internet's rapid diffusion and digitization of economic activities, cyber-crime has gained momentum in developing economies. Many developing countries are top cybercrime sources (see Tables 7.1, 7.2, and 8.1). Businesses and consumers in developing countries have also become victims of domestic as well as international cybercrimes. Since most of the growth in the global PC market in the near future is likely to be from the developing countries (Miller, 2008), cybercrimes in these countries deserve special attention. Analyzing the trend of cybercrime activities across countries, analysts have suggested 10–15% Internet penetration as the threshold level for the generation of significant hacking activities (Reilly, 2007). It is important to note that Internet penetrations in many developing countries have reached this level.

N. Kshetri, *The Global Cybercrime Industry*, DOI 10.1007/978-3-642-11522-6_8,
© Springer-Verlag Berlin Heidelberg 2010

Table 8.1 Cybercrime situations in selected developing countries

Country	Internet users (% of population 2005)	International cybercrimes originated	Cybercrime victims
Brazil	19.5	2003: World's 10 most active cyber-criminal groups were based in Brazil (Smith, 2003) 2004: Two-thirds of the world's pedophile pages were hosted in Brazil (Leyden, 2004)	• Online financial fraud exceeds the loss through bank robberies (Leyden, 2004) • 2006: Over half of firms with Internet access were virus-attack victims (ITU, 2007)
China	8.5	According to a Symantec report, 5% of the world's malware-infected computers were in Beijing in 2006 Overtook the United States in the number of malware hosts	• 2007: Attacks on PC rose by 2125% (WEBWIRE, 2008) • 2004: 58% of large government, educational, and commercial entities experienced cybercrimes (US, Commercial Service, 2004)
India	5.5	Data frauds have been reported in call centers in Pune, Hyderabad, Bangalore, and Gurgaon (tribuneindia.com 2005; Schwartz 2005, Fest 2005)	• The Cyber Crime Investigation Cell (CCIC) recorded 159 cases in 2006, 344 in 2007, 775 in 2008, 718 in the first 8 months of 2009 (Sawant, 2009) • 2006: 565 people arrested on cybercrime-related charges (Expressindia, 2008) • Cybercrime cases increased by 200% in Delhi in 2007 and credit card fraud in the city went up by 500% (hindu.com, 2008) • August 2007: Bank of India's network was attacked with Mpack-created virus, which forwarded financial data to Russian Business Network (RBN) (Krebs, 2007) • Mid-2007–mid-2008: 10 ministry websites were attacked (Raghav, 2008) • During September 2007–September 2009, Indian banks experienced over 1,000 unique phishing attacks (Indiatimes, 2009) • Cybercrime cases in Mumbai: 142 in 2005, to 159 in 2006, 344 in 2007, and 775 in 2008 (Hindustan Times, 2009)

Table 8.1 (continued)

Country	Internet users (% of population 2005)	International cybercrimes originated	Cybercrime victims
Panama	6.4	Over 100 portals with child pornography content hosted in 2007 (Frayssine, 2007)	
Poland	26.2	An ISP produced 5% of the world's spam in 2007 (Greenberg, 2007)	
Romania	20.8	Cybercrime industry is bigger than drug smuggling or human trafficking industries (Wylie, 2007)	
Russian Federation	15.2	Russians have a profitable niche in Internet dating fraud (Wylie, 2007)	
South Africa	10.9		• 2005: About 12,000 computer crimes were registered (BBC Monitoring International Reports, 2006) • Cybercrime is the fastest growing white collar crime • 2007: PricewaterhouseCoopers' biennial Global Economic Crime Survey: 72% companies became cybercrime victims in the previous 2 years (Africa News, 2007)
The Philippines	5.4	A Philippino hacker launched the "Love Letter" virus in 2000. Estimated damage in the US: $4–15 billion (Adams, 2001)	• 2007: More than 330 cyberattacks per day, the sixth highest cybercrime target country in the world (Conti, 2007)

The underlying notion in this chapter is that cybercrimes in developing and developed countries are characterized by important structural differences. The sources, targets as well as other ingredients structurally differ in developing and developed countries. First, as we have demonstrated, economic factors facing cyber-criminal and cybercrime victims are significantly different in developing and developed countries. They include nature and quality of hardware, software, and infrastructure; targetability of victims; stock of cybercrime skills; and associated opportunity costs and benefits.

A second, probably more significant factor, relates to formal and informal institutions in these economies. As explained in Chap. 3, cyber-criminals' activities can be explained in terms of Baumol's (1990) destructive entrepreneurship. The society's "rules of the game," known as institutions affect the extent of such activities (Baumol, 1990; North, 1990, 1996).

Institutions can be better understood in the context of the tasks for which they were created (Holm, 1995). Relevant institutions from the standpoint of cybercrimes include the availability of jurisdictional arbitrage and strength of rule of law and stigmatization issues associated with becoming a cyber-criminal or a cybercrime victim.

A final reason why cybercrimes in developing and developed countries are likely to differ is related to cognitive factors. Cyber-criminals as well as cybercrime victims in these two groups of countries are likely to differ in terms of confidence, skills, and experiences.

8.2 A Brief Survey of Cybercrimes in Developing Countries

Tables 7.1 and 7.2 (Chap. 7) presented quantitative indicators related to cybercrimes in developing countries. Table 8.1 presents some qualitative indicators. In some cities such as Mumbai in India, there have been more cybercrime cases being registered with the police than conventional crimes such as murder, burglary, and arson (Hindustan Times, 2009).

An increasing number of cyberattacks targeting developing countries are international in nature. For instance, it is reported that cyber-criminals from Malaysia, Japan, Korea, the United States, and China have targeted computers in the Philippines (Conti, 2007). In a well-publicized case, it was found that Canada-based hackers employed about 100,000 poorly protected "zombie" computers mainly in developing countries such as Poland, Brazil, and Mexico and stole US $44 million (Harwood, 2008). Experts argue that this is an indication of a change in the victim/victimizer pattern and an unusual case of role reversal.

In Chap. 1, we discussed Gordon and Ford's (2006) classification of Type I and Type II cybercrimes. Because of their lower digitization, Type II cybercrimes, which mainly involve human elements are likely to be proportionately higher in developing countries compared to those in industrialized countries. For instance, many

Indians are reported to be victims of various versions of "Nigerian 419"[1] fraud, which involve criminal–victim interaction (Srivastava, 2009).

8.2.1 Broadband Connections and Increase in Cybercrimes

In a discussion of cybercrimes in developing economies, the rapid proliferation of broadband connections in these economies deserves special attention. At this point, we should emphasize that one reason why US computers are attractive targets for cyber-criminals is because they are always online and have broadband connections. Note that serious cybercrimes require bandwidth intensive applications. A related point is that African networks do not attract the same level of attention from hackers as other regions of the world because of the low level of connectivity of the region and low broadband penetration. From the criminal's standpoint, the African environment is thus highly unreliable for carrying out cyberattacks effectively (Reilly, 2007). Not that typical "bot-herders" control tens of thousands and even millions of "zombie" computers.

Not long ago, most African economies lacked fiber-optic cable and relied on slower satellite links to connect to the World Wide Web, which meant longer time to attack local websites (Kinyanjui, 2009). In June 2009, East Africa got its first fiber-optic submarine cable. Two additional companies are expected to complete similar projects by the end of 2009. The project is expected to speed up the connections in Kenya, Burundi, Rwanda, Tanzania and Uganda, Somalia, Ethiopia, and Sudan. Analysts argue that Africa and other developing countries are likely to experience a rapid growth of cybercrime as broadband technology takes off in these economies (Africa News, 2007; The Economist, 2009). For instance, Kenya experienced about 800 bot attacks per day in July 2009, which is expected to increase to 50,000 per day after the fiber connectivity goes live (Kinyanjui, 2009b).

Most obviously, cybercrime proliferation is associated with and facilitated by the growth of broadband networks. In the early 2000s, estimates suggested that about one-third of spam came from zombie computers with broadband connections (Kotadia, 2003). Estimates suggested that in recent years, Zombie computers are almost always connected to broadband Internet.

A number of developing countries are experiencing rapid broadband growth. Analysts argue that increased penetration of broadband in developing countries is likely to make these countries a fertile ground for hackers. It is argued that rise of cybercrime in China can be mainly attributed to the rapid growth of broadband users in the country (Business Daily Update, 2006). China's broadband subscriber base, for instance, grew by 114% in 2004, 57% in 2005 and 38% in 2006 and is expected to experience a double-digit growth for the next few years. China's broadband subscriber base is expected to surpass that of the United States in 2008 (Chan, 2007).

Likewise, broadband connections in Latin America increased by 41% in 2007 and by 2013, average consumer broadband penetration in the region is expected to reach 30 % (Screen Digest, 2008). In particular, in Peru, the number of broadband subscribers rose by over 80% annually during 2001–2006 and it reached about half a million in 2006 (ITU, 2007).

8.3 Economic and Institutional Factors Related to Cybercrimes in Developing Economies

8.3.1 Formal Institutions: Permissiveness of Regulatory Regimes

Most cybercrimes in recent years are committed by organized criminal groups. To understand organized criminal groups' operations, it may be helpful to consider them as rational economic actors with profit maximization goal (Becker, 1968; Ehrlich, 1973; Freeman, Grogger, & Sonstelie, 1996; Sjoquist, 1973; Viano, 1999). Their profit depends upon capability to emulate market mechanisms. This may require formation of strategic alliances, making appropriate capital investment decision, identifying new growth areas, investing in R&D, adopting modern accounting systems, and insuring against risks (Mittelman & Johnston, 1999).

The research literature provides abundant evidence that like multinational firms, organized crime groups consider a number of factors to make decisions related to geographic location of their activities. Perhaps the most important factor influencing the location decision is the strength of the rule of law. A person's decision to participate in an illegal activity is a function of the expected probability of apprehension and conviction and the expected penalty if convicted (Ehrlich, 1996). Many developing countries' weak rule of law and permissiveness of regulatory regimes provide a fertile ground for criminal activities (Mittelman & Johnston, 1999; Vassilev, 2003).

Developing economies are at different degrees of readiness in terms of regulative institutions to deal with cybercrimes. In Africa, for instance, as of September 2009, Kenya and Rwanda recognized electronic signature and electronic crimes. In Tanzania and Uganda, on the other hand, the bills to recognize electronic signature and electronic crimes were at the parliament level (Mark, 2009).

While an increasing number of developing economies have enacted laws to deal with cybercrimes, they lack enforcement mechanisms. As one might expect, developing countries lack judges, lawyers, and other law-enforcement manpower, who understand cybercrimes. For instance, Malaysia's HeiTech Padu Berhad's director noted that out of the country's 40,000 lawyers, only four were able to handle cybercrimes (Ismail, 2008). Similarly, in 2004, of the 4,400 police officers in India's Mumbai city, only five worked in the cybercrime division (Duggal, 2004).

Cybercrime awareness level is very low among the law-enforcement community. For instance, it was reported that when a police officer was asked to seize the hacker's computer in an investigation of a cybercrime in India, he brought the hacker's monitor. In another cybercrime case, the police seized the CD-ROM drive from a hacker's computer instead of the hard disk (Aggarwal, 2009). Likewise, eBay's Albena Spasova, who worked in promoting law reform in Moldova and

Bulgaria noted: "Even in 2001, I was meeting judges who thought cybercrime was someone stealing a computer" (Wylie, 2007).

Regulative institutions in developing economies are also insufficient and impractical to deal with some forms of cybercrimes. Experts, for instance, say that Indian law on computer crime is "fuzzy" (Ribeiro, 2006). India's IT Act 2000, for instance, did not cover phishing, cyberstalking, and cyberharassment (Hindustan Times, 2006). The IT (Amendment) Act 2008, however, has specific provisions on how various cybercrimes such as publishing sexually explicit material, cyber-terrorism, Wi-Fi hacking, sending and viewing child pornography, identity theft, and spam are punished (Deshpande, 2009).

Similarly, due to a lack of cybercrime laws, Indonesian police used a "red book," a manual to conduct credit card investigations available since 1997, to handle Internet credit card fraud (Darmosumarto, 2003). Likewise, according to Brazil's legislation enacted in 1988, a hacker cannot be charged for breaking into a site, or distributing a virus, unless it is proven that the action resulted in a crime (Smith, 2003). In the same vein, Romanian law requires cybercrime victims to send police a signed complaint and be represented at the hearing (Wylie, 2007). It is thus virtually impractical for most US-based eBay fraud victims to bring a case in the Romanian courts.

In Indonesia, only 15% of reported incidents are actually investigated (Shubert, 2003). In India about 10% cybercrimes are reported of those reported about 2% is actually registered. The conviction rate is as low as 2% (Hindustan Times, 2006). As of 2006, no one charged for data fraud in India was convicted (Ribeiro, 2006). As of August 2009, only four people were convicted for cybercrime (Aggarwal, 2009).

One reason why industrialized economies are forced to develop legal and regulatory infrastructures to deal with cybercrimes is because they experience more cybercrimes compared to developing economies. In industrialized countries, while most laws have focused in increasing the severity of punishment for cyber-criminals (Walker, 2004), some also require businesses to enhance defense against cyber-crimes. An estimate suggested that US banks spent US $60 million in 2002 on technology to comply with the requirements of the Patriot Act (McGeer, 2002).

Although criminals in general are emboldened if laws are weak, a much higher degree of jurisdictional arbitrage is available in digital crimes. Not surprisingly, organized cybercrimes are initiated from countries that have few or no laws directed against cybercrimes and little capacity and willingness to enforce existing laws. Commenting on Africa's currently low level but high-growth potential of cyber-crimes, Hamadoun Toure, secretary-general of the ITU put this issue this way: "At the moment, cybercriminals see Africa as a safe haven to operate illegally with impunity" (Africa News, 2007).

We noted above that national level institutions dealing with cybercrimes in developing countries are thin and dysfunctional. Equally problematic are institutions at industry and inter-organizational levels. For instance, there is no insurance company in India that offers a comprehensive anti-cybercrime policy for a company (Syed and D'monte, 2008).

8.3.1.1 Resources to Fight Cybercrimes

Developing economies lack resources to build institutions to combat cybercrimes (Cuéllar, 2004). For instance, consider Ramnicu Valcea town of Romania, where a large number of eBay fraud cases originate. In 2005, two law-enforcement officers in the town were dealing with over 200 eBay cases with a 9-year-old computer that had no Internet connection. And to connect to the Internet they had to use the same cafes as used by cyber-criminals for eBay fraud (Wylie, 2007). Similarly, in the ITU Regional Cybersecurity Forum for Eastern and Southern Africa held in Zambia in 2008, an expert from Democratic Republic of Congo stated that factors such as the lack of legal experts in ICT and poor understanding of ICTs and its added value in the national economy hindered the adoption of cybersecurity-related legislation in the country (ITU, 2008). Likewise, in Bangladesh cellphones with unregistered subscriber identity module (SIM) cards have been increasingly used for extortion activities. However, the cybercrime unit of Dhaka Metropolitan Police (DMP) has not been equipped to handle such crimes (The New Nation, 2009).

8.3.1.2 Cyber-Criminals' Confidence

Increased success is sending positive cognitive messages and making cyber-criminals more brash and disrespectful of law-enforcement agencies (Kshetri, 2005). Because of weak law-enforcement machinery in developing countries, cyber-criminals in these countries are more confident than those in developed countries. A computer forensics expert in Sao Paolo, Brazil noted that Internet crime gangs in the country do not use techniques to hide themselves (Warren, 2007). Likewise, it is reported that many developing world-based hackers targeting the US networks do not conceal their real identities or origin of their mailings (Vardi, 2005).

8.3.2 Informal Institutions: Social Legitimacy and Cybercrime

We noted above how regulative permissiveness has been a driving force behind the growth of the crime industry. But the more immediate—and also the more foundational—reason behind the rapidly rising global cybercrimes relates to the degree of social legitimacy to such crimes. As discussed in Chap. 5, condemnation of an act such as a cybercrime leads to internalization of norms against the act among the "condemners" and as well as the "condemned" (Kahan, 1996). Proponents of "gay rights" legislation, for instance, argue that the real battle centers on gaining social and cultural acceptability, achieving social legitimacy of such rights (Hu, 2001; Shilts, 1991), and stigmatizing "orthodox religious believers" (Duncan, 1994).

As noted in Chap. 2, various factors lead to less guilt in cybercrimes compared to conventional crimes (Kallman & Grillo, 1996; Phukan, 2002). Most obviously, these conditions are more pervasive in developing countries as many Internet users in these countries are connected to the Internet for the first time (redherring.com, 2005). A related point is that developing and developed countries may also differ in terms of social stigma associated with becoming a cybercrime victim. In sum, cybercrimes tend to be more justifiable in developing countries than in developed countries.

8.3.3 Defense Mechanisms Against Cybercrimes

Countries across the world differ in the deployment of security products to address such holes. In 2002, North America accounted for 58% of the global security product market (Europemedia, 2002).

An estimate suggested that in 2006, about 3 million of Brazil's small- and medium-sized enterprises (SMEs) lacked anti-virus software in their PCs (Business Wire, 2006). Likewise, 60% of Kenyan banks are reported to have insecure systems (Kinyanjui, 2009).

The concept of "hollow diffusion" of Internet and e-commerce technologies among firms in developing economies such as China may help understand weak defense mechanisms (Otis and Evans, 2003: 49). The basic idea behind "hollow diffusion" is simple: Many companies adopting e-commerce, especially in developing countries, lack technological and human resources, and other fundamental ingredients needed for long-term success. In short, they lack true depth of Internet adoption. "Hollow diffusion" can take place in human terms (lack of skill and experience) as well as in technological terms (failure to use security products) (Otis & Evans, 2003). It is argued that organizations that adopt Internet technologies without considering the costs and efforts needed to maintain those systems generate a negative externality (Otis & Evans, 2003). A related point is that compared to dominant multinationals, ICT vendors in developing countries tend to be smaller businesses and later entrants into the global ICT market (Denardis, 2007).

8.3.3.1 Hardware and Software Used in Developing Economies

Of equal importance in the discussion of cybercrimes in developing countries that follows below is the nature of hardware and software in these countries. According to the product-cycle approach, ICT products are adapted in developing countries to meet the conditions of local markets and processes to local technological capacity (Nordas, 1996). Most ICT products targeted for developing countries are low-cost versions as advanced features make them unaffordable (Dairy Industries International, 1998). At the same time, universities and other organizations are taking measures to make products available at low cost in developing countries. For instance, Universities Allied for Essential Medicines (UAEM) has called for "open-access" patents from universities to increase low-income countries' access to medicines (Kim, 2007). In some cases, entirely new products are developed for developing world-based consumers. A case in point is Whirlpool's launch of the world's cheapest automatic washer in the US $150–200 price range (Jordan & Karp, 2003).

As an example of entirely new products designed for developing world-based consumers, the One Laptop per Child (OLPC) program deserves special attention. The program aims to provide low-cost computers to children in developing countries. The goal of the OLPC project was to deploy 100 million laptops in the first year (Naraine, 2006). While this goal has not been materialized, the OLPC program has made a significant progress. As of the early 2008, there were an estimated 250,000 children from developing countries across the world, who owned laptops under the OLPC program (South Africa: The Good News, 2008). These computers run on Linux and have a security system called BitFrost (Reilly, 2007). BitFrost's built in features prevent viruses and other programs from "damaging the computer, stealing files, or spying on the user" (Brandt, 2007). It has been robust against viruses so far. Analysts however, argue that hackers may find previously unknown flaws in BitFrost (Reilly, 2007). To substantiate this claim, we draw a parallel with recent intensification of cybercrimes targeting Macs. It is worth noting that cybercriminlas have extended their efforts beyond Windows and such efforts are becoming more sophisticated over time. For instance, while some viruses targeting Macs existed before, Apple's computers experienced financially motivated attacks from organized criminal groups for the first time in 2007 (sophos.com, 2008).

The OLPC program is facing a competition from Intel's low-cost Classmate computers designed for children in developing countries (Clark 2008). Intel sold "tens of thousands" of its first generation of Classmate PCs, which were launched in the early 2007 (thestate.com, 2008). The company announced its plan to start selling a new generation of Classmate PCs starting April 2008. The Classmate computers operate on Windows' cut-down versions (Reilly, 2007). As noted above, most viruses and botnets attack Windows.

8.3.3.2 Internet Users' Skills

Another problem is related to the lack of skills. Many Internet users in developing economies such as China are inexperienced and not technically savvy. A high proportion of them are getting computers and connecting them to the Internet for the first time (redherring.com, 2005). A majority of new Internet users in developing countries also lack English language. While the developments of user-friendly software and interfaces have reduced the complexity and consumer learning requirements (Gatignon & Robertson, 1985) for computer and Internet use, such developments have not taken place in the development of security products.

Most of the information, instructions, and other contents for security products are available in English language only (Information Today, 2008). Many Internet users in developing countries are unable to use IT security products developed in English language. For instance, even if Microsoft publishes a security bulletin in Chinese, it is unlikely to do so in all the 20 dialects of China (redherring.com, 2005).

8.3.3.3 International Hierarchical Pattern in the Diffusion of Security Products

It is also important, in this context, to look at the connection between a country's market size and the availability of technology products in the country. Most developing countries lack market and infrastructures for such products (Brown, Malecki, & Spector, 1976). Put differently, international diffusion of technology products exhibits a "hierarchical pattern" (Gatignon & Robertson, 1985, p. 858). As is the case of other technologies, commercial distributors of IT security products often find developing countries unprofitable for their markets, which lead to adverse international hierarchical pattern of such products. A related point is that the international "hierarchical pattern" is more adverse for security products. While the top security software firms are US-based, businesses and consumers in some developing countries (e.g., Southeast Asia), mainly because of nationalism, prefer to buy domestically manufactured software (Information Today, 2008).

8.3.4 Concentration of Crimes

Deutsch, Hakim, and Weinblatt (1984) suggested that the return to crime is positively related to the concentration of criminals in a neighborhood. Criminals tend to focus their efforts in a few neighborhoods, or crime hot spots, "overwhelming" the law-enforcement agencies and police forces in those neighborhoods (Freeman et al., 1996; Weisburd, Bushway, Lum, & Yanz, 2004). As middle classes tend to avoid "high crime areas," crime hot spots tend to be inner city low-income neighborhoods (Lianos & Douglas, 2000). It is also suggested that sparsely populated neighborhoods are associated with a high rate of violent crimes (Browning, Feinberg, & Dietz, 2004; Wilson, 1987). Note that in the conventional world, most crimes are committed close to home. Criminals travel far only if there are sufficient incentives to leave known territory (van Koppen & Jansen, 1998).

It was apparent from our review that cybercrimes targeting developing economies exhibit a heavy concentration in specific industry sectors. In China, businesses in the online gaming industry and gamers have been attractive targets for hackers (Kshetri, 2009b). These hackers steal gamers' passwords and login information (e.g., World of Warcraft). The stolen virtual items and identities are then auctioned online (Greenberg, 2007). Experts say that an online gaming account in China can be sold for up to US $1,000 compared to US $5–10 for stolen credit card data (Fong, 2008).

In Brazil, a large number of cybercrimes involve malicious codes, most notably keylogging viruses, designed to steal banking passwords (Greenberg, 2007). E-mail spam is getting more personalized (ITU, 2007). Cyber-criminals also use sophisticated social engineering scams to trick Brazilians into giving up personal information. According to the Brazilian Banks Association, estimated losses associated with virtual fraud in 2005 were US $165 million (PR Newswire, 2008). Cyber-criminals also make a rapid adaptation in password-stealing malware to the changes made by banks (PR Newswire, 2008). Likewise most high-profile and widely publicized cybercrimes in India are concentrated in the offshoring sector (Hindustan Times, 2006). For instance, data frauds have been reported in call centers in Pune, Hyderabad, Bangalore, and Gurgaon. The British Tabloid, Sun, reported that an Indian call center employee sold confidential information of 1,000 bank accounts to its reporter working as an undercover (tribuneindia.com, 2005; Hindustan Times, 2006). In another case, call center workers at Pune, India, subsidiary of Mphasis, a provider of outsourcing services, transferred about US $500,000 from four Citibank customers' accounts to their personal accounts (Schwartz, 2005; Fest, 2005). It is reported that in major Indian cities, there are "data brokers," who obtain data illegally from people that are working in offshoring companies (Aggarwal, 2009).

The common denominator to the above examples is that businesses and consumers in leading e-commerce sectors in a developing economy are more likely to be cybercrime targets compared to other less e-commerce ready industries. In China, for instance, online games generated US $1.8 billion in 2007 (China Daily, 2008). Buying and selling of virtual items has been a "mini-economy" in China (Nystedt, 2004).

Similarly, a majority of Brazilians do banking activities online (PR Newswire, February 21, 2008). Indeed, financial services are among the leading e-commerce sectors and banks are positioned to be leaders in e-marketplaces and in e-payment solutions in Brazil and other Latin American countries (Kshetri & Dholakia, 2002). Likewise, Indian offshoring industry's revenue grew from US $4.8 billion in fiscal year 1997–1998 to US $47.8 billion in 2006–2007 (Indo-Asian News Service, 2007).

8.3.5 Path Dependence Externalities Generated by Conventional Crimes and Cybercrimes

As discussed in Chap. 4, due to path dependence of crimes, other things being equal, the more a particular type of crime a society previously had, the higher the odds of observing crimes of the type in the society.

Given the cybercrime environment and feedback loops, increasing returns could manifest themselves in many ways. For instance, cyber-criminals may "invent" sophisticated and new tools that law-enforcement agencies face increased difficulty in tracing. Cyber-criminals could also operate from countries with weak cybercrime laws (Kshetri, 2009a). The externality could also arise because at a given level of law-enforcement resources, an increase in the number of cyber-criminals reduces the probability that a cyber-criminal will be caught (Freeman et al., 1996).

As discussed in Chap. 4, developing countries also differ in terms of leadership in a cybercrime category and the patterns of international cybercrimes originated from these countries. More fully developed examples of cybercrimes are found in East European countries. In Chap. 4, we discussed Romanian and Ukrainian cyber-criminals' specialization in Internet auction frauds and online credit card related crimes (Wylie, 2007). Bulgarian and Chinese cyber-criminals have reportedly specialized in intellectual property theft (Vardi, 2005). For instance, in 2005, a Trojan horse code named Myfip was sending data from the networks of US-based companies to an Internet user in Tianjin, China. Myfip reportedly sent sensitive documents such as CAD/CAM files that stored mechanical designs, electronic circuit board schematics, and layouts (Vardi, 2005). In 2005, a Chinese intern working in Valeo was detained in France for alleged "illegal database intrusion" aimed at intellectual property theft (Luard, 2005).

8.3.6 Cybercrime Business Models in Developing Economies

Developing world in general lags behind the developed world in the availability of IT skills. There are, however, highly skillful organized crime groups in some developing countries. Note that specialized organized crime groups are increasingly engaged in cybercrime activities (Hawser, 2007; Giannangeli, 2008). Indeed, cybercrime has been one of the most important revenue sectors for global organized crime groups (M2 Presswire, 2007). In many cases, organized criminals also buy high-skilled coders as well as low-skilled IT workforce to engage in cybercrimes.

To launder funds stolen through cybercrime operations, organized crime groups often lure and recruit money mules. The mules help to move stolen money from one account to another. Most often they take the stolen funds into their own account before sending as a wire transfer to the criminal groups (Sullivan, 2007). They receive commissions for doing that. For instance, most of Romanian cyber-criminals' auction fraud victims are in the United States, Canada, Britain, Spain, or Italy. Romanian mules are found to pick up money in these countries. In 2006, US law-enforcement agencies arrested an eBay fraud ring in Chicago, which was traced to have connections with cyber-criminals in Pitesti, Romania (Wylie, 2007).

Here is why "money mules" are needed. Cyber-criminals know that credit card transactions initiated from Eastern Europe and some developing countries have a low probability of success. In such cases, they recruit "money mules" in countries where the credit card holder is located (e.g., United States). A US-based "money mule", for instance, uses the stolen credit card to make a transaction in a US bank and then sends the money to the cyber-criminal. One estimate suggested that international cybercrime groups had set up about 44,000 post office boxes and residential addresses in the United States in 2004 (Acohido & Swartz, 2005). US-based online retailers are cautious of shipping across borders. Cybercrime groups, however, know that if an online transaction is approved, shipments inside the United States are rarely scrutinized. They thus recruit US-residents as mules, whose homes are used as shipment drop points.

In some cases, money mules are unaware that they are engaged in illegal activities. Worse still, the mules themselves could become scam victims (Claburn, 2008). To take another example, consider the Nigerian check scam. In this type of scam,

Nigerians send fake documents, which look like Wal-Mart money orders, Bank of America checks, US Postal Service checks, and American Express traveler's checks[2] (Gohring, 2008). They provide a money mule with instructions on filling out the checks and where they would go. The mule cashes the checks and sends most of the check amount to Nigerian cyber-criminals. However, when the check is found to be a fake one, the mule would be responsible for the entire amount.

Location and number of money mules and functions they perform also vary across the type of cybercrimes. Some transactions involve "money mules" located in a number of countries. In a case reported in Sullivan (2007), a cybercrime victim, an online CD and DVD retailer, paid a ransom of US $40,000 to a hacker based in Balakov, western Russia. The fund was wired to 10 different bank accounts in Riga, Latvia. The mules then wired the money to accounts in St. Petersburg and Moscow. Another set of mules brought the money to Balakov. The computer server used by the Balakov-based hacker to launch the botnet attacks was in Houston.

In an interesting pattern of international division of labor, in the early 2008, a criminal group involved in botnet attacks set up offices in India to process applications that cannot be completed automatically (Arnott, 2008). IT workers in the India offered help to facilitate signing up of free e-mail accounts.

8.3.7 Motivations Behind Cybercrimes

As noted in Chap. 2, crime rates are tightly linked to the lack of economic opportunities. A large number of cyberattacks originate from Eastern Europe and Russia because there are a large number of students good at mathematics, physics, and computer (Blau, 2004). Speaking of the social emphasis on mathematics skills among Romanians, a senior research scientist at the Institute of Mathematics in Bucharest put the issue this way: "The respect for math is inside every family, even simple families, who are very proud to say their children are good at mathematics" (Wylie, 2007).

Consistent with history and theory bot herders and other types of cyber-criminals tend to be from locations where high-paying legitimate IT jobs are unavailable (Sullivan, 2007). In industrialized countries, people with IT skills can easily find legitimate IT jobs. In many developing economies, IT job growth is lower than Internet penetration growth (Sulaiman, 2007). The primary reason why some people are attracted into cybercrime in Eastern Europe and Russia is because of high unemployment and low wages. Organized crime groups in countries such as Russia, Romania, and Brazil are thus tapping into the technical skills available in those countries to expand their operations.

The combination of over-educated and under-employed computer experts has made Russia and other Eastern European countries fertile ground for hackers. While IT industries are developing in these economies, the growth rate is far from enough to absorb students and the workforce with IT skills. Students good at mathematics, physics, and computer science are having difficulties to find jobs in these countries (Blau, 2004). Beyond all that, in Russia a financial crash in 1998 left many computer programmers unemployed. In Russia, top university graduate are paid by organized crime groups up to 10 times as much as from legitimate IT jobs (Warren, 2007).

A related point is that notwithstanding India's huge IT talents, the country accounts for proportionately fewer cybercrimes compared to other developing countries. For instance, according to Sophos researchers, the United Kingdom and India together contributed 1.3% of the world's malware. While they could not separate malware originated from the United Kingdom and India as both use British English, the United Kingdom is considered to account for more crimes than India (Greenberg, 2007). The primary reason behind India's low cybercrime profile is the development of legitimate IT industry in the country. Speaking of a low rate of cybercrimes in the country, Nandkumar Saravade, director of cybersecurity for India's National Association of Software and Service Companies noted: "Today ? any person in India with marketable computer skills has a few job offers in hand" (Greenberg, 2007).

8.4 Concluding Comments

This chapter has contributed to the conceptual and empirical understanding of the structure of cybercrimes in the context of the developing world. The analyses indicated that the nature of the source of a web attack is a function of the nature of institutional legitimacy to a cyber-criminal; and stocks of hacking skills relative to the availability of economic opportunities; and potential victims' defense mechanisms. Table 8.2 presents economic and institutional factors facing cybercrime offenders and victims in a developing economy.

Anti-cybercrime institutions are developing rapidly in industrialized economies because of exogenous shocks, pressures to change organizational logics and other

Table 8.2 Economic and institutional factors facing offenders and victims

	Economic factors	Institutional factors
Offender	[1] • Lack of availability of other economic opportunities	[3] • Jurisdictional arbitrage: No or few laws dealing with cybercrimes • More confident cyber-criminals • Novelty factor and stigmatization • Path dependence and specialization in specific crimes
Victim	[2] • Heavy concentration of cybercrimes in specific industry sectors • Hierarchical pattern of the diffusion of security products • Hollow diffusion of Internet and e-commerce	[4] • Stigmatization • Lack of strong security mechanisms • Less experienced computer users—weak psychological/behavioral defense

forces of gradual changes. In many developing economies, on the other hand, formal institutions are weak because these countries lack laws that recognize cybercrime, they lack judges, lawyers, and other law-enforcement manpower who understand cybercrimes, and they lack resources to build institutions to combat cybercrime. Governments' measures to combat cybercrimes too often remain pure lip service. One reason for this problem is a lack of resources to build formal institutions to deal with cybercrimes (Cuéllar, 2004). Equally problematic are institutions at industry and inter-organizational levels. Because of weak law-enforcement machinery in developing countries, cyber-criminals in these countries are more confident than those in developed countries.

Cybercrimes may be more justifiable if informal institutions (or social and internalized norms) against them are weaker in a society. These conditions are more pervasive in economies, in which many Internet users are connected to the Internet for the first time (redherring.com, 2005). Moreover, cybercrime victimization level is relatively low in these economies.

As noted earlier, most people involved in using computer networks unethically and illegally do not perceive their actions' ethical implications. Factors giving rise to such conditions are stronger in developing countries. This is because the Internet is new for many users in developing countries. A related point is that many organizations and individuals are unaware of cybercrimes. Cybercrimes are more justifiable in developing countries than in developed countries. As pointed out by social identity theory argues (Hamner, 1992; Tajfel & Turner, 1986), as more and more individuals and organizations become cybercrime victims and they belong to the in-group of cybercrime victims the perceived social stigma associated with a cyber-criminal may increase and that of becoming a cybercrime victim may reduce. Based on above discussion, the following proposition is presented.

Many Internet users in developing economies are inexperienced and not technically savvy. Most organizations adopt these technologies without considering security and other related problems. Even if organizations are willing to secure their systems, because of the adverse international "hierarchical pattern" for security products, these products are less likely to be available in these economies.

Thin and dysfunctional institutions and a lack of resources are among the biggest roadblocks for combating cybercrimes in developing countries. A lack of international cooperation and coordination is equally problematic in fighting cybercrimes originated in developing countries.

Yet, notwithstanding the political, legal, cultural, and economic barriers, some economies are making some great leaps. Some developing countries are also modernizing their crime-fighting efforts. It was, for instance, reported in 2006 that Kenya was in advanced stages for assembling a cybercrime laboratory, which could be used by police in Eastern African countries (Kornakov, 2006). In September 2009, Antigua opened a state-of-the-art cyberforensics facility to serve the entire Caribbean region to fight cybercrimes. Montserrat, Barbados, St Kitts Nevis, and Antigua and Barbuda would use the lab. The United States provided over US $500,000 to establish the lab and US $200,000 to train the workforce (caribbean360.com, 2009).

Indian offshoring industry provides a remarkable example of industry-government collaboration in combating against cybercrime (Box 8.1). Especially the National Association of Software and Services Companies (NASSCOM) has played an exemplary role in bringing institutional changes in cybercrime-related institutions (Kshetri & Dholakia, 2009).

Box 8.1 NASSCOM's Efforts in Fighting Cybercrimes in the Indian Offshoring Industry

Indian offshoring industry provides a remarkable example of industry-government collaboration in combating against cybercrime. India's National Association of Software and Services Companies (NASSCOM) works with police officers, lawyers, and industry bodies to ensure enforcement. NASSCOM meets with bar councils in different cities to educate legal communities. It also educates police officers about cybersecurity and trains them to recognize and prosecute cybercrimes (Ticoll, 2004). NASSCOM started working with Mumbai police since 2003 (Saravade & Saravade, 2007). NASSCOM helped police departments of Mumbai and Thane in establishing a cybercrime unit and in training officers to investigate data theft (Indo-Asian News Service, 2006). In 2005, NASSCOM announced a training initiative for Pune's cybercrime unit, which caught data crime perpetrators from MphasiS, a major ICT company (Cone, 2005). A third cybercrime unit established in Bangalore in January 2007 has resources to train more than 1,000 police officers and other law-enforcement personnel annually (COMMWEB, 2007). Similar units were planned for other cities. NASSCOM also offered to work with authorities in the United Kingdom and India to investigate cases involving identity theft (tribuneindia.com, 2005).

The Data Security Council of India (DSCI), a self-regulatory member organization set up by NASSCOM, has the ability to expel non-compliant members or call in police (McCue, 2007). Companies that fail to secure their data may have to pay up to US $1 million (Hindustan Times, 2006). NASSCOM has also established a CyberCop committee and a member of the committee serves as a technical advisor to the Indian CyberCrime Investigation Cell.

NASSCOM asked the Indian government to create a special court to try people accused of cybercrimes and other violations of the country's Information Technology Act. The Indian government is considering NASSCOM's request in establishing such courts (Ribeiro, 2006). NASSCOM has also launched a registry of IT employees, which allows employers to perform background checks on existing or prospective employees (Hindustan Times, 2006; Trombly, 2006; Trombly & Yu, 2006). Creation of criminal and public records databases has been a part of the program (Fest, 2005).

In September 2007, the Indian government announced a grant of US $900 thousand to Central Bureau of Investigation (CBI) for combating cybercrime (BBC Monitoring South Asia, 2007).

NASSCOM's measures have paid off brilliantly. Studies conducted by Forrester Research and by the UK's Banking Code Standards Board indicated that security standards in Indian call centers are among the best in the world and there were more security breaches in the United Kingdom and the United States in 2005 than in India (Precision Marketing, 2006).

We noted above that growth of Internet and broadband penetrations in developing countries is likely to lead to a more rapid growth of cybercrimes in these countries than in developed countries. Other economic factors related to cybercrimes such as availability of resources to fight cybercrimes and availability of economic opportunities are likely to change at slower rates. Institutions related to cybercrimes are even slower to change, especially informal institutions.

On the bright side, developing world-based firms have also increased investments in security. The security market in China showed a 24% increase during 2006 (Hope, 2008). Factors such as the 2008 Olympics in Beijing, the 2010 World Expo in Shanghai, and a steady rise in broadband usage as a vehicle for online entertainment have boosted the growth (Hope, 2008). Likewise, small and medium businesses in Brazil spent an estimated US $260 million in 2007 on IT security solutions (Business Wire, 2006).

Cybercrimes catching international attention have been an important trigger for the strengthening of cybercrime laws in some developing economies. For instance, the Philippine Republic Act 8792 came following the love bug virus attack. The act laid out how cybercrimes should be punished in the country (Evans, 2000).

Other developing countries are also taking some measures against cybercrimes. In November 2006, the Bangladesh hosted a regional cybercrime seminar to exchange experience on combating cybercrime and foster future cooperation, leading towards a strong regional response to cybercrime. Experts dealing with cybercrime issues from Australia, Hong Kong, Sri Lanka, and Nepal participated. The Australian Federal Police supported the seminar (Asia Pulse, 2007).

It is also important to include developing economies in international level policy initiatives. In the first UN forum on Internet governance some developing countries such as Iran and South Africa complained that they had not been given an opportunity to adequately express their views on ethical issues and other concerns (RTÉ, 2006).

Economic factors related to cybercrimes such as hardware and software used, broadband connections, stock of cybercrime skills, availability of economic opportunities, diffusion of security products are changing in developing economies. Institutions related to cybercrimes, on the other hand, tend to be persistent (Parto, 2005), durable (Hodgson, 2003), and stable (Scott, 1995, 2001) and hence are slower to change. Moreover, in most cases, compared to formal institutions, de-institutionalization and re-institutionalization of social practices, cultural values, and beliefs occur very slowly (Clark & Soulsby, 1999; Ibrahim & Galt, 2002, p. 109; North 1990; Zweynert & Goldschmidt, 2006). Informal institutions such as those related to stigmatization of a cyber-criminal and a cybercrime victim are thus likely to change more slowly than formal institutions such as strength of rule of law.

Notes

1. Nigerian 419 fraud is named for a section of the Nigerian criminal code.
2. Edna Fiedler of the Washington State pleaded guilty in March 2008 for a scam of this type.

References

Acohido, B., & Swartz, J. (2005, July 11). Cybercrooks lure citizens into international crime. *USA Today*. http://www.usatoday.com/tech/news/2005-07-10-cyber-mules-cover_x.htm. Accessed 5 October 2009.

Adams, J. (2001, May/June). Virtual defense. *Foreign Affairs*, 98–112.

Africa News. (2007, October 24). South Africa; Internet banking fraud on the increase.

Aggarwal, V. (2009, August 3). Cyber crime's rampant. *Express Computer*. http://www. expresscomputeronline.com/20090803/market01.shtml. Accessed 27 October 2009.

Arnott, S. (2008, March 22). Cyber crime stays one step ahead. http://www.independent. co.uk/news/business/analysis-and-features/cyber-crime-stays-one-step-ahead-799395.html. Accessed 27 October 2009.

Asia Pulse. (2007, November 6). Cybercrime cost is a burden on developing countries: Bangladesh.

Baumol, W. J. (1990). Entrepreneurship: Productive, unproductive, and destructive. *Journal of Political Economy, 98* (5), 893–921.

BBC Monitoring International Reports. (2006, September 30). Kazakhstan Russian police chief urges cis efforts against cybercrime.

BBC Monitoring South Asia. (2007, September 15). India takes steps to tackle cybercrime.

Becker, G. S. (1968). Crime and punishment: An economic approach. *Journal of Political Economy, 76*, 169–217.

Blau, J. (2004, May 28). Viruses: From Russia, with love? *IDG News Service*. http://www. pcworld.com/news/article/0,aid,116304,00.asp. Accessed 27 October 2005.

Brandt, R. L. (2007). Ivan Krstic, 21. *Technology Review, 110*(5), 54–55.

Brown, L., Malecki, E., & Spector, A. (1976). Adopter Categories in a Spatial Context: Alternative explanations for an empirical regularity. *Rural Sociology, 41*, 99–118.

Browning, C. R., Feinberg, S. L., & Dietz, R. D. (2004). The paradox of social organization: Networks, collective efficacy, and violent crime in urban neighborhoods. *Social Forces, 83*(2), 503–534.

Business Daily Update. (2006, September 28). China tops globe in robot PCs.

Business Wire. (2006, November 20). SMBs in Brazil to Spend $260USM on IT Security in 2007; – Up to 72% of Brazil-based MBs Cited Enhanced Data Security and Privacy as Key Factors Influencing IT Purchases, AMI Partners Study Finds.

caribbean360.com. (2009, September 28). Regional cyber lab opens in Antigua. http://www. caribbean360.com/News/Caribbean/Stories/2009/09/28/NEWS0000008964.html. Accessed 27 October 2009.

Chan, I. (2007, July 26). China's Disturbing Broadband Decline: A digital divide between saturated urban areas and underserved rural markets is behind the slowdown. http://www. businessweek.com/globalbiz/content/jul2007/gb20070726_579284.htm?campaign_id=rss_as. Accessed 27 October 2009.

China Daily. (2008, May 5). China gets its game on. http://www.chinadaily.com.cn/bizchina/2008-05/05/content_6661519.htm. Accessed 2 October 2008.

Claburn, T. (2008, April 9). The Cybercrime Economy. http://www.informationweek.com/blog/main/archives/2008/04/the_cyber_crime.html. Accessed 7 October 2008.

Clark, D. (2008). PC makers race to market with low-cost 'Netbooks'. *Wall Street Journal* (Eastern edition), B.1.

Clark, E., & Soulsby, A. (1999). *Organisational change in post-communist Europe*. London: Routledge.

COMMWEB. (2007, January 4). India will train police to catch cybercriminals.

Cone, E. (2005). Is offshore BPO running around? *CIO Insight, 53*, 22.

Conti, M. K. C. (2007). Firms warned vs. cybercrimes. *BusinessWorld*, S1/7.

Cuéllar, M. (2004). The mismatch between state power and state capacity in transnational law enforcement. *Berkeley Journal of International Law, 22*(1), 15–58.

Dairy Industries International. (1998). No fuss printing basics assist third world trade, *63*(2), 48.

Darmosumarto, S. (2003, December 8). Battle on Internet credit card fraud still long. *The Jakarta Post*. http://www.crime-research.org/news/2003/12/Mess0802.html. Accessed 27 October 2005.

Denardis, L. (2007, November 11). Internet standards and developing countries: Problems and opportunities. Giganet second annual symposium, Rio De Janeiro, Brazil. http://www.igloo.org/community.igloo?r0=community-download&r0_script=/scripts/document/download.script&r0_pathinfo=%2F%7B58dacb33-31ea-4219-9124-89a75ffe71d0%7D%2FPublic%20Library%2Fpapers~1%2Fdenardis&r0_output=xml. Accessed 27 October 2009.

Deshpande, S. (2009, October 28) New cyber law casts its net wide. *The Economic Times*. http://economictimes.indiatimes.com/infotech/internet/New-cyber-law-casts-its-net-wide-/articleshow/5170897.cms. Accssed 29 October 2009.

Deutsch, J., Hakim, S., & Weinblatt, J. (1984). Interjurisdictional criminal mobility: A theoretical perspective. *Urban Studies, 21*, 451–458.

Duggal, P. (2004). What's wrong with our cyber laws? http://www.expresscomputeronline.com/20040705/newsanalysis01.shtml

Duncan, R. (1994). Who wants to stop the church: Homosexual rights, legislation, public policy, and religious freedom. *Notre Dame Law Review, 69*, 393.

Ehrlich, I. (1973). Participation in illegitimate activities: A theoretical and empirical investigation. *Journal of Political Economy, 81*, 521–565.

Ehrlich, I. (1996). Crime, punishment, and the market for offenses? *Journal of Economic Perspectives, 10*(1), 43–67.

Europemedia. (2002, June 13). Terrorist attacks mean bid e-security spending, 1.

Evans, J. (2000). Cyber-crime laws emerge, but slowly. http://archives.cnn.com/2000/TECH/computing/07/05/cyber.laws.idg. Accessed 27 October 2005.

Expressindia. (2008, January 7). Cyber crime in India on the decline: Report. http://www.expressindia.com/latest-news/Cyber-crime-in-India-on-the-decline-Report/258638/.

Fest, G. (2005). Offshoring: Feds take fresh look at India BPOs; Major theft has raised more than a few eyebrows. *Bank Technology News, 18*(9), 1.

Fong, C. (2008, May 8). Fighting the agents of organized cybercrime. http://www.cnn.com/2008/TECH/05/08/digitalbiz.cybercrime. Accessed 27 October 2009.

Frayssine, F. (2007). Latin America: New 'Cyber Paradise' for Paedophiles and Racists? *ipsnews.net* http://ipsnews.net/news.asp?idnews=40072. Accessed 11 April 2010.

Freeman, S., Grogger, J., & Sonstelie, J. (1996). The spatial concentration of crime. *Journal of Urban Economics, 40*(2), 216–231.

Gatignon, H., & Robertson, T. S. (1985). A propositional inventory for new diffusion research. *Journal of Consumer Research, 11*, 849–867.

Giannangeli, M. (2008). Are we ready for Russian Mafia's crime revolution? *Sunday Express*, Scottish Edition, 4.

Gohring, N. (2008, June 25). Woman gets two years for aiding Nigerian internet check scam. *PC World*. http://www.pcworld.com/businesscenter/article/147575/woman_gets_two_years_for_aiding_nigerian_internet_check_scam.html.

Gordon, S., & Ford, R. (2006). On the definition and classification of cybercrime. *Journal in Computer Virology, 2*, 13–20.

Greenberg, A. (2007, July 17). The top countries for cybercrime. *Forbes.com*. http://www.forbes.com/2007/07/13/cybercrime-world-regions-tech-cx_ag_0716cybercrime.html. Accessed on 9 April 2008.

Hamner, K. M. (1992). Gay-bashing: A social identity analysis of violence against Lesbians and Gay Men. In G. M. Herek & K. Berrill (Eds.), *Hate crimes: Confronting violence against Lesbians and Gay Men* (pp. 179–190). Newbury Park, CA: Sage.

Harwood, M. (2008, February 22). Quebec police break up hacking syndicate. *Security Management*. http://www.securitymanagement.com/news/quebec-police-break-hacking-syndicate.

Hawser, A. (2007). Banks on the spot over internet fraud. *Global Finance, 21*(8), 8.

Hindustan Times. (2006, October 22). Securing the web.

Hindu.com. (2008, April 1). Delhi Police to train officers on combating cyber crime. http://www.hindu.com/thehindu/holnus/002200804011653.htm

Hindustan Times. (2009, October 24). Wired for trouble. http://www.tmcnet.com/usubmit/2009/10/24/4442635.htm. Accessed on 29 October 2009.

Hodgson, G. M. (2003). The hidden persuaders: Institutions and individuals in economic theory. *Cambridge Journal of Economics, 27*, 159–175.

Holm, P. (1995). The dynamics of institutionalization: Transformation processes in Norwegian fisheries. *Administrative Science Quarterly, 40*(3), 398–422.

Hope, C. (2008, March 20). UK security threat from cyber crime. http://www.telegraph.co.uk/news/main.jhtml?xml=/news/2008/03/19/nterror319.xml. Accessed 27 October 2008.

Hu, V. T. (2001). Nondiscrimination or secular orthodoxy? Religious freedom and breach of contract at Tufts University. *Texas Review of Law & Politics, 6*(1), 289–333.

Ibrahim, G., & Galt, V. (2002). Bye-bye central planning, hello market hiccups: Institutional transition in Romania. *Cambridge Journal of Economics, 26*(1), 105.

Indiatimes. (2009, September 24). Phishing attacks on Indian brands rising. *Symantec*. http://economictimes.indiatimes.com/infotech/software/Phishing-attacks-on-Indian-brands-rising-Symantec/articleshow/5051231.cms. Accessed 27 October 2009.

Indo-Asian News Service. (2007, January 23). Indian IT revenue grows 10-fold in decade. *NASSCOM*.

Information Today. (2008, February). Challenges in the East. *25*(2), 22.

Ismail, I. (2008). Understanding cybercriminals. *New Straits Times* (Malaysia), 12.

ITU. (2007). *World Information Society Report 2007*, International Telecommunication Union. http://www.itu.int/osg/spu/publications/worldinformationsociety/2007. Accessed 27 October 2009.

ITU. (2008). ITU Regional Cybersecurity Forum 2008 Lusaka, Zambia, Meeting Report: ITU Regional Cybersecurity Forum for Eastern and Southern Africa, Lusaka, Zambia, 25–28 August 2008, 29 August 2008. http://www.itu.int/ITU-D/cyb/events/2008/lusaka/docs/lusaka-cybersecurity-forum-report-aug-08.pdf. Accessed 5 October 2009.

Jordan, M., & Karp, J. (2003). Machines for the masses; Whirlpool aims cheap washer at Brazil, India and China; Making due with slower spin. *Wall Street Journal*, A.19.

Kahan, D. M. (1996). What do alternative sanctions mean? *63 U. Chicago Law Review, 591*, 603–604.

Kallman, E. A., & Grillo, J. P. (1996). *Ethical decision making and information technology, 2e*. New York: McGraw Hill.

Kim, J. Y. (2007). Toward a golden age. *Harvard International Review, 29*(2), 20–25.

Kinyanjui, K. (2009). High speed Internet exposes Kenya to cybercrime. http://www.businessdailyafrica.com/-/539444/638794/-/rx1rgv/-/. Accessed 5 October 2009.

Kinyanjui, K. (2009b, September 8). Watchdog warns of increased cybercrime threat. http://www.businessdailyafrica.com/Company%20Industry/-/539550/654440/-/u765i9z/-/. Accessed 5 October 2009.

Kornakov, K. (2006, September 8). Police forces in East Africa will have a new hi-tech lab. http://www.viruslist.com/en/viruses/news?id=197753850. Accessed 27 October 2007.

Kotadia, M. (2003, December 3). Report: A third of spam spread by RAT-infested PCs. *CNET News.com*. http://www.news.com/Report-A-third-of-spam-spread-by-RAT-infested-PCs/2100-7355_3-5113080.html. Accessed 27 October 2005.

Krebs, B. (2007, October 13). Taking on the Russian business network. http://blog.washingtonpost.com/securityfix/2007/10/taking_on_the_russian_business.html. Accessed 27 October 2008.

Kshetri, N. (2005). Pattern of global cyber war and crime: A conceptual framework. *Journal of International Management, 11*(4), 541–562.

Kshetri, N. (2009a). Positive externality, increasing returns and the rise in cybercrimes. *Communications of the ACM, 52*(12), 141–144.

Kshetri, N. (2009b). The evolution of the chinese online gaming industry. *Journal of Technology Management in China, 4*(2), 158–179.

Kshetri, N., & Dholakia, N. (2002). Determinants of the global diffusion of B2B e-commerce. *Electronic Markets, 12*(2), 120–129.

Kshetri, N., & Dholakia, N. (2009). Professional and trade associations in a nascent and formative sector of a developing economy: A case study of the NASSCOM effect on the Indian Offshoring industry. *Journal of International Management, 15*(2), 225–239.

Leyden, J. (2004, September 23). US credit card firm fights DDoS attack. http://www.theregister.co.uk/2004/09/23/authorize_ddos_attack. Accessed 27 October 2005.

Lianos, M., & Douglas, M. (2000). Dangerization and the end of deviance. *The British Journal of Criminology, 40*(2), 261–278.

Luard, T. (2005, July 22). China's spies come out from the cold. http://news.bbc.co.uk/2/hi/asia-pacific/4704691.stm. Accessed 27 October 2007.

M2 Presswire. (2007, July 13). Frost & Sullivan: Correction: Cybercrime drives growth and increased competition in the global anti-malware market.

Mark, O. (2009). ICT experts gear up for war against e-crime. http://www.businessdailyafrica.com/Company%20Industry/-/539550/655032/-/u75jcqz/-/. Accessed 5 October 2009.

McCue, A. (2007, June 7). India gets offshore cyber crime watchdog. *silicon.com*. http://services.silicon.com/bpo/0,3800004865,39167417,00.htm.

McGeer, B. (2002). Security: Bankers fight a new battle it adjustments, purchases Part of Patriot Act. *Bank Technology News, 15*(11), 1.

Miller, N. (2008). Casting a wide net for cyber crimes. *The Age* (Melbourne, Australia), 6.

Mittelman, J. H., & Johnston, R. (1999). The globalization of organized crime, the courtesan state, and the corruption of civil society. *Global Governance, 5*(1), 103–126.

Naraine, R. (2006). Money Bots: Hackers cash in; Research group details how lucrative PC hijacking can be. *eWeek*, 27.

Nordas, H. K. (1996). South African manufacturing industries – Catching up or falling behind? *The Journal of Development Studies, 32*(5), 715–733.

North, D. C. (1990). *Institutions, institutional change and economic performance*. Cambridge, MA: Harvard University Press.

North, D. C. (1996). Epilogue: Economic Performance Through Time. In L. J. Alston, T. Eggertsson, & D. C. North (Eds.), *Empirical studies in institutional change* (pp. 342–355). Cambrige, PA: Cambridge University Press.

Nystedt, D. (2004). Online gaming growing fast in China, study says. http://archive.thestandard.com/movabletype/datadigest/archives/003210.php. Accessed 27 October 2005.

Otis, C., & Evans, P. (2003). The Internet and Asia-Pacific security: Old conflicts and new behavior. *Pacific Review, 16*(4), 549–550.

Parto, S. (2005). Economic activity and institutions: Taking stock. *Journal of Economic Issues, 39*(1), 21–52.

Phukan, S. (2002, June). IT ethics in the Internet age: New dimensions. *InSITE*. http://proceedings.informingscience.org/IS2002Proceedings/papers/phuka037iteth.pdf. Accessed 27 October 2005.

PR Newswire. (2008, February 21). New McAfee research shows regionalized malware rising; More attacks tailored to different cultures and technologies.

Precision Marketing. (2006, October 6). India call centres set to triple US Bank work. *18*(42).

Raghav, K. (2008, June 26). Cyber attacks will be disruptive, not destructive. http://www.livemint.com/2008/06/26001839/Cyber-attacks-will-be-disrupti.html. Accessed 27 October 2009.

redherring.com. (2005, April 5). China's Zombie PCs. http://www.redherring.com/Home/11708. Accessed 27 October 2006.

Reilly, M. (2007). Beware, botnets have your PC in their sights. *New Scientist, 196*(2634), 22–23.

Ribeiro, J. (2006, September 7). India's Nasscom calls for special cybercrimes court. *Network World*. http://www.networkworld.com/news/2006/090706-indias-nasscom-calls-for-special.html. Accessed 27 October 2007.

RTÉ. (2006, November 2). Global forum on Web bridges 'cultural gap'. *RTÉ Commercial Enterprises*. http://www.rte.ie/business/2006/1102/internet.html. Accessed 1 October 2009.

Saravade, P., & Saravade, N. (2007). A public-private partnership in India: Broken windows in cyberspace. *The Police Chief, 74*(3), 16.

Sawant, N. (2009, October 5). Virtually speaking, crime in the city on an upward spiral. *The Times of India*. http://timesofindia.indiatimes.com/news/city/mumbai/Virtually-speaking-crime-in-the-city-on-an-upward-spiral/articleshow/5087668.cms. Accessed 27 October 2009.

Schwartz, K. D. (2005). The background-check challenge. *InformationWeek*, 59–61.

Scott, R. (1995). *Institutions and organizations*. Thousand Oaks, CA: Sage.

Scott, R. (2001). *Institutions and organizations*. Thousand Oaks, CA: Sage.

Screen Digest. (2008). Telefonica takes the lead in Latin America. http://www.screendigest.com/press/releases/press_releases_22_01_2008/view.html

Shilts, R. (1991, January). The queering of America. *The Advocate*, 1.

Shubert, A. (2003, February 6). Taking a swipe at cyber card fraud. *CNN.com*. http://www.cnn.com/2003/WORLD/asiapcf/southeast/02/06/indonesia.fraud. Accessed 27 October 2005.

Sjoquist, D. L. (1973). Property crime and economic behavior. *American Economic Review, 63*, 439–446.

Smith, T. (2003, October 27). Technology; Brazil becomes a cybercrime lab. http://query.nytimes.com/gst/fullpage.html?res=9F02E3DA1131F934A15753C1A9659C8B63&sec=&spon=&pagewanted=2. Accessed 27 October 2005.

sophos.com. (2008, July 23). Police crack suspected online extortion ring. *Sophos reports*. http://www.sophos.com/virusinfo/articles/extortion.html. Accessed 27 October 2009.

South Africa: The Good News. (2008, April 8). SA kids benefit from one Laptop per child campaign. http://www.sagoodnews.co.za/education/sa_kids_benefit_from_one_laptop_per_child_campaign_.html. Accessed 27 October 2008.

Srivastava, M. (2009, September 14). Pros of con; From credit card fraud to drug peddling and job scams, Nigerians seem to be everywhere in the crime business. *India Today*. http://indiatoday.intoday.in/index.php?option=com_magazine&opt=section&sectionid=36&issueid=127&Itemid=1. Accessed 27 October 2009.

Sulaiman, H. (2007). Quest to fight cybercrime. *New Straits Times*, 13.

Sullivan, B. (2007, April 10). Who's behind criminal bot networks? http://redtape.msnbc.com/2007/04/whos_behind_cri.html. Accessed 27 October 2009.

Syed, F., & D'monte, L. (2008, April 7). India lags in cybercrime insurance. http://www.rediff.com/money/2008/apr/07cyber.htm. Accessed 27 October 2009.

Tajfel, H., & Turner, J. C. (1986). The social identity theory of intergroup behavior. In S. Worchel & W. G. Austin (Eds.), *Psychology of intergroup relations* (pp. 7–24). Chicago, IL: Nelson-Hall.

The Economist. International: It may make life easier and cheaper; East Africa gets broadband. *391*(8636), 46.

The New Nation. (2009, October 5). Cell phone crime rise: Extortions go on unabated. Internet Edition. http://nation.ittefaq.com/issues/2009/10/05/news0827.htm. Accessed 5 October 2009.

thestate.com. (2008, April 15). Intel adds new features to low-cost laptops. http://www.thestate.com/business/story/376162.html. Accessed 27 October 2009.

Ticoll, D. (2004, October). IT industry trade associations and the globalization of knowledge work. *Review of NASSCOM and the Irish Software Association*. http://www.itac.ca/Archive/PolicyandAdvocacy/Outsourcing/04OctITIndustryTrade-AReviewofNASSCOM.pdf. Accessed 27 October 2005.

tribuneindia.com. (2005, June 25). Outsourcing crime Call centre expose can wreak havoc. http://www.tribuneindia.com/2005/20050625/edit.htm. Accessed 27 October 2006.

Trombly, M. (2006). India tightens security. *Insurance Networking & Data Management, 10*(1), 9.

Trombly, M., & Yu, W. (2006). Outsourcing resilient in India. *Securities Industry News, 18*(26), 1–21.

US Commercial Service. (2004, October 15). Approximately 58% of China's internet users experience security problems. China Commercial Brief – American Embassy, Beijing, 2(168). http://www.buyusa.gov/china/en/ccb041015.html. Accessed 27 October 2005.

van Koppen, P. J., & Jansen, R.W. J. (1998). The road to the robbery: Travel patterns in commercial robberies. *The British Journal of Criminology, 38*(2), 230–246.

Vardi, N. (2005). Chinese take out. *Forbes*, 54.

Vassilev, R. (2003). De-development problems in Bulgaria. *East European Quarterly, 37*(3), 345.

Viano, E. C. (1999). *Global organized crime and international security*. Burlington, VT: Ashgate Publishing.

Walker, C. (2004, June). Russian Mafia extorts gambling websites. http://www.americanmafia.com/cgi/clickcount.pl?url=www.americanmafia.com/Feature_Articles_270.html. Accessed 27 October 2005.

Warren, P. (2007, November 15). Hunt for Russia's web criminals the Russian Business Network – Which some blame for 60% of all internet crime – Appears to have gone to ground. *The Guardian*. http://www.guardian.co.uk/technology/2007/nov/15/news.crime. Accessed 5 October 2009.

WEBWIRE. (2008, June 25). First told of Chinese PC hijack explosion. http://www.webwire.com/ViewPressRel.asp?aId=68776. Accessed 27 October 2009.

Weisburd, D., Bushway, S., Lum, C., & Yang, S. M. (2004). Trajectories of crime at places: A longitudinal study of street segments in the city of Seattle. *Criminology, 42*(2), 283–320.

Wilson, W. J. (1987). *The truly disadvantaged*. Chicago: University of Chicago Press.

Wylie, I. (2007). Internet; Romania home base for EBay scammers; The auction website has dispatched its own cyber-sleuth to help police crack fraud rings. *Los Angeles Times*, C.1.

Zweynert, J., & Goldschmidt, N. (2006). The two transitions in Central and Eastern Europe as processes of institutional transplantation. *Journal of Economic Issues, 40*(4), 895–918.

Chapter 9
Institutional and Economic Foundations of Cybercrime Business Models

Four pence – that's the price of your credit card number (a headline in independent.co.uk, Cavaglieri, 2009).
Once you build a better mousetrap, hackers build better mice (Lance Hayden, a manager of professional services in the Cisco Secure Consulting Services group, cf. Grimes, 2001).

Abstract Cybercrime business models are rapidly evolving. It is argued that cyber-criminals closely imitate business models of legitimate corporations. Cybercrime firms and legitimate businesses, however, differ in terms of the important sources of core competence. Legitimate businesses' core processes are centered around creating the most value for customers. Most cyber-criminals' core processes, however, involve extorting and defrauding prospective victims and minimizing the odds of getting caught. Cyber-criminals and legitimate businesses also differ in terms of the legitimacy related to regulative institutions and inter-organizational arrangements. This chapter disentangles the mechanisms behind the cybercrime business models and examines the contexts and processes associated with such models.

9.1 Criminal Entrepreneurship and Business Models in the Digital World

A framework for theorizing and organizing illegal activities as entrepreneurial activities has recently gained popularity (Kshetri, 2009; Warner & Daugherty, 2004). It is argued that Schumpeter's (1934) list of entrepreneurial activities can be expanded to include unproductive and even destructive activities such as trying a previously unused legal gambit (Baumol, 1990). Consistent with this theory, in prior theoretical and empirical research, scholars have examined a range of quasi-criminal (Warner & Daugherty, 2004) and criminal activities such as fraud in the health insurance industry (Tillman, 1998) and drug dealing under the concept of entrepreneurship.

In a justly influential paper, Baumol (1990, pp. 897–898) states: "If entrepreneurs are defined, simply, to be persons who are ingenious and creative in finding ways that add value to their own wealth, power, and prestige, then it is to be expected that not all of them will be overly concerned with whether an activity that achieves these goals adds much or little to the social product or, for that matter, even whether it is an actual impediment to production . . .." Cyber-criminals are coming up with new and creative ways to make money for themselves. Baumol's (1990) central hypothesis is that "the exercise of entrepreneurship can sometimes be unproductive or even destructive, and that whether it takes one of these directions or one that is more benign depends heavily on the structure of payoffs in the economy—the rules of the game" (p. 895).

In destructive entrepreneurship, entrepreneurs are engaged in detrimental activities such as those related to criminal behaviors, which lead to net social loss (Hall & Rosson, 2006). Baumol (1990, p. 894) pointed to the possibility that entrepreneur may even lead a "parasitical existence" upon the economy and hypothesized that the relative payoffs a society offers to different forms of entrepreneurial activities (e.g., productive, unproductive, and destructive) influence the distribution of such activities.

The extent of criminal entrepreneurship in the digital world is powerfully illustrated in an increasing pervasiveness of extrinsically motivated cybercrimes. Berinato (2008) notes, "Criminal hacking has spawned a full-blown service economy—one that supports growing legions of relatively lower-skilled but fulsomely larcenous hackers."

Cybercrime business models are rapidly evolving. In the early 2000s, experts argued that cybercrime was in its infancy and cybercrime business models were similar to those of high-technology companies in the early 1990s (Graft, 2000; Katyal, 2001). A popular view in recent years has been that cyber-criminals have learnt from and closely imitate legitimate businesses such as eBay, Yahoo, Google, and Amazon (ITPRO, 2008; Thomson, 2008). Indicators such as those related to high degree of professionalism among cyber-criminals (Warren, 2007), use of advanced social engineering tools (Rodier, 2007), supermarket-style pricing, outsourcing and sub-contracting of businesses and business functions (Carvajal, 2008), international price differentials in the value of stolen data (Thomson, 2008) point to the maturity of cybercrime business models.

Scholars have routinely pointed out that to understand organized criminal groups' operations, it may be helpful to consider them as rational economic actors with profit maximization goal (Becker, 1968; Ehrlich, 1973; Freeman, Grogger, & Sonstelie, 1996; Sjoquist, 1973; Viano, 1999). Their profit depends upon capability to emulate market mechanisms. This may require formation of strategic alliances, making appropriate capital investment decision, identifying new growth areas, investing in R&D, adopting modern accounting systems, and insuring against risks (Mittelman & Johnston, 1999). It is thus tempting to view cybercrime business models as having essential features fundamental to the success of legitimate businesses. There are, however, important differences between legitimate businesses and cyber-criminals' businesses in terms of the actors they deal with and their goals.

As noted in Chap. 3, economic actors are embedded in formal and informal institutions. Institutional theory frames a business model as the product of a social process, which is shaped by various actors' persuasive and coercive strategies and tactics to advance their interests (DiMaggio & Powell, 1983). A related point is that a business model is also affected by broad "macro-cultural discourse" and associated institutions, which extend beyond the boundaries of the business (Berger & Luckmann, 1967; Lawrence & Phillips, 2004).

Cybercrime firms and legitimate businesses face different economic conditions and are embedded in different types of institutions. Studying the contrast between economic and institutional conditions facing cyber-criminals and legitimate businesses raises important questions about the validity of some popular views on cybercrime business models. It would thus be only half-right to say that cyber-criminals have imitated legitimate companies' business models.

Economic and institutional conditions facing cyber-criminals also differ from those facing conventional criminals. For instance, the e-marketplace has unique characteristics related to quality uncertainty, technological information, and market information, which provide irresistible economic temptation to engage in frauds.

9.2   Business Model and Their Components: Applying in the Context of the Cybercrime Industry

According to Hamel (2002), a business model is a business concept put into practice. He proposed four major components of a business concept: core strategy, strategic resources, customer interface, and value network. Table 9.1 presents some examples of the similarities and differences between business models of a cyber-criminal and a legitimate business in terms of the four components and their elements.

The four components are linked and related by other three elements: configuration of competencies (intermediating between core strategy and strategic resources), customer benefits (intermediating between core strategy and customer interface), and company boundaries (intermediating between strategic resources and value network) (Hamel, 2002, p. 96).

9.2.1   Configuration of Competencies

9.2.1.1   The Internet and Cyber-Criminals' Configuration of Competencies

Configuration is related to "the unique way in which competencies, assets and processes are combined and interrelated in support of a particular strategy" (Hamel, 2002, p. 81). Configuration of competencies enables a firm to adapt to changing market conditions in order to achieve a competitive advantage (Eisenhardt, Martin, & Jeffrey, 2000; Zahra & George, 2002).

Core competencies are related to "skills and unique capabilities" (Hamel, 2002, p. 77). Cyber-criminals' business models involve interesting linkages between competencies, assets, and processes and how they manage the linkages (Hamel, 2002, p. 81). Coalition with other criminals, advanced technology and social engineering

Table 9.1 Similarities and differences between business models of cyber-criminals and legitimate businesses

Component of a business model and its sub-components	Similarities	Differences
Core strategy: • *Mission* • *Product/marker scope* • *Basis for differentiation*	• Product/market scope: cyber-criminals define the products and markets on which they concentrate (naive users' poorly protected computers; second, to avoid detection, click fraudsters are more likely to target companies that buy more terms, most obviously, companies that buy higher-priced search terms are more likely to fall victim of click fraud)[a] • Differentiation: Some cyber-criminals differentiate from competitors in dimensions important to "customers" (e.g., Mpack monitors the success of the operations through various metrics on its online, password protected control and management console; some offer free research tools to confirm the validity of a stolen credit card number or learning about security weaknesses, others handle the details of complex deals)[b]	• A mission "projects a sense of worth and intent that can be identified and assimilated by company outsiders."[c] A cybercrime player's mission cannot have this element
Strategic resources: • *Core competencies* • *Strategic assets* • *Core processes*	• Some cyber-criminals possess strategic assets that are rare and "valuable" (e.g., Mpack creates unique infectious programs that exploit known software security holes in several different kinds of Internet browsers)[d]	• Cyber-criminals' core processes relate to extorting and defrauding prospective victims (mostly licit actors) by gaining unfair or dishonest advantage[e]
Value network: • *Suppliers* • *Partners* • *Coalitions*	• *Coalition of criminals:* Cybercrime players cooperate through the formation of strategic alliances or subcontracting (e.g., some Japanese gangs hire Russian hackers to	• Structures like e-synchronized supply chains and e-marketplaces, which closely link "suppliers' suppliers" and "customers' customers" to facilitate information

Table 9.1 (continued)

Component of a business model and its sub-components	Similarities	Differences
	attack law-enforcement agencies' databases; Australian swindlers have established links with Russian and Malaysian organized crime networks to transfer stolen money from overseas banks)[f]	sharing, interaction, and supply chain integration (Andersen Consulting, 1999). In illegal activities in general, a player knows only immediate supplier and buyer and has no idea of the network's structure[g]
Customer interface: • *Target customer* • *Fulfillment and support* • *Information and insight* • *Pricing structure*	• Some features of pricing structure in the cybercrime industry resemble those in the legitimate industries. They include price differentials in the value of stolen data, adoption of supermarket-style pricing, etc.	• Fulfillment and support: cyber-criminals have limited channels and ways to reach "customers" and interact with them • Customer support is irrelevant for cyber-criminals interacting with victims

[a] Milyan (2007).
[b] Acohido and Swartz (2006).
[c] Pearce (1982, p. 74).
[d] Krebs (2007).
[e] GAO Reports (2007).
[f] Foreign Policy (2005).
[g] Paoli (2001).

tools have enhanced and promoted their capabilities. It is also important to note that cyber-criminals are getting better at protecting themselves from law-enforcement (publictechnology.net, 2008). Lance Hayden, a manager of professional services in the Cisco Secure Consulting Services group put the issue this way: "Once you build a better mousetrap, hackers build better mice" (Grimes, 2001).

Cyber-criminals have extended their efforts beyond PCs and Windows to other technology targets such as VoIP and RFID. For instance, while some viruses targeting Macs existed before, Apple's computers experienced financially motivated attacks from organized criminal groups for the first time in 2007 (sophos.com, 2008). Analysts suggest that new technologies such as Bluetooth, RFID, and mobile phones are likely to be increasingly popular targets (Security Director's Report, 2007). It is also reported that bots are performing an increasing proportion of click frauds.

Cyber-criminals' efforts have become more sophisticated over time. They have also developed a number of novel techniques and approaches. An international organized crime group involving 38 individuals based in Romania and the United States charged in two indictments in May 2008, for instance, used encoders. Encoders are hardware products that record the fraudulently obtained information onto the magnetic strips of credit and debit cards or hotel keys. The successful or "cashable" cards were used to withdraw money from ATMs or point of sale terminals (US Fed News Service, Including US State News, 2008).

A typical cybercrime business model involves different sets of people. They include high-skilled coders or programers, low-skilled workforce, organized crime groups, and money "mules" (Lovet, 2006). High-skilled coders develop ready-to-use tools or services. Low-skilled workforce, on the other hand, uses the tools developed by high-skilled coders for phishing activities and to steal bank accounts or other sensitive data. They typically employ IRC "carding" channels for these activities.

9.2.2 Company and Firm Boundaries

Critical resources also lie outside a firm's control. Legitimate businesses draw such resources from value network, which include suppliers, partners, and coalitions. By their very nature, many cyber-criminals lead a "parasitical existence" (Baumol, 1990, p. 894). While cyber-criminals have value networks, they also draw such resources from licit sources (Table 9.2).

Cybercrime firms are looking beyond their firm boundaries and have extended their value chain to coalition partners. For instance, consider click fraud. Networks of human clickers engaged in click fraud are reported to be operating from developing economies such as India, Russia, and other former Soviet Union countries, South Africa, Bulgaria, Czech Republic, Egypt, Ukraine, Botswana, Mongolia, and Syria (Chapell, 2006; Einhorn, 2006; Marketing, 2006; Vidyasagar, 2004; Grow, Elgin, & Herbst, 2006; Lynn, 2006; Motlogelwa, 2007).

Table 9.2 Some examples of licit and illicit actors and actions related to cybercrimes

Actors ⇒ Actions ⇓	Licit	Illicit
Licit	o Legitimate advertisers (e.g., Vonage) signing up partners to distribute Internet ads (which through a layers of eight sub-distributors illegally downloaded to users' PCs)[a]	o Cyber-criminals publishing pictures of their adversaries on the Internet[b]
Illicit	o Legitimate online casinos paying ransom to cyber-extortionists[c] o Money mules unknowingly cashing checks for cyber-criminals in Nigerian check scams[d]	o Organized criminal groups' engagement in cyber-extortions[c] o Cyber-criminals in Nigerian check scams[d]

[a]Businessweek.com (2006).
[b]Etges and Sutcliffe (2008).
[c]Kshetri (2005).
[d]Gohring (2008).

9.2.2.1 Coalitions: Cyber-Criminals' Networks Strategy

Criminal alliances are transnational as well as sub-national (Cao, 2004). London's Metropolitan Police (2006) identified four types of criminal networks—family-based, culture-based, proximity-based, and virtual (Internet-based).

As is the case of most global criminal networks, some cyber-criminals leverage the pre-existing ethnic ties (Cao, 2004). These networks can be family-based, culture-based, or proximity-based (Metropolitan Police, 2006). For instance, most of Romanian cyber-criminals' auction fraud victims are located in countries such as the United States, Canada, Britain, Spain, or Italy. Romanian mules picked up money in these countries. In 2006, the US law-enforcement agencies arrested an eBay fraud group in Chicago, which was traced to have links with cybercrime outfits in Pitesti, Romania (Wylie, 2007).

Internet-based networks are increasingly used by cyber-criminals. As noted in Chap. 8, in order to launder funds stolen through cybercrime operations, organized crime groups often lure and recruit money mules.

9.2.2.2 Licit and Illicit Actors and Actions Involved in Cybercrime Activities

Prior researchers have recognized that illicit actors employ sophisticated telecommunications technology to engage in criminal activities (Naím, 2005). Some organized crime groups are capturing potential economies of scope well as the advantages of digitization and are expanding their operations into the cyberworld. The Russian Business Network (RBN), for instance, offered spyware, trojans, and botnet command and control systems and also laundered money (Warren, 2007). Russian organized crime groups arguably include "underworld" criminals as well as "overworld" figures from the former Communist Party (Paoli & Fijnaut, 2006). It is argued that RBN had political protection (Warren, 2007).

Prior researchers have also noted that it is difficult to distinguish between licit and illicit markets (Naím, 2005; Nordstrom, 2004). These two markets are directly or indirectly connected and seemingly legitimate businesses "dabble in the shadows" (Dillman, 2007). In some cases, underground, shadow, and illicit activities interact with each other and contribute to the success of legal businesses (Hampton & Levi, 1999).

Legitimate businesses sometimes deliberately, consciously, and willfully participate in transactions with illicit actors and may act in a criminal manner (Dillman, 2007). For instance, many licit actors are found to participate in global commodity chains linking producers and consumers (Dillman, 2007). Many legitimate businesses also engage in legitimate transactions with other businesses, which subsequently lead to illicit actions without their knowledge.

As is the case of conventional world's shadow economy (Dillman, 2007), many actors tied to cybercrimes may not realize their connections to such crimes. Table 9.1 presents some examples of licit and illicit actors and actions related to cybercrimes. To take one example, legitimate Internet advertisers are paying cyber-criminals and in many cases they may not realize. An estimate suggested that in 2004 advertisers paid over US $1 billion for spyware placements (Edelman, 2007). In 2007, a New Zealand-based hacker admitted in a court that he was involved in international botnet conspiracies. He confessed of making more than US $36,000 for this work (Gleeson, 2008). New Zealand Police linked the payments to the Dutch company, ECS International. ECS International had been prosecuted for engaging people to use their botnets to secretly install adware on computers. In another case, a Bot herder group in California, which pled guilty to hospital hack, earned more than US $100,000 in affiliate advertising income.

9.2.2.3 Market-Based Cybercrimes and Customer Benefits

In Chap. 1, we discussed two types of cybercrimes: predatory and market-based (Glaser, 1971; Naylor, 2005). In a predatory cybercrime, often a criminal victimizes his/her intended target. A market-based cybercrime, on the other hand, is associated with a criminal-to-criminal (C2C) transaction rather than a criminal-to-victim (C2V) transaction in a typical predatory cybercrime.

Some C2C operators focus on customer benefits in their engament with their clients. These players supply their products and services to other cyber-criminals and are more market-oriented than C2V players. In order to support their market-based objectives, they need to be market-oriented. C2C cybercrime operators, for instance, provide training sessions on issues such as new scams and vulnerabilities and changing credit card billing addresses and PINs (Rodier, 2007). Some crimeware writers also offer service contracts to their customers, which involves sending another malware if the sold malware is blocked (Thomson, 2008). Others offer free technical support for renting their botnets (Rodier, 2007). Some C2C cybercrime operators who rent bots to others also emphasize that their networks have a 99% reliability and are checked every 5 min (Warren, 2007).

9.2.2.4 Predatory Cybercrimes: Dream Customers vs. Ideal Victims

Here is another unhappy parallel. Just like legitimate businesses have their dream customers (e.g., those spending more money, and building a deeper relationship with the brand), cyber-criminals have their dream victims. C2V players focus on vulnerable and rewarding victims and targets. From a cyber-criminal's standpoint, the longer a crimeware goes undetected, the higher the profit. Naive Internet users, who have poorly protected computers, are thus cyber-criminals' ideal victims.

9.3 The Internet and Organized Crime Groups' Reinvention of Business Models

Reputed legitimate businesses' core processes are centered around creating the most value for customers. While this may also be true for some cyber-criminals, most criminals' core processes also involve extorting and defrauding prospective victims and minimizing the odds of getting caught.

As noted earlier, most cybercrimes in recent years are committed by organized crime groups. Many organized criminal groups operate large-scale businesses,
which need computers to run their businesses efficiently and effectively (Katyal,
2001).

Organized crime groups also need to develop computer capabilities to engage
in crime against individuals and organizations using computers. The Internet has
helped organized criminal groups expand the product market scope. The opportunity
for expansion in their product/marker scope led to a change in organized criminal
groups' core strategy.

Additionally, from the standpoint of organized criminal groups, part of the
fascinating character of the Internet stems from the fact that the cyber-space is characterized by less governance and weak rule of law (Aguilar-Millan, Foltz, Jackson,
& Oberg, 2008). As noted earlier, most criminals' core processes are also centered around minimizing the odds of getting caught. The unregulated cyber-space
provides organized crime groups with a unique opportunity to combine their competencies, assets, and processes to support their strategy of defrauding victims with
a minimal chance of being detected and caught. Finally, law-enforcement agencies use computers to investigate and prosecute organized crime groups. On this
front, crime organizations can employ their technical capability to attack the tools
used in tracking their activities (Katyal, 2001). For instance, in August 2009, a
hacker reportedly broke into the Australian federal police's computer system and
accessed police evidence and intelligence. At that time, the police were monitoring
the hacker's activities and his cybercrime group (Moses, 2009).

9.4 Cybercrime Operators and Legitimate Businesses: Selling Concept vs. Marketing Concept

Compared to legitimate businesses, cyber-criminals deal with a drastically different social environment. Legitimate businesses and cyber-criminals thus differ in
their persuasive and coercive measures and tactics. Given the distinction between
legitimate firms' and cyber-criminals' natures of businesses, it is likely that their
orientation towards the market would be different. Evidence of market orientation
is more readily apparent in C2C cybercrime operators, who supply their products
and services to other cyber-criminals.

Criminal organizations' modus operandi can be better explained by selling concept rather than marketing concept. Note that the philosophy of selling concept
focuses on the needs of the seller, involves aggressively pushing sales, and is best
for short-term purposes. Selling concept is practiced for unsought goods, which
focuses on creating sales transaction rather than on building long-term profitable
relationships with customers (Kotler & Armstrong, 2005).

Prior researchers have recognized that when the interests of a firm's senior
management are closely aligned with the long-term interests of the firm, they
are unlikely to engage in deception intentionally due to the incentive structures

(Arlen & Carney, 1992). For one thing, as is the case of any organized crime groups, we can assume that relationships among different players in the cybercrime industry are characterized by minimal trust and short-term orientation (Etges & Sutcliffe, 2008).

Successful legitimate businesses such as Yahoo, Google, and Amazon want to achieve competitive advantage and operate according to marketing concept philosophy. Note that marketing concept is customer-centered philosophy. This means that they are interested in long-term customer satisfaction and engage in creating, delivering, and communicating customer value.

Some of the business concepts and tools that legitimate businesses apply to create customer benefits are used by cyber-criminals' to defraud prospective victims and gain unfair or dishonest advantage. For instance, cyber-criminals are generating more targeted products. They deliver specialized and localized crimeware for various geographical regions (publictechnology.net, 2008).

9.4.1 Marketing Mix of C2C vs. C2V Operators

Cyber-criminals' pricing strategy is based on consumers' perceptions of values. In the cybercrime industry, there are price differentials in the value of stolen data. For example, it was found that in 2008, a stolen US credit card could be sold for only 40 cents, while prices for EU and Asian cards could be up to US \$20 (Thomson, 2008). Cyber-criminals have also adopted a supermarket-style or quantity discount pricing strategy such as "two for the price of one" for stolen credit card information (Carvajal, 2008).

In most cases, cyber-criminals obviously cannot use mainstream media for promotion. They mostly employ bulletin boards, which work in the same manner as eBay (Rodier, 2007). They also employ a reputation system. In chat rooms, they advertise their products and recruit new members (Rodier, 2007).

9.5 Quality Uncertainty, Technological Information, and Market Information

As noted earlier, most cyber-criminals prey on the ignorance of Internet users. The concepts of quality uncertainty, technological information, and market information would be helpful to understand this dynamic.

9.5.1 The Problem of Quality Uncertainty in an e-Marketplace

To understand the problem of distribution of information in an e-marketplace, it may be helpful to consider the problem of quality uncertainty. Market uncertainty and technological uncertainty superimpose in a unique interaction in e-marketplaces, which provide incentives to create information disparity (Wurth, 1992/1993).

In electronic channels, buyers are unable to physically evaluate a product until it is delivered, which leads to uncertainty about the product condition (Ghose, 2009). The lack of spatial proximity between buyers and sellers hinders the transfer of complex information about some products. Transfer of such information may require face-to-face contacts (Zazzaro, Fratianni, & Alessandrin, 2009). In some cases, insufficient telecommunications bandwidth does not allow the electronic channel to transmit pictures, graphics, video, and other bandwidth intensive information. This limitation of electronic channel, which is related to the absolute level of information about product quality, is referred as technological uncertainty. This type of uncertainty is the result of complexity of quality measurement and the bounded rationality of individuals (Williamson, 1975, 1985; Simon, 1957). Most buyers interested in online channels accept this unmeasurable quality related to technological uncertainty as "fate" or the "state of things" (Wurth, 1992/1993).

The most serious concern for online buyers, however, is the likelihood that the sellers may provide incomplete or false information. In their product description in online auctions, some sellers misrepresent what is being offered. For instance, in online auctions, buyers complained that some sellers omit important product details in the description and receive items that are different from purchased and of substandard quality (Gregg & Scott, 2008). Non-delivery fraud, sales of illegal goods, and failure to take remedial actions to correct defects are other problems in online auctions (Australia Treasury, 2001). A survey found that in 8% of the complaints filed on online auctions, buyers reported that they received damaged or defective goods (Gregg & Scott, 2008).

In general, electronic channels are susceptible to higher opportunism, which increases the possibility of deception through a deliberate creation of information advantage by a potential seller (Barkhi et al., 2008; Williamson, 1975, 1985). The problem here is thus related to the distribution of information about product quality, where potential traders possess different levels of information. Quality uncertainty in such cases is a problem of market uncertainty instead of technological uncertainty (Wurth, 1992/1993).

9.5.2 *Technological Information and Market Information in an e-Marketplace*

Creativity in cybercrimes requires a combination of various types of knowledge as well as the interaction between various actors with different skills, expertise, and experience. Economists employ the concept of technological information and market information to understand the functioning of a marketplace (Hirshleifer, 1971; Hirshleifer & Riley, 1979; Koopmans, 1957; Wurth, 1992/1993). According to Machlup (1962, p. 3), technological information refers to "knowledge of the technology of the time" and market information is "knowledge of the markets." These can be framed as opportunities for production and exchange (Wurth, 1992/1993).

As noted above, many organized crime groups invest in R&D (Mittelman & Johnston, 1999). Likewise, instead of focusing on a wide range of skills, criminals are specializing in specific areas of criminal activities (Sutherland, 2008). The division of labor has allowed some criminals to have better technological information. As discussed earlier Mpack, which was created by RBN, efficiently monitors the success of a cybercrime operation through various metrics (Symantec, 2007). Cyber-criminals using the superior technological information created by RBN are thus economizing on the use of resources for criminal activities. In this case, the technological information is a source of efficiency improvement (Wurth, 1992/1993).

It is reported that attitudes toward services of many C2C cyber-criminals exhibit a high degree of professionalism (Warren, 2007). The C2C e-marketplaces can thus be considered as having essential features of a positive-sum-game, which is characterized by education and teaching rather than exploitation and deception (Wurth, 1992/1993). As noted above, in order to support their market-based objectives, C2C operators provide training sessions on various issues, offer service contracts, and free technical support to their customers. In sum, the C2C operators do not simply secure a "political gain" by deceiving those with the lesser information (Wurth, 1992/1993). That is, most C2C operators in the cyberworld make money by delivering value to their customers.

A different picture, however, emerges when looking into the operations of cyber-criminals that directly victimize consumers. Illicit and predatory actions of C2V operators are motivated purely by "political gains," which come at the expense of victims that are uninformed or inadequately informed (Wurth, 1992/1993). For instance, in many cases, money mules are unaware that they are engaged in illegal activities and they themselves become victims (Claburn, 2008). In the cyberworld, various types of deception and exploitation can be seen in their extreme form. Most of these are related to the problem of distribution of information.

9.6 Development of Dynamic Capabilities

As noted earlier, a business model is a business concept put into practice. The development of a sound business concept and ability to put such concept into practice can be expressed as a function of the development of dynamic capabilities.

Prior literature has successfully shown that a firm's use of resources in integrating, building, and reconfiguring competencies is of paramount importance to succeed in the rapidly changing environments (Eisenhardt et al., 2000; Teece, Gary, & Amy, 1997). The concept of dynamic capabilities (Teece et al., 1997) provides helpful perspectives for understanding the processes associated with gaining competitive advantages in the cybercrime world. Eisenhardt et al. (2000) define dynamic capabilities as: "The firm's processes that use resources—specifically the process to integrate, reconfigure, gain and release resources—to match and even create market change. Dynamic capabilities thus are the organizational and strategic routines, by which firms achieve new resources configurations as markets emerge, collide, split, evolve, and die" (1107).

Firms can build dynamic capabilities in several ways (Eisenhardt et al., 2000). First, some dynamic capabilities entail integrating resources within a firm. A firm can combine diverse skills and backgrounds of its employees to develop new products and services (e.g., Clark & Fujimoto, 1991). For example, cyber-criminals can develop new virus to attack new technologies such as Bluetooth, RFID, and mobile phones or focus on delivering specialized and localized crimeware for various geographical regions (publictechnology.net, 2008; Security Director's Report, 2007).

Second, dynamic capabilities can be built by reconfiguring resources within a firm. As noted earlier, cyber-criminals are specializing in specific areas of criminal activities, which has allowed them to get better at what they do (Sutherland, 2008).

Third, a firm can build dynamic capabilities by gaining resources through processes such as "new thinking" (e.g., Helfat, 1997) as well as alliance and acquisition, which bring new resources from external sources. As discussed in Chap. 2, some Australian cybercrime groups were reported to have links with Russian and Malaysian organized crime networks to transfer stolen money from overseas banks they have cracked into (Foreign Policy, 2005). Likewise, cyber-criminals extensively recruit money mules.

Finally, exit strategies that involve getting rid of resources that no longer provide competitive advantage can also help develop dynamic capabilities. For instance, the Russian Business Network (RBN) stopped operations in November 2007. Some analysts suspected that "whatever protection RBN enjoyed was withdrawn because the group had overreached itself" (Espiner, 2007). Analysts also suggested that the group operating RBN may have shifted its operations to China and other Asian countries (Blakely, Richards, & Halpin, 2007).

9.7 Concluding Comments

As is the case of many conventional crimes, cybercrime typically involves coercion (e.g., cyber-extortion), deception, and cyber-violence such as internet stalking, harassing, virus infection, and online defamation. The discussion above indicates that cyber-criminals have enhanced and promoted their capabilities by combining disruptive technologies and novel business concepts. They are discovering new business models and ways to innovate. Cyber-criminals' core processes also entail taking advantage of jurisdictional arbitrage. As noted earlier, institutions dealing with cybercrimes are not developed at the same rate across countries.

The widespread view is that cyber-criminals closely imitate legitimate businesses. The research presented in this chapter suggests that these views are partly right, but incomplete. Cyber-criminals and legitimate businesses differ in terms of the legitimacy related to regulative institutions and inter-organizational arrangements. For instance, cyber-criminals are less likely to adopt the marketing concept compared to legitimate businesses. However, C2C players, which appear to follow legitimate businesses' models closely, are more likely to operate according to the marketing concept philosophy compared to C2V operators.

References

Acohido, B., & Swartz, J. (2006, October 11). Cybercrime flourishes in online hacker forums. *USA Today*. http://www.usatoday.com/tech/news/computersecurity/infotheft/2006-10-11-cybercrime-hacker-forums_x.htm. Accessed 27 October 2008.

Aguilar-Millan, S., Foltz, J. E., Jackson, J., & Oberg, A. (2008). The globalization of crime. *Futurist, 42*(6), 41–50.

Andersen Consulting. (1999). *e-Europe Takes off*. http://www.ac.com. Accessed 29 November 1999.

Arlen, J. H., & Carney, W. J. (1992). Vicarious liability for fraud on securities markets: Theory and evidence. *The University of Illinois Law Review, 691*, 724–727.

Australia. Treasury. (2001) *Dispute resolution in economic commerce*. Canberra: Consumer Affairs Division, Department of the Treasury.

Barkhi, R., Belanger, F., & Hicks, J. (2008). A model of the determinants of purchasing from virtual stores. *Journal of Organizational Computing & Electronic Commerce, 18*(3), 177–196.

Baumol, W. J. (1990). Entrepreneurship: Productive, unproductive, and destructive. *Journal of Political Economy, 98*(5), 893–921.

Becker, G. S. (1968). Crime and punishment: An economic approach. *Journal of Political Economy, 76*, 169–217.

Berger, P. L., & Luckmann, T. (1967). *The social construction of reality: A treatise in the sociology of knowledge*. New York: Doubleday.

Berinato, S. (2008). Service Economy the cybercrime, breakthrough ideas for 2008. *Harvard Business Review, 86*(2), 17–45.

Blakely, R., Richards, J., & Halpin, T. (2007, November 10). Cybergang raises fear of new crime wave. *The Times* (London), 13.

Businessweek.com. (2006, April 24). Your ad here. And here. And here. http://www.businessweek.com/magazine/content/06_17/b3981046.htm. Accessed 27 October 2008.

Cao, L. (2004). The transnational and sub-national in global crimes. *Berkeley Journal of International Law, 22*(1), 59–97.

Carvajal, D. (2008, April 7). Cybercrime evolves as it grows. *The International Herald Tribune, 10*.

Cavaglieri, C. (2009, September 27). Four pence – That's the price of your credit card number, independent.co.uk. http://www.independent.co.uk/money/spend-save/four-pence-ndash-thats-the-price-of-your-credit-card-number-1793741.html. Accessed 27 October 2009.

Chapell, A. (2006, October 13). Re-Evaluating Click Fraud. http://www.imediaconnection.com/printpage/printpage.aspx?id=11361. Accessed 27 October 2008.

Claburn, T. (2008, April 9). The Cybercrime Economy. http://www.informationweek.com/blog/main/archives/2008/04/the_cyber_crime.html. Accessed 27 October 2008.

Clark, K. B., & Fujimoto, T. (1991). *Product development performance: Strategy, organization, and management in the world auto industry*. Boston: Harvard Business School Press.

Dillman, B. (2007). Introduction: Shining light on the shadows: The political economy of illicit transactions in the Mediterranean. *Mediterranean Politics, 12*(2), 123–139.

DiMaggio, P. J., & Powell, W. W. (1983). The iron cage revisited: Institutional isomorphism and collective rationality in organizational fields. *American Sociological Review, 48*, 147–160.

Edelman, B. (2007, January 25). Why I can never agree with adware and spyware. *The Guardian*.

Ehrlich, I. (1973). Participation in illegitimate activities: A theoretical and empirical investigation. *Journal of Political Economy, 81*, 521–565.

Einhorn, B. (2006). Advertisers in China are getting burned, too. *Business Week, 4003*, 54.

Eisenhardt, K., Martin, M., & Jeffrey, A. (2000, October/November). Dynamic capabilities: What are they? *Strategic Management Journal, 21*(10/11), 1105–1121.

Espiner, T. (2007, November 9). Infamous Russian malware gang vanishes. *CNET News.com*. http://news.cnet.com/Infamous-Russian-malware-gang-vanishes/2100-7355_3-6217852.html Accessed 27 October 2009.

Etges, R., & Sutcliffe, E. (2008). An overview of transnational organized cyber crime. *Information Security Journal: A Global Perspective, 17*(2), 87–94.

Foreign Policy. (2005, March/April). Caught in the net: Australian teens, 92.

Freeman, S., Grogger, J., & Sonstelie, J. (1996). The spatial concentration of crime. *Journal of Urban Economics, 40*(2), 216–231.

GAO Reports. (2007, June 22). *Public and private entities face challenges in addressing cyber threats*. RPT-number: GAO-07-705.

Ghose, A. (2009). Internet exchanges for used goods: An empirical analysis of trade patterns and adverse selection. *MIS Quarterly, 33*(2), 263–291.

Glaser, D. (1971). *Social deviance*. Chicago, IL: Markham.

Gleeson, S. (2008). Superhacker convicted of international cyber crime, April 2. http://www.nzherald.co.nz/category/story.cfm?c_id=30&objectid=10501518.

Gohring, N. (2008, June 25). Woman gets two years for aiding Nigerian internet check scam. *PC World*. http://www.pcworld.com/businesscenter/article/147575/woman_gets_two_years_for_aiding_nigerian_internet_check_scam.html. Accessed 27 October 2008.

Graft, M. (2000). Cyber threats and the U.S. economy: Hearing before the joint economic committee on *Cyber Threats and the US Economy*, The One Hundred Sixth United States Congress.

Gregg, D. G., & Scott, J. E. (2008, April). A typology of complaints about ebay sellers. *Communications of the ACM, 51*(4), 69–74.

Grimes, B. (2001, July 31). The right ways to protect your net. *PC World*. http://www.pcworld.com/howto/article/0,aid,56423,00.asp. Accessed 27 October 2005.

Grow, B., Elgin, B., & Herbst, M. (2006, October 2). Click fraud. *Business Week, 4003*, 46.

Hall, J., & Rosson, P. (2006). The impact of technological turbulence on entrepreneurial behavior, social norms and ethics: Three Internet-based cases. *Journal of Business Ethics, 64*(3), 231–248.

Hamel, G. (2002). *Leading the revolution*. Boston: Harvard Business School Press.

Hampton, M. P., & Levi, M. (1999). Fast spinning into oblivion? Recent developments in money-laundering policies and offshore finance centres. *Third World Quarterly, 20*(3), 645–656.

Helfat, C. E. (1997). Know-how and asset complementarity and dynamic capability accumulation. *Strategic Management Journal, 18*(5): 339–360.

Hirshleifer, J. (1971). The private and social value of information and the reward to inventive activity. *American Economic Review, 61*, 561–574.

Hirshleifer, J., & Riley, J. G. (1979). The analytics of uncertainty and information: An expository survey. *Journal of Economic Literature, 17*, 1375–1421.

ITPRO. (2008). RSA 2008 – Spamming a shadow economy. http://www.itpro.co.uk/blogs/maryb/2008/04/10/rsa-2008-spamming-a-shadow-economy. Accessed 27 October 2009.

Katyal, N. K. (2001). Criminal law in cyberspace. *University of Pennsylvania Law Review, 149*(4), 1003–1114.

Koopmans, T. (1957). *Three essays on the state of the economic science*. New York: McGraw-Hill.

Kotler, P., & Armstrong, G. (2005). *Principles of marketing*. NJ: Prentice Hall.

Krebs, B. (2007). Taking on the Russian Business Network, October 13, 2007. http://blog.washingtonpost.com/securityfix/2007/10/taking_on_the_russian_business.html. Accessed 27 October 2008.

Kshetri, N. (2005). Hacking the Odds. *Foreign Policy*, May/June, 93.

Kshetri, N. (2009). Entrepreneurship in post-socialist economies: A typology and institutional contexts for market entrepreneurship. *Journal of International Entrepreneurship, 7*(3), 236–259.

Lawrence, T. B., & Phillips, N. (2004). From Moby Dick to Free Willy: Macro-cultural discourse and institutional entrepreneurship in emerging institutional fields. *Organization, 11*, 689–711.

Lovet, G. (2006). Dirty money on the wires: The business models of cyber criminals. *Virus Bulletin Conference.*

Lynn, M. (2006, October 7). Why Google has already passed its peak. *The Spectator.*

Machlup, F. (1962). *The production and distribution of knowledge in the United States.* Princeton, NJ: Princeton University Press.

Marketing. (2006, July 19). Media Analysis: Click fraud rears its head.

Metropolitan Police. (2006). *Criminal networks, a new approach.* London: Metropolitan Police.

Milyan, A. (2007, May 14). Developing click fraud standards: Q&A with Tom Cuthbert l Click Forensics. http://www.searchmarketingstandard.com/articles/2007/05/developing-click-fraud-standards-qa-with-tom-cuthbert-l-click-forensics.html. Accessed 27 October 2008.

Mittelman, J. H., & Johnston, R. (1999). The globalization of organized crime, the courtesan state, and the corruption of civil society. *Global Governance, 5*(1), 103–126.

Moses, A. (2009, August 18). Hackers break into police computer as sting backfires. *The Age.* http://www.theage.com.au/technology/security/hackers-break-into-police-computer-as-sting-backfires-20090818-eohc.html. Accessed 27 October 2008.

Motlogelwa, T. (2007, October 5). Cyber crime law gets teeth. mmegi Online. http://www.mmegi.bw/index.php?sid=1&aid=30&dir=2007/October/Friday5. Accessed 27 October 2009.

Naím, M. (2005). *Illicit: How smugglers, traffickers, and copycats are hijacking the global economy.* New York: Doubleday.

Naylor, R. T. (2005, Winter/Spring). The rise and fall of the underground economy. *Brown Journal of World Affairs, 11*(2), 131–143.

Nordstrom, C. (2004). *Shadows of war: Violence, power, and profiteering in the twenty-first century.* Berkeley: University of California Press.

Paoli, L., & Fijnaut, C. (2006). Organized crime and its control policies. *European Journal of Crime, Criminal Law & Criminal Justice, 14*(3), 307–327.

Paoli, L. (2001). Drug trafficking in Russia: A form of organized crime? *Journal of Drug Issues, 31*(4), 1007–1037.

Pearce, J. A. (1982, Spring). The company mission as a strategic tool. *Sloan Management Review, 23*(3), 15–24.

publictechnology.net. (2008). The latest Cybercrime Business Model... Crimeware-as-a-Service, 11 April. http://www.publictechnology.net/modules.php?op=modload&name=News&file=article&sid=15173. Accessed 27 October 2008.

Rodier, M. (2007). Thwarting Hackers; As hacking increases, experts say firms must use a blend of multifactor authentication, risk analysis and people to protect themselves. *Wall Street & Technology*, October 1, 17.

Security Director's Report. (2007, July). Cybercrime in 2007–2008. 7(7), 8.

Simon, H. A. (1957). *Models of men, social and rational.* New York: Wiley and Sons.

Sjoquist, D. L. (1973). Property crime and economic behavior. *American Economic Review, 63*, 439–446.

sophos.com. (2008, 22 January). Sophos security threat report reveals cybercriminals moving beyond Microsoft. http://www.sophos.com/pressoffice/news/articles/2008/01/security-report.html. Accessed 27 October 2008.

Sutherland, B. (2008). The rise of black market data; Criminals who steal personal data often don't exploit it. Instead, they put it up for sale on one of the many vibrant online markets. *Newsweek, 152*(24), (International ed.).

Symantec. (2007, September 17). Symantec reports cyber criminals are becoming. http://www.prwire.com.au/pdf/symantec-reports-cyber-criminals-are-becoming-increasingly-professional. Accessed 27 October 2008.

Teece, D., Gary, P., & Amy, S. (1997). Dynamic capabilities and strategic management. *Strategic Management Journal, 18*(7), 509–533.

Thomson, I. (2008). Malware mimicking legitimate business: R&D budgets, outsourcing models and support services. Vnunet.com, 08 Apr. http://www.vnunet.com/vnunet/news/2213747/malware-mimicking-legitimate. Accessed 27 October 2008.

Tillman, R. (1998). *Broken promises: Fraud by small business health insurers.* Boston: Northeastern University Press.

US Fed News Service, Including US State News. (2008, May 19). *38 Individuals in US, Romania charged in two related cases of computer fraud involving international organized crime.* Washington, DC.

Viano, E. C. (1999). *Global organized crime and international security.* Burlington, VT: Ashgate Publishing.

Vidyasagar, N. (2004). India's secret army of online ad 'clickers'. http://timesofindia.indiatimes.com/articleshow/msid-654822,curpg-1.cms. Accessed 27 October 2008.

Warner, M., & Daugherty, C. W. (2004). Promoting the 'civic' in entrepreneurship: The case of rural Slovakia. *Journal of the Community Development Society, 35*(1), 117–135.

Warren, P. (2007, November 15). Hunt for Russia's web criminals, The Russian Business Network – Which some blame for 60% of all internet crime – Appears to have gone to ground. *The Guardian.* http://www.guardian.co.uk/technology/2007/nov/15/news.cri. Accessed 27 October 2009.

Williamson, O. E. (1975). *Markets and hierarchies: Analysis and antitrust implications.* New York: Free Press.

Williamson, O. E. (1985). *The economic institutions of capitalism.* New York: Free Press.

Wurth, A. H., Jr. (1992/1993). Policy information or information policy? Information types in economics and policy. *Knowledge & Policy, 5*(4), 65–81.

Wylie, I. (2007). Internet; Romania home base for EBay scammers; The auction website has dispatched its own cyber-sleuth to help police crack fraud rings. *Los Angeles Times,* C.1.

Zahra, S., & George, G. (2002). Absorptive capacity: A review, reconceptualization, and extension. *The Academy of Management Review, 27*(2), 185–203.

Zazzaro, A., Fratianni, M., & Alessandrin, P. (2009). *The changing geography of banking and finance.* Chapter 3: Financial centers between centralization and virtualization. New York: Springer US.

Chapter 10
The Global Click Fraud Industry

"Computer-based detection gives the defender economies of scale, but the attacker can use those same economies of scale to defeat the detection system" (Schneier, 2009).

"Cybercriminals used to be individual hooligans showing off their prowess, but the fact that it is so profitable, so easy to do and comparatively low-risk has made cybercrime an extremely attractive felony and, as a result, it has mushroomed into a giant global industry that is unlikely to stop growing anytime soon," Maxim Shirokov, Kaspersky Lab's regional director for the Middle East and Africa (cf. Naidu, 2008).

Abstract Click fraud is arguably the cyberworld's biggest scam. How do click fraudsters frame their actions? What are the characteristics of click fraud victims? How do formal and informal institutions affect click fraudsters' actions? We address these questions by examining the contexts, mechanisms, and processes associated with the click fraudsters' profitability and performance. We also discuss some attempts to criminalize and stigmatize click fraudsters.

10.1 Introduction

Click fraud is pervasive and is arguably the cyberworld's biggest scam (Agarwal, Athey, & Yang, 2009; Arnott, 2008). Illegitimate and unwanted clicks on paid advertisements have raised the ire of advertisers and rekindled debate about the effectiveness of online advertising. Cyber-criminals involved in diverse activities such as online pornography and software piracy are capturing potential economies of scope and are expanding their operations into lucrative businesses in the search advertising industry. Search engine network partners, competitors, and unhappy employees are receiving financial and psychic benefits from their engagements in generating illegitimate clicks. In 2004, Google's chief financial officer noted: "Click fraud is the biggest threat to the Internet economy" (Veverka, 2006).

A related, but less well-known phenomenon is impression fraud, in which ads are placed on invisible web pages and are not presented to Internet users. Such ads

N. Kshetri, *The Global Cybercrime Industry*, DOI 10.1007/978-3-642-11522-6_10,   207
© Springer-Verlag Berlin Heidelberg 2010

are opened when an Internet user visits a website (Leggatt, 2009). It is reported that advertisers such as Kraft Foods, Greyhound, and Capital One have fallen victim of such a scam. In this chapter, we examine the contexts, mechanisms, and processes associated with the click fraud industry.

10.2 Clicks and Value Creation in the Internet Economy

As an advertising medium, part of the fascinating character of the Internet stems from its measurability and instant feedback. The basic idea behind search advertising and pay per click (PPC) model is simple: From a marketer's standpoint, a genuine click represents the clicker's personal choice, which provides an opportunity to create and deliver value and make money (Cart, 2000). Businesses are thus understandably willing to invest in generating clicks to attract consumers (Cell I, Table 10.1).

The Internet's measurability, which is a driving force behind the rapid growth of online advertising, is however, more complicated than first meets the eye. As illustrated in Table 10.1, a click does not necessarily represent the clicker's interest in the product, service, or content. Some websites pay people for clicking on ads or typing certain words into search engines. Some sites also run forums to exchange click fraud tips (Kehaulani, 2006). These fraudulent clicks arise from a malicious intent of a user to make an advertiser pay for unwanted and invalid clicks (Cells II and IV, Table 10.1), which have raised the question of infallibility of the Internet's measurability. In Parker's (1976, 17–21) typology of computer crimes, click fraud thus involves a computer as the "instrument" of the offense as well as its "symbolic"

Table 10.1 Click and value creation in the Internet economy

Value created⇒ Payment ⇓	Positive	Zero
Paid clicks	[I] • Genuine click on ads distributed by a PPC provider • Paying to *create positive brand* value through consumer-generated contents	[III] • Bogus and fake clicks (human- or machine-generated) on ads distributed by a PPC provider
Free clicks	[II] • Managing user-generated content to *create positive brand* value	[IV] • Advertisers and providers agree as "garbage traffic" or an invalid click

representation. This last point may warrant elaboration. In click frauds, computers are used symbolically to "deceive or defraud victims" (Parker, 1976). That is, click frauds "rely partially on the perceived infallibility of computer-generated information" (Hollinger & Lanza-Kaduce, 1988, p. 103).

Advertisers and search providers differ widely in their assessment of the proportion of clicks that belong to Cell III and IV in Table 10.1. PPC providers such as Google and Yahoo maintain that invalid clicks that are not proactively detected (Cell III, Table 10.1) account for less than 0.02% of total clicks. Advertisers think that this proportion is higher and argue that PPC providers' secretive techniques to detect invalid clicks have held them at bay.

Faced with massive click frauds, advertisers have challenged the infallibility and reliability of click-related data. There have been legitimate arguments about whether the current approach of measuring and counting clicks and identifying invalid clicks is equitable. Attacking the symbolic basis of PPC, advertisers have complained that search providers such as Google and Yahoo have not taken enough measures to protect them from illegitimate clicks and have provided tacit support for click fraud activities (Leonard, 2006).

To move to a different issue, some companies pay to generate clicks on consumer-generated contents (Cell III, Table 10.1). However, critics are concerned about manipulation of consumer reviews and paid reviews (Sullivan, 2008). China's public relations (PR) firms such as Daqi.com, Chinese Web Union, and CIC charge US $500–25,000 monthly to monitor online postings for a business. They help minimize the impact of negative information and create positive brand value for the company. There are reports that these PR firms hire college students to write good postings about certain brands and to criticize the competition (Roberts, 2008). In other cases, traffics on consumer-generated contents (e.g., reviews on products or the company) may result in actionable sales leads, for which businesses do not pay (Cell III, Table 10.1). There is increasing evidence to suggest that user-generated content, consumer-generated product reviews, and word-of-mouth are beginning to shape consumers' perception of a company and its offerings (Clemons, 2008). Indeed, consumer-generated Internet content is increasingly displacing other media (Martin & Smith, 2008). One estimate suggested that about a third of the top 300 retail websites offer consumer-generated reviews (Sullivan, 2008). Most consumers, however, do not realize that they could be charging for the contents they produced (Cart, 2000).

10.3 A Survey of Click Fraud

Consumers are increasingly relying on the Internet for information search. In 2007, Internet users worldwide conducted 61 billion searches per month (Burns, 2007). In December 2008, Americans conducted 12.7 billion online searches (Sullivan, 2009). Businesses are gearing up to respond to this surge in online searches. The global

Internet advertising was worth US $27 billion in 2006 and is expected to reach US $61 billion by 2010 or 20% of total ad spending (The Economist, November 25, 2006). An estimate suggested that about 40% of all Internet ads belong to the PPC category (Kehaulani, 2006). In 2006, advertisers worldwide spent US $15 billion on PPC advertising (Epstein, 2007). One estimate suggests that US businesses will spend US $12.3 billion in online search advertising in 2009 (Emarketer, 2009). Google dominates the PPC business. The company had a 61.2% share of searches in October 2008 compared with 16.9% for Yahoo and 11.4% for Microsoft (USA Today, December 17, 2008).

Studies vary as to the size of the problem as the proportion of fraudulent clicks is difficult to quantify. Estimates of fraudulent clicks as a proportion of total clicks vary from 10 to 50% (Mann, 2006). Most academics and consultants who study online advertising estimate that 10–20% of ad clicks are fake (Table 10.2). Others put it at 30% (Lynn, 2006). Automated scripts or computer programs are being increasingly used by click fraudsters to generate fake and bogus clicks, which imitate a legitimate user clicking on an ad (Table 10.2).

Estimates suggest that the United States and Canada account for as much as 90% of click frauds (Gonsalves, 2006; Utter, 2006). Top click fraud originating countries outside North America include India, China, Russia, the UK, France, Germany, Monaco, and Ghana (Table 10.2). Networks of human clickers engaged in click fraud are also reported to operate from former Soviet Union economies, South Africa, Bulgaria, Czech Republic, Egypt, Ukraine, Botswana, Mongolia, Vietnam, Honduras, Syria, and others (Chapell, 2006; Einhorn, 2006; Marketing, 2006; Vidyasagar, 2004; Grow, Elgin, & Herbst, 2006, Lynn, 2006; Motlogelwa, 2007). Some website owners have formed international networks to click on ads on each other's sites. One such network, Mutualhits.com, was reported to have over 2,000 members in 2006 (Kehaulani, 2006). Recent surge in click frauds are also associated with and facilitated by parked sites. These sites have little or no content except for Internet ads supplied by search providers such as Google and Yahoo.

Click fraudsters mostly target the US online advertising industry. However, click fraud's footprints across the world economy are getting bigger. In South Korea, there were over 134 million cases of click fraud in the first three quarters of 2006. Click frauds accounted for 11% of clicks on ads provided by Overture Korea in the first 9 months of 2006 (chosun.com, 2006). Likewise, the market research firm Analysys' survey in China conducted in 2006 indicated that one-third of respondents believed they had been click fraud victims (Einhorn, 2006).

As is the conventional world's shadow economy (Dillman, 2007), many legitimate actors are knowingly or unknowingly tied to click frauds. Legitimate Internet advertisers are indirectly funding click fraud activities. An estimate suggested that in 2004 advertisers paid over US $1 billion for spyware placements (Edelman, 2007). In 2007, a New Zealand-based hacker admitted his involvement in secretly installing the Dutch company, ECS International's adware on computers. He reportedly earned more than US $36,000 for this work (Gleeson, 2008). In another case, a Bot herder group in California, which pled guilty to a hospital hack, earned more than US $100,000 in affiliate advertising income.

Table 10.2 Some click fraud-related indicators

Year	Study conducted by	Fraudulent clicks as a proportion of total clicks	Top click fraud originating countries outside North America	Remarks
2005	Yankee group	10%		Click frauds cost advertisers US $500 million (PPC ads generated $5 billion)
2006Q1	ClickForensics	13.7%	China and France	Tier 1 search providers: 12.1%, Tier 2: 21.3%, Tier 3: 29.8%
2006Q2	ClickForensics	14.1% (20.2% for higher-priced ads)	India (increased by 26% during the quarter)	Higher-priced ads > $2 per click
2007Q1	ClickForensics	14.8% (22.2% for higher-priced ads)		Botnets accounted for about 9% of all click frauds
2007Q4	ClickForensics	16.6%	India (4.3%), Germany (3.9%), and South Korea (3.7%)	Botnets accounted for 22% of all click frauds
2008Q1	ClickForensics	16.3%	Monaco and Ghana: (each 3.1%).	Botnets accounted for 23.5% of all click frauds
2008Q2[a]	Click fraud network	16.2%	China (4.3%), Russia (3.5%), France (3.2%)	Botnets accounted for 25% of all click frauds
2008Q4	ClickForensics	17.1%		Botnets accounted for over 31.4% of all click frauds (compared to 27.6% in 2008Q3)

[a] Higgins (2008).

10.4 A Click Fraudster's Cost–Benefit Calculus

As noted in Chap. 2, economists consider financial as well as psychic costs and benefits to analyze individuals' propensity to engage in criminal activities. Equation 2.1 in Chap. 2 is specified to capture the behavior observed in an individual criminal. Nonetheless, the logics associated with the parameters can be extended at the firm level to investigate the firm's engagement in click fraud activities or incentives to discourage them. For instance, O_{cm} can capture a firm's potential reputation damage for engaging in click fraud. Likewise, P_a in Eq. 2.1 (Chap. 2) can be mapped with the probability of click fraud detection. In this section, we examine the parameters of Eq. 2.1 by analyzing the characteristics of offenders and victims associated with click frauds as well as institutions in which they are embedded.

10.4.1 The Offenders

10.4.1.1 Reputation, External Visibility, and Measures to Prevent Click Frauds

Click fraud rates vary across ads provided by various search providers. For instance, click fraud rates for Tier 1 search providers (e.g., Yahoo and Google) are higher than those for Tier 2 providers (e.g., Ask, MSN, Lycos) and Tier 3 ones (e.g., Dogpile) (Table 10.2). Google also offers three choices to advertisers: (1) advertising on Google.com only, (2) Google.com and major search partners such as AOL and AskJeeves, and (3) Google.com and the network of its affiliates. Click fraud rates are the highest in (3) and the lowest in (1) (Vise, 2005). Likewise, a study by China IntelliConsulting found that Baidu had a click fraud rate of 34%, compared to Google's 24% in China (Greenberg, 2007). In 2006, a Beijing hospital claimed that Baidu directed a scheme in which one of its affiliates maliciously generated fake clicks on the hospital's ads (Barboza, 2006).

Click fraud rates thus tend to be higher for ads involving less visible players. Why might this be the case? One reason behind a higher click fraud rates for ads distributed by smaller search providers, distributors, and affiliates may be that they are less likely to be spotlighted by the media. To examine why firms show a differential tendency to engage in and respond to potentially demeaning and reputation-damaging activities such as click fraud it would be helpful to consider the stigmatization process associated with such activities. A central concept here is *arbiters*. Wiesenfeld, Wurthmann, and Hambrick (2008) argue that arbiters' "constituent-minded sensemaking" influences the stigmatization process. Wiesenfeld et al. (2008) have identified three categories of "arbiters"—social, legal, and economic. Social arbiters include members of the press, governance watchdog groups, academics, and activists. Legal arbiters are those who enforce rules and regulations. Economic arbiters make decisions about engaging in economic exchange with individuals.

The media reports serve as an intermediary affecting the perceptions of market audience about a firm's scandalous and "nonconforming" behaviors (Rindova, Pollock, & Hayward, 2006). Media reports have played a critical role in the criminalization of computer crimes (Hollinger & Lanza-Kaduce, 1988).

Prior research indicates that the extent to which arbiters and other external actors criticize, devalue, or question a firm following a reputation-damaging event is a function of the firm's external visibility and reputation (Rhee & Valdez, 2009). In the automobile industry, for instance, media are more likely to target and write negative comments on recalls by higher reputation automakers than on by higher reputation automakers (Haunschild & Rhee, 2004; Rhee & Haunschild, 2006). Consistent with theory, search providers with a higher degree of external visibility seem to direct more efforts toward preventing click frauds. In 2006, Yahoo announced that the company developed a technology for collecting "traces" of Internet advertising users' paths (Leonard, 2006). The technology did not require to record Internet users' data. In 2006, Google launched a feature for advertisers to see the invalid clicks detected by the company (Los Angeles Times, 2006). That may be a small comfort for online advertisers. Google has sued click fraudsters and credited advertisers when click fraud is detected.

10.4.1.2 Hypermediation and Click Fraud

A central feature of the Internet economy is a near zero transaction cost. An emerging body of literature asserts that business is undergoing hypermediation as opposed to disintermediation, as some analysts had suggested (Cart, 2000). New intermediaries have emerged to provide services such as aggregating, matching suppliers and customers, providing trust, and providing inter-organizational market information (Bailey & Bakos, 1997).

The roots of the click fraud lie partly in this hypermediation. An increase in the number of sub-distributors increases the probability of click frauds. Portals and PPC providers such as Yahoo and Google do not normally disclose the chain of intermediaries involved in online advertising. Identifying them from outside is difficult. To understand hypermediation-led click frauds, consider one detail. It was found that a Vonage ad passed through layers of eight sub-distributors and was "illegally" downloaded to users' PCs (Businessweek.com, April 24, 2006). Likewise, an online ad of Dell, which was carried by Yahoo in 2005 was sent to distributor InfoSpace, which was then delivered to Direct Revenue. Direct Revenue put the ad in a pop-up (Elgin, 2006).

In the early days, PPC ads were displayed only as Search Engine results pages. PPC was thus called Search Engine advertising. The PPC syndication networks can be viewed as intermediaries, which match advertisers with relevant audience (Bailey & Bakos, 1997). In some cases, the PPC syndication networks are a better match than Search Engine results pages and provide high-conversion rates at low CPCs (Epstein, 2007).

Site owners of programs such as Google's AdSense, Yahoo's Publisher Network, or other contextual networks earn a part of the PPC charge for clicks on ads generated on their sites. Ad network partners, for instance, accounted for at least 30% of Google's revenue in 2008 and were paid about 25% of the company's revenue as commissions (Perez, 2009).

The hypermediation in the online search industry has acted as a crime generator by bringing potential click fraudsters in the value chain of the industry. PPC syndication networks consist of players with different sizes, reputations, and external visibility. A Google "help" page entitled "Where will my ads appear?", for instance, mentions brand names such as AOL.com and New York Times (Grow et al., 2006). In the early 2005, Google's AdSense program had about 200,000 websites consisting of individual bloggers, small businesses, and other websites (Graham, 2005).

We noted above that a firm's external visibility is negatively related to its engagement in reputation-damaging activities such as click fraud. Following this logic, we can argue that small sub-distributors and small Adsense affiliates are more likely to engage in click fraud-related activities compared to websites with higher external visibility such as AOL.com and New York Times. The publishers and search engine network partners benefit directly from click frauds. They have an incentive to develop creative ways to click on ads on their websites. Note too that these site owners lack external visibility and thus are less likely to be targeted by media.

10.4.1.3 The Economic Geography: Locations of Click Fraud Operations

It is tempting to employ low-wage workers from developing countries to generate clicks on ads, and collect commission from PPC programs. As noted above, most search terms cost just US $0.10—0.15 per click. Let's assume that it takes 8 seconds for an individual to click on an ad and view a page and the advertiser has to pay US $0.10 to a PPC provider for the click. At this rate, the clicker's activities generate US $45 per hour. Even if we assume that PPC providers and other intermediaries involved in click fraud activities take 90% of this amount, the clicker can still make US $4.50 per hour. This amount is much higher than many people make in developing countries. Declining connectivity and computer costs have made this a reality. There are reports that housewives, college graduates, and working professionals in India make US $100–200 per month by clicking on Internet ads (Vidyasagar, 2004).

The low-wage workers, however, may face an entry barrier if advertisers and PPC engines activate geo-targeting and monitor traffic originated from unusual geographical locations. Note that search engines allow an advertiser to choose the countries it would like to target and offer services related to IP address filtering (Mello, 2006). For instance, Overture South Korea's "continental cut-off" services block clicks from Africa (chosun.com, 2008).

A country's size of the online advertising industry is positively related to the attractiveness of click fraud activities generated in the country. The US, for instance, has the world's biggest online advertising industry. In 2008, about half of Google's revenue came from the United States (Perez, 2009). Unsurprisingly, suppliers pay more for adware installs in a US computer compared to those in other countries. Adware suppliers such as the Dutch firm E.C.S. International reportedly paid 30 cents for each install in the United States (Businessweek.com, April 24, 2006). The rates for non-US machines were: 20 cents for Canada, 10 cents for the UK, and 1–2 cents in most other countries (Espiner, 2007).

10.4.1.4 Economics of Labor versus Technology and Technological Economies of Scope

Click fraudsters are also confronted with the problem of whether to employ the seemingly bottomless source of human clickers in developing countries or technologies enabling click fraud. In this regard, it is important to note that most organizations take a reactive approach to click fraud. Click fraud-enabling technologies are developing more rapidly than anti-click fraud technologies developed according to advertisers' reactive decisions (Matin, 2007). For instance, spyware is used to generate pop-up ads (Robertson, 2006). Fraudsters also use automated clicking models such as "Hitbots" or "Clickbots" (Graham, 2005).

As noted above, advertisers and PPC providers employ mechanisms such as geo-targeting and IP address filtering to detect click frauds. In such cases, botnet generated click frauds are more effective as they are less detectable compared to those associated with click fraud farms (Perez, 2009). Botnet generated click frauds come from a large numbers of home computers that are geographically distributed and have unique IPs and hence mimic legitimate clicking behavior. Algorithms used by PPC providers and third-party auditors, which look for unusual traffic patterns, thus may fail to identify botnet generated click frauds. From the click fraudster's standpoint, click fraud-enabling technologies may reduce the proportion of defective products. Click fraud-enabling technologies can be viewed as process innovations, which change the production process, leading to a higher level of "quality" (Standing, 1984). They can also be viewed as improvement innovations, which help "extend a branch of industry" and reduces production costs (Standing, 1984; p. 128).

Consumers are duped by "free" software, video games, and pornography. For instance, Easycracks.net, the Armenia-based company, which describes itself as "one of the biggest cracks database on the internet" and boasts itself as having "a complete list of cracks, serials, nocds patches and keygens" (www.easycracks.net). Easycracks lures consumers by offering free download of unauthorized copies of Windows XP and video games, which also requires the installation of ECS International's software, ActiveX controls. When users approve the installation, 16 other pieces of adware are downloaded to the user's machine without permission, which delivers up to five pop-up ads per minute (Businessweek.com, April 24, 2006).

Economies of scope exist if a technology is used in a variety of activities. For instance, easycracks describes itself as "a site for all your software needs." Botnets, which were mainly used to perpetrate spam in the past, is being used for click fraud (Mindlin, 2008). According to Click Forensics, in the second quarter of 2008, botnets accounted for more than a quarter of all click frauds. Cyber-criminals have used botnets to fraudulently increase traffic to specific online ads and generate false clicks in massive numbers. For instance, the KMeth worm targeted Yahoo! Messenger users. The worm directed infected users to a website hosting Google AdSense ads related to mesothelioma (Leyden, 2006).

Online pornographers are turning to the click fraud industry. For instance, Internet users are lured to click on naked pictures, which takes them to a legitimate site and registers as a click (Mello, 2006). Note that the PPC model is based on the premise that each click represents a personal choice. In such a case, the clicker actually visited the advertiser's website without an interest to do so.

10.4.1.5 Economic and Psychic Benefits of Wasting Competitor's Ad Budget

There are economic and psychic benefits (satisfaction) associated with wasting a competitor's advertising budget. Some illegitimate and malicious clicks are funded by companies to waste their competitors' online ad budgets (Marketing, 2006). There have been arrests related to such frauds (Zaharov-Reutt, 2008).

Businesses usually have limits on how much they would spend on PPC advertising. Once they reach the limit, search engines do not display their ads. Pushing competitors' links off the search sites help the fraudsters ads receive a higher priority for the keyword search and are displayed more prominently (Matin, 2007). Such frauds thus mainly victimize small businesses with limited budget in competitive spaces with PPC costs. Some also benefit psychically from wasting a competitor's advertising budget. Psychologists refer this phenomenon as enjoyment-based intrinsic motivation (Deci & Ryan, 1985). Olsen (2004) reported that the chief executive of an Internet marketing company enjoyed clicking on his competitors' ads on Google and Yahoo. The executive said that clicking on competitors' ads is "an entertainment."

Many companies have reported that they have suffered from competitor-generated bogus clicks on their ads. The Atlanta-based insurance company, MostChoice.com reported that its ads were clicked by competitors (Vise, 2005). Likewise, Karaoke Star reported that one of its competitors employed an automated click fraud program to target Karaoke Star and other online Karaoke stores (Penenberg, 2005). Similarly, JetNetwork, a charter-jet service in Miami Beach, claimed that over 40% of the clicks on the company's ads came from a single IP address belonging to a rival (Mann, 2006).

10.4.1.6 Institutions and Click Fraud

Institutional perspective thus can help us understand complex causes and roots associated with click fraud. It is important to note that institutional theory is described as "a theory of legitimacy seeking" (Dickson & BeShers, 2004, p. 81). To gain legitimacy, organizations adopt behaviors irrespective of the effect on organizational efficiency (Campbell, 2004, p. 18). Institutional influence on the click fraud industry thus becomes an admittedly complex process when organizations have to derive legitimacy from multiple sources such as the state, trade and professional

Table 10.3 Institutional mechanisms associated with criminalizing and stigmatizing click frauds

Level of institutions	Mechanisms	Remarks/examples
National/state	• *Adoption of statutes* and regulations addressing click frauds	• Click fraud is a felony covered by Penal code 502 in California and the Computer Misuse Act 1990 in the United Kingdom
	• Strengthening cybercrime-related rule of law	• 2007: 17 US states had adopted statutes *to* deal with spyware (Skrzycki, 2007)
Industry, trade/professional associations	• Codes of ethics require members to maintain higher standards of conduct than required by law	• Direct Marketing Association's *guidelines* for software downloading
		• The Click Measurement Working Group launched by the Interactive Advertising Bureau (IAB)
Inter-organizational	• *Economic exchange-related* responses	• 2006: A coalition of brands such as Expedia and LendingTree pressured Google and Yahoo to be more accountable (Grow et al., 2006)
		• 2006: A group of advertisers, including PepsiCo, Hewlett-Packard, and Kimberly-Clark demanded audited numbers and common measurement standards (Leonard, 2006)
Intra-organizational	• *Intra-organizational rules, norms*, and culture to deal with click frauds	• 2005: Priceline.com started working on a draft of the company's adware policy (Heun, 2005)
Individual	• Feeling of guilt or remorse	• Many clickers in developing countries click on ads just to make money and do not know that some *businesses are victimized* by their activities

associations, business partners, and individuals. These institutions thus exist at various levels (Table 10.3), which affect financial and psychic costs and benefits in equation (2.1, Chap. 2) by attacking the ingredients and ecosystems of click frauds and influencing factors such as arrest, stigma, and earnings associated with (McCarthy, 2002).

10.4.1.7 Regulative/Formal Institutions and Click Fraud

In nascent and formative sectors such as Internet advertising, there is no developed network of regulatory agencies comparable to established industrial sectors (Powell, 1993). Governments are adopting statutes and regulations to deal with click frauds.

For instance, click fraud is considered as a felony in some economies. As of 2007, there was no federal law prohibiting spyware in the United States. Nonetheless, many states had adopted statutes to deal with spyware, which is used to generate pop-up ads (Skrzycki, 2007).

Law-enforcement agencies are also beginning to take a closer look at click fraud and criminalize associated activities. In the United States, the Securities and Exchange Commission (SEC) filed fraud charges in 2005 against operators of 12dailypro.com, which allegedly operated a pay-to-read advertising (Kehaulani, 2006). In September, 2006, a cybercrime unit led by the FBI and US Postal Inspection Service assigned analysts to examine possible violation of federal laws by click frauds. The Senate Judiciary Committee has launched its own informal probe (Grow et al., 2006). In the same year, a federal grand jury also indicted a Pennsylvania man for allegedly operating a click fraud network (Kehaulani, 2006).

Countries with weak rule of law and permissiveness of regulatory regimes have provided a fertile ground for click fraud activities (Mittelman & Johnston, 1999; Vassilev, 2003). In the United States, the FBI acted on after the agency noticed suspected cyber-criminals discussing click frauds in secret chat rooms (Grow et al., 2006). In India, on the other hand, companies openly advertised in national newspapers looking for people, who would use home computers to click on Internet ads (Kehaulani, 2006). To return to the Easycracks.net and ECS International example above, ECS International was prosecuted for engagement in cybercrimes thanks to the Netherlands' strong cybercrime laws (Gleeson, 2008). Easycracks.net is, however, likely to be safer because of Armenia's weak enforcement of such laws (Giragosian, 2006, 2007). Higher-level institutions and exogenous parameters have thus been favorable to Easycracks.net (Snidal, 1994, 1996).

Because of low-opportunity costs of conviction and low values of P_a and P_c because of weak law-enforcement measures, the expected penalty (O_{cm}, P_a, P_c) in Eq. (2.1) of engaging in click fraud is low in developing countries such as India and Armenia.

10.4.1.8   Informal Institutions and Click Fraud

Edelman and Suchman (1997) note: "the legal rules 'cause' the organizational practices (or vice versa) is, at best, a gross simplification." Anti-click fraud norms and practices are evolving at the industry, inter-organizational, and intra-organizational levels to deal with click frauds and to criminalize and stigmatize such activities.

In prior literature, researchers have noted professional and trade associations constitute the "most elaborate and intricate organizational arrangements" (Scott, 1992, p. 253) and play a significant role in legitimating institutional changes (Greenwood, Suddaby, & Hinings, 2002, Kshetri & Dholakia, 2009). For instance, trade and professional associations have codes of ethics, which require members to maintain higher standards of conduct than required by law (Backoff & Martin, 1991). The Direct Marketing Association issued guidelines, which require marketers to give clear and conspicuous notice to consumers to download software and an easy way to uninstall it (Skrzycki, 2007). In 2006, the Center for Democracy and Technology asked the Federal Trade Commission to take action against an adware company, which repeatedly and intentionally attempted to trick Internet users into download-ing intrusive software (Chabrow, 2006). In August 2006, the Interactive Advertising Bureau (IAB) launched The Click Measurement Working Group to create a set of Click Measurement Guidelines. Members include search vendors such as Yahoo, Google, Microsoft, and Ask.com, and industry body the Media Rating Council (MRC) (IT Week, 2006). In South Korea, small-scale online businesses have estab-lished the Online Advertisers Association, which has voiced concerns click fraud (chosun.com, 2008).

To understand inter-organizational relations, it may be helpful to consider the roles of economic arbiters, which make economic exchange-related decisions. In this regard, advertisers are actively mobilizing discourses against technology and service providers to take anti-cybercrime measures. In the United States, advertis-ers have pressured Google and Yahoo to be more accountable and have demanded audited numbers and common measurement standards (Grow et al., 2006; Leonard, 2006). Inter-organizational relations are also shaped by broad "macro-cultural dis-course" and associated institutions, which extend beyond the boundaries of the business (Berger & Luckmann, 1967; Lawrence & Phillips, 2004). Search engines in China do not face such pressures and thus tend to be more lenient on click fraud (Lu, 2007).

An important question is: Do click fraudsters have a feeling of guilt or remorse for engaging in click frauds? As discussed earlier, most of those who make unethical uses of computer networks may not perceive their actions' ethical implications. For instance, many clickers in India click on ads just to make money and do not know that some businesses are victimized by their activities. Social identity theory also points to the possibility of ethnocentric bias (Hamner, 1992; Tajfel & Turner, 1986). This means that the level of perceived guilt is smaller for out-group victims than for ingroup ones.

10.4.2 The Victims

10.4.2.1 Profiles of Click Fraud Victims and Targets

Prior research indicates that crime opportunity is a function of target attractiveness, which is measured in monetary or symbolic value (Clarke, 1995). To put things in context, two observations are worth making regarding the targets of click fraud. The first observation is that return to click fraud or the monetary benefit (M_b in 2.1, Chap. 2) is positively related to the price of a search term. As noted above, site owners of programs such as Google's AdSense, Yahoo's Publisher Network or other contextual networks earn a percentage of the PPC charge for every click on ads on their sites. While some search terms cost just 10–15¢ per click, others cost several hundred dollars. Search terms related to law, medicine, finance, and travel industries are among the most expensive ones (Liptak, 2007). For instance, in 2005, for "D.C. Hair Laser Removal," maximum cost per click was US $146 and average cost per dick was US $69 (Penenberg, 2005). Most obviously, companies that buy higher-priced search terms are more likely to fall victim of click fraud (Milyan, 2007).

Second, to avoid detection, click fraudsters are more likely to target companies that buy more terms (Matin, 2007). Advertising networks and third-party auditors employ various methods to identify invalid clicks. The method perhaps most often utilized entails identifying clicks that significantly deviate from the past clicking history. Likewise, according to rules-based algorithms, a click is considered as invalid if click fraud filters identify "specific conditions or a series of conditions" defined by the algorithms (Matin, 2007, p. 542). If different keywords bought by a competitor are searched, instead of a single term, fraudulent clicks could be considered as legitimate competitor analysis and research.

10.4.2.2   Poorly Protected Computers and Weakness of Defense Mechanisms

Click frauds have mainly victimized advertisers. It would be erroneous, however, to assume that advertisers are the only victims of click fraud. Note too that weakness of defense mechanism co-varies positively with the likelihood of becoming a crime victim (Glaeser & Sacerdote, 1999). Consumers are both instrument and victim of click fraud schemes. Other things being equal, naive users' poorly protected computers are more susceptible to such schemes. Their compromised computers are infested with annoying pop-up ads and are also used as vehicles to perform click fraud. For instance, in 2005, the Russian website, iFrameCash.biz exploited a Microsoft Windows security hole to distribute adware products. Microsoft promptly patched the hole. Many computers around the world, however, remained vulnerable for a long time (Anderson, 2008).

Internet users in developing economies are attractive targets for botnet generated click frauds. As discussed in Chap. 8, in developing countries, many Internet users connected to the Internet for the first time are not security oriented (Information Today, 2008; redherring.com, 2005).

10.4.2.3   Preventing Click Fraud: The Cost–Benefit Calculus

Prior research indicates that individuals and organizations can reduce the probability of becoming crime victims and losses by buying insurance policies or by using safety measures such as anti-burglar systems and safety deposit boxes, or by living in safe neighborhoods (Ehrlich & Becker, 1972). From a potential victim's perspective, the cost–benefit calculus associated with preventing click fraud activities involves determining the optimum investment as well as types of measures needed (Anderson & Schneier, 2005). For small companies, identifying fraudulent clicks may be a challenge. Tools such as Click Lab, Click Defense, and Click Detective are available to identify fake and bogus clicks. Such tools, however, cost from

US $30 to several thousand dollars per month (Penenberg, 2005). Click frauds are especially painful and frustrating for small companies, which are overwhelmed by search engine marketing budgets and thus are forced to accept fraudulent clicks as a cost of doing business.

10.5 Concluding Comments

Click fraud has been an uncomfortable reality facing the search advertising industry and has posed a threat to the growth of this industry. The presumed infallibility of click measurement is eroding because of massive click frauds. We examined the contexts, mechanisms, and processes associated with the click fraudsters' profitability and performance.

Various groups of arbiters are providing legal, ethical, and economic pressures to firms associated with click fraud. They are directing efforts toward criminalizing and stigmatizing click frauds, which may change the fraudsters' cost–befit calculus. The above analysis indicates that the roots of click frauds lie partly in asymmetric hypermediation consisting of a dense network of organizations in the supply side such as PPC providers, sub-distributors, and affiliates; and thin and dysfunctional institutions to perform trust-producing roles.

The above discussion also indicates that advertisers need to be vigilant about click fraudsters' creative ways to increase profitability. They need to take measures to minimize victimization. As noted above, the differences in click frauds can be partly explained by differing reputation levels of the players involved in the value chain of Internet advertising. There is thus a complex trade-off between minimizing victimization by paying a higher rate to search providers with a high degree of external visibility or accepting a higher click fraud rate with less reputed search providers. Small companies that cannot afford tools to identify fake and bogus clicks may look for unusual clicking behavior and regularly track conversion rates to see whether their PPC ads are working.

Many analysts argue that anti-click fraud actions of Yahoo and Google are only symbolic, which are designed to appease the advertisers and thus lacked substantiveness. PPC providers' anti-click fraud measures thus need to be driven by substantive considerations. Well-coordinated, well-funded campaign can create the perception of infallibility, validity, and reliability of PPC information, and reassure advertisers that their ad dollars are effectively spent. We noted above the emergence of new intermediaries to match suppliers and customers. Increasing pervasiveness of click frauds has also created a compelling need for new types of intermediaries. Establishment of intermediaries to provide a third-party measurement system capable of producing trust may address some of the concerns in the search advertising industry.

Finally, businesses need to direct more efforts toward harnessing the power of consumer reviews, blogs, and other forms of online endorsement as an alternative to PPC advertising. Most often, these are less costly, relatively fraud free, and are becoming more effective. While practices such as hiring consumers to write good things about a company and manipulation of consumer reviews have ethical implications, businesses can find ethical ways to manage consumer-generated contents. For instance, according to Amazon.com's conditions of use statement, the company reserves "the right (but not the obligation)" to edit or remove user-generated content.

References

Agarwal, N., Athey, S., & Yang, D. (2009). Skewed bidding in pay-per-action auctions for online advertising. *American Economic Review, 99*(2), 441–447.

Anderson, M. (2008, July 2008). Crimeware pays: Adware, phishing, and spam are a strange—and big—business. *IEEE Spectrum.* http://www.spectrum.ieee.org/jul08/6375. Accessed 2 October 2008.

Anderson, R., & Schneier, B. (2005). Counterpane internet security guest editors introduction: Economics of information security. *IEEE Security & Privacy, 3*(1), 12–13.

Arnott, S. (2008, March 22). Cyber crime stays one step ahead. http://www.independent.co.uk/news/business/analysis-and-features/cyber-crime-stays-one-step-ahead-799395.html. Accessed 2 October 2008.

Backoff, J. F., & Martin, Jr., C. L. (1991). Historical perspectives: Development of the codes of ethics in the legal, medical and accounting professions. *Journal of Business Ethics, 10*, 99–110.

Bailey, J. P., & Bakos, Y. (1997). An exploratory study of the emerging role of electronic intermediaries. *International Journal of Electronic Commerce, 1*(3), 7–20.

Barboza, D. (2006, September 17). The Rise of Baidu (That's Chinese for Google). http://www.nytimes.com/2006/09/17/business/yourmoney/17baidu.html?pagewanted=3&_r=1. Accessed 2 October 2008.

Berger, P. L., & Luckmann, T. (1967). *The social construction of reality: A treatise in the sociology of knowledge.* New York: Doubleday.

Burns, E. (2007, October 15). Worldwide Internet: Now Serving 61 Billion Searches per Month Search Engine Watch. http://searchenginewatch.com/3627304. Accessed 2 October 2008.

Businessweek.com. (2006, April 24). Your ad here. And here. And here. http://www.businessweek.com/magazine/content/06_17/b3981046.htm. Accessed 2 October 2008.

Campbell, J. L. (2004). *Institutional change and globalization.* Princeton, NJ: Princeton University Press.

Cart, N. G. (2000). Hypermediation: Commerce as Clickstream. *Harvard Business Review, 78*(1), 46–47.

Chabrow, E. (2006). The spies inside. *InformationWeek, 1082*, 34–40.

Chapell, A. (2006, October 13). Re-evaluating click fraud. http://www.imediaconnection.com/printpage/printpage.aspx?id=11361. Accessed 2 October 2008.

Chosun.com. (2006, October 31). Click fraud sets back internet advertising. http://english.chosun.com/w21data/html/news/200610/200610310025.html. Accessed 2 October 2008.

Chosun.com. (2008, July 15). Online advertisers demand industry reforms.

Clarke, R.V. (1995). Situational crime prevention. In Tonry, M. & Farrington, D. P. (Eds.), *Building a safer society. Strategic approaches to crime* (pp. 91–150). Chicago: University of Chicago Press.

Clemons, E. K. (2008). How information changes consumer behavior and how consumer behavior determines corporate strategy. *Journal of Management Information Systems, 25*(2), 13–40.

Deci, E. L, & Ryan, R. M. (1985). *Intrinsic motivation and self-determination in human behavior.* New York: Plenum Press.

Dickson, M., & BeShers, R. G. V. (2004). The impact of societal culture and industry on organizational culture: Theoretical explanations. In R. J. House, P. J. Hanges, M. Javidan, P. W. Dorfman, & V. Gupta (Eds.), *Culture, leadership, and organizations: The GLOBE study of 62 societies.* Thousand Oaks, CA: Sage Publications.

Dillman, B. (2007). Introduction: Shining light on the shadows: The political economy of illicit transactions in the Mediterranean. *Mediterranean Politics, 12*(2), 123–139.

Edelman, B. (2007, January 25). Why I can never agree with adware and spyware. *The Guardian.*

Edelman, L. B., & Suchman, M. C. (1997). The legal environments of organizations. *Annual Review of Sociology, 23,* 479–515.

Ehrlich, I., & Becker, G. (1972). Market insurance, serf-insurance and serf-protection. *Journal of Political Economy, 80*(4), 623–648.

Einhorn, B. (2006). Advertisers in China are getting burned, too. *Business Week, 4003,* 54.

Elgin, B. (2006). Yahoo's pop-up connection. *Business Week,* July 17 (3993), 45.

Emarketer. (2009, February 6). US Search Ad Spending Falters? http://www.emarketer.com/Article.aspx?id=1006902. Accessed 2 October 2009.

Epstein, A. J. (2007, April 23). Online merchant's guide to pay per click advertising. *AuctionBytes.com.* http://www.auctionbytes.com/cab/abn/y07/m04/i23/s03. Accessed 2 October 2008.

Espiner, T. (2007, December 14). Cracking open the cybercrime economy. *ZDNet News.* http://news.zdnet.com/2100-1009_22-180416.html. Accessed 2 October 2008.

Giragosian, R. (2006). Redefining Armenian national security. *Demokratizatsiya, 14*(2), 223–234.

Giragosian, R. (2007). Armenia on the move: A comparative assessment. *AGBU, 17*(1), 22–24.

Glaeser, E. L., & Sacerdote, B. (1999). Why is there more crime in cities? *The Journal of Political Economy, 107*(6), 225–258.

Gleeson, S. (2008, April 2). Superhacker convicted of international cyber crime. http://www.nzherald.co.nz/category/story.cfm?c_id=30&objectid=10501518. Accessed 2 October 2008.

Gonsalves, A. (2006, April 24). Click fraud less than expected. *Monitoring Firm Says.* http://www.informationweek.com/news/security/cybercrime/showArticle.jhtml?articleID=186700544. Accessed 2 October 2008.

Graham, J. (2005, November 3). Google's AdSense a bonanza for some websites. *USA Today.*

Greenberg, A. (2007, July 3). More Evil than Google? http://www.forbes.com/2007/07/03/google-evil-competition-tech-techbiz-cx_ag_0703googevil.html. Accessed 2 October 2008.

Greenwood, R., Suddaby, R., & Hinings, C. R. (2002). Theorizing change: The role of professional associations in the transformation of institutionalized fields. *Academy of Management Journal, 45*(1), 58–80.

Grow, B., Elgin, B., & Herbst, M. (2006). Click fraud. *Business Week, 4003,* 46.

Hamner, K. M. (1992). Gay-bashing: A social identity analysis of violence against Lesbians and Gay Men. In G. M. Herek & K. Berrill (Eds.). *Hate crimes: Confronting violence against Lesbians and Gay Men* (pp. 179–90). Newbury Park, CA: Sage.

Haunschild, P. R., & Rhee, M. (2004). The role of volition in organizational learning: The case of automotive product recalls. *Management Science, 50,* 1545–1560.

Heun, C. T. (2005). Can spyware ever come in from the cold? *InformationWeek, 1061,* 70–71.

Higgins, K. J. (2008, July 28). Botnets behind one fourth of click fraud. *DarkReading.* http://www.darkreading.com/security/government/showArticle.jhtml?articleID=211201369.

Hollinger, R., & Lanza-Kaduce, L. (1988). The process of criminalization: The case of computer crime laws. *Criminology, 26,* 101–126.

Information Today. (2008). *Challenges in the East, 25*(2), 22.

IT Week. (2006, August 14). Advertising body fights click fraud, 13.

Kehaulani, S. (2006, October 22). 'Click Fraud' threatens foundation of web ads; Google faces another lawsuit by businesses claiming overcharges. *The Washington Post,* A.1.

Kshetri, N., & Dholakia, N. (2009). Professional and trade associations in a nascent and formative sector of a developing economy: A case study of the NASSCOM effect on the Indian offshoring industry. *Journal of International Management, 15*(2), 225–239.

Lawrence, T. B., & Phillips, N. (2004) From Moby Dick to Free Willy: Macro-cultural discourse and institutional entrepreneurship in emerging institutional fields. *Organization, 11,* 689–711.

Leggatt, H. (2009, October 13). Online advertisers duped by 'invisible' ads. *BizReport*. http://www.bizreport.com/2009/10/online_advertisers_duped_by_invisible_ads.html. Accessed 27 October 2009.

Leonard, D. (2006). When is a click not a click? *Fortune, 154*(5), 53.

Leyden, J. (2006, October 6). Worm automates Google AdSense fraud. . http://www.theregister.co.uk/2006/10/06/google_adsense_worm. Accessed 2 October 2008.

Liptak, A. (2007, October 15). Competing for clients, and paying by the click. *The New York Times*. http://www.nytimes.com/2007/10/15/us/15 bar.html. Accessed 27 October 2009.

Los Angeles Times. (2006, August 3). In brief/internet; Search engines unite to fight 'Click Fraud', C.4.

Lu, P. B. (2007, March). CIC China search engine advertisers survey brief 1Q2007. http://www.researchinchina.com/headline/download/ChinaPaidSearchAdvertisersSurvey1Q2007.pdf. Accessed 2 October 2008.

Lynn, M. (2006, October 7). Why Google has already passed its peak. *The Spectator*.

Mann, C. C. (2006, January). How click fraud could swallow the internet. *WIRED Magazine, 14*(1). http://www.wired.com/wired/archive/14.01/fraud.html. Accessed 27 October 2008.

Marketing. (2006, July 19). Media analysis: Click fraud rears its head. http://www.accessmylibrary.com/coms2/summary_0286-33091453_ITM. Accessed 2 October 2008.

Martin, K. D., & Smith, N. C. (2008). Commercializing social interaction: The ethics of stealth marketing. *Journal of Public Policy & Marketing, 27*(1), 45–56.

Matin, S. (2007). Clicks Ahoy! Navigating online advertising in a sea of fraudulent clicks. *Berkeley Technology Law Journal, Annual Review, 22*(1), 533–554.

McCarthy, B. (2002). New economics of sociological criminology. *Annual Review of Sociology, 28*, 417–442.

Mello, J. P. Jr. (2006, May 1). Pornographers turn to click fraud. *E-Commerce Times*. http://www.ecommercetimes.com/story/48135.html. Accessed 2 October 2008.

Milyan, A. (2007, May 14). Developing click fraud standards: Q&A with Tom Cuthbert 1 Click Forensics. http://www.searchmarketingstandard.com/articles/2007/05/developing-click-fraud-standards-qa-with-tom-cuthbert-l-click-forensics.html. Accessed 2 October 2008.

Mindlin, A. (2008, June 16). Rogue computers used in ad fraud; [Business/Financial Desk]. *New York Times,* (Late Edition (East Coast)), C.4.

Mittelman, J. H., & Johnston, R. (1999). The globalization of organized crime, the courtesan state, and the corruption of civil society. *Global Governance, 5*(1), 103–126.

Motlogelwa, T. (2007, October 5). Cyber crime law gets teeth. http://www.mmegi.bw/index.php?sid=1&aid=30&dir=2007/October/Friday5. Accessed 27 October 2009.

Naidu, E. (2008, May 11). Cybercrime expert comes to SA. http://www.iol.co.za/index.php?set_id=1&click_id=139&art_id=vn20080511082218330C406913 Accessed 1 October 2008.

Olsen, S. (2004, July 19). Exposing click fraud. *CNET News*. http://news.cnet.com/Exposing-click-fraud/2100-1024_3-5273078.html. Accessed 2 October 2008.

Parker, D. B. (1976). *Crime by computer*. New York: Charles Scribners' Sons.

Penenberg, A. L. (2005). So many clicks, so few sales. *Inc, 27*(8), 29–30.

Perez, J. C. (2009, January 26). Google Q4 earnings plummet, revenue up 18%. http://www.techworld.com.au/article/274113/google_q4_earnings_plummet_revenue_up_18. Accessed 2 October 2009.

Powell, W. W. (1993). *The social construction of an organizational field: The case of biotechnology*. Paper presented at the Warwick-Venice workshop on Perspectives on Strategic Change, University of Warwick.

redherring.com. (2005, April 5). China's Zombie PCs. http://www.redherring.com/Home/11708. Accessed 2 October 2008.

Rhee, M., & Haunschild, P. R. (2006). The liability of good reputation: A study of product recalls in the US automobile industry. *Organization Science, 17*, 101–117.

Rhee, M., & Valdez, M. E. (2009). Contextual factors surrounding reputation damage with potential implications for reputation repair. *Academy of Management Review, 34*(1), 146–168.

Rindova, V. P., Pollock, T. G., & Hayward, M. L. A. (2006). Celebrity firms: The social construction of market popularity. *Academy of Management Review, 31*, 50–71.

Roberts, D. (2008). Inside the war against China's Blogs; Vengeful bloggers? Flaming posts? PR firms help global brands navigate the country's perilous Web. *Business Week, 4089*, 60.

Robertson, B. (2006, October 23). China's Internet Mess; Search-engine firms routinely use spyware to capture market share. Now they face allegations of click fraud. *Newsweek* (International ed.)..

Schneier, B. (2009, October 15). Why framing your enemies is now virtually child's play. *The Guardian*. http://www.guardian.co.uk/technology/2009/oct/15/bruce-schneier-internet-security. Accessed 22 October 2008.

Scott, W. R. (1992). *Organizations: Rational, natural and open systems*. Englewood Cliffs, NJ: Prentice Hall.

Skrzycki, C. (2007). Stopping Spyware at the source. *The Washington Post*, D.1.

Snidal, D. (1994). The politics of scope: Endogenous actors, heterogeneity and institutions. *Journal of Theoretical Politics, 6*(4), 449–472.

Snidal, D. (1996). Political economy and international institutions. *International Review of Law and Economics, 16*(1), 121–137.

Standing, G. (1984). The notion of technological unemployment. *International Labour Review, 123*(2), 127–147.

Sullivan, E. A. (2008, February 15). Consider your source. *Marketing News, 42*(3), 16–19.

Sullivan, L. (2009, February 6). Brick-and-Mortar retailers losing search battle. *MediaPost*. http://www.mediapost.com/publications/?fa=Articles.showArticle&art_aid=99829. Accessed 2 October 2008.

Tajfel, H., & Turner, J. C. (1986). The social identity theory of intergroup behavior. In S. Worchel & W. G. Austin (Eds.), *Psychology of intergroup relations* (pp. 7–24). Chicago, IL: Nelson-Hall.

The Economist. (2006). *Leaders: Truth in advertising; Internet commerce, 381*(8505), 12.

USA Today. (2008, December 17). Marketers hone the focus of search ads.

Utter, D. A. (2006). High-priced keyword click fraud rises. http://www.webpronews.com/insiderreports/2006/07/17/highpriced-keyword-click-fraud-rises, July 17. Accessed 2 October 2008.

Vassilev, R. (2003). De-development problems in Bulgaria. *East European Quarterly, 37*(3), 345.

Veverka, M. (2006). How Click Fraud Just Got Scammier; Calling All "Bot" Busters!. *Barron's*, 44.

Vidyasagar, N. (2004, May 3). India's secret army of online ad 'clickers'. http://timesofindia.indiatimes.com/articleshow/msid-654822,curpg-1.cms. Accessed 2 October 2008.

Vise, D. A. (2005). Clicking to steal: When advertisers pay by the look. *The Washington Post*, F01. http://www.washingtonpost.com/wp-dyn/articles/A58268-2005Apr16.html. Accessed 2 October 2008.

Wiesenfeld, B. M., Wurthmann, K. A., & Hambrick, D. C. (2008). The stigmatization and devaluation of elites associated with corporate failures: A process model. *Academy of Management Review, 33*(1), 231–251.

Zaharov-Reutt, A. (2008, November 30). Click fraud: Advertisers to watch closely. *ITWire*. http://www.itwire.com/content/view/21990/53. Accessed 28 October 2009.

Chapter 11
Concluding Remarks and Implications

"When good gains a foot, evil adds a yard. As you upgrade your knowledge, skills and equipment, you can be sure that criminals are doing the same." Singaporean Prime Minister Lee Hsien Loong (cf. Joshi, 2009).

"... [P]olicing cyberspace will require a different approach than traditional law enforcement. Streets are public, but telecommunications lines are not" (a Boston Globe article, October 21, 2009, Reed and Dunkelman, 2009).

Abstract This concluding chapter provides insights into some possible forces and mechanisms that are likely to influence the trajectory of the future cybercrime landscape. It also discusses possible measures that can be taken at various levels to combat this new form of criminality. Implications for businesses, consumers, and policy makers are discussed and directions for future research are pointed out. Integrative approaches that combine policy and technological measures at various levels are likely to make the cyberworld more secure.

11.1 Where Do We Go from Here?

The size of the cyberspace is tremendously huge and is increasing exponentially. According to internetworldstats.com (2009), there were 1.7 billion Internet users in the world in the mid-2009. A calculation based on data available from Euromonitor's Global Market Information Database (GMID) indicates that there were more than 414 million broadband Internet subscribers in 77 countries in 2008. Likewise, the consulting firm Ovum estimated that there will be 2 billion mobile broadband subscribers worldwide by 2014 and 258 million of them will access the mobile broadband services through laptops (O'Halloran, 2009). A calculation from Euromonitor's GMID data also suggested that in 2007, Internet retailing exceeded US $213 billion in just 48 countries. It is an accepted axiom that crime follows opportunity. Growth in the size of the cyberspace and an increasing digitization of value chains and business processes would offer an attractive opportunity for cyber-criminals.

N. Kshetri, *The Global Cybercrime Industry*, DOI 10.1007/978-3-642-11522-6_11,
© Springer-Verlag Berlin Heidelberg 2010

The ubiquity of cyberspace, the existence of many small players, and a lack of face-to-face relations mean that the occurrence of opportunism is more likely in the cyberworld than in the physical world. As discussed in Chap. 10, most cybercrimes involve less visible players, which are less likely to be spotlighted by the media. The discussion in this book also indicates that organized crime groups are benefiting from economies of scope as well as the advantages of digitization and are expanding their operations into the cyberworld. Cybercrimes are thus likely to become more pervasive and sophisticated. It is reasonable to expect that cyber-criminals will invent increasingly new and rare forms of cybercrimes. At the same time, IT companies are in a time of unprecedented opportunity to develop sophisticated security products.

A more fascinating question probably concerns the changes in formal and informal institutions. As discussed earlier, various components of institutions are subject to change. Compared to economic and technological factors, however, formal and informal rules of the game change relatively slowly (Baumol, 1990). Prior research, for instance, has suggested that the legal system in an industry evolves more slowly compared to the development of the technology (e.g., see Weniz, 2007 for the medical industry).

We can expect that organizations and government agencies may singly or cooperatively make efforts to minimize institutional forces that promote deviant cyber behavior and improve the security of the cyberworld. In addition to enacting new laws to minimize cyber threats (change in regulative institutions), they can devise strategy to change social norms (change in normative institutions) that influence hackers' behavior. Over time, there will be dense and extended networks of institutions, actors, laws, and norms developed to combat cybercrimes. For instance, regulators are likely to expand the scope of the reach of their policy in light of the increasing cybercrime activities. Organizations are likely to be more vigilant to ensure that measures are taken to deal with governments', organized criminals' and individuals' ICT-created positive and negative asymmetries. Likewise, Internet users are likely to have better cognitive abilities and skills and develop mechanisms to defend against cyberattacks of varying severity.

11.2 Implications for Businesses

Management of security risks is a critical practical challenge that organizations face in the digital economy. There are two interrelated reasons why security risks matter for companies. First, in prior theoretical and empirical research, scholars have viewed "channel opportunism" concerns related to quality uncertainty and risk as the principal barriers in the adoption of electronic channels (Barkhi, Belanger, & Hicks, 2008). Overby and Jap (2009), for instance, found that products that involved a low degree of quality uncertainty and were relatively rare were more likely to be bought and sold in the electronic channels compared to those that involved high-quality uncertainty and were widely available. Measures taken to address the problems related to quality uncertainty and risk would help expand e-commerce to a wider spectrum of products. A second, probably more significant factor, concerns the importance of addressing the cyberattack-related threats facing the company. In this regard, this book has important managerial implications.

11.2.1 All Firms Are Not Equally Susceptible to the Vulnerability of Various ICT-Created Security Risks

The global cybercrime landscape is moving toward a higher proportion of targeted attacks. All organizations, however, are not equally attractive cybercrime targets. Whereas symbolic significance and criticalness of a network attract intrinsically motivated cyber-criminals, larger businesses and those with a high dependence on digital technologies are lucrative targets for financially motivated hackers.

According to a Verizon Business study conducted in 2009, 30% of all cyber-crimes take place through the retail industry (Asch, 2009). As noted in Chap. 7, some computer hackers' interests are also framed by fight against capitalism, who are likely to attack networks of big companies. Similarly, terrorist are more likely to target the networks of sensitive organizations such as hospitals and critical infrastructures. Likewise, as discussed in Chap. 1, exploiting online casinos' dependence on Internet technologies, cyber-criminals have extorted millions of dollars with them. A firm's management of security risks requires an understanding of its position on the spectrum of positive and negative asymmetries created by ICTs. It is thus important for firms to assess the risks of their networks being cybercrime targets and devise appropriate defense mechanisms.

11.2.2 Some Firms Are More Affected by the Government's Measure

Regulatory landscape influencing the cybercrime industry is changing very rapidly. New laws may force companies to change business models to minimize nations' and citizens' negative asymmetries as well as to restrict adversaries (e.g., terrorists and hostile nations) from gaining symmetric advantages. For instance, the *US Patriot Act* required banks to spend on technology to enhance security. Compliance with other new laws written for electronic criminal activities may provide similar pressures. Some firms are more affected than others by governments' measures to deal with cybercrimes.

11.2.3 Consideration of Security Risks in ICT and Competitive Strategies

ICT and competitive strategies such as outsourcing should go beyond obvious considerations such as core competence, human resource, and service quality (e.g., Goo, Kishore, & Rao, 2000). For instance, origination and destination countries in offshore business process and information technology offshoring may differ on regulative, normative, and cognitive institutions (Kshetri, 2007). In some cases, such differences can translate to negative asymmetries for a party. The Pakistani medical transcriber discussed earlier took advantage of institutional differences in the United States (outsourcing origination) and Pakistan (destination). Such differences produced negative asymmetry for the US hospital and positive asymmetry for the Pakistani medical transcriber. Each move that involves ICT should be evaluated in terms of new vulnerabilities that adversaries can potentially exploit.

11.2.4 The Rank Effect

Like other technologies, deployment of defense mechanisms tends to diffuse from large to small organizations. This is commonly known as the *rank effect* in the economics literature (Gotz, 1999). As large companies put stronger defense mechanisms against cyberattacks, small and medium-sized enterprises (SMEs) are more likely to become cybercrime targets. The proportion of total cybercrimes that target SMEs is thus likely to increase. A survey conducted by Panda Security during December 2008–May 2009 among SMEs indicated that 44% of the US respondents and 58% worldwide were "recently" infected by Internet threats (PR Newswire July 24 2009).

11.2.5 Importance of Reporting

In the physical world, research has indicated that time taken to report a crime is one of the most important factors in determining the probability of arrest (National Institute of Justice, 2001). As discussed earlier, cybercrimes are among the most under-reported forms of criminality. Many companies probably have the misguided belief that they can resolve problems related to attacks on their networks internally. But this is definitely not the case with most cybercrimes. Timely reporting of cyberattacks to authorities is thus likely to strengthen the rules of law and help combat cyber threats in the long run. This is especially important for crimes for which the proper preservation of evidence is critical for a successful prosecution. For many cybercrimes, a successful prosecution of the offender may require the preservation of physical as well as digital evidence.

11.2.6 Measures to Avoid Positive Feedbacks to Cyber-Criminals

Some companies have set a dangerous precedent of negotiating with cyber-criminals by paying ransoms. Experts argue that gambling sites alone have paid millions of dollars to cyber-extortionists annually. But this pragmatic and probably not entirely wrong-headed response has created negative externalities for consumers and businesses and has thus at a great cost.

Ransom money sends positive cognitive messages and will fuel further cyberattacks by making criminals more sophisticated and organized. As criminals' skill, organization, and intelligence co-vary positively with the odds of getting away with crimes (National Center for Policy Analysis, 2002), paying ransom would contribute to the vicious circle of cybercrimes.

11.2.7 Combining Technological and Behavioral/Perceptual Measures

Ensuring that both technological and behavioral/perceptual factors are given equal consideration in the design and implementation of a computer network is crucial. Technological measures range from simply disconnecting databases containing sensitive information from the Internet to the deployment of sophisticated anti-fraud technologies. Some examples of such technologies include eBay's "spoof detector," which enables users to receive alerts when eBay/PayPal passwords are entered in inappropriate log-in screens and some financial companies' deployment of dummy accounts to trap phishers and tools to detect fake e-commerce/bank websites.

Similarly, simple behavioral measures can stop some serious cybercrimes. A simple training strategy aimed at improving the ability of employees to distinguish a fraudulent e-mail with a real one may reduce a significant proportion of such crimes.

11.2.8 Managing Market Information

Due to increasing cybercrimes, many e-commerce transactions are zero sum game or "political gains" (Wurth, 1992/1993). E-commerce providers such as eBay need to develop new methods for managing market information to reduce market uncertainty. Overcoming an informational disadvantage facing the consumer can help transform structure of e-marketplaces from a zero-sum game to a positive sum game.

11.2.9 Collaborating with Government Agencies

Businesses can lobby governments for enactment and tougher enforcement of laws. Organizations may also benefit from their measures to educate people involved in law-enforcement, law making, and law interpretation. For instance, Microsoft finances cybercrime conferences and training programs to judges and law-enforcement agencies. Likewise, eBay has been educating Romanian prosecutors about cybercrimes including explaining to a judge using layman's language (Wylie, 2007). As discussed in Chap. 8, India's NASSCOM works with police officers and lawyers, and works with industry bodies and the government. Organizations based and developed as well as developing economies can borrow a page from eBay's and NASSCOM's lesson books.

11.2.10 Harnessing the Power of Attachment in Online Communities

Some scholars argue that due to the drawbacks of the traditional law-enforcement model in combating cybercrimes, it is important to look for alternatives (Jones, 2007). Community policing, which places primary emphasis on the relationships between police and citizens and employed extensively in the 1970s and 1980s to fight crimes in inner cities of the United States may be especially effective to fight cybercrimes (Forman, 2004; Greene, 2004). There are a number of community policing methods employed in the cyberworld. They include user rating systems on e-commerce websites like eBay (http://www.ebay.com) and Craigslist (http://www.craigslist.org) (Jones, 2007). The various drawbacks of these methods are pointed out earlier.

Organizations can harness the power of attachment in various online communities (Ren, Kraut, & Kiesler, 2007) to increase the effectiveness of community policing. For instance, community-based clan control can be effectively combined with formal control mechanisms to fight some types of cybercrimes such as internet auction fraud (Chua, Huang, Wareham, & Robey, 2007). Originally proposed by (Shaw & McKay, 1942), and later developed and refined by other scholars (Anderson, 1999; Sampson, Morenoff, & Gannon-Rowley, 2002; Triplett, Gainly, & Sun, 2003), social disorganization theory argues that weak and disorganized communities are likely to experience a higher degree of crime. One of the central tenets of social disorganization theory is that a member's attachment to the community is positively associated with his/her engagement in crime fighting activities.

Measures taken to build a stronger attachment to the online community would thus help fight cybercrimes. Prior research indicates that some important features of websites that have strong online community include the existence of repeat and regular visitors; discussions in which participants reply to one another; new and innovative interaction designs with browsing and searching capabilities; and interfaces for tagging, ratings, and RSS feeds (Harper, Raban, Rafaeli, & Konstan, 2008). These and other related efforts toward increasing attachments to online community can serve as an important cybercrime-fighting tool.

11.2.11 Employing Online Security as a Competitive Advantage Tool

The ubiquity of cybercrimes also provides businesses an opportunity to employ online security as a competitive advantage tool. For instance, recently, there have been instance in which cyber-criminals have pretended to be well-known advertising agencies and have duped media outlets such as *New York Times* into running fake ads, which are loaded with malicious codes (Kravets, 2009). In order to address these issues and ensure safe and malware-free ads, the New York-based advertising company, Epic Advertising hired a former FBI cybercrime agent as the head of a division in the company that scrutinizes and evaluates potential advertisers (Poulsen, 2009). Additional measures taken to ensure cybersafety would give businesses such as Epic Advertising a competitive advantage.

11.3 Implications for Consumers

We discussed above that technological and behavioral/perceptual factors are crucial in the design and implementation of a computer network. The same is true of consumers. Technological measures range from simply disconnecting databases containing sensitive information from the Internet to the deployment of sophisticated anti-fraud technologies. Similarly, it is important to think carefully and act thoughtfully for all online activities. For instance, before opening an e-mail, it is important to know who the sender is.

11.3.1 Revisiting a Cognitive Framework Related to Cybercrimes

Before making decision to engage in an electronic transaction, consumers screen the transaction and categorize it as legitimate or fraudulent. False-positive and false-negative rates associated with the screening process are high, which can be attributed to the difference between an individual's subjective and objective vulnerability to cybercrimes.

We noted earlier that, as a precaution to avoid being victimized by cyber-criminals, many consumers do not shop online. Consumers' ability to avoid false-positive and false-negative categorizations is a function of their skills, education, and experience.

Deception works by exploiting systematic weaknesses in the potential victim's cognitive systems (Grazioli & Jarvenpaa, 2003). Naïve Internet users are victims, targets, and instruments in cybercrimes. Consumers thus need to pay close attention to such processes as perception, learning, and cognition with respect to cybercrimes.

Consumers also need to be aware that anti-virus software is necessary and that it needs to be regularly updated. Equally important are consumers' experience, expertise, skills, and knowledge about how to evaluate fake and genuine security products. Some cyber-criminals have been able to sell fake anti-virus products by capitalizing on consumers' fear of becoming a cybercrime victim. For instance, in March 2009, San Jose, California-based web security company, Finjan detected a Ukraine-based cybercrime organization, which was selling fake anti-virus software (The New Zealand Herald, April 23, 2009). According to Symantec, there were 250 varieties of fake security software products in 2009, which were installed in tens of millions of computers (Reuters, 2009). For instance, fraudsters who tricked New York Times into running a fake ad hijacked readers' browsers, which displayed a fake virus-scan (Kravets, 2009). Instead of reducing risks, the fake security software products make computers more vulnerable to cybercrimes.

As noted earlier, many consumers are reluctant to engage in online transactions because of concerns related to cybercrimes. While there are some well-founded rationales against online transactions, there are also a number of misinformed and ill-guided viewpoints. In this regard, a proper education process could prevent the harboring of unnecessary fears about cybercrimes.

11.3.2 Tracking the Performance Indicators Frequently

A frequent tracking of some performance indicators would help consumers evaluate how successful they are in terms of achieving the goals related to cybersafety. For instance, consumers need to evaluate their awareness level of various types of cyber threats and check credit reports frequently.

11.3.3 Minimizing Activities, Websites, Channels, and Networks Associated with Cybercrimes

Consumers can minimize the chance of becoming a cybercrime victim by avoiding financial transactions and mechanisms widely used by criminal groups such as wire transfer services. Consumers need to be suspicious of highly unusual and too good to be true offers, requests, and opportunities such as winning a lottery, clicking on web links, and downloading free software.

11.3.4 Understanding Communication Modes of Legitimate and Criminal Enterprises

An understanding of communication modes used by legitimate businesses and criminal enterprises may also help to minimize the chance of becoming a cybercrime victim. For instance, most legitimate businesses may not ask their customers to provide personal information by e-mail (Rubenking, 2009).

11.3.5 Need to Be Watchful for e-Commerce Activities That Have Relatively High Incidence of Cybercrimes and Cyber-frauds

E-commerce transactions vary in terms their proneness to crime. For products that can be delivered digitally such as software, music, and video, the delivery is instantaneous. The shorter time lag between online transaction and delivery reduces the chance for an opportunistic behavior (Chatterjee & Datta, 2008). The risk of opportunism in e-shopping *is* higher for products that require physical delivery than those that can be delivered digitally (Scott, 2004). Consumers need to be especially watchful for these and other e-commerce activities that have relatively high incidence of cybercrimes and cyber-frauds. These include online auctions.

11.3.6 Staying Safe Offline

While precaution online is important, it is also crucial to stay safe offline. According to Measurement Evaluation Learning (MEL), the British research and consultancy firm, 77% of UK household waste contains one or more items, which may lead to identify theft (euromonitor.com, 2007).

The issue of physical security is even more important. Hardware items such as laptop computers, PDAs, cellphones, flash drives, and important documents such as birth certificates and social security cards need to be locked securely.

11.3.7 Monitoring Children's Online Activities

One problem that has been noted by cybersecurity analysts is that children's online activities are not sufficiently monitored. For instance, many parents do not know availability of parental controls options at latest versions of operating systems such as Microsoft's Vista and Apple's Mac OS X Tiger. Of particular importance is thus parental awareness of risk factors associated with children's online activities and the availability of various options to control and monitor children's online activities.

11.3.8 Assessing the Credibility and Reputation of Parties Involved in Economic Transactions

Cyber-frauds come in all shapes and sizes. It is important to assess the credibility of and reputation of the parties involved in economic transactions. As more and more economic activities are digitized, fraudsters can convincingly pretend as individuals and organizations involved in various transactions to victimize consumers. For instance, a cybercrime outfit reportedly broke the secret computer code and algorithm used in generating Amazon.com vouchers, which were being offered at a half price (Kendall, 2009).

A mule interviewed by Krebs (2009) reported that a criminal group, pretending to be a legitimate company, e-mailed her to offer a work-at-home "financial manager" job. The e-mail mentioned that the group found her resume on Careerbuilder.com. The mule needed to provide the criminal outfit with personal and financial information such as name, address, Social Security number, bank account and routing numbers, and a scanned copy of driver's license (Krebs, 2009). The lesson of this story: it is important to verify the background of any company, which offers a job. For instance, it needs to be checked that the company has a registered address.

11.3.9 Knowing About How Information Is Handled by Parties Involved in Various Transactions

Some organizations such as hospitals, schools, universities require personal information in order to provide services. In such cases, it is important to know how the information is handled by various transacting parties. If personal informal needs to be provided, it would be important to make sure that the information is secured properly.

11.4 Implications for Policy Makers

The interaction of market uncertainty and technological uncertainty contributes to market failure (Williamson, 1975, 1985; Wurth, 1992/1993). In general, dealing with technological information (dismantling cyber-criminals' technological system) and market information (providing accurate information to businesses and consumers) require different combinations of public policy, focusing on production and distribution of information (Wurth, 1992/1993).

   The government needs to pursue various goals with respect to diverse array of cyber-criminal activities. Policy makers need to establish the right balance between promoting the use of e-commerce to achieve economic growth and efficiency and controlling cybercrimes. Adequate public policies will obviously play a major role in combating cybercrimes and dismantling the underground e-marketplaces. The framework developed in this book has some clear implications for policy makers.

11.4.1 Cooperation and Collaboration Among National Governments, Computer Crime Authorities, and Businesses

There is no pure technological fix for security-related problems involving technologies (Carblanc & Moers, 2003; Skolnikoff, 1989). Cooperation and collaboration among national governments, computer crime authorities, and businesses are critical to combat cyberattacks and enhance cybersafety (Table 7.4). If national governments work with one another as well as with business communities to modify institutions by defining appropriate policies for the security of the digital world, it will result in lower transaction costs. Some signs of success have materialized, but nations have very far to go before they can achieve even a moderate level of success.

11.4.2 Paying Attention to Wider Institutional Fields

As noted in Chap. 7, the United States is the world's top cybercrime target. Increasingly new forms of cybercrimes are emerging that require the participation or cooperation of many countries. However, the necessary cooperation is lacking in many cases. Institutional change measures are thus needed to foster and enhance the level of international cooperation. As noted earlier, doing so requires an understanding of other "higher" level existing institutions and exogenous parameters (Snidal, 1994, 1996). Institutional change measures that pay attention as to how they are embedded in the "wider institutional field" (Lawrence, Hardy, & Phillips, 2002) or "networks of other already legitimate institutions" (Suchman, 1995) are more likely to be successful. Put differently, the patterns of international cooperation on cybercrime-related issues also need to be seen against the backdrop of the current international political situation and legal regime rather than as a self-contained phenomenon.

At the broadest level, the context in which new fields emerge is constituted by macro-cultural discourse. This includes the broad discourses and associated sets of institutions that extend beyond the focal institutional field's boundaries and are widely understood and accepted in a society (Berger & Luckmann, 1967; Lawrence & Phillips, 2004). For instance, associated sets of institutions include integration with the global economy and war on terror.

Law-enforcement agencies in some developing countries continue to neglect and dismiss cybercrimes as being exaggerated and frame them as Wetsern propaganda. To get developing countries' cooperation, it would be important to include them in international discourses. In the first UN forum on Internet governance, some developing countries such as Iran and South Africa complained that they had not been given an opportunity to adequately express their views on ethical issues and other concerns (Hadoulis, 2006).

11.4.3 Measures to Increase Reporting Rate

Enacting laws that require organizations to deploy appropriate defense mechanisms and making reporting of cybercrimes mandatory can help combat such crimes. Since the mid-2004, South Korea's National Cyber Security Center has mandated that all Internet-related hacking incidents must be reported (Ho, 2004). Likewise, the State of California's Senate Bill 1386 requires public organizations to report computer security breaches (Walden, 2005). Many countries, however, do not have such laws.

11.4.4 Certainty vs. Severity of Punishment

Most measures taken so far have emphasized on increasing penalty rather than on increasing the probability of arrest. Many countries are changing the regulative landscape toward severity of punishment. The US government, for instance, requires commercial banks to secure their networks. The *Patriot Act* and the *Gramm Leach Bliley (GLB) Act* require new security measures including customer identification and privacy protection. Despite the existence of similar regulations for decades, *the Patriot Act* reflected a change in the US banking landscape. The *US Patriot Act* brought cyberattacks into the definition of terrorism with penalties of up to 20 years in prison.

The probability of arrest in cybercrimes is, however, very low since conventional law-enforcement authorities lack skills required in dealing with such crimes. The severity of punishment is important, but what is still more critical in enhancing cybersafety is the certainty of punishment (Becker, 1995). The probability of arrest is likely to increase with more investments in the development of law-enforcement capabilities. Vinton Cerf, the co-designer of the Internet's basic architecture noted: "You should not pass legislation that cannot be enforced... When [the legislation] can not be enforced, that is when people ignore laws" (The Industry Standard, 2001).

11.4.5 Developing Economies' Negative International Image and Exclusion from the Digital World

Cyber-criminals have created a negative international image for some developing economies. Speaking of their association with cybercrime activities, a Telegraph article noted: "Trust in Nigerian businessmen and princes" described as "50 things that are being killed by the internet" (Moore, 2009). In August 2009, Haruna Iddrisu, Minister of Communication of Ghana noted that a failure to address cybercrime and cybersecurity would tarnish the country's image and hinder its ability to create an enabling environment for ICT and stimulate socio-economic development (Ghana News Agency, 2009). Likewise, the Head Pastor of a Christian Center in Ghana noted that cybercrime originated from Ghana created a bad image for the country and urged Christians to defend and restore the country's image (ghanabusinessnews.com, 2009). Note that Ghana is among the top 10 countries in terms of perpetrators based on complaints made to the I3C in the second half of 2007 (Table 7.2) as well as a top source country for click fraud activities (Table 10.2).

As noted earlier, organizations in developing countries that are adopting the Internet without considering the costs and efforts needed to secure the systems have generated a negative externality (Otis & Evans, 2003). Some ISPs in industrialized countries reportedly block contents originated from problematic networks based in developing countries (Garfinkel, 2002).

Prior research indicates that some criteria that lack precise quantitative data and are nonspecific measures (e.g., those related to a group in which the transacting entity belongs to) can be utilized as quality indicators to assess the transacting entity. This may be necessary when information on the quality of the individual transacting party is unavailable or is too costly to measure. Prior researchers have recognized that variables such as race, age, and gender are used by buyers to as indicators of seller quality (Akerlof, 1970). The US online merchants, for instance, consider Indonesia as one of the high-risk countries and block all orders from the country (Richmond, 2003). Indonesia was banned for some time from eBay auctions after a carder manipulated sellers under a false identity and card number (Lim, 2001). From the developing countries' perspective, a failure to control international cybercrimes originated from these countries thus may lead to their exclusion in the digital world.

11.4.6 Helping Small and Poor Countries Develop Anti-cybercrime Capabilities

As noted above, cybercrimes have a high degree of globalization. Cyber-criminals can make more effective use of safe haven than most other crimes. Because of its cross-border character, cybercrime is becoming a pressing international relations issue. For industrialized economies, the battle against cybercrime is about more than developing capacity on the home front. Enormous and vexing troubles related to developing countries' lack of resources and lack of cooperation frustrate developed world-based law-enforcement agencies' anti-cybercrime efforts. Thus, helping developing countries build anti-cybercrime institutions is of paramount importance. Developed nations' assistance to these countries, especially those with high rates of origin of cybercrimes, is urgently needed to combat global cyber threats originating from these countries. Especially cooperation of government in countries that have high degrees of concentration of cybercrimes is critical to fight cybercrimes that originate in these countries.

11.4.7 Collaborations with Businesses

It would be erroneous, however, to assume that legislative and law-enforcement solutions alone would reduce cybercrime. A simple training strategy to improve the ability of consumers, employees, and the public to distinguish a fraudulent e-mail with a real one may significantly reduce cybercrimes. It would be also important to include cybersafety, cybersecurity, and cyberethics-related courses in school and college curricula. These measures are even more important in the developing world. Multinationals must cooperate with local organizations to help consumers understand cybercrimes and to encourage the evolution of ethical standards (Donaldson, 1996). For instance, Microsoft has teamed up with Paradigm Initiative Nigeria (PIN) to educate Nigerians on cybercrimes and to create economic opportunities (Zulu, 2008). The country's Economic and Financial Crimes Commission (EFCC), which announced in October 2009 that it shut down about 800 websites associated with cybercrimes and arrested 18 e-mail fraudster groups, noted that "smart technology" provided by Microsoft helped it (Awolusi, 2009).

11.4.8 Measures to Educate Consumers and Increase the Distribution of and Access to Information

As indicated earlier, cyber-criminals prey on the ignorance of some consumers. It is thus a matter of central importance for policy makers to get information to the less informed (Machlup, 1962). It is argued that, policy makers have arguably placed too much emphasis on increasing "technological" information in order to encourage innovation and discovery (Wurth, 1992/1993). Very little efforts have been made to broaden access and distribution or to increase "market" information (Wurth, 1992/1993). We can draw a parallel of the above example to the context of the cyberworld. The efforts have been primarily directed toward controlling the activities of cyber-criminals, for instance, by shutting down their networks (e.g., during 2004–2005, the US Secret Service shut down an online criminal outfit with 4,000 members, Chap. 1). Measures to educate the consumers have been purely a lip service. Distribution of information has thus been relatively neglected.

The public's lack of education is also associated with technological, behavioral/perceptual weaknesses. Experts say that the key to combat phishing lies in consumer's ability to distinguish between real and fraudulent e-mails. The Chronicle of Higher Education (2007) put the issue this way: "We continue to seek technological, legislative, and law-enforcement solutions to what is largely an educational problem. ... Meanwhile, our schools have failed to systematically incorporate Internet safety, information security, and cyberethics instruction into curricula."

The governments need to develop educational outreach programs to create a greater awareness of cybercrimes. In Canada, the government and businesses have collaborated to promote each October as Cyber Security Awareness Month. Public Safety Canada, the Royal Canadian Mounted Police (RCMP), and the Retail Council of Canada have teamed up to increase cybersecurity awareness (Marketwire October 02, 2009).

11.4.9 Broadband Penetrations and Cybercrime in Developing Economies

In a discussion of cybercrimes in developing economies, an issue that deserves mention relates to rapid growth in Internet and broadband penetrations. Serious cybercrimes require bandwidth intensive applications. Most developing countries' networks attract little attention from hackers because of low connectivity. These networks are unreliable to carry out sophisticated cyberattacks (Reilly, 2007). Developing countries, however, may experience a rapid cybercrime growth with an increase in broadband penetration in the future. Note that broadband networks are growing rapidly in these countries.

11.4.10 Dealing with Various Types of Online Communities

In Chap. 2, we noted that community policing may be effective to fight cybercrimes (Forman, 2004; Greene, 2004). It should, however, be noted that communities with various stages of development orientation differ in terms of their relationships with the formal control mechanisms (Nolan, Conti, & McDevitt, 2004). Prior research indicates that dissatisfied communities are likely to behave antagonistically toward the authorities while the interdependent communities tend to cooperate (Nolan et al., 2004). One-size-fits-all approach, thus may not work in organizations' approach in dealing with online communities.

11.5 Directions for Future Research

There obviously is a need for more research on the global cybercrime industry. Future researchers on this topic can help us better understand the phenomenon of cybercrimes that is becoming pervasive, and perhaps to find better ways of controlling it. The evolution of new types of cybercrimes and associated institutional changes will also provide many interesting and fruitful avenues for future research. Before concluding, we suggest several potentially fruitful avenues for future research.

11.5.1 Institutional Analysis of Cybercrime

Formal and informal institutions' connections with criminal activities in the cyber-world might be worthwhile target of study. Prior research indicates that individuals differ in terms of fear associated with the social stigma of lawbreaking. White-collar offenders, for instance, are likely to feel the stigma of prison more strongly than low-end criminals (Braithwaite, 1989). Researchers could examine whether hackers and cyber-criminals in different economic, professional socio-cultural backgrounds differ in terms of the feeling of guilt, shame, and embarrassment.

Roles of the government: Our study highlighted an important role of the government in fighting cybercrimes. One way to understand the government's role would be to incorporate the ideas of institutional field and field dominance. Note that dominant field members exert control and influence in the development of structures and practices and shape institutional evolution (Phillips, Lawrence, & Hardy 2000). In this book, we did not extensively pursue this line of reasoning for the sake of simplicity. It may, however, be a future research area when constructing more comprehensive model of cybercrimes. Further theoretical and empirical research is needed to gain a better understanding of the natures of the government's "formal authority, resources and discursive legitimacy" (Phillips et al., 2000, p. 33) needed to dominate cybercrime-related institutional field.

Institutions and institutional field at the global level: This book (Chaps. 3 and 5) mainly focused on institutions and institutional field at the intra-countrylevel. One extension of the present work would be to investigate international level institutions related to cybercrime. As discussed earlier, cybercrime has also opened up new discourses in international relations. One extension thus would be to investigate institutional fields formed around cybercrimes and cyber-war at the global level. Studies of discourses and resources associated with cyber-war and cyber-attacks can provide new insights on global cybercrimes and global cyber-war. As discussed earlier (Chap. 6), Chinese military strategists have written openly about exploiting the vulnerabilities associated with the US military's reliance on ICTs and traditional infrastructure used to conduct operations (GAO Reports, 2007). Interplay of resources, authority, and discursive legitimacy in institutional fields formed around cybercrime and cyber-war at the global level thus might be worthwhile target of study.

International variation: Researchers could also examine whether specific institutions are linked with particular forms of cybercrimes. Preliminary evidence, for instance, indicates that cyberattacks originated from Asia tend to exploit vulnerabilities in common software applications to steal personal information. Eastern European cyber-criminals, on the other hand, are linked with organized crime networks and are associated with identity theft. Likewise, hackers from Middle Eastern countries deface websites (Fitzgerald, 2008). In the same vein, Skorodumova (2004) provides some evidence linking national sub-culture with different characteristics of intrinsically motivated hacking. Future research might also examine institutional foundation of regional specialization in cybercrimes.

Ingroup/out-group dynamics: Our discussion of ingroup/out-group dynamics related to stigmatization and sympathy mainly focused on victimization and offending as grouping variables. Another interesting study would be to examine the ingroup/out-group effects by using other grouping variables such as nationality, ethnicity, race, etc. For instance, are people likely to sympathize more with victims and cyber-criminals of their own ethnic group than those of different ethnic groups? Does this tendency vary across cultures? For instance, prior researchers have found that Asians have a tendency to distrust out-group and are more trusting of ingroup (Fukuyama, 1995; Osland & Cavusgil, 1996). In this regard, our work also opens new areas of research in terms of how various elements of a culture influence stigmatization and sympathy of victims and cyber-criminals.

Interaction of institutions and cybercrime types: Researchers could examine whether institutional drivers differ across different forms of cybercrimes. Preliminary evidence noted in this book indicates regional and country-specific specialization in intrinsically as well as extrinsically motivated cybercrimes (Fitzgerald, 2008; Skorodumova, 2004). Researchers could thus look at whether specialization in cybercrimes can be attributed to regional or country-specific institutions.

11.5.2 Empirical Analysis

Further research is needed to extend, refine, enhance, validate, and test the framework presented in this book. Primary or secondary data on constructs related to institutional and economic processes can be collected. An important area of future research concerns operationalizing the various constructs discussed in this book and testing some of the models. One such model is Fig. 7.1. Two possible approaches can be employed for this purpose. The first approach entails testing the model based on country-level data. Although Fig. 7.1 employs different levels of analysis, sources and target characteristics can be aggregated at the country level. For this purpose, Table 7.3 provides some measures of cybersafety and a non-exhaustive list of factors that reflect and determine the cybersafety environment.

The second approach is to apply economics of crimes to test the influence of characteristics of the source nation on hackers' willingness to commit cybercrimes. As noted in Chap. 2, a cyber criminal weighs benefits and costs to make decision about engaging in a crime. A cybercrime is thus committed if the sum of perceived monetary benefits and perceived psychic benefits exceeds perceived psychic costs of committing a cybercrime plus the expected penalty effect (which is the product of the probability of arrests, the probability of conviction, and perceived monetary opportunity costs of conviction) (Probasco & Davis, 1995). Surveys consisting of impacts of regulative, normative, and cognitive institutions; and availability of economic opportunities on hackers' assessment of perceived cost–benefit of cybercrimes can be employed to test the model presented in Fig. 7.1. For institutional processes affecting cybercrimes, survey instruments designed in other fields such as entrepreneurship (e.g., Busenitz, Gomez, & Spencer, 2000) can be modified and used for primary data collection. Respondents could be hackers and/or computer network experts from a number of countries. Similarly, surveys can also be conducted to predict profiles of target organization that different categories of hackers consider worthwhile to attack.

11.5.3 Inter-organizational Studies

As mentioned earlier, not all companies report attacks on their networks. Additional research is also needed to identify the determinants of self-selection bias in the reporting of cyberattacks. What factors distinguish firms that report attacks on their networks from those that do not? Are there international variations in the reporting patterns?

11.5.4 ICT-Created Positive and Negative Asymmetries

An important area of future research concerns testing propositions related to ICT-created positive and negative asymmetries discussed in this book. Positivist qualitative research, which emphasizes causality, can be employed to test the propositions (Myers, 1997; Orlikowski & Baroudi, 1991, p. 5). Especially, case studies can provide a clearer understanding of complex phenomena such as utilization of ICT tools to manage asymmetries by nation and non-nation entities. Efficacy of case study research lies in addressing research questions related to "hows" and "whys" of the complex process of ICT deployment in creating positive asymmetries and dealing with negative asymmetries (Oz, 2004; Yin, 1994, pp. 3–6). In-depth longitudinal examination of a case related to the management of ICT-related asymmetries would also reveal interesting multivariable patterns (Hitt, Harrison, Ireland, & Best, 1998).

Future research is also recommended to better understand how ICT-created asymmetry interacts with other forms of asymmetry (e.g., method, will, morale, organization, and patience). For instance, a question related to interaction between an ICT-created asymmetry and an asymmetry related to organization would be: How do non-state/non-nation entities organized as networks (e.g., Al Qaeda) differ from nations in terms of their capabilities to create positive asymmetries and deal with negative asymmetries. In this book, we discussed a number of ICT functions that contribute to create asymmetric advantages. They include employing ICT tools to fight a war against an enemy (e.g., development of cyber-war technologies in some nations), communicating (e.g., Al Queda's Internet network), detecting threats from enemies (e.g., deployment of smart containers), etc. Future research is also required to construct a clearer taxonomy of ICT functions that are used to create positive asymmetries and to deal with the vulnerabilities of negative asymmetries. Furthermore, it is important to explore how different entities differ with respect to the taxonomy. Some research questions include the following: How nations and non-nation organizations differ in terms of the taxonomy of ICT functions related to positive and negative asymmetries? How nations at different levels of economic development differ with respect to the taxonomy?

11.5.5 Modus Operandi of Various Types of Cyber-Criminals

In this book, we examined various elements of cyber-criminals' business models (Chap. 9). Some cyber-criminals operate through *well*-organized, legitimate channels such as eBay. Many organized and semi-organized illegitimate and criminal organizations are reported to have their own channels to engage in cybercrime activities. Finally, there are also petty identity thieves working alone or in unorganized small groups. In this regard, our work also opens new areas of research in terms of how various cybercrime groups differ in terms of their modus operendi. In future conceptual and empirical work scholars need to compare and contrast the various operational processes of legitimate companies and cyber-criminals such as R&D and offshoring.

11.5.6 Examination of Non-state Actors

The discussion in this book indicated that some non-state actors (e.g., Al Qaeda) have gained access to tangible and intangible resources to develop cyber-war capabilities (Chap. 6). Future research would shed more light on the natures of these non-state actors' tangible and intangible resources from the standpoint of their cyber-war capability.

11.5.7 Longitudinal Analysis of Hackers

Preliminary evidence discussed in this book indicates the shift in hackers' motivations from intrinsic to extrinsic. In this regard, another fruitful avenue for future research is to understand the determinants of the turning point. In-depth interviews with extrinsically motivated hackers would help understand how institutional and economic factors discussed in this book transform motivations of attacking computer networks.

11.5.8 The Nature of Hot Products

One issue that was raised in this book but not fully developed concerns the nature of "hot products" (Clarke, 1999, Chap. 7). For instance, some years ago, cyber-extortionists focused mainly on online casinos, banks, and e-commerce hubs. Recent reports have indicated that they have targeted the networks of utility companies in developing countries such as India, Nigeria, Vietnam, and those in the Middle East (Grant, 2008). Further inquiry is needed to investigate whether cyber-criminals have "hot products" in terms of target attractiveness and how they change.

11.5.9 Portability in Cybercrimes

As noted in this book, portability is related to target attractiveness (Clarke, 1995). Digitization of wealth is an obvious factor facilitating portability in cybercrimes. Cyber-criminals, however, have utilized the services of financial companies such as Western Union and their access to social networks to transfer money stolen from overseas victims (Kshetri, 2005a; Foreign Policy, 2005). Researchers could look at how these factors are related to portability in cybercrimes.

11.5.10 Applying a Game-Theoretic Approach

It is argued in social, biological, and economic sciences *that* a game-theoretic approach would enrich the analysis of the problems of cheating and lying (Maynard

Smith, 1982; Hirschauer & Musshoff, 2007). Game theory can capture behaviors of various actors in cybercrimes, in which an actor's success in making choices is a function of the choices of other actors such as businesses, consumers, and the government. In a game theory framework, the decision-making environment of the actors are defined by rules "including who they are, what they can do, what they know and what will happen according to their actions" (Snidal, 1996, p. 128). A game-theoretic analysis of the cybercrime industry thus might be worthwhile target of study.

11.5.11 Developing a Typology of Cybercrimes

In future research scholars should also attempt to develop a typology of cybercrimes based on various dimensions. The possible dimensions for this purpose include (a) associated motivations (intrinsic and extrinsic) and (b) predatory vs. market-based. For instance, intrinsically motivated cyber-criminals can be predatory (e.g., Chinese hackers who defaced several Taiwanese websites, Chap. 7) as well as market-based (e.g., efforts of individuals who engage in unpaid activities and provide volunteer services in the hacking and cyber-criminal community) (Naylor, 2005). Characteristics of cybercrimes that belong to different combinations of these dimensions can be explored and compared.

11.5.12 Country-Level Case Studies of Cybercrimes

Future research also needs to provide country-level case studies of cyber-crimes. Researchers can look at the social, economic, and institutional drivers of cybercrimes in a country. Country-level case studies can also bring together in concrete and detailed ways the impacts of cybercrimes on businesses and consumers.

11.5.13 Cybercrime Operations as a Born Global Phenomenon

Various examples presented in this book indicate that cybercrime groups derive most of their revenue from international operations. Cybercrime outfits can thus be considered as interesting examples of born global companies, which are also referred as "international new ventures" (McDougall, Shane, & Oviatt, 1994), "instant internationals" (Preece, Miles, & Baetz, 1999), and "global startups" (Oviatt & McDougall, 1994). Several important insights can be derived from the examination of cybercrime operations from the born global approaches.

11.6 Final Thought

The distinctive geography of cyberspace provides an ideal environment for engaging in opportunistic behavior. There is a high temptations for rule-breaking in the cyberspace. The cyberspace possesses all the characteristics of a crime-prone neighborhood. At the same time, hacking technologies are improving at an alarming rate and cyber-criminals are orchestrating new variations of social engineering. The fact that cyber-criminals have been able to dupe the US FBI director into believing that the e-mail originated from his bank (Chap. 4) and businesses such as *New York Times* into running malware-infected ads tells a lot about the sophistication of their operations.

While IT companies are putting some efforts in developing security products, they appear to be far from bulletproof. There have been an increasing number of attacks on computer networks notwithstanding significant investments in security.

The battle against cybercrimes must be waged on many fronts. Integrated approaches that combine technology and policy measures are needed. Organizations need to redesign their "institutional filter" to provide more secure defense mechanisms. Supranational institutions, national governments, private companies, non-profit and non-government organizations, and consumers can work together to deal with forces that influence global security. The global nature of the cybercrime industry inherently downplays the role of localized law-enforcement agencies. Cybercrimes probably require more international collaborations and information sharing than any other crimes. The framework, concepts, and examples discussed in this book would help understand the contexts, mechanisms, and processes associated with the development of strong regulative institutions to fight cybercrimes, anti-cybercrime societal norms, and anti-cybercrime cognitions.

References

Akerlof, G. A. (1970). The market for 'lemons': Qualitative uncertainty and the market mechanism. *Quarterly Journal of Economics, 84*, 488–500.

Anderson, E. (1999). *Code of the street: Decency, violence, and the moral life of the inner city*. New York: W. W. Norton.

Asch, A. (2009, October 23–29). California's proposed cyber-crime legislation could resurface in 2010. *Apparel News*. http://www.apparelnews.net/features/industry_issues/102309-Californias-Proposed-Cyber-Crime-Legislation-Could-Resurface-in-2010. Accessed 27 October 2009.

Awolusi, B. (2009, October 23). EFCC shuts 800 scam web sites – Daily trust. *Nigerian Bulletin*. http://nigerianbulletin.com/summary-plus-news/efcc-shuts-800-scam-web-sites-daily-trust/23102009/10753/

Barkhi, R., Belanger, F., & Hicks, J. (2008, July–September). A model of the determinants of purchasing from virtual stores. *Journal of Organizational Computing & Electronic Commerce, 18*(3), 177–196.

Baumol, W. J. (1990). Entrepreneurship: Productive, unproductive, and destructive. *Journal of Political Economy, 98*(5), 893–921.

Becker, G. S. (1995, Fall). The economics of crime. *Cross Sections*, 8–15, http://www.rich.frb.org/pubs/cross/crime/crime.pdf. Accessed 27 October 2005.

Berger, P. L., & Luckmann, T. (1967). *The social construction of reality: A treatise in the sociology of knowledge*. New York: Doubleday.

Braithwaite, J. (1989). *Crime, shame and re-integration*. Cambridge University Press.

Busenitz, L. W., Gomez, C., & Spencer, J. W. (2000). Country institutional profiles: Unlocking entrepreneurial phenomena. *Academy of Management Journal, 43*(5), 994–1003.

Carblanc, A., & Moers, S. (2003). Towards a culture of online security. *The OECD Observer*, 30.

Chatterjee, S., & Datta, P. (2008). Examining inefficiencies and consumer uncertainty in e-commerce. *Communications of AIS, 22*, 525–546.

Chua, C., Huang, E., Wareham, J., & Robey, D. (2007). The role of online trading communities in managing internet auction fraud. *MIS Quarterly, 31*(4), 759–781.

Clarke, R. V. (1995). Situational crime prevention. In M. Tonry & D. P. Farrington (Eds.), *Building a safer society. Strategic approaches to crime* (pp. 91–150). University of Chicago Press.

Clarke, R. V. (1999). Hot products: Understanding, anticipating, and reducing demand for stolen goods. *Police Research Paper*, 112. London: Home Office.

Donaldson, T. (1996). Values in tension: Ethics away from home. *Harvard Business Review, 74*(5), 48–57.

euromonitor.com. (2007, December 21). Consumer privacy – Protecting the consumer (from himself?). http://www.portal.euromonitor.com/passport/ResultsList.aspx. Accessed 27 October 2009.

euromonitor.com. (2008, April 7). Cybercrime: The global impact on consumer behaviour. http://www.portal.euromonitor.com/passport/ResultsList.aspx. Accessed 27 October 2009.

Fitzgerald, P. (2008, September/October). Crash of civilizations. *Foreign Policy*, 122.

Foreign Policy. (2005, March/April). Caught in the net: Australian teens, 92.

Forman, J., Jr. (2004). Community policing and youth as assets. *Journal of Criminal Law and Criminology, 95*(1), 1–48.

Fukuyama, F. (1995). *Trust: Social virtue and the creation of prosperity*. New York: The Free Press.

GAO Reports. (2007, July 23). *Cybercrime: Public and private entities face challenges in addressing cyber threats* (pp. 1–59). GAO-07-705.

GAO Reports. (2007, June 22). *Public and private entities face challenges in addressing cyber threats*. RPT-number: GAO-07-705.

Garfinkel, S. (2002). Leaky cyber borders: The net effect. *Technology Review*. http://www.technologyreview.com/articles/garfinkel0602.asp. Accessed 27 October 2004.

Ghana News Agency. (2009, August 31). Anomabu township gets ICT centre for students. http://www.ghananewsagency.org/s_social/r_7939. Accessed 27 October 2009.

ghanabusinessnews.com. (2009). Church prays against cyber crime in Ghana. http://ghanabusinessnews.com/2009/06/01/church-prays-against-cyber-crime-in-ghana. Accessed 27 October 2009.

Goo, J., Kishore, R., & Rao, H. R. (2000). A content-analytic longitudinal study of the drivers for information technology and systems outsourcing. *Proceedings of the twenty first international conference on Information systems*.

Gotz, G. (1999). Monopolistic competition and the diffusion of new technology. *The Rand Journal of Economics, 30*(4), 679–693.

Grant, I. (2008, March 19). The UK's dependence on the internet is putting more than half of its economy at risk, says the government. *ComputerWeekly.com*. http://www.computerweekly.com/Articles/2008/03/19/229932/uk-government-warns-of-economys-reliance-on-internet.htm. Accessed 27 October 2009.

Grazioli, S., & Jarvenpaa, S. L. (2003). Deceived: Under target online. Association for computing machinery. *Communications of the ACM, 46*, 196.

Greene, J. R. (2004). Community policing and organization change. In W. Skogan (Ed.), *Community Policing: Can it Work*? Belmont, CA: Wadswort.

Hadoulis, J. (2006, November 3). Global Internet forum closes with call vs. online repression. *Agence France-Presse/INQUIRER.net*. http://services.inquirer.net/print/print.php?article_id=30328. Accessed 27 October 2009.

Harper, F. M., Raban, D., Rafaeli, S. & Konstan, J. A. (2008, April 5–10). *Predictors of answer quality in online Q&A sites* (pp. 865–874). Proceeding of the twenty-sixth annual SIGCHI conference on Human Factors in Computing Systems, Florence, Italy.

Hirschauer, N., & Musshoff, O. (2007). A game-theoretic approach to behavioral food risks: The case of grain producers, *Food Policy, 32*, 246–265.

Hitt, M., Harrison, J., Ireland, R. D., & Best, A. (1998). Attributes of successful and unsuccessful acquisitions of US firms. *British Journal of Management, 9*, 91–114.

Ho, S. (2004, November/December). Haven for hackers. *Foreign Policy*.

internetworldstats.com. (2009). Top 20 countries with the highest number of internet users. http://www.internetworldstats.com/top20.htm. Accessed September 30, 2009.

Jones, B. R. (2007). Comment: Virtual neighborhood watch: Open source software and community policing against cybercrime. *Journal of Criminal Law &Criminology, 97*(2), 601–629.

Joshi, V. (2009, October 12). Officials: Criminals cooperate better than police. *The Boston Globe*. http://www.boston.com/news/world/asia/articles/2009/10/12/officials_criminals_cooperate_better_than_police/ Accessed 27 October 2009.

Kendall, N. (2009, August 1). What the cybercrime fraudsters get up to. *Times Online*. http://www.timesonline.co.uk/tol/news/uk/crime/article6735761.ece. Accessed 27 October 2009.

Kravets, D. (2009, September 14). New York times reforms online ad sales after Malware Scam. *wired.com*. http://www.wired.com/threatlevel/2009/09/nyt-revamps-online-ad-sales-after-malware-scam/. Accessed 27 October 2009.

Krebs, B. T. (2009, September 24). 'Money Mule' recruitment network exposed. http://voices.washingtonpost.com/securityfix/2009/09/money_mule_recruitment_101.html?wprss=securityfix. Accessed 27 October 2009.

Kshetri, N. (2005a). Pattern of global cyber war and crime: A conceptual framework. *Journal of International Management, 11*(4), 541–562.

Kshetri, N. (2007). Institutional factors affecting offshore business process and information technology outsourcing. *Journal of International Management, 13*(1), 38–56.

Lawrence, T. B., & Phillips, N. (2004). From Moby Dick to Free Willy: Macro-cultural discourse and institutional entrepreneurship in emerging institutional fields. *Organization, 11*, 689–711.

Lawrence, T. B., Hardy, C., & Phillips, N. (2002). Institutional effects of interorganizational collaboration: The emergence of proto-institutions. *Academy of Management Journal, 45*(1), 281–290.

Lim, M. (2001). *From real to virtual (and back again): Civil society, public sphere, and the Internet in Indonesia*. Paper presented at Internet Political Economy Forum conference, Singapore.

Machlup, F. (1962). *The production and distribution of knowledge in the United States*. Princeton, NJ: Princeton University Press.

Marketwire. (2009, October 2). October is cyber security awareness month. http://www.marketwire.com/press-release/Public-Safety-Canada-1054181.html. Accessed 27 October 2009.

Maynard, S. J. (1982). *Evolution and the theory of games*. Cambridge: Cambridge University Press.

McDougall, P. P., Shane, S., & Oviatt, B. M. (1994). Explaining the formation of international new ventures: The limits of theories from international business research. *Journal of Business Venturing, 9*, 469–487.

Moore, M. (2009, September 4). 50 things that are being killed by the internet. *Telegraph.co.uk*. http://www.telegraph.co.uk/technology/6133903/50-things-that-are-being-killed-by-the-internet.html. Accessed 27 October 2009.

Myers, M. D. (1997). Interpretive research in information systems. In J. Mingers & F. A. Stowell (Eds.), *Information systems: An emerging discipline?* (pp. 239–266). London: McGraw-Hill.

National Center for Policy Analysis. (2002). Crime and punishment in Texas: Update. http://www.ncpa.org/pub/st/st202/st202c.html. Accessed 27 October 2009.

National Institute of Justice. (2001, August). 2000 Annual report to congress. http://www.ncjrs.
    org/txtfiles1/nij/189105.txt. Accessed 27 October 2005.
Naylor, R. T. (2005, Winter/Spring). The rise and fall of the underground economy. *Brown Journal
    of World Affairs, 11*(2), 131–143.
Nolan, III, J. J., Conti, N., & McDevitt, J. (2004). Situational policing: Neighborhood development
    and crime control. *Policing & Society, 14*(2), 99–117.
O'Halloran, J. (2009, March 30). Two billion mobile broadband users by 2014. *com-
    puterweekly.com*. http://www.computerweekly.com/Articles/2009/03/30/235455/two-billion-
    mobile-broadband-users-by-2014.htm. Accessed 30 September 2009; Accessed 27 October
    2009.
Orlikowski, W. J., & Baroudi, J. J. (1991). Studying information technology in organizations:
    Research approaches and assumptions. *Information Systems Research, 2*(1), 1–28.
Osland, G. E., & Cavusgil, S. T. (1996). Performance issues in US-China joint ventures. *California
    Management Review, 38*(2), 106–130.
Otis, C., & Evans, P. (2003). The Internet and Asia-Pacific security: Old conflicts and new behavior.
    Pacific Review, 16(4), 549–550.
Overby, E., & Jap, S. (2009). Electronic and physical market channels: A multi-year investigation
    in a market for products of uncertain quality. *Management Science, 55*(6), 940–957.
Oviatt, B. M., & McDougall, P. (1994). Toward a theory of international new ventures. *Journal of
    International Business Studies, 25*(1), 45–64.
Oz, O. (2004). Using Boolean- and fuzzy-logic-based methods to analyze multiple case study
    evidence in management research, *Journal of Management Inquiry, 13*(2), 166–179.
Phillips, N., Lawrence, T. B., & Hardy, C. (2000). Inter-organizational collaboration and the
    dynamics of institutional fields. *Journal of Management Studies, 37*(1), 23–43.
Poulsen, K. (2009, October 27). Cybercrooks trick Gawker into serving Malware-Laced Ad.
    wired.com. http://www.wired.com/threatlevel/2009/10/gawker/. Accessed 27 October 2009.
PR Newswire. (2009). Forty-four percent of US SMBs admit to falling victim to cyber-
    crime. According to Latest Panda Security Survey. http://news.prnewswire.com/
    DisplayReleaseContent.aspx?ACCT=104&STORY=/www/story/07-24-2009/0005065647&
    EDATE=. Accessed 27 October 2009.
Preece, S.B., Miles, G., & Baetz, M.C. (1999). Explaining the international intensity and global
    diversity of early-stage technology-based firms. *Journal of Business Venturing, 14*(3), 259–281.
Probasco, J. R., & Davis, W. L. (1995). A human capital perspective on criminal careers. *Journal
    of Applied Business Research, 11*(3), 58–64.
Reed, B., & Dunkelman, M. (2009, October 21). Policing our cyberstreets. *The Boston Globe.*
    http://www.boston.com/bostonglobe/editorial_opinion/oped/articles/2009/10/21/policing_our_
    cyberstreets/ Accessed 27 October 2009.
Reilly, M. (2007). Beware, botnets have your PC in their sights. *New Scientist, 196*(2634), 22–23.
Ren, Y., Kraut, R., & Kiesler, S. (2007). Applying common identity and bond theory to design of
    online communities. *Organization Studies, 28*(3), 377–408.
Reuters. (2009, October 20) Fake security software in millions of computers. *Newsday*, A43.
Richmond, R. (2003, January 27). Selling strategies – Scammed! Web merchants use new tools to
    keep buyers from ripping them off. *Wall Street Journal*, R.6.
Rubenking, N. J. (2009, July 10). Top cybercrime fighters discuss their trade. *PC Magazine.com*.
    Accessed 27 October 2009.
Sampson, R. J., Morenoff, J. D., & Gannon-Rowley, T. (2002). Assessing 'neighborhood effects':
    Social processes and new directions for research. *Annual Review of Sociology, 28*, 443–478.
Scott, C. (2004, July–October). Regulatory innovation and the online consumer. *Law & Policy,
    26*(3/4), 477–506.
Shaw, C. R., & McKay, H. D. (1942). *Juvenile delinquency and urban areas.* Chicago: University
    of Chicago Press.
Skolnikoff, E. B. (1989). Technology and the world tomorrow. *Current History, 88*(534), 5–13.
Skorodumova, O. (2004). Hackers as information space phenomenon. *Social Sciences, 35*(4),
    105–113.
Smith, M. J. (1982). *Evolution and the theory of games.* Cambridge: Cambridge University Press.

Snidal, D. (1994). The politics of scope: Endogenous actors, heterogeneity and institutions. *Journal of Theoretical Politics, 6*(4), 449–472.

Snidal, D. (1996). Political economy and international institutions. *International Review of Law and Economics, 16*(1), 121–137.

Suchman, M. C. (1995). Managing legitimacy: Strategic and institutional approaches. *Academy of Management Review, 20*, 571–610.

The Chronicle of Higher Education. (2007). *We must educate young people about cybercrime before they start college, 53*(18), B.29.

The Industry Standard. (2001, July 17). More laws, cops won't stem cybercrime, Execs say. *PC World.* http://www.thestandard.com/article/0,1902,27996,00.html. Accessed 27 October 2004.

The New Zealand Herald. (2009, April 23). Global botnet hits Kiwis too.

Triplett, R. A., Gainly, R. R., & Sun, I. Y. (2003). Institutional strength, social control, and neighborhood crime rates. *Theoretical Criminology, 7*(4), 439–467.

Walden, I. (2005). Crime and security in cyberspace. *Cambridge Review of International Affairs, 18*(1), 51–68.

Weniz, M. (2007). Offshore radiology: The legal questions. *Journal of the American College of Radiology, 4*(1), 5–7.

Williamson, O. E. (1975). *Markets and hierarchies.* New York: Free Press.

Williamson, O. E. (1985). *The economic institutions of capitalism.* New York: The Free Press.

Wurth, A. H. J. (1992/1993, Winter). Policy information or information policy? Information types in economics and policy. *Knowledge & Policy, 5*(4), 65–81.

Wylie, I. (2007, December 26). Internet; Romania home base for EBay scammers; The auction website has dispatched its own cyber-sleuth to help police crack fraud rings. *Los Angeles Times,* C.1.

Yin, R. K. (1994). *Case study research: Design and methods.* Thousand Oaks, CA: Sage.

Zazzaro, A., Fratianni, M., & Alessandrin, P. (2009). Chapter 3: Financial centers between centralization and virtualization. *The changing geography of banking and finance.* New York: Springer US.

Zulu, B. (2008). Microsoft combats cybercrime in Nigeria. http://www.pcworld.com/businesscenter/article/152784/microsoft_combats_cybercrime_in_nigeria.html. Accessed 27 October 2009.

Printed by Printforce, the Netherlands